全国高等学校外语教师丛书·教学研究系列

英语语言教学材料：理论与实践

English Language Teaching Materials: *Theory and Practice*

Nigel Harwood（英）编著

剑桥大学出版社
CAMBRIDGE UNIVERSITY PRESS

外语教学与研究出版社
FOREIGN LANGUAGE TEACHING AND RESEARCH PRESS
北京 BEIJING

京权图字：01-2012-7770

图书在版编目（CIP）数据

英语语言教学材料 ：理论与实践 ：英文 /（英）哈伍德（Harwood, N.）编著．—— 北京 ：外语教学与研究出版社，2013.3（2018.1 重印）
（全国高等学校外语教师丛书．教学研究系列）
书名原文：English language teaching materials: theory and practice
ISBN 978-7-5135-2846-7

Ⅰ．①英… Ⅱ．①哈… Ⅲ．①英语－语言教学－教学研究－高等学校－英文 Ⅳ．①H319

中国版本图书馆 CIP 数据核字（2013）第 050444 号

出 版 人　徐建忠
项目负责　段长城
责任编辑　毕　争
责任校对　郑丹妮　丁　雪
封面设计　覃一彪　天泽润
版式设计　吴德胜
出版发行　外语教学与研究出版社
社　　址　北京市西三环北路 19 号（100089）
网　　址　http://www.fltrp.com
印　　刷　北京九州迅驰传媒文化有限公司
开　　本　650×980　1/16
印　　张　34.5
版　　次　2013 年 3 月第 1 版 2018 年 1 月第 5 次印刷
书　　号　ISBN 978-7-5135-2846-7
定　　价　126.90 元

购书咨询：（010）88819926　电子邮箱：club@fltrp.com
外研书店：https://waiyants.tmall.com
凡印刷、装订质量问题，请联系我社印制部
联系电话：（010）61207896　电子邮箱：zhijian@fltrp.com
凡侵权、盗版书籍线索，请联系我社法律事务部
举报电话：（010）88817519　电子邮箱：banquan@fltrp.com
法律顾问：立方律师事务所　刘旭东律师
　　　　　中咨律师事务所　殷　斌律师
物料号：228460101

Contents

总　序

“全国高等学校外语教师丛书”是外语教学与研究出版社高等英语教育出版分社近期精心策划、隆重推出的系列丛书，包含理论指导、科研方法和教学研究三个子系列。本套丛书既包括学界专家精心挑选的国外引进著作，又有特邀国内学者执笔完成的“命题作文”。作为开放的系列丛书，该丛书还将根据外语教学与科研的发展不断增加新的专题，以便教师研修与提高。

笔者有幸参与了这套系列丛书的策划工作。在策划过程中，我们分析了高校英语教师面临的困难与挑战，考察了一线教师的需求，最终确立这套丛书选题的指导思想为：想外语教师所想，急外语教师所急，顺应广大教师的发展需求；确立这套丛书的写作特色为：突出科学性、可读性和操作性，做到举重若轻，条理清晰，例证丰富，深入浅出。

第一个子系列是“理论指导”。本系列力图为教师提供某学科或某领域的研究概貌，期盼读者能用较短的时间了解某领域的核心知识点与前沿研究课题。以《二语习得重点问题研究》一书为例。该书不求面面俱到，只求抓住二语习得研究领域中的热点、要点和富有争议的问题，动态展开叙述。每一章的写作以不同意见的争辩为出发点，对取向相左的理论、实证研究结果差异进行分析、梳理和评述，最后介绍或者展望国内外的最新发展趋势。全书阐述清晰，深入浅出，易读易懂。再比如《认知语言学与二语教学》一书，全书分为理论篇、教学篇与研究篇三个部分。理论篇阐述认知语言学视角下的语言观、教学观与学习观，以及与二语教学相关的认知语言学中的主要概念与理论；教学篇选用认知语言学领域比较成熟的理论，探讨将之应用到中国英语教学实践中的可能性；研究篇包括国内外将认知语言学理论应用到教学实践中的研究综述、研究方法介绍以及对未来研究的展望。

第二个子系列是“科研方法”。本系列介绍了多种研究方法，通常是一书介绍一种方法，例如问卷调查、个案研究、行动研究、有声思维、语料库研究、微变化研究和启动研究等。也有一书涉及多种方法，综合描述量化研究或者质化研究，例如《应用语言学中的质性研究与分析》、《应用语言学中的量化研究与分析》和《第二语言研究中的数据收集方法》等。凡入选本系列丛书的著作人，无论是国外著者还是国内著者，均有高度的读者意识，乐于为一线教师开展教学科研服务，力求做到帮助读者“排忧解难”。例如，澳大利亚Anne Burns教授撰写的《英语教学中的行动研究方法》一书，从一线教师的视角，讨论行动研究的各个环节，每章均有“反思时刻”、“行动时刻”等新颖形式设计。同时，全书运用了丰富例证来解释理论概念，便于读者理解、思考和消化所读内容。凡是应邀撰写研究方法系列的中国作者均有博士学位，并对自己阐述的研究方法有着丰富的实践经验。他们有的运用了书中的研究方法完成了硕士、博士论文，有的是采用书中的研究方法从事过重大科研项目。以秦晓晴教授撰写的《外语教学问卷调查法》一书为例，该书著者将系统性与实用性有机结合，根据实施问卷调查法的流程，系统地介绍了问卷调查研究中问题的提出、问卷项目设计、问卷试测、问卷实施、问卷整理及数据准备、问卷评价以及问卷数据汇总及统计分析方法选择等环节。书中对各个环节的描述都配有易于理解的研究实例。

第三个子系列是“教学研究”。本系列与前两个系列相比，有两点显著不同：第一，本系列侧重同步培养教师的教学能力与教学研究能力；第二，本系列的撰稿人主要为中国学者。有些著者虽然目前在海外工作和生活，但他们出国前曾在国内高校任教，也经常回国参与国内的教学与研究工作。本系列包括《英语教学中的学习策略培训：阅读与写作》、《英语听力教学与研究》、《英语写作教学与研究》、《阅读教学与研究》、《口语教学与研究》、《翻译教学与研究》等。以《英语听力教学与研究》一书为例，著者王艳博士拥有十多年的听力教学经验，同时听力教学研究又是她博士论文的选题领域。《英语听力教学与研究》一书，浓缩了她多年听力教学与听力教学研究的宝贵经验。全书分为两部分：教学篇与研究篇。教学篇中涉及了听力教学的各个重要环节以及学生在听力学习中可能碰到的困难与应对的办法，所选用的案例均来自著者课堂教学的真实活动。研究篇中既有著者的听力教学研究案例，也有著者从国内外文献中筛选出的符合中国国情的听力教学研究案例，综合在一起加以分析阐述。

教育大计，教师为本。“全国高等学校外语教师丛书”内容全面，出版及时，必将成为高校教师提升自我教学能力、研究能力与合作能力的良师益友。笔者相信本套丛书的出版对高校外语教师个人专业能力的提高，对教师队伍整体素质的提高，必将起到积极的推动作用。

文秋芳
北京外国语大学中国外语教育研究中心
2011年7月3日

导　读

由Niger Harwood担任主编、剑桥大学出版社2010年出版的《英语语言教学材料：理论与实践》（*English Language Teaching Materials: Theory and Practice*）是近些年来教材研究方面的一部力作。尽管教材在教学中的作用非常重要，但教材研究一直是语言教学研究领域的弱项。正如Jack Richards在该书的序言中所说，教材研究一直不受重视，有人还认为教材研究没有学术价值。一些教师教育课程也不重视教材研究。很多接受过教师教育或培训的毕业生对于英语教材的设计与评价知之甚少。Harwood和Richards都呼吁加强对英语教材的开发与设计的研究。本书各章的作者都是英语作为外语或第二语言教学方面的专家，且在英语教材开发与设计方面有丰富的研究和实践经验。

本书涵盖了英语教材开发与设计的方方面面，既有理论探讨，也有很多实际案例。理论探讨包括教材研发与设计中的问题、二语习得研究对语言教学材料的启示、教材设计和任务设计中的技术应用、有效教材设计的基本原理等等。实践探讨的章节包括如何编写基于内容的阅读教材、如何编写基于体裁法的写作教材，以及如何设计听力教材、口语教材、学术论文写作教材等。除此以外，本书还涉及一些专门用途英语教材的设计，如国产医学博士后学术写作教材、护理专业英语教材、商务会谈教材、社区成人英语学习者教材。

需要指出的是，本书所说的教材是广义的教材，即有利于促进教学的各种学习材料，甚至学习活动，而不只是大多数国内读者心中的各种教科书。

以下是各章主要内容简介，供读者参考。

第一章　教材研发与设计中的问题

在本书的第一章中，作者介绍了本书的目标读者、撰写背景以及教材设计研究的重要性和紧迫性，并简要介绍了后面各章的内容。

本书的目标读者是英语语言教学领域的学习者、教师、教师培训者和研究者。本书中的“教材”是指在语言教学中任何可以被教师或学习者用来促进语言学习的材料和任务，可以是文字材料、视觉材料、有声材料等，它们的形式可以是纸质的印刷品、视频/音频材料或基于这些材料的练习和活动。

本章首先讨论了为什么要研究教材的设计与开发问题以及教材研究在教师教育课程中的重要性。本章的重点是回顾内容层面的教材分析与研究。英语教材内容分析，是指对教授的语言或主题内容的分析。在语言内容分析方面，研究者不断探索教材与真实口语和书面语的匹配程度。Sheldon（1988）认为，市场上销售的教材（commercial materials）在编写时，没有参照像West（1953）提出的词表等体系作为词汇选择的依据。好在近年来语料库的发展给我们提供了真实语料使用数据。一系列基于语料库的研究发现，以商业为目的开发的教材与真实语言使用之间存在差异。还有一些研究证实，教材中的对话并不是基于真实交谈，而是教材作者的直觉发挥。在文化内容分析上，很多英语教材出版商着力排除那些潜在的有可能冒犯学生或老师的话题，以至于大多数教材中的话题都极其类似。鉴于以上原因，作者呼吁研究者在未来加强教材方面的研究。

第二章　二语习得研究与语言教学材料

本章是第二部分的开篇，由二语习得研究领域的权威专家Rod Ellis撰写，主要介绍了如何将二语习得（SLA）理论应用于指导任务型教学和语法教学，并给那些对此领域不甚了解的读者介绍了很多二语习得研究领域的参考文献。

Ellis在二语习得与任务型教学部分共讲述了四方面内容。他首先明确定义了任务型活动，并清楚地解释了任务型活动和基于语境的语法学习活动之间的差别。其次，他又指出了非聚焦任务（unfocused task）与聚焦任务（focused task）的区别：前者并不是针对具体语言特征的任务，而后者是针对具体语言特征的任务。但无论是采用非聚焦任务还是聚焦任务，其最重要的目的还是促进学习者的交流。再次，Ellis讨论了任务型活动的理论基础。作为二语习得领域重要的教学途径，任务型活动分为任务支持型语言教学（task-supported language teaching）和基于任务的语言教学（task-based language teaching）。任务支持型活动可以作为传统的PPP（present-practice-produce）教学步骤中的最后一步。它的理论基础来源于技能学习理论（skill-learning theory）。基于任务的活动是由一系列难度不同的任务组成的有组织的教学活动。最后作者介绍了任务设计方法。作者列出了Ellis（2003）提出的任务设计特征框架，但同时他也强调此框架对二语习得的推动效果还有待研究。同时，作者还介绍了Johnson（2000）提出的不同的任务设计方式。Johnson指出任务设计者可从三个方面着手设计任务：任务功能、任务语类和任务组织（task function, task genre and task frame）。经验不足的设计者通常先从任务组织出发设计任务，而有经验的设计者则首先考虑的是任务语类。

Ellis在二语习得与语法教学部分讨论了演绎活动（interpretation activity）和培养意识任务（consciousness-raising tasks）。演绎活动是指让学习者在学习的过程中逐渐归纳出目标语的语法结构知识，而不是将知识直接灌输给学习者。演绎活动共分为两类：强化输入活动（input-enrichment activities）和结构输入活动（structure-input activities）。前者意欲通过不断的有针对性的语言输入来使学习者领悟语法知识，而后者则在输入的基础上加以引导，以驱使学习者着重练习某项语法知识。仅仅培养学习者的语法意识是不够的，我们还需要通过意识启发活动来引起学习者的注意以促使其将知识内化。培养意识任务是启发学习者在语料中自行观察和归纳出语法结构知识的活动。实践证明，意识启发要比直接教授效果好，但意识启发活动有可能在低龄学习者身上不是很适用。

导读者认为，Ellis从二语习得理论高度深入浅出地阐释了任务型教学和语法教学。本章作为第二部分的开篇章意义非凡，特别是对于那些对此领域不甚了解的读者来说，它能够让其迅速了解此领域的一些基本理论和概念，为读者读后续章节奠定了一定的理论基础。

第三章　教材设计和任务设计中技术应用的理论与实践

技术在当今语言教材设计方面扮演着重要的角色。本章作者首先对比了计算机辅助语言学习（CALL）和传统非计算机辅助语言教学的特征，以及这些特征如何影响教材设计，然后阐述了计算机辅助语言学习的理论依据。最后从实践、教法和理论角度介绍了计算机辅助语言学习教材研发的最新尝试。

计算机辅助语言学习教材包括任务、网站、软件、课件、网络课程和模拟学习环境。首先，与传统教材相比，基于计算机辅助语言学习的教材在组织上有以下优势：学习者的学习进程和测试结果能被自动记录下来，并随时供人查阅，这不仅对教师，而且对学习者也是大有裨益的；计算机辅助语言学习教材还十分便于分享和不断更新，而且从长远来看十分节约成本；基于计算机辅助语言学习的教材也具有教法上的优势：它能利用语料库来促进真实语料的使用和发展，并能通过游戏、拟真课外交流活动等方式帮助学习者接触和感受真实的语言使用。计算机辅助语言学习的最大优势就是它有助于促进学习者的交流和语言使用。

在理论方面，作者列举了一些以往对计算机辅助语言学习的研究，其中包括Chapelle（2001）提出的计算机辅助语言学习任务设计标准，以及Doughty和Long（2003）提出的十条设计原则。但同时作者也指出，二语习得理论与教材设计实践之间仍然存在脱节的现象。

作者在实例介绍部分介绍了两个项目：远程网络教学和网络自主学习。作者首先介绍了Hampel（2006）在理论和实践上对远程网络教学的探索。Hampel（2006）利用一个由英国开放大学开发的、称作Lyceum的语言学习系统来进行远程网络教学。他积极采用人机互动教学模式，取得了良好的教学效果。但此项目也存在一些不足，那就是并没能将所有学生的积极性都调动起来。随后，作者又介绍了奥克兰大学研发的一个网络自主学习项目。奥克兰大学推出了一个名为ELSAC的网络自主学习终端，目的是为其众多多元化的学生和教员提供帮助。此终端包含大型电子资源数据库和一些帮助学习者进行需求分析、设定学习计划、记录学习进程和提供参考策略的辅助学习工具。此项目在学习者和教学者中都获得了良好反响，但也存在不足之处。鉴于此，设计者又推出了一个ELSAC的升级版本，名为My English。My English力图加强学习者和教师之间的交流互动，以便让学习者能更多地获取教师的支持与帮助。

第四章　有效教材设计的基本原理

本章指出，教材应该在语言习得和教学的理论指导下设计，而不是随意设计或抄袭市场上发行的畅销教材。本章首先进行了文献综述，然后介绍了六点语言习得的原理和四点语言教学原理。作者提出了教材设计的一些原则，其中着重强调了教材设计应遵守语言习得和发展的理论和教学原理。

以下是本章作者总结的六条英语语言习得原理：

· 让学习者最大限度地接触和使用丰富的、有意义的和难度适宜的语言
· 尽量促使学习者在情感和认知上投入
· 态度积极的学习者可能比其他学习者进行更多的交际实践活动
· 学习和使用第一语言过程中所用到的心智资源也对二语习得大有裨益
· 要使学习者注意到语言输入中的凸显特征
· 应该为学生提供语言实践的机会以达到交际的目的

以下是本章作者总结的四条语言教学原理：

· 教学内容和方法应与课程目标相吻合，应该满足学习者的需求
· 教学不应只停留在语言习得层面，还要能有助于促进学习者的语言发展
· 教学应能为学习者创造学习锻炼机会，使其变得更成熟，更有批判意识、创造力、建设性、协作性，更有能力和有信心。
· 教师应该能将教材内化，以便使其适应当地学生，并且能做到针对各个学生的不同需求和学习风格因材施教

作者还给出了与上述这些原理相对应的教材设计建议（详见相应章节，在此不再赘述）。

第五章　批判性教学理论指导下的教材开发：以美国校园征兵材料为例

本章讨论如何在批判性教学理论指导下进行教材设计。批判性教学是一种教学方法，主张批判地探索语言使用的条件以及语言使用的社会和文化目的，而不只是传授语言、文化和其他信息。批判应用语言学是把批判理论

的原理和方法应用在语言教育、文化、话语分析等领域的语言问题的研究范式。本章介绍的是在批判性教学理论指导下的教学实践。作者指出，我们不应只把语言当成一个交流的媒介，语言更是一种社会实践。

美国通过的一项法案规定，学校不能拒绝征兵人员到校园征兵，在此背景下，就产生了关于国家是否应该允许校园征兵，校园是否可以拒绝征兵的争论。作者将这个社会争论引入了英语作为第二语言（ESL）的课堂教学中。他收集了一些支持或反对校园征兵的材料，并在课堂上呈现给学生，让学生进行讨论，引发学生的思考，加深他们对此问题的认识和理解。作者详细介绍了他如何将此话题引入课堂，学生对此问题的反应，以及他作为教师是如何根据学生的反馈来调整自己的教学过程的，并且指出教材的设计和教学实践具有互动关系。

作者还提出，本章介绍的批判性教学是一项探索性教学活动，不是传统的教学者单向给学习者传授知识的过程，而是一个教师和学习者互相学习，共同促进对社会问题的深化认识的过程。在本章最后作者指出，其本人一直纠结是否应将自己对征兵这一问题的看法在课堂上透露给学生。作者也明确指出自己在课外是校园征兵的反对者。

第六章　基于内容的阅读教材设计原则

本章介绍了阅读教材的设计原则：针对性（responsiveness）、衔接性（cohesion）和稳定性（stability）。本章介绍的教材是一种供中高级（low-advanced）英语水平、生物学专业学生使用的大学英语阅读教材。该课程的目的是为学生提供机会，使其提高英语水平，增强阅读学术文章的能力。

作者首先介绍了阅读课教材的设计原则：针对性、衔接性和稳定性。针对性是其中最重要最核心的一条原则，是指设计任何教材的第一步都是需求分析，要使教材满足各方面尤其是学习者的需求。衔接性是指课程要在其不同级别、课时、技能和教材等各方面相互关联、贯通一致。其中，教材的衔接性是指每节课、每章以及各个教学活动之间要存在内部联系。课程要保持相对稳定性是指对课程的任何调整都要建立在审慎、细致的调查研究的基础上，且必须要在正确的语言教学和语言习得理论原则指导下调整。在设计原则这一部分的最后作者指出，阅读教材设计一定要同时兼顾这三点原则。

在介绍了设计原则之后，本章提供了一篇关于光合作用的阅读材料范例，并对此教材在阅读前、阅读中和阅读后三个阶段中的每个任务设计是如何贯彻针对性、衔接性和稳定性原则进行了详细的注释。

第七章　基于体裁法的写作教材设计

本章首先回顾了以往有关体裁写作教学研究的文献，然后讨论了学习者和教师的需求以及如何在教材设计上满足这些需求，最后展示了一系列基于体裁法的写作教材范例。体裁是用在特定情景中、具有可被辨认的模式和结构组织的话语类型。不同的体裁具有不同的特定交际功能，例如商务报告、新闻广播、演讲、书信、广告。

本章第一部分作者在回顾了现有文献之后，提出了自己的观点：英语作为外语的写作教学不能只停留在教授写作方法上，还要让学习者明白不要只把眼光局限在课堂内，写作中创作的文章应该能够起到一定社会作用，产生一定的社会影响。教育者要帮助学习者挑战这一新的角色和目标。其中教师所面临的挑战是如何帮助学生获取其需要的各种体裁的写作经验，并且确保学生在完成任务的过程中充分利用与任务相关的语言和认知资源。

第二部分分别介绍了学习者和教师的需求。要撰写文章，作者需要了解以下几个方面的知识：内容知识、背景知识、语言系统知识和写作流程知识。而教师则需要在课上给学习者提供范文输入、内容焦点、语言焦点和任务焦点（Hutchinson & Waters 1987；Hyland 2003：101）。

本章介绍的写作教材是针对剑桥初级英语证书考试（Cambridge First Certificate in English，简称FCE）而设计的。此考试难度相当于欧洲语言参考架构的2B级水平，由英国剑桥ESOL考试中心推出。

本章第三部分详细介绍了如何设计剑桥初级英语证书考试的写作教材。作者将写作教学分成了五个步骤：第一步是建立语境。这是指教师要给学习者提供一系列教具、印刷材料、音频/视频等资源以激发学习者兴趣，引发学习者讨论。第二步是示范和重构语篇。学习者首先要对所要撰写的文体的基本结构有所了解。此步意在辅助学习者构建起一个对应写作体裁的文章框架模版。在这一步中教师能否为学生选出优质的范文就显得尤为重要了。这些范文的主题既要与学生的写作题目不同，又要能诠释该类体裁文章的结构和主要特征。一旦学习者明白了此体裁下的文章的撰写方法后，就开始第三步和第四步教学，即合作构思起草文章和独立构思起草文章。在这两步里学习者要在教师的指导和辅助下多次修改文章。第五步是将本体裁文章与其他体裁文章联系比较，这能够加深学习者对目标体裁特征的认识。

第八章　强调过程的听力教学活动：自我评估和自我管理式听力活动

听力能力的提高需要多种技巧和不断练习。听的过程也涉及到学习者的认知、情感等方面的需求。本章的目的是针对这些认知、情感需求，提供一些理论框架和实践经验，以便使学习者发展自主提高听力水平的能力。作者建议使用元认知理论来引导学习者学会如何听，而不是只让学习者停留在听什么的层面上。元认知是指不同类型的学习所涉及的心理认知过程。元认知策略是一种学习策略，包括对学习过程中所运用的心理过程的思考、学习时对学习的监控以及学习后对学习结果的评估。

在听力训练中使用元认知策略有以下三个方面的好处：第一，能增强学生的信心，激发学生的动机和兴趣；第二，能增加学生对听力过程和对自己作为二语听力学习者的认识；第三，能发展有助于听力理解的技巧和策略。作者回顾了其他研究者在此方面做过的研究。这些研究结果显示，元认知策略不仅能大大调动学习者对听力的积极性，而且能着实提高学生的听力成绩。它对听力能力薄弱的学习者尤为有效，并且有研究证实此策略也适合低龄学习者使用。

关于如何引导学习者利用元认知策略提高听力水平，本章提出了以下两方面的建议：一体化体验式听力任务和教师指导下的听力反思。下面就对这两方面分别进行详细的说明。关于一体化体验式听力任务，作者介绍了以下五项活动：

- 元认知听力顺序：（1）计划；（2）听力I；（3）双人讨论；（4）听力II；（5）全班讨论；（6）听力III；（7）文本与录音对照；（8）自省

- 自主听力：计划、监控、评估
- 听力伙伴：与一个伙伴一起进行听力练习活动
- 同学间听力任务设计：学生组成4人左右的小组共同学习，轮流担任教师角色，计划并组织小组听力活动
- 课后听力活动：使学生可以在没压力的情况下提高听力

关于教师指导下的听力反思，作者介绍了以下四项活动：

- 听力日记：鼓励学生记录下个人的听力经验、感受、遇到的问题、使用的策略等
- 焦虑和动机图表：引导学生利用图表记录自己一段时间的焦虑和动机变化
- 基于过程的讨论：可以在单独的讨论课上也可以在听力前阶段组织
- 自省报告单：学生填写的报告单一定要避免冗长繁复

第九章　口语教材的设计

本章主要讨论如何设计训练口语技能的教材。本章所讲的教材设计最适宜的目标群体是中高级和高级学习者。在口语教学方面，研究者们已经进行了很多理论研究，如：口语语料库研究、话语语篇分析、语用学研究、语言创造性研究、互动语言学研究和话语过程与心理语言学研究。其中互动语言学理论很重要，但在此方面的进一步研究还很缺乏。本章就是对在此理论指导下的口语教材设计进行的探索性研究。

本章给读者提供了三篇教材设计范例，目的是想展示如何在课堂上引导学生学会处理简单的交互式的反馈，以增强学习者信心和提高口语能力。人在说话的同时所得到的一些反馈，例如uh、yeah、really、微笑、摇头和咕噜声这些反应，表明交际的成功或失败。范例1探索如何让学生在听别人讲话时，给出对所听内容表示感兴趣的反馈，如right、mmm、wow等。范例2尝试让学习者体会和学习前台电话服务用语中的常用短语的语言节奏。范例3力图帮助学习者掌握中途打断对方说话的方法。

第十章　针对学术研讨中学科专业词汇和短语的教材设计

词汇在学术英语的学习中起重要作用。以往的大多数研究主要探讨如何根据学术写作研究的结果进行教材设计，而本章讨论了如何根据学术研讨（academic seminars）中使用的学科专业口语词汇来设计教材，以促进专门学科的词汇、短语的教学。

Jones（2003b）进行了一个小规模的需求分析，并在此分析基础上推出了一个名为NDSC的需求驱动口语语料库。NDSC共包含三个子语料库，本章所讨论的教材设计是基于其中的学术子语料库。作者把学术研讨会中的词汇、短语语料与英国国家语料库中的口语语料（BNC Spoken Sample，本族语语料）相比较，发现NDSC语料中普遍多用单数普通名词、复数普通名词、冠词和形容词。根据比较结果，作者选出以下三类词汇和短语作为教材设计的目标词汇：专业词汇（technical）、一般词汇（general）和口语词汇（colloquial）。

作者根据所选目标词汇制作成了一个计算机学习程序，用来帮助学习者学习专业词汇和短语。作者还进行了一个实验性研究，来检验学习者使用该学习程序的效果。实验对象由两组构成，一组是法律和经济学专业的学生，另一组是来自日本的英语教师。第一组对象的英语能力相当于国际英语语言测试系统（雅思）测试成绩6.5—7.0分的水平，第二组相当于雅思测试成绩5.5—6.5分的水平。对目标学习者的教学分为两部分：第一部分是教师引导的课堂教学，第二部分是学习者自己使用以上学习程序练习和巩固词汇。实验结果显示，两组学习者都能良好地掌握所学词汇和短语。总之，此实验研究能初步证明以上介绍的学习程序对专门学科词汇和短语的教学有一定促进作用。

第十一章　大学学术论文写作教材的设计

本章作者任教于英国伯明翰大学，主要教授该大学各专业国际学生英语写作技能。本章作者主要分享了在学术论文写作课上的一些教学探索。该写作课所使用的教材是由作者与其同事共同设计的，不是市场上购买的教材。

作者认为，学术论文是作者针对某一话题的观点而撰写的短篇文章。此观点可以是学生报告的其他作者的观点，也可以是学生自己的观点，文章中要有支持观点的论据。Bazerman（1981）认为，论文写作包括四个方面的内容：论题、此领域文献、预期读者和作者自己的观点。教师应当鼓励学生表达自己的观点。

本章的教材设计在很大程度上是受语类分析理论的影响。本章详细讲述的教材范例共有五个教学任务：第一，提出论题（making claims）；第二，提供论据（providing evidence）；第三，论据种类（types of evidence）；第四，以修辞目的组织信息（organizing information for rhetorical purpose）；第五，学生的观点（the student's position）。

第十二章　基于语料库的围产医学博士后学术写作教材设计

本章介绍了一门15学时的旨在帮助围产医学博士后撰写和发表学术论文的写作培训课程。此课程是根据一个小型的自建学术论文语料库设计的，课程的目标群体是一群在围产医学领域卓有成绩且有论文发表经历的专家。这是一门针对专业学生的英语课程。本章重点展示作者为这门课程所设计的一些教材。

本课程使用的语料为2004至2006年间发表的140篇文章。这些文章来自于围产医学领域权威的期刊杂志，共包含约450,000词。

首先作者设计了一系列的活动来引导学习者将目光放在语篇上而不是只关注文章所提供的医学内容；其次，引导学生不仅从宏观上关注这些文章的特征，还要注意文章内细小的具体特征；再次，鼓励学生通过观察思考来得出结论，使其克服之前的盲目依赖英语教科书或教师的习惯；最后，为学生提供了一些新的富有启发性的教学内容。

第十三章　为研究生解开学术引证谜团的教材设计

本章主要讨论研究生在学术写作中的引证（academic citation）问题。本章介绍的教材是根据对计算机专业和社会学专业的学者的采访而设计的。作者指出，学习者不仅缺乏如何使用引证的知识，而且不明白使用引证的原因和引证的不同功能，因此这方面的研究和教学都很有意义。

以往的研究都是在文本分析的基础上研究学术引证的功能。这样的研究可能曲解作者的引证目的，因此，本章使用的是以语篇为基础的采访研究方式。为了做到文理科兼顾，作者分别调查采访了计算机专业和社会学专业的学者，考察他们在其发表的文章中使用引证的情况。此研究的目的是揭示使用频率最高的一些引证功能以及引证功能的具体使用方式。

根据调查研究结果可知，观点综述引证（position citations）、佐证引证（supporting citations）和归功引证（credit citations）这三种引证在两个被调研学科的论文中被高频率地使用。观点评述引证（engaging citations）在社会学论文中被广泛使用，而文献指引引证（signposting citations）则在计算机专业的文章中使用最为广泛。

在此研究基础之上，本章给读者列出了一些教材设计的范例，并在最后指出以下三个方面还有待进一步研究：学习者使用的引证功能、学科内与学科间的引证区别，以及引证的恰当性与引证资源的选择问题。

第十四章　专业学术写作实践突破：以研究为基础的提高英语写作能力的策略

本章主要讨论非英语本族语学者如何在探究式策略（heuristics）的指导下准备学术会议论文摘要并在国际学术期刊上发表英文论文。探究式策略是引导学习者通过经验或亲身探究进行学习的一种教学方法。大多数英语学术写作课程都只停留在教授语言修辞层面，而并没有指导学者如何参加社会学术实践活动。而学者想要撰写英文学术会议摘要或在国际英文期刊上发表文章的话，还要开阔思路，要借助研究网络和学术经纪人等方面的社会资源的辅助。研究网络是指由一系列的社会资源和人员而构成的网络，是由语言专家、修辞专家、研究专家和专业领域专家等构成的人脉网。学术经纪人主要有两类：语言专业经纪人和学术专业经纪人。

作者举了三位不同学者的例子来启发读者思考，鼓励读者借鉴。

例一：Fidel是名具有14年教龄的资深教师，在欧洲南部一所大学工作，他还定期到美国和英国进修。他具有较高的英语水平，曾发表过46篇文章，其中9篇是英文文章。作者详细介绍了Fidel如何有效地利用资源，组成共有

13位研究者的协作团队，积极推进手头上的两个项目。通过Fidel的例子，作者启发读者思考以下问题：你加入了什么样的研究网络？你在其中起什么作用？你需要别人哪方面的支持？你能列出你的研究网络人员名单吗？作者又进一步给读者提出以下建议：（1）争取更多的撰写学术会议摘要、撰写国际期刊文章的机会，以提高学术论文产量；（2）与他人合作以提高效率；（3）努力构建本地的学术网络，谋求与志同道合的学者或研究生的共同合作。

例二：Istvan是一名在中欧工作的从事心理学研究的教授，有25年工龄。在学术英语阅读方面他驾轻就熟，但在口语和学术英语写作上并不擅长。他扬长避短，积极寻求合作，在一位擅长英语的学生、一位自己实验室的研究员和两位美国研究员的支持下，成功地将自己的研究成果发表在了国际期刊上。从中我们可以借鉴以下几点：要与其他研究者多沟通联络，努力争取各种资源，比如来自政府或学术机构等的资金支持，并积极与研究团队成员沟通交流，以增进合作。

例三：Carla是名心理学副教授，任职于欧洲南部的一所大学，有17年工作经验。她英语水平很高，曾发表过5篇英文文章和10篇本族语文章。她和英国的同行共同进行了长期的实验研究合作，还与临近城市的一名同行共同从事研究工作。她的成功离不开学术经纪人的帮助。在语言文字润色方面的学术经纪人能给学者提供很大帮助。他们可以帮助学者争取发表机会、撰写英文论文、确定目标期刊、修改润色文章语句以及提供对文章的批评意见。因此，作者建议学者们加强与学术经纪人的交流合作。当然，作者还要用批判的眼光看待不同经纪人对自己文章给予的批评建议。

第十五章　护理专业英语：特殊专业的教材设计

本章指出，在美国学习护理专业的移民学生人数在不断上升。这些学生大部分在英语学习方面存在困难，但是针对这一现状的研究和教材开发又十分欠缺。因此，本章致力于探讨针对护理专业学生的以英语作为第二语言的教材设计问题。

作者调查了护理专业非英语本族语学习者的需求，并总结出被调查者具有个人、学术、语言和文化四方面的需求，其中最大的问题是语言方面的障碍，另外文化差异也是学习者在临床环境中交流的另一大障碍。尽管在此方面不乏研究，但是其中大多数都是在研究学习者的社会文化和学术需求，只有极少数研究涉及护理专业所需要的语言技能，更罕有专门针对护理专业的英语作为第二语言的教材研究。

Bosher（2006）对美国2000—2001年四年制本科护理专业的英语作为第二语言的学习者进行了需求分析。调查结果显示，学术技能和临床技能两方面都对学习者至关重要。本章展示的教材设计就是建立在此调查研究的基础上的。教材话题的选择都是与护理相关的，其中的各种学习活动都是为了锻炼学习者的语言和学术技能，以帮助这些学习者顺利获得学位。随后，本章从以下几个方面详细介绍了本研究的教材和课堂活动范例：

· 批判性阅读/思考：评价信息资源
· 发展批判思维：使用元话语知识来评价信息
· 撰写病情发展记录：用电报式言语撰写
· 临床环境的倾听：倾听并记录交班记录
· 临床环境交流：自信心建立训练
· 文化内容：反思学生的视角
· 学习策略：解构选择题

第十六章　利用教材和真实对话材料来教授商务会谈中的话轮转换技巧

本章探讨如何利用真实对话材料来补充商务英语教材，以教授商务会谈中的话轮转换技巧。本章意在研究真实的商务会谈的特征以及如何教授商务会谈技巧。

本章的真实商务会谈语料来自于7家欧洲的国际公司的21段平均长度为56分钟的会议录音。作者对这些数据进行分析，并与6种教授商务英语的教材进行比较，发现这些教材中教授的话轮转换技巧在真实语料中从来没有被使用过，教材并没能抓住灵活而复杂的交流互动本质。因此，为了使学习者在将来能尽快、更好地适应工作环境中的英语交流，应着力培养学习者的观察和分析能力。

最后作者分享了其设计的一份教材范例，这是对如何结合教材和真实语料而进行的教学探索。本章还提议教材设计应具有灵活性，以便适应大量商务专业学生的需求。另外教材编写者、出版社、研究者和学者应多多交流合作。

第十七章　针对英语作为第二语言的社区成人英语学习者的教材设计

本章探讨针对美国等国家的成人移民二语习得者的教材设计问题，力图帮助这些移民更好地适应在移民国家的工作和生活。尽管美国移民人数不断上升，关于成人英语作为第二语言课程的研究却还很缺乏。本章就着力研究针对美国成人英语二语教育的教材设计。

美国的英语二语教育是美国成人基础教育（ABE）项目的组成部分，起初主要教授基本口语（也称为“生存英语”），后来开始逐步转向以教授阅读和写作为主。成人基础教育项目在实施过程中面临着优质师资匮乏和教学效果不显著等各种挑战。本章探讨了在这一背景下，针对成人基础教育项目的三种不同的英语二语教材设计的理论框架和实践活动：基础英语二语教育或以技能为基础的教育（CBE）、综合语言能力/语言经验教学法（LEA）、弗洛姆（Freirean）/参与式英语二语教学。

基础英语二语教育或以技能为基础的教育（CBE）是最核心和最基础的，主要教授和评估学生生存所需的最基础的与读写相关的语言能力。综合语言能力/语言经验教学法（LEA）是建立在被广泛运用的儿童听说读写全方面语言教学的基础上的。顾名思义，语言经验教学法（LEA）是利用儿童个人生活中的经历及他们在课堂外发展语言技能的方法。弗洛姆（Freirean）/参与式英语二语教学与语言经验教学法比较近似，是一种以学生为中心的合作式或协作式教学方法。它以内在激励和外在激励的关系理论以及弗洛姆（Freirean）的期望理论为基本原理。

程晓堂　　　郭海燕
北京师范大学　首钢工学院
2013年1月

Contributors

Neil J. Anderson, Brigham Young University, USA
Jo Angouri, University of the West of England, UK
Sarah Benesch, City University of New York, USA
Susan Bosher, St. Catherine University, USA
Mary Jane Curry, University of Rochester, USA
Rod Ellis, University of Auckland, New Zealand
Norman W. Evans, Brigham Young University, USA
Christine B. Feak, University of Michigan, USA
Christine Goh, National Institute of Education, Singapore
Linda Harklau, University of Georgia, USA
K. James Hartshorn, Brigham Young University, USA
Nigel Harwood, University of Essex, UK
Martin Hewings, University of Birmingham, UK
Rebecca Hughes, University of Nottingham, UK
Cori Jakubiak, University of Georgia, USA
Martha Jones, University of Nottingham, UK
Theresa Lillis, Open University, UK
Hayo Reinders, Middlesex University, UK
Norbert Schmitt, University of Nottingham, UK
John M. Swales, University of Michigan, USA
Brian Tomlinson, Leeds Metropolitan University, UK
Christopher Tribble, University of London, UK
Cynthia White, Massey University, New Zealand

Preface

A fact of life in the majority of language-learning classrooms around the world is that commercial or teacher-made materials generally provide the core resources that teachers and students depend on. Despite the opportunities provided by blended learning and other Web-based initiatives, traditional books or print-based learning materials continue to play an important role in the lives of the majority of teachers and learners.

The reasons for this are various. Although "authentic materials" are often recommended as an alternative to commercial materials, the scope of language teaching around the world today is such that few teaching institutions have the resources to abandon commercial materials. And Web-dependent learning is not always an option since, in many places, adequate resources for technology-based learning are not available. Learning contexts, too, are often situation specific, and when commercial materials do not provide a good fit with learners' needs, teachers are often required either to adapt available materials or to design their own materials for a specific teaching-learning context. In addition, the majority of the world's English language teachers are not native speakers of English and may have limited teacher training – for such teachers, well-designed materials can provide rich sources of learning input as well as facilitate teacher development.

In second language teacher-education programs, however, insufficient attention is often given to the role of materials in language teaching. Teachers sometimes graduate from such programs with limited experience in materials design, evaluation, adaptation, and implementation. The status of materials design is sometimes undervalued in graduate education, where it is regarded as a relatively trivial and theory-free activity. However, whereas materials design may seem an eminently practical activity, sound instructional materials cannot be created in a theoretical vacuum. They draw on a wide variety of theoretical foundations, since they reflect particular assumptions about the nature of language, of second language learning, and of second language teaching. They should hence be informed by research and current knowledge drawn from relevant domains of applied linguistics, including corpus linguistics, discourse analysis, genre analysis, pragmatics, and sociocultural theory.

Materials design is also a special case of the application of the sophisticated kind of thinking that expert teachers possess, which is sometimes called *pedagogical reasoning skills*. These are the special skills that enable language teachers to do the following:

- To analyze potential lesson content (i.e., a piece of realia, a text, an advertisement, a poem, a photo, etc.) and identify ways in which it could be used as a teaching resource.
- To identify specific linguistic goals (i.e., in the area of speaking, vocabulary, reading, writing, etc.) that could be developed from the chosen content.
- To anticipate any problems that might occur and ways of resolving them.
- To make appropriate decisions about time, sequencing, and grouping arrangements.
- To develop appropriate instructional tasks as the basis for the lesson.

Shulman[1] described these abilities as a process of transformation, in which the teacher turns the subject matter of instruction into forms that are pedagogically powerful and that are appropriate to the level and ability of the students. Experienced and competent teachers use these skills every day when they plan their lessons, when they decide how to adapt lessons from their course book, and when they search the Internet and other sources for materials and content that they can use in their classes. It is one of the most fundamental dimensions

[1] Shulman, L. S. (1987). Knowledge and teaching: Foundations of the new reform. *Harvard Educational Review* 57(2): 4-14.

of teaching, one that is acquired through experience, through accessing content knowledge, and through knowing what learners need to know and how to help them acquire it. This is also one of the core skills of an expert materials writer.

At the same time, materials design is also, to some extent, art rather than science. The ability to design materials that are pedagogically sound and yet also show evidence of the writers' creativity and imagination depends on considerable skill and ingenuity. The best instructional materials not only serve their pedagogic goals but also hopefully provide the basis for memorable and enjoyable classroom experiences for both teachers and students. The ingredients needed to achieve this level of engagement, however, are often difficult to quantify.

The present book, therefore, provides a timely overview of the current state of materials writing in language teaching, surveying both the theoretical and practical issues involved in the design, implementation, and evaluation of materials in language programs, as well as providing case studies of materials design projects in a wide variety of settings and contexts. Nigel Harwood has assembled a stimulating collection of original papers that describe different approaches to materials design, including teacher-developed classroom materials and commercial materials, as well as technology-driven materials. The contributors describe the theories and principles underlying their approaches to materials design, the issues that need to be resolved, problems that have been encountered, and the solutions that were arrived at. The papers in the book hence provide invaluable documentation of the processes and resources employed by materials writers and, as such, can serve as guidelines for both new and experienced teachers who are involved in materials design projects in their own institutions.

Jack C. Richards

PART A
INTRODUCTION

1

Issues in materials development and design

Nigel Harwood

This book is intended for students, teachers, teacher-trainers, and researchers in the field of English Language Teaching (ELT)/Teaching English to Speakers of Other Languages (TESOL) with an interest in teaching materials. Drawing on Brown (1995) and Mishan (2005), *materials* is a term used here to encompass both texts and language-learning tasks: texts presented to the learner in paper-based, audio, or visual form, and/or exercises and activities built around such texts. This definition is intentionally broad in order to include locally produced handouts a teacher uses with a single class, as well as the textbooks produced by major publishing houses and distributed globally. As its title suggests, *English Language Teaching Materials: Theory and Practice* discusses materials development and design by bringing together theoretical and practical/pedagogical perspectives, and the authors in this volume describe and justify materials produced for a variety of local and international, commercial and noncommercial contexts. A wealth of research on teaching materials and textbooks can be found in a number of disciplines, including the fields of mainstream (i.e., non-TESOL) education and sociology. Whereas this introductory chapter seeks to alert readers to what I consider to be the most relevant work for TESOL researchers and professionals, informative reviews focusing on non-TESOL research include Johnsen (1993), Mikk (2000), Nicholls (2003), and Pingel (1999).[1]

[1] To take one example, Mikk (2000) features an extended section on research on materials evaluation.

Why talk about materials design?

As Heilenman (1991), Richards (2006), and Samuda (2005) have pointed out, materials development and design is often mistakenly seen as unworthy of serious study, being "an essentially atheoretical activity" (Samuda 2005: 232). As this volume makes clear, however, materials designers draw on a wide array of theories and frameworks. Some may question the relevance of this collection to many of the teachers around the world who are restricted in the amount of materials they can produce: Time is short, teaching schedules are heavy, and practitioners are sometimes not permitted to deviate from a rigid syllabus by introducing their own materials. Yet, as Allwright (1981) argues, and even well-known textbook writers (e.g., Hutchinson & Torres 1994; O'Neill 1982) concede, no pre-prepared materials can ever meet the needs of any given class precisely; some level of adaptation will be necessary. Indeed, the commercial textbooks that teachers may be required to stick to should be seen as resources rather than courses (Bell & Gower 1998; Richards 1993), constituting a "jumping-off point for teacher and class" (O'Neill 1982: 110). Hence, as Dudley-Evans and St. John (1998: 173) claim, whereas most teachers may not be obliged to *create* materials from scratch, *providing* them in a suitable form for the local context is another matter. Dudley-Evans and St. John go on to suggest that a good provider of materials will be able to:

1. Select appropriately from what is available.
2. Be creative with what is available.
3. Modify activities to suit learners' needs.
4. Supplement by providing extra activities (and extra input).

Dudley-Evans & St. John (1998: 173)

As Samuda (2005) puts it, teachers engage in "re-design" work, "tweaking, adjusting and adapting materials to suit particular needs" (p. 235). The problem, however, is that it is sometimes assumed that all teachers are equipped with this ability to redesign as part of their "normal professional repertoire"; it is seen as something "easily picked up," "essentially unproblematic" (p. 236). Such assumptions can be questioned – Samuda (2005) cites the case of the inexperienced teacher in Tsui's (2003) study of expertise who did not "have any principles on which to base her judgment of whether the activities [were] well designed" (p. 213). And Ball and Feiman-Nemser's (1988) impressive longitudinal study also found that novice teachers had problems using and adapting textbook materials. Hence a number of researchers agree with Samuda (2005) and Ball and Feiman-Nemser (1988) that materials design should be studied and theorized, proposing that it be incorporated into pre- and in-service teacher education programs (e.g., McGrath 2002; Richards 1993; Tomlinson 2003b). Some, like Tomlinson (2003b), place more emphasis on getting teachers to design their own materials, whereas others, like Hutchinson and Torres (1994), are more concerned with training teachers to "become better consumers of textbooks" (p. 327), but the argument that materials design should play a part in teacher education is consistent. It is anticipated that this book could be used in these education programs, and that the range of theories and sample activities in this volume will enhance teachers' awareness of the pedagogical options available to them. They will then need to critically evaluate how suitable these options are when (re)designing materials appropriate for their context.

Materials and the TESOL curriculum

In order to get a sense of the many considerations designers must take into account when writing or adapting materials, a good starting point is to consider the place of materials in the TESOL curriculum. Good overviews of theories of curriculum are provided by Brown (1995), Graves (2008), Richards (2001), and Richards and Rodgers (2001). Using Richards and Rodgers's (2001) terminology, designers will need to determine their *approach*, *design*, and *procedure*, which refer respectively to (i) approach: the nature of language and of language teaching and learning; (ii) design: the specification of content, and of the roles of teachers, learners, and materials; and (iii) procedure: the variety of pedagogical activities that can be drawn on. Materials will be shaped by these considerations. In addition, as Brown (1995) argues, it will also be necessary to evaluate the curriculum in general, and the materials in particular.

Some of the key elements associated with approach, design, and evaluation are now discussed in more detail. Materials writers will wish to consult the second-language acquisition (SLA) literature, especially when considering which language structures to focus on, and how and when to present them (see Ellis 2006). Genre-specific computer corpora, that is, electronically stored databases of authentic spoken and/or written text (see Hunston 2002; Sinclair 2004), will also be invaluable when specifying language content. Although the pros and cons of using "authentic" texts and materials (however one defines the term) are much discussed (e.g., Gilmore 2007; Lee 1995; Mishan 2005), it is fair to say that most materials writers nowadays would agree with Carter (1998) that both authentic and inauthentic texts can inform the curriculum. Despite being a corpus linguist, Carter (1998) argues that patently *in*authentic as well as authentic texts are pedagogically exploitable (see also Shortall 2007). Rather than aiming to expose learners to how English is spoken by native speakers, these artificial texts may intentionally contain a high frequency of a particular language item to alert learners to its existence, and to provide them with practice in manipulating it. Carter (1998) also points out that authentic dialogs can be modified somewhat to make them more accessible to learners, while retaining some of the more intriguing features of naturally occurring discourse. However, just because materials are authentic, there is no guarantee learners will find them interesting (Prodromou 1988). There is much to be said, then, for producing materials on a local rather than a global level, connecting them meaningfully with the context and with the learners' own lives (Rossner 1988; Rubdy 2003; Tomlinson 2003a). Materials writers will therefore need to consider their purposes and priorities carefully when choosing texts and balancing the authentic against the inauthentic.

Materials writers should also consider whose authentic English is to inform the curriculum. It has often been pointed out that there are far more nonnative than native speakers of English around the world nowadays, and that nonnatives are far more likely to need to speak English with other nonnatives (e.g., Crystal 2003). The question then arises as to whether and to what extent these Englishes in the expanding circle (Kachru 1985) should be governed by those of the inner circle. Many researchers feel such considerations should be linked with international intelligibility: Those deviations by nonnative speakers that do not lead to miscommunication should be distinguished from those that do, with only the latter type pointed out by teachers (see Jenkins 1998, 2000, 2002; Seidlhofer 2005). Although a number of arguments have been put forward in favor of an English as a Lingua Franca (ELF) model (e.g., Seidlhofer 2005), Kuo (2006) and Timmis (2002) remind us that some nonnative speakers wish to sound like native speakers. Whatever variation of English is chosen, however, issues of identity loom large.

The content of the curriculum generally, and of the resulting materials in particular, is often seen as governed by "needs," although the meaning of "needs" is far from straightforward (does it refer to any or all of the learners' "lacks," "necessities," and/or "wants," to use Hutchinson and Waters's 1987 terms?). The literature is replete with discussions about whose needs materials writers should take into account (see Long 2005 and West 1994 for helpful overviews) and what instruments materials developers should use to conduct needs analyses (e.g., Jordan 1997, who lists 14 different methods). Whereas it was the language "expert" who traditionally identified needs (e.g., Munby 1978), more recent approaches have recommended that a number of parties should have a say, including teachers, education authorities, and other stakeholders (e.g., parents, sponsors), as well as the learners themselves. Writing specifically about English for Academic Purposes (EAP) contexts, Swales *et al.* (2001) note that although many useful insights into academic genres have been provided by corpus studies like Hyland's (e.g., 2000), many researchers question whether these findings should be unquestioningly transmitted by teachers – and unquestioningly imitated by students. The aim of such a "pragmatic" approach to needs analysis and to materials design is to identify the dominant discourse norms, and to ensure these norms are mastered by the students. However, Swales *et al.* (2001) make it clear that others believe instead that students and lecturers should "negotiate" discoursal norms as part of a more equal relationship. Hence Benesch (2001) and Pennycook (1997) have introduced elements of Freireian critical pedagogy into EAP, resulting in "critical EAP" or "critical pragmatic EAP" (see Harwood & Hadley 2004). Regardless of which pedagogy is chosen, though, this will impact on how the materials construct teacher and learner roles.

Continuing to focus on teacher and learner roles, a number of researchers have stressed the need to promote learner independence. Breen and Littlejohn (2000), Clarke (1989), Littlejohn (1985), Nunan (1988), and Tudor (1996) all offer accounts of how a learner-centered curriculum can be implemented. Clarke (1989), for instance, suggests that a learner-centered approach can be fostered by getting learners to adapt materials for their own or other classes, even where materials are imposed by some official curriculum or institutional requirement. This will lead to enhanced interest on the part of learners, and a shift in their roles from "language receiver" to "collaborator"; from "assimilator" to "knower," since by adapting or designing new tasks that focus on form, learners become "expert" in those areas and are then able to transmit their knowledge to others (p. 135). In line with Tudor (1992), McGrath (2002) argues that learner-centeredness is a matter of degree. Whereas some of the activities he proposes feature relatively modest amounts of learner-centeredness, more radical proposals include an approach akin to learner-based teaching (Campbell & Kryszewska 1992).

With regard to the variety of pedagogical activities designers can draw on, a wide and diverse range is justified and explicated by the authors in this volume, and an overview of contents is provided at the end of this chapter. Whatever the activity selected, designers will also wish to evaluate the effectiveness of the curriculum in general and the materials in particular, and a plethora of criteria can inform evaluation checklists (see, for instance, Breen & Candlin 1987; Chambers 1997; Cunningsworth 1995; Tomlinson *et al.* 2001; Williams 1983; see also Mikk's 2000 survey of the evaluation schemes used in mainstream education). As Roberts (1996) has argued, however, one of the problems with evaluation checklists is that they are all to some extent context-specific, and will therefore not be unproblematically transferrable to any given situation and set of materials; hence they "should be regarded as illustrative and suggestive only" (p. 381). There will thus be a need for what Roberts (1996) calls a "pre-evaluation phase," during which the teacher defines his or her own context, and on this basis draws up locally appropriate criteria to be evaluated.

Another important contribution to thinking on materials evaluation has come from Ellis (1997). Like Roberts (1996), Ellis highlights the need for *retrospective*, *empirical*, as well as *predictive* evaluations, since, no matter how systematic (predictive) checklists may appear, they will always be to some extent intuitive and subjective (Sheldon 1988). While Ellis (1997) acknowledges that most teachers informally conduct micro-evaluations (normally mentally and on the fly), there is much to be gained from formalizing the process, since the result is likely to be better thought out and more rigorous. Tomlinson (2003c) also argues for a more systematic, empirical approach to evaluation, using pre- and posttests, exams, interviews, questionnaires, learner diaries, and so on, although he acknowledges the time and expertise such a systematic approach would require. However, one of the chapters in this volume (Jones & Schmitt, Chapter 10) provides an account of empirical post-use evaluation, and other contributors discuss how their materials have been (or could be) modified as a result of classroom trialing.

I now review some of the key literature featuring an analysis of materials at the level of content. Although this literature has focused on commercial materials that are widely available, there are also useful messages here for teachers who are producing or adapting in-house materials.

Content analysis

As Pingel (1999) explains, quantitative content analysis of materials and textbooks involves counting the number of references to a particular topic/item, or identifying content categories and calculating the percentage of space devoted to each category. In contrast, qualitative content analysis is more overtly interpretive, seeking to uncover meanings and values transmitted by the materials. De Posada (1999) argues that content analyses can show materials writers' "pedagogical, psychological, and epistemological positions" (p. 425), as well as revealing "cultural patterns" and "the focus of societal attention" (Wasburn 1997: 473), since materials are at some level representative of the world in which they originate. In TESOL, then, content analysis of textbooks/materials normally focuses on the language taught or the thematic content, and both types of study are now reviewed, before the limitations of this body of work are discussed.

(a) Linguistic content analyses

Researchers have wondered for some time how closely the language textbooks teach matches the language speakers and writers use (e.g., Ewer & Boys 1981). Sheldon (1988) judged that commercial materials writers selected and presented vocabulary "without system" and without consulting sources like West's (1953) service list. It seemed "a closed circle" was in operation,

> ... wherein textbooks merely grow from and imitate other textbooks and do not admit the winds of change from research, methodological experimentation, or classroom feedback. (Sheldon 1988: 239)

The compilation of corpora in recent years has provided us with databases of authentic language use, making it possible to investigate this issue systematically, and the results are not encouraging: It would seem that much of the language taught in commercial materials differs markedly from the language that is actually used in spoken and written discourse. Some of what follows draws on Gilmore's (2007) useful review, and whereas all of the content analyses discussed here are preoccupied with language, I draw a (convenient but artificial) distinction between those focusing on language, pragmatics, and genre.

(i) Language

A number of corpus-based studies have identified a linguistic gap between commercial materials and actual language use. Hence ELT textbooks misrepresent the range of modal language (Holmes 1988; Hyland 1994; McEnery & Kifle 2002; Römer 2004) and reported speech (Barbieri & Eckhardt 2007) found in native speaker corpora, and textbooks' treatment of the linking adverbial *though* (Conrad 2004) and the present continuous tense (Römer 2005) comes up short. Carter (1998), Cullen and Kuo (2007), and McCarthy and Carter (1995) show how corpora distinguish spoken and written grammar, suggesting that standard grammars and materials that are not informed by corpus data fail to account for some pervasive spoken discourse features (such as ellipsis and vague language). A number of studies, including Jones (1997) and Levis (1999), have also highlighted the unsatisfactory treatment of pronunciation in textbooks, and research in other areas (such as textbooks' treatment of formulaic language) is ongoing (see Gouverneur 2008).

(ii) Pragmatics

It is difficult for language learners to achieve pragmalinguistic competence, as Bardovi-Harlig *et al.* (1991) argue, because speech acts are not easily transferred from one language to another (see also Rose & Kasper 2001; Thornbury & Slade 2006); however, "[s]peakers who do not use pragmatically appropriate language run the risk of appearing uncooperative at the least, or, more seriously, rude or insulting" (p. 4). For instance, Bardovi-Harlig *et al.* (1991) point out that the way conversations are closed varies from culture to culture, with some cultures having minimal closing requirements, and others (including American and British) having far more elaborate ones. Their study of ELT textbooks' treatment of closing conversations finds the advice given wanting. Chan (2009b) and Jiang (2006) found shortcomings in textbooks' coverage of suggestions, and Boxer and Pickering (1995) found advice on the language of complaints similarly inadequate. This shows, Boxer and Pickering believe, that textbook dialogs "are not based on spontaneously occurring conversations but rather on authors' intuitions" (p. 47). Hence,

> ... many ELT texts ... continue to concentrate on the acquisition of linguistic competence, with insufficient attention to a fuller communicative competence.
>
> (Boxer & Pickering 1995: 52)

(iii) Genre

Several studies have compared textbooks' language syllabi in specific genres with real-life data in the realms of academic and business discourse. Williams (1988) and Chan (2009a), for instance, contrast the language that features in textbooks with that in real-life business meetings. Candlin *et al.* (2002) focus on legal English materials. In trying to locate suitable legal writing materials for Hong Kong EAP learners, they found that, of the 56 books available, "[f]ew, if any, are premised on any type of research-based linguistic analysis of legal texts and language" (p. 300). Finally, Paltridge (2002), in common with Harwood (2005b) and Hyland (1994, 1998), finds that textbooks offering advice to EAP students on writing often do so anecdotally (that is, "[f]ew ... include an examination of actual texts" [p. 126]), and that such advice as is presented is incomplete.

(b) Cultural content analyses

As well as being carriers of linguistic content, materials have also been seen as cultural artifacts because of their thematic content (e.g., Apple 1984; Liu 2005; Luke 1988). One example of a cultural content analysis was conducted by Shardakova and Pavlenko (2004), who object to the construction of the target culture in two Russian language textbooks. In one of the books, women are reportedly depicted "as less socially engaged, situated predominantly in the family domain" (p. 36), despite the fact that the majority of women in Russia work outside the home. Both books stereotype women as being preoccupied with romantic relationships, whereas men are more concerned with their careers (see also Porreca 1984, who found gender stereotyping in TESOL textbooks). Both books also (inaccurately) portray Russia as an ethnically homogeneous society, and one of the books is said to present students with a crudely stereotypical view of Russian society by informing readers that many Russian businessmen "clearly have connections with organized crime" (p. 34). Another well-known study of the cultural messages transmitted by language textbooks is Canagarajah (1993a), who argues that the (US) textbook he used in Sri Lanka presented his Tamil learners with an alien, consumerist culture:

> ... the situations represented – such as commuting frequently by air, performing instant cooking, or doing department store shopping – assume an urbanised, Western culture that is foreign to the rural, "third world" students. (p. 147)

It should be noted, however, that a more recent article by Gray (2002) suggests that ELT publishers are concerned with eliminating any content that may offend teachers or learners. Gray (2002) illustrates this by showing how women occupy positions of power in a bestselling UK textbook, and men are shown "in situations where they wear aprons, prepare meals for their female partners, and talk knowledgeably about housework" (p. 159). Gray (2002) explains how some ELT publishers rely on the acronym PARSNIP (politics, alcohol, religion, sex, narcotics, -isms, and pork) to determine the subject matter best avoided (p. 159). However, he argues that the downside of all of this is that textbooks can become "bland" and "begin to look very much alike" as materials writers opt for the same "safe" topics (p. 159).

(c) The limitations of content analysis

Both quantitative and qualitative forms of content analysis have been critiqued (e.g., Johnsen 1993). The former is guilty of "enabl[ing] breadth at the expense of depth" (Nicholls 2003), revealing which aspects of language, culture, and content feature heavily in the materials, but telling us little about how these aspects are presented. The latter approach, unless conducted rigorously and systematically, suffers from reliability issues. For instance, it is noticeable that neither Canagarajah (1993a) nor Shardakova and Pavlenko (2004) include any mention of inter-rater reliability testing of their analyses. Qualitative content analysis may also be felt to lack generalizability, having limited relevance to other materials beyond the scope of the investigation.

As Shardakova and Pavlenko (2004) acknowledge, because it is confined to an analysis of the printed page, content analysis suffers from the weakness of being disconnected from the context in which the materials are presented – the classroom – and can take no account of the learners' and teachers' reactions to, and adaptations/subversions of, the materials to truly gauge their impact. Hence it is necessary to speak to the users of materials, as Gray (2000) has done in his questionnaire-based study of teachers' attitudes. What is significant about this study is that it provides evidence that the (undesirable) cultural messages that Shardakova and Pavlenko, Canagarajah, and others claim to be present in textbooks do not only exist in content analysts' minds: All of the teachers Gray surveyed reported sometimes feeling "uncomfortable" with the messages conveyed by the textbook they were using. This concern related to "stereotypical representations, mainly of Britain," and "irrelevant, outdated, and sexist content" (p. 276). Whereas some teachers objected to the portrayal of their own (British) culture in the textbooks – two teachers felt uncomfortable by an unfavorable image of parenting, for instance – others were more concerned "with the potentially alienating effect of the material on their students" (p.

277). One teacher reports there being "dozens" of references to drinking and pubs throughout the textbook, which "seem to imply a culture obsessed with the stuff " which he "didn't feel like having to defend" when teaching in Egypt (p. 277). Most of the teachers surveyed felt the textbook constructed British teenagers as deceitful and sexually promiscuous, and that learners could be given the impression that the textbooks implicitly condoned these attitudes. Yet Gray also found that 11 of the 12 teachers surveyed deleted or adapted materials they felt were culturally inappropriate, or would do so now if asked to teach the same materials. Hence, however (in)appropriate textbook content may be, teachers (and students) may operationalize this material in a very different way to that envisaged by the textbook author, making the lesson in turn more or less ideologically (in)appropriate. These findings are in agreement with those of other studies from TESOL (Hutchinson & Torres 1994) and ethnographies from mainstream education (Alvermann 1987, 1989; Hinchman 1987), which also show that teachers' use of the same set of materials can vary considerably and can be exploited to achieve different aims.

In light of such findings, I will argue that further research relating to how materials are used in the classroom is necessary. However, I first discuss another set of literature describing materials writers' accounts of the design process.

The challenge of materials writing: Authors' and publishers' accounts

There are a number of materials writers' accounts of the design process, all of which underscore its complexity and formidable nature. I focus first of all on an innovative study by Johnson (2003).

The materials writers in Johnson's (2003) investigation were asked to design a task that focused on teaching learners how to describe people, with the informants thinking aloud about what they were doing during the exercise. Eight experienced and eight novice materials designers took part, the experienced informants having written commercial textbooks. Johnson found that experienced designers are more likely to "complexify" than the novices: that is, the experienced materials writers spent far more time considering alternative ways of designing the task, whereas the inexperienced designers tended "to think of one configuration, and immediately go with that" (pp. 99-100). One of the experienced writers, for instance, considered using as many as six different types of tasks before making a final decision. She then spent an hour exploring the task type she thought would work, but eventually ruled it out, moving on to consider an alternative task type. Johnson (2003) uses this episode to make two points:

> ... the possibility of dead ends can never be eliminated even by the most experienced designers. Secondly, it is noteworthy that this designer is able, ready and willing to abandon a possibility even though such an amount of time and effort has been put into it. (pp. 97-8)

Experienced materials designers are therefore said to have an "easy abandonment capacity" compared to inexperienced designers. Like the "expert" teacher in Tsui's (2003) study, then, experienced designers constantly question and problematize what they are doing. In sum, Johnson's (2003) research highlights the effort and rigor needed to produce materials. Indeed, Samuda (2005), who worked with Johnson on the project, sums it up as follows:

> ... the overall message from this work is that the process of task design is certainly not a matter of working through the development of a task from beginning to end in a linear fashion, nor does it entail orderly progressions through checklists of guiding principles. Task design is a complex, highly recursive and often messy process, requiring the designer to hold in mind a vast range of task variables relating to the design-in-process. (p. 243)

Richards (2006) offers another recent account of the complexities of the design process, describing how the research literature has altered and influenced his approach. For instance, he has reconsidered his approach to the teaching of listening, and to the materials he produces, as a result of advances in SLA research. He also used his own listening research to shape his materials. And he describes how he consulted corpus research and academic word lists like Coxhead's (2000) when designing reading materials, whereas the selection of grammar items was influenced by the corpus-based Cobuild grammar (Collins Cobuild 2005). Nevertheless, he argues that not all research findings and data sources are equally relevant or applicable for materials writers. Authentic conversational interaction may well prove inappropriate for incorporation into activities because of its primarily phatic nature, offering little of what Richards wants his dialogs to contain: "a repertoire of essential vocabulary, grammar, functions, and communication strategies" (p. 20). As well as research findings, materials writers must also bear other factors in mind; that is,

> ... *contextual factors* (the kinds of grammatical items specified in national syllabuses in countries where the courses were to be marketed), as well as *teacher factors* (information from teachers and consultants on grammatical items they would expect to see included at different levels). (p. 11)

Whether these expectations and requirements are appropriate or not, to a certain extent materials writers are obliged to heed them and meet the users where they are:

> The route from research to application ... is by no means direct, since language teaching materials are also shaped by many other factors and constraints and the success of teaching materials is not dependent upon the extent to which they are informed by research. It is not difficult to find examples of widely used teaching materials that succeed despite their archaic methodology because they suit the contexts in which they are used. (p. 23)

Materials writers are faced with a number of competing demands, then. They need to make their materials suitable for a wide variety of teachers, who have different amounts of experience, are more or less qualified, and who may have differing teaching styles and beliefs. As Johnson *et al.*'s (2008) study shows, experienced and inexperienced teachers may be looking for different things from materials. Textbook writers need to make their materials easy enough to follow for the inexperienced teacher by, for instance, making activities build upon one another in a transparent and predictable sequence, or by providing detailed teachers' notes, while at the same time ensuring the materials are flexible enough for the more experienced teacher to adapt in any number of ways. In the words of a textbook editor, then, authors are trying "to please all the people all the time" (Young 1990: 77; see also Mares 2003). Producing truly innovative materials could lead to resistance on the part of teachers: The textbook writers in Littlejohn's (1992) study say that many of the teachers who are likely to use their materials will teach in a "traditional," teacher-centered manner, wanting a textbook they can follow to the letter. These teachers will "have certain expectations about what should be in a language course and will reject anything that differs markedly" (p. 147). In addition,we have seen that materials writers are obliged to satisfy curriculum requirements and other stipulations made by educational authorities and political policymakers (Altbach 1991; Richards 2006). These requirements can be extremely rigid: In the mainstream education context, individual US states can make highly specific (indeed, frequently absurd) curricular demands (e.g., Ravitch 2003). And even in TESOL, Freebairn (2000) points out that no matter how "brilliant or suitable in most respects," textbooks can "be dismissed out of hand because of one ill-advised reference to a controversial topic" (p. 3). She also points out that a topic that provokes lively exchanges in one context may be taboo in another.

Materials writers obviously need to bear in mind the needs of the context and their audience; however, some of the challenges they face appear to derive from the fact that, as Apple (1984) and Apple and Christian-Smith (1991) have argued, textbooks are commercial artifacts, profit being the first priority in the eyes of the industry (although it should be acknowledged that some publishers operate as nonprofit charities). Silverman (1991), an editor of American university textbooks, says that money is "the bottom line," and she compares textbooks to "breakfast cereals or automobiles or shoes," in that all of these are "products," "manufactured and sold for the purpose of making a profit" (p. 163). This is why, as Mehlinger (1991) says, textbooks produced in the West "approach the visual quality of coffee-table volumes" (p. 149). All of this presentational detail is designed to win the approval of what tends to be a cursory evaluation by potential users:

> One reason so much expense is lavished on visual qualities in American textbooks is that publishers believe that, in order to be adopted, their books must pass the "flip test" – a hypothetical test performed by teachers and school administrators who, lacking time to read each text presented for adoption, merely "flip" through the pages while trying to form an impression of the quality of the book. It is surely the case that publishers spend as many hours agonizing over color, layout, illustration, and design as they do over editorial style and content. (p. 150)

Other accounts confirm this preoccupation with presentational details. Young (1990), for instance, talks about how her publishing house was concerned when it learned that its new textbook launch had been preempted by a rival's. Notice how her account focuses on the look of the rival's book rather than its content:

> ... we found ourselves somewhat scooped by a new biology textbook put out by [another publisher]. They ... had remarkably beautiful photos and art, and they tried a new format. They concluded discussion of a topic at the bottom of the page; there was no need to turn the page to conclude the reading and no beginning of topics, or ending, in the middle of a page. (p. 82)

And Bell and Gower's (1998) fascinating insight into the "compromises" they were obliged to make when writing their successful textbook also confirms that the publishers placed a much higher priority on how the textbook looked than on what it did.

In contrast to Bell and Gower's (1998) account, which describes a relatively happy experience of textbook authoring despite the odd "compromise" along the way, Olson (1999) describes his bitter experience of producing a composition textbook for the US market. Olson was contracted by a major publisher to write an innovative process-oriented composition textbook which, when completed, was organized like a traditional rhetorical book at the editor's insistence:

> Despite our protestations that arranging a "process-oriented"

> book according to the rhetorical modes exhibited a ridiculous inconsistency and would certainly discourage any truly progressive compositionist from adopting the book, the editor prevailed, arguing that "the progressive people are always a minority; we're targeting the majority – where the money is." (p. x)

Unsurprisingly, the result satisfied neither the traditionalists nor the innovators.

I close this section on a happier note, by reviewing some of Swales's accounts of textbook writing. In common with the other publications reviewed here, these illustrate the amount of reflection, attention to detail, and research that should go into materials design, at the same time highlighting the challenging nature of the design task itself. Swales's position, in common with that of Alred and Thelen (1993), is that textbook writing should be seen as a scholarly, rather than a low-status, activity. Accordingly, Swales (1995) makes clear how one of his textbooks coauthored with Feak (Swales & Feak 1994) was shaped by research into academic discourse across the academy. Swales and Feak drew on their own and existing EAP writing research, and, where less research existed, invited students and teachers to conduct further research to complement that reported in the textbook. In a more recent account, Swales (2002) describes how he collects findings from corpus studies, which can then be incorporated into new materials, and also mentions that the draft materials under discussion have been modified "as a result of two class trials" (p. 162). Another account that shows how materials writing can be research-led is Swales *et al.* (2001). In designing EAP materials for postgraduate architecture students, the researchers

> ... interviewed architecture students and faculty, conducted a literature review of architectural discourse ..., observed design studios, examined student written assignments and their responses to those assignments, recorded, transcribed and analysed a number of ... sessions from the studios, read and studied a wide range of architecture texts, reflected upon the numerous displays that line the corridors of the building, and used the Michigan Corpus of

Academic Speech in English (MICASE) for corpus linguistic work. (p. 442)

Materials writers can learn much from these and from other recent thoughtful, detailed accounts of the materials design process by Stoller and colleagues (Stoller *et al.* 2005, 2006), Lee (2007), and Reaser and Adger (2007).

Accounts like those above illustrate the formidable nature of principled materials design because the process clearly required considerable time, resources, and expertise. Swales *et al.* (2001), for instance, describe a process that took place over a period of four years. Most materials designers will not be in a position to perform such a lengthy period of research (although note that Feak and Swales in this volume explain how they were able to research and compile a perinatology corpus relatively quickly). Stoller and colleagues are also at an advantage in that their audiences are very specific (chemists). But where, for instance, would a textbook author of a global "general" English textbook begin his/her investigations? What kind of data should s/he collect? And even in more specific EAP contexts, things are rarely straightforward. Consider the EAP textbook writer, for instance, who only has access to corpora of "expert" writing (i.e., journal articles). Given that we know that expert writing is markedly different from (successful) student writing, even in the same discipline (e.g., Harwood 2005a; Samraj 2002, 2004), these corpora will not be sufficient: The materials writer should also have access to corpora of student writing (Harwood 2005c). If s/he does not, one must be built, and textbook writers' (Bell & Gower 1998) and publishers' (Young 1990) accounts suggest that production schedules are often very tight, which would preclude such corpus compilation taking place. Researchers and/or textbook authors therefore need to alert publishers to the difficulties industry norms cause them, and publishers should strive to ensure that textbook writers are provided with the time and resources to do their job well.

The final section in this chapter presents other proposals that I argue need to be acted upon to improve the quality of TESOL materials, as well as our understanding of the materials design process itself.

Future research, future challenges for materials design

Peters *et al.* (1997) argue that we still do not have "[a] commonly accepted and elaborated 'theory of textbooks'" because our "knowledge about the way in which the textbooks are used by teachers and pupils alike at school and at home is limited" (p. 476). How can such a theory of textbooks – and indeed of materials generally – be arrived at? The key would appear to be ethnographic studies of materials production and use.

(a) Ethnographies of materials production

Apple (1984), like Johnsen (1993), has called for textbook ethnographies tracing a book's "writing to its selling (and then to its use)" (p. 319). What is needed initially, then, are ethnographies of materials production, involving interviews with publishers and authors as a product unfolds in order to gain an insight into the factors that shape the eventual form of the materials. As Venezky (1992) puts it, "we have no case studies on the design of new textbook series that would allow insights into the origins of textbook innovations or the decision-making processes that lead to the retention or rejection of specific content or design" (p. 444). There is the need for TESOL practitioners and researchers to understand the conditions in which materials and textbooks are produced: What are publishers' priorities? In Littlejohn's (1992) words, "Why are ELT materials the way they are?" Accounts such as these will allow researchers to understand the pressures editors and materials writers operate under, but will also enable researchers to interrogate and critique the standard practices and assumptions of the industry, and to suggest alternatives.

(b) Ethnographies of materials use

As Kalmus (2004), Lebrun *et al.* (2002), Johnsen (1993), Schudson (1994), Wade (1993), Zahorik (1991), and others argue, although it is easy to critique materials using content analysis, it is less easy to predict what effect these texts will have when they are put to use in the classroom. Two studies that have investigated the effect of materials in use are Canagarajah (1993b) and Yakhontova (2001). Canagarajah (1993b) writes of how the textbook's "communicative" pedagogy was resisted by his Tamil learners. He explains how he tried to get his students to take a collaborative approach to learning, rearranging the desks in a circle for textbook pairwork activities. However, before each class, students moved the desks back into traditional rows. Students also often missed classes when they knew communicative activities would be the focus, yet attended those lessons devoted to "the more overtly grammar-oriented sections of the textbook" (p. 616). These findings bring to mind well-known work by Holliday (1994) and Kumaravadivelu (1994), which appeals for locally appropriate methodology to be employed. Also relevant is Kerfoot's (1993) call for materials designers to address local concerns by taking teachers' and learners' evaluations into account during the development and piloting stages.

Yakhontova (2001) conducted a study in a Ukranian university setting of students' reactions to the (Ukranian) writing teacher's use of an American textbook designed for nonnative students studying in the West. Yakhontova (2001) describes how the contextual conditions are at odds with those of the students for whom the book was authored. Despite generally favorable reactions to the materials and an appreciation that it was raising awareness of written discoursal features, that the Ukranian system does not emphasize, there was some learner resistance due to the cultural strangeness of the book and the lack of references to Russian and / or to the Ukranian context therein. Yakhontova (2001) argues that authors could design local versions of materials and textbooks, which could include comparisons between the students' first language (L1) and English "in order to stimulate analytical contemplation of culture-specific differences in English and native academic discourses" (p. 412). An advantage of this approach would be to enable the students to make informed choices as to the conventions they wish to follow: In other words, the materials Yakhontova proposes would feature a critical element (cf. Benesch 2001; Pennycook 1997).

Canagarajah and Yakhontova's ethnographies provide us with insights into contextual conditions and requirements. Clearly, future studies also need to focus on students' reactions to and comprehension of classroom materials, as well as on teachers' interpretations of the materials. Peacock (1997) and Huang *et al.* (2006) are two other studies that have attempted to investigate things from the learners' perspective, whereas McGrath (2006) surveys both teachers' and learners' perspectives. Although there have been occasional studies of this type, then, there is the need to pursue this line of enquiry further, and Kalmus (2004) contains many useful methodological proposals for ensuring such investigations are as valid and reliable as possible, proposing pre- and posttests, questionnaires, interviews, systematic classroom observations, focus-group sessions, and analyses of learners' writing as a result of interacting with the materials.

Last but by no means least, there needs to be better dialog and communication between materials writers, researchers, and publishers. Gilmore (2007) concludes his comprehensive review of authenticity in ELT materials by highlighting the need for better communication between theorists and practitioners. He quotes Bouton (1996), who argues that "[p]oor communication between researchers and teachers means that potentially useful findings from research often 'linger in journals' instead of making it into the classroom" (p. 112). With the exception of people like Swales, many researchers interested in materials design do not write textbooks, and textbook writers do not conduct research into materials. This book therefore aims to stimulate such dialog, and to cause materials writers to become researchers and researchers to become materials writers, ensuring that such research becomes "less of an 'after the event' activity and more of an integrated part of the development and use of textbooks" and materials (Johnsen 1993).

Overview of this volume

After this introduction, Part B of this volume, "Perspectives on materials," begins with Rod Ellis's chapter, which explains and illustrates how second language acquisition (SLA) research has contributed to two areas of materials development: the design of communicative tasks and grammar-teaching activities. In addition, Ellis provides numerous signposts to SLA literature, which will be of interest to those readers less familiar with the area. Hayo Reinders and Cynthia White also refer to the literature on task design and second language acquisition in their discussion and exemplification of the design of computer-assisted language-learning (CALL) materials. Brian Tomlinson's chapter outlines a number of principles which it is argued should inform materials development, and are drawn from the SLA and the language-teaching literature. The section concludes with Sarah Benesch's account of how she developed a set of materials dealing with the issue of military recruitment, exemplifying how a critical element can be built into the curriculum. In the spirit of such an approach, there is a notable element of self-questioning and self-criticism woven into the chapter involving a reevaluation of the materials.

The chapters in Part C focus on discrete elements of the language syllabus. Norman Evans, James Hartshorn, and Neil Anderson explain and illustrate how three principles – responsiveness, cohesion, and stability – inform their development of reading materials. Chris Tribble shows how genre theory can inform the teaching of writing, exemplifying his approach by applying it to the teaching of the discursive essay to Cambridge First Certificate in English (FCE) candidates. Christine Goh focuses on metacognitive listening instruction, providing a wide range of activities that can be used to develop learners' sense of *how* to listen, which are suitable for a range of levels and ages. Rebecca Hughes's chapter concentrates on the speaking skill, explaining how authentic data can be exploited to develop learners' spontaneous speech. The final chapter in this section, by Martha Jones and Norbert Schmitt, explains how a needs analysis and subsequent compilation of a spoken corpus were used to inform the teaching of disciplinary vocabulary and collocations relevant for speaking in academic seminars. They include an account of how a post-use evaluation of the materials was carried out.

Part D examines materials designed for particular specific and academic purposes. A number of chapters focus on academic contexts. Both Martin Hewings's and Christine Feak and John Swales's chapters discuss materials developing university-level writing in specific disciplines. Offering in-sessional language support to postgraduate students, Hewings draws on genre analysis and argumentation research to provide rhetorical models for essay writing. Feak and Swales's chapter explains how the learners, whose subject knowledge may far exceed the teacher's, can themselves inform materials design. Assigned with developing a course to develop postdoctoral perinatologists' writing skills, Feak and Swales also show how a discipline-specific corpus was inexpensively constructed to compare and contrast writing practices in the discipline with other fields. In contrast, Nigel Harwood focuses on how postgraduates from across the disciplinary spectrum can be taught about the rhetorical functions of citation using data from an interview-based research project. Mary Jane Curry and Theresa Lillis's chapter is devoted to a type of nonnative speaker often neglected in discussions of materials design: the scholar wishing to publish in English. Their sample materials are founded on extensive ethnographic research that will equip scholars with a range of strategies they can use when writing and publishing. Susan Bosher's chapter on nursing English shows how her materials were written after a principled needs analysis, and will be a useful resource for ESP practitioners facing the challenge of providing a similar course appropriate for their context. The final two chapters in this section concern nonacademic contexts. Focusing on business English, Jo Angouri compares turn-taking patterns in real-life business meetings with textbook dialogs, suggesting ways in which materials can more effectively prepare learners for workplace interactions. Finally, Cori Jakubiak and Linda Harklau discuss materials design for immigrant ESL learners looking to live and work in predominantly English-speaking countries, such as the United States.

A series of discussion questions and tasks follow each chapter, asking readers to *reflect on*, *evaluate*, and *adapt* or *design* materials relevant to the issues raised.

References

Allwright, R. L. (1981). What do we want teaching materials for? *ELT Journal* 36(1): 5-18.

Alred, G. J., & Thelen, E. A. (1993). Are textbooks contributions to scholarship? *College Composition & Communication* 44(4): 466-77.

Altbach, P. G. (1991). The unchanging variable: Textbooks in comparative perspective. In P. G. Altbach *et al.* (eds.). *Textbooks in American society: Politics, policy, and pedagogy*. Albany: State University of New York Press, pp. 237-54.

Alvermann, D. E. (1987). The role of textbooks in teachers' interactive decision making. *Reading Research & Instruction* 26(2): 115-27.

Alvermann, D. E. (1989). Teacher-student mediation of content area texts. *Theory into Practice* 28(2): 142-7.

Apple, M. W. (1984). The political economy of text publishing. *Educational Theory* 34(4): 307-19.

Apple, M. W., & Christian-Smith, L. K. (1991). The politics of the textbook. In M. W. Apple & L. K. Christian-Smith (eds.). *The politics of the textbook*. London: Routledge, pp. 1-21.

Ball, D. L., & Feiman-Nemser, S. (1988). Using textbooks and teachers' guides: A dilemma for beginning teachers and teacher educators. *Curriculum Inquiry* 18(4): 401-23.

Barbieri, F., & Eckhardt, S. E. B. (2007). Applying corpus-based findings to form-focused instruction: The case of reported speech. *Language Teaching Research* 11(3): 319-46.

Bardovi-Harlig, K., Hartford, B. A. S., Mahan-Taylor, R., Morgan, M. J., & Reynolds, D. W. (1991). Developing pragmatic awareness: Closing the conversation. *ELT Journal* 45(1): 4-15.

Bell, J., & Gower, R. (1998). Writing course materials for the world: A great compromise. In B. Tomlinson (ed.). *Materials development in language teaching*. Cambridge: Cambridge University Press, pp. 116-29.

Benesch, S. (2001). *Critical English for Academic Purposes: Theory, politics, and practice*. Mahwah, NJ: Lawrence Erlbaum Associates.

Bouton, L. F. (1996). Pragmatics and language learning. In L. F. Bouton (ed.). *Pragmatics and Language Learning Vol. 7*. Urbana-Champaign, IL: University of Illinois, Division of English as a Foreign Language, pp. 1-20.

Boxer, D., & Pickering, L. (1995). Problems in the presentation of speech acts in ELT materials: The case of complaints. *ELT Journal* 49(1): 44-58.

Breen, M. P., & Candlin, C. N. (1987). Which materials? A consumer's and designer's guide. In L. E. Sheldon (ed.). *ELT textbooks and materials: Problems in evaluation and development*. London: Modern English Publications/The British Council, pp. 13-27.

Breen, M. P., & Littlejohn, A. (2000). *Classroom decision-making: Negotiation and process syllabuses in practice*. Cambridge: Cambridge University Press.

Brown, J. D. (1995). *The elements of language curriculum: A systematic approach to program development*. Boston: Heinle & Heinle.

Campbell, C., & Kryszewska, H. (1992). *Learner-based teaching*. Oxford: Oxford University Press.

Canagarajah, A. S. (1993a). American textbooks and Tamil students: Discerning ideological tensions in the ESL classroom. *Language, Culture & Curriculum* 6(2): 143-56.

Canagarajah, A. S. (1993b). Critical ethnography of a Sri Lankan classroom: Ambiguities in student opposition to reproduction through ESOL. *TESOL Quarterly* 27(4): 601-26.

Candlin, C. N., Bhatia, V. K., & Jensen, C. H. (2002). Developing legal writing materials for English second language learners: Problems and perspectives. *English for Specific Purposes* 21: 299-320.

Carter, R. (1998). Orders of reality: CANCODE, communication, and culture. *ELT Journal* 52(1): 43-56.

Chambers, F. (1997). Seeking consensus in coursebook evaluation. *ELT Journal* 51(1): 29-35.

Chan, C. S. C. (2009a). Forging a link between research and pedagogy: A holistic framework for evaluating business English materials. *English for Specific Purposes* 28: 125-36.

Chan, C. S. C. (2009b). Thinking out of the textbook: Toward authenticity and politeness awareness. In L. Savova (ed.). *Using textbooks effectively*. Alexandria: TESOL, pp. 9-20.

Clarke, D. F. (1989). Materials adaptation: Why leave it all to the teacher? *ELT Journal* 43(2): 133-41.

Collins Cobuild (2005). *Collins Cobuild English grammar* (2nd ed.). London: Harper Collins.

Conrad, S. (2004). Corpus linguistics, language variation, and language teaching. In J. Sinclair (ed.). *How to use corpora in language teaching*. Amsterdam: John Benjamins, pp. 67-85.

Coxhead, A. (2000). A new academic word list. *TESOL Quarterly* 34(2): 213-38.

Crystal, D. (2003). *English as a global language* (2nd ed.). Cambridge: Cambridge University Press.

Cullen, R., & Kuo, I.-C. (2007). Spoken grammar and ELT course materials: A missing link? *TESOL Quarterly* 41(2): 361-86.

Cunningsworth, A. (1995). *Choosing your coursebook*. Oxford: Heinemann.

de Posada, J. M. (1999). The presentation of metallic bonding in high school science textbooks during three decades: Science educational reforms and substantive changes of tendencies. *Science & Education* 83: 423-47.

Dudley-Evans, T., & St. John, M. J. (1998). *Developments in ESP: A multidisciplinary approach*. Cambridge: Cambridge University Press.

Ellis, R. (1997). The empirical evaluation of language teaching materials. *ELT Journal* 51(1): 36-42.

Ellis, R. (2006). Current issues in the teaching of grammar: An SLA perspective. *TESOL Quarterly* 40(1): 83-107.

Ewer, J. R., & Boys, O. (1981). The EST textbook situation: An enquiry. *The ESP Journal* 1(2): 87-105.

Freebairn, I. (2000). The coursebook – future continuous or past? *English Teaching Professional* 15 (April): 3-5.

Gilmore, A. (2007). Authentic materials and authenticity in foreign language learning. *Language Teaching* 40: 97-118.

Gouverneur, C. (2008). The phraseological patterns of high-frequency verbs in advanced English for general purposes: A corpus-driven approach to EFL textbook analysis. In F. Meunier & S. Granger (eds.). *Phraseology in foreign language learning and teaching*. Amsterdam: John Benjamins, pp. 223-43.

Graves, K. (2008). The language curriculum: A social contextual perspective. *Language Teaching* 41(2): 147-81.

Gray, J. (2000). The ELT coursebook as cultural artefact: How teachers censor and adapt. *ELT Journal* 54(3): 274-83.

Gray, J. (2002). The global coursebook in English Language Teaching. In D. Block & D. Cameron (eds.). *Globalization and language teaching*. London: Routledge, pp. 151-67.

Harwood, N. (2005a). "I hoped to counteract the memory problem, but I made no impact whatsoever": Discussing methods in computing science using *I*. *English for Specific Purposes* 24(3): 243-67.

Harwood, N. (2005b). "We do not seem to have a theory ... The theory I present here attempts to fill this gap": Inclusive and exclusive pronouns in academic writing. *Applied Linguistics* 26(3): 343-75.

Harwood, N. (2005c). What do we want EAP teaching materials for? *Journal of English for Academic Purposes* 4: 149-61.

Harwood, N., & Hadley, G. (2004). Demystifying institutional practices: Critical pragmatism and the teaching of academic writing. *English for Specific Purposes* 23(4): 355-77.

Heilenman, L. K. (1991). Material concerns: Textbooks and teachers. In E. S. Silber (ed.). *Critical issues in foreign language instruction*. New York: Garland Publishing, pp. 104-30.

Hinchman, K. (1987). The textbook and three content-area teachers. *Reading Research & Instruction* 26(4): 247-63.

Holliday, A. R. (1994). *Appropriate methodology and social context*. Cambridge: Cambridge University Press.

Holmes, J. (1988). Doubt and certainty in ESL textbooks. *Applied Linguistics* 9(1): 21-44.

Huang, S.-C., Cheng, Y.-S., & Chern, C.-L. (2006). Pre-reading materials from subject matter texts: Learner choices and the underlying learner characteristics. *Journal of English for Academic Purposes* 5: 193-206.

Hunston, S. (2002). *Corpora in applied linguistics*. Cambridge: Cambridge University Press.

Hutchinson, T., & Torres, E. (1994). The textbook as agent of change. *ELT Journal* 48(4): 315-28.

Hutchinson, T., & Waters, A. (1987). *English for Specific Purposes: A learning-centred approach*. Cambridge: Cambridge University Press.

Hyland, K. (1994). Hedging in academic writing and EAP textbooks. *English for Specific Purposes* 13(3): 239-56.

Hyland, K. (1998). *Hedging in scientific research articles*. Amsterdam: John Benjamins.

Hyland, K. (2000). *Disciplinary discourses: Social interactions in academic writing*. Harlow: Longman.

Jenkins, J. (1998). Which pronunciation norms and models for English as an International Language? *ELT Journal* 52(2): 119-26.

Jenkins, J. (2000). *The phonology of English as an international language*. Oxford: Oxford University Press.

Jenkins, J. (2002). A sociolinguistically based, empirically researched pronunciation syllabus for English as an International Language. *Applied Linguistics* 23(1): 83-103.

Jiang, X. (2006). Suggestions: What should ESL students know? *System* 34: 36-54.

Johnsen, E. B. (1993). *Textbooks in the kaleidoscope: A critical survey of literature and research on educational texts*. Oslo: Scandinavian University Press. Accessed online at: www-bib.hive.no/tekster/pedtekst/kaleidoscope/forside.html, April 30, 2008.

Johnson, K. (2003). *Designing language teaching tasks*. Basingstoke: Palgrave Macmillan.

Johnson, K., Kim, M., Ya-Fang, L., Nava, A., Perkins, D., Smith, A. M., Soler-Canela, O., & Lu, W. (2008). A step forward: Investigating expertise in materials evaluation. *ELT Journal* 62(2): 157-63.

Jones, R. H. (1997). Beyond "listen and repeat": Pronunciation teaching materials and theories of second language acquisition. *System* 25(1): 103-12.

Jordan, R. R. (1997). *English for Academic Purposes: A guide and resource book for teachers*. Cambridge: Cambridge University Press.

Kachru, B. B. (1985). Standards, codification and sociolinguistic realism: The English language in the outer circle. In R. Quirk and H. Widdowson (eds.). *English in the world: Teaching and learning the language and literatures*. Cambridge: Cambridge University Press, pp. 11-30.

Kalmus, V. (2004). What do pupils and textbooks do with each other? Methodological problems of research on socialization through educational media. *Journal of Curriculum Studies* 36(4): 469-85.

Kerfoot, C. (1993). Participator education in a South African context: Contradictions and challenges. *TESOL Quarterly* 27(3): 431-47.

Kumaravadivelu, B. (1994). The postmethod condition: (E)merging strategies for second/foreign language teaching. *TESOL Quarterly* 28(1): 27-48.

Kuo, I.-C. (2006). Addressing the issue of teaching English as a lingua franca. *ELT Journal* 60(3): 213-21.

Lebrun, J. *et al.* (2002). Past and current trends in the analysis of textbooks in the Quebec context. *Curriculum Inquiry* 32(1): 51-83.

Lee, D. J. (2007). Corpora and the classroom: A computer-aided error analysis of Korean students' writing and the design and evaluation of data-driven learning materials. Unpublished PhD thesis, University of Essex, UK.

Lee, W. Y.-C. (1995). Authenticity revisited: Text authenticity and learner authenticity. *ELT Journal* 49(4): 323-8.

Levis, J. M. (1999). Intonation in theory and practice, revisited. *TESOL Quarterly* 33(1): 37-63.

Littlejohn, A. (1985). Learner choice in language study. *ELT Journal* 39(4): 253-61.

Littlejohn, A. (1992). Why are English language teaching materials the way they are? Unpublished PhD thesis, University of Lancaster, UK.

Liu,Y. (2005). The construction of pro-science and technology discourse in Chinese language textbooks. *Language & Education* 19(4): 304-21.

Long, M. H. (2005). Methodological issues in needs analysis. In M. H. Long (ed.). *Second language needs analysis*. Cambridge: Cambridge University Press, pp. 19-76.

Luke, A. (1988). *Literacy, textbooks, and ideology: Postwar literacy instruction and the mythology of Dick and Jane*. London: Falmer Press.

McCarthy, M., & Carter, R. (1995). Spoken grammar: What is it and how can we teach it? *ELT Journal* 49(3): 207-18.

McEnery, T., & Kifle, N. A. (2002). Epistemic modality in argumentative essays of second-language writers. In J. Flowerdew (ed.). *Academic discourse*. Harlow: Longman, pp. 182-95.

Mares, C. (2003). Writing a coursebook. In B. Tomlinson (ed.). *Developing materials for language teaching*. London: Continuum, pp. 130-40.

McGrath, I. (2002). *Materials evaluation and design for language teaching*. Edinburgh: Edinburgh University Press.

McGrath, I. (2006). Teachers' and learners' images for coursebooks. *ELT Journal* 60(2): 171-80.

Mehlinger, H. D. (1991). American textbook reform: What we can learn from the Soviet experience. In P. G. Altbach *et al.* (eds.). *Textbooks in American society: Politics, policy, and pedagogy*. Albany: State University of New York Press, pp. 145-60.

Mikk, J. (2000). *Textbook: Research and writing*. Frankfurt: Peter Lang.

Mishan, F. (2005). *Designing authenticity into language learning materials*. Bristol: Intellect.

Munby, J. (1978). *Communicative syllabus design*. Cambridge: Cambridge University Press.

Nicholls, J. (2003). Methods in school textbook research. *International Journal of Historical Learning, Teaching and Research* 3(2). Accessed online at: www.centres.ex.ac.uk/historyresource/journal6/nichollsrev.pdf, May 1, 2008.

Nunan, D. (1988). *The Learner-centred curriculum*. Cambridge: Cambridge University Press.

O'Neill, R. (1982). Why use textbooks? *ELT Journal* 36(2): 104-11.

Olson, G. A. (1999). Foreword: Be just a little bit innovative – but not too much. In X. L. Gale & F. G. Gale (eds.). *(Re)visioning composition textbooks: Conflicts of culture, ideology, and pedagogy*. Albany: State University of New York Press, pp. ix-xi.

Paltridge, B. (2002). Thesis and dissertation writing: An examination of published advice and actual practice. *English for Specific Purposes* 21: 125-43.

Peacock, M. (1997). Comparing learner and teacher views on the usefulness and enjoyableness of materials. *International Journal of Applied Linguistics* 7(2): 183-200.

Pennycook, A. (1997). Vulgar pragmatism, critical pragmatism, and EAP. *English for Specific Purposes* 16(4): 253-69.

Peters, M., Ono, Y., Shimizu, K., & Hesse, M. (1997). Selected bioethical issues in Japanese and German textbooks of biology for lower secondary schools. *Journal of Moral Education* 26(4): 473-89.

Pingel, F. (1999). *UNESCO guide on textbook research and textbook revision.* Hannover: Verlag Hahnsohe Buchhandlung.

Porreca, K. L. (1984). Sexism in current ESL textbooks. *TESOL Quarterly* 18(4): 705-24.

Prodromou, L. (1988). English as cultural action. *ELT Journal* 42(2): 73-83.

Ravitch, D. (2003). *The language police: How pressure groups restrict what students learn.* New York: Alfred Knopf.

Reaser, J., & Adger, C. (2007). Developing language awareness materials for nonlinguists: Lessons learned from the *Do you speak American?* curriculum development project. *Language & Linguistics Compass* 1(3): 155-67.

Richards, J. C. (1993). Beyond the text book: The role of commercial materials in language teaching. *RELC Journal* 24(1): 1-14.

Richards, J. C. (2001). *Curriculum development in language teaching.* Cambridge: Cambridge University Press.

Richards, J. C. (2006). Materials development and research – Making the connection. *RELC Journal* 37(1): 5-26.

Richards, J. C., & Rodgers, T. S. (2001). *Approaches and methods in language teaching.* Cambridge: Cambridge University Press.

Roberts, J. T. (1996). Demystifying materials evaluation. *System* 24(3): 375-89.

Römer, U. (2004). A corpus-driven approach to modal auxiliaries and their didactics. In J. Sinclair (ed.). *How to use corpora in language teaching.* Amsterdam: John Benjamins, pp. 185-99.

Römer, U. (2005). *Progressives, patterns, pedagogy: A corpus-driven approach to English progressive forms, functions, contexts and didactics.* Amsterdam: John Benjamins.

Rose, K. R., & Kasper, G. (2001). *Pragmatics in language teaching.* Cambridge: Cambridge University Press.

Rossner, R. (1988). Materials for communicative language teaching and learning. *Annual Review of Applied Linguistics* 8: 140-63.

Rubdy, R. (2003). Selection of materials. In B. Tomlinson (ed.). *Developing materials for language teaching*. London: Continuum, pp. 37-57.

Samraj, B. (2002). Texts and contextual layers: Academic writing in content courses. In A. M. Johns (ed.). *Genre in the classroom: Multiple perspectives*. Mahwah, NJ: Lawrence Erlbaum Associates, pp. 163-76.

Samraj, B. (2004). Discourse features of the student-produced academic research paper: Variations across disciplinary courses. *Journal of English for Academic Purposes* 3(1): 5-22.

Samuda, V. (2005). Expertise in pedagogic task design. In K. Johnson (ed.). *Expertise in second language learning and teaching*. Basingstoke: Palgrave Macmillan, pp. 230-54.

Schudson, M. (1994). Textbook politics. *Journal of Communication* 44(1): 43-51.

Seidlhofer, B. (2005). English as a lingua franca. *ELT Journal* 59(4): 339-41.

Shardakova, M., & Pavlenko, A. (2004). Identity options in Russian textbooks. *Journal of Language, Identity, & Education* 3(1): 25-46.

Sheldon, L. E. (1988). Evaluating ELT textbooks and materials. *ELT Journal* 42(4): 237-46.

Shortall, T. (2007). The L2 syllabus: Corpus or contrivance? *Corpora* 2(2): 157-85.

Silverman, N. (1991). From the ivory tower to the bottom line: An editor's perspective on college textbook publishing. In P. G. Altbach *et al.* (eds.). *Textbooks in American society: Politics, policy, and pedagogy*. Albany: State University of New York Press, pp. 163-84.

Sinclair, J. (2004). *How to use corpora in language teaching*. Amsterdam: John Benjamins.

Stoller, F. L., Horn, B., Grabe, W., & Robinson, M. S. (2006). Evaluative review in materials development. *Journal of English for Academic Purposes* 5(3): 174-92.

Stoller, F. L., Jones, J. K., Costanza-Robinson, M. S., and Robinson, M. S. (2005). Demystifying disciplinary writing: A case study in the writing of chemistry. *Across the disciplines: Interdisciplinary perspectives on language, learning, and academic writing* 2. Accessed online at: www.wac.colostate.edu/atd/lds/stoller.cfm, May 9, 2007.

Swales, J. M. (1995). The role of the textbook in EAP writing research. *English for Specific Purposes* 14(1): 3-18.

Swales, J.M. (2002). Integrated and fragmented worlds: EAP materials and corpus linguistics. In J. Flowerdew (ed.). *Academic discourse*. Harlow, UK: Longman, pp. 150-64.

Swales, J. M., & Feak, C. B. (1994). *Academic writing for graduate students*. Ann Arbor: University of Michigan Press.

Swales, J. M., Barks, D., Ostermann, A. C., & Simpson, R. C. (2001). Between critique and accommodation: Reflections on an EAP course for Masters of Architecture students. *English for Specific Purposes* 20: 439-58.

Thornbury, S., & Slade, D. (2006). *Conversation: From description to pedagogy*. Cambridge: Cambridge University Press.

Timmis, I. (2002). Native-speaker norms and international English: A classroom view. *ELT Journal* 56(3): 240-49.

Tomlinson, B. (2003a). Humanizing the coursebook. In B. Tomlinson (ed.). *Developing materials for language teaching*. London: Continuum, pp. 162-73.

Tomlinson, B. (2003b). Materials development courses. In B. Tomlinson (ed.). *Developing materials for language teaching*. London: Continuum, pp. 445-61.

Tomlinson, B. (2003c). Materials evaluation. In B. Tomlinson (ed.). *Developing materials for language teaching*. London: Continuum, pp. 15-36.

Tomlinson, B., Dat, B., Masuhara, H., & Rubdy, R. (2001). EFL courses for adults. *ELT Journal* 55(1): 80-101.

Tsui, A. M. (2003). *Understanding expertise in teaching: Case studies of second language teachers*. Cambridge: Cambridge University Press.

Tudor, I. (1992). Learner-centredness in language teaching: Finding the right balance. *System* 20(1): 31-44.

Tudor, I. (1996). *Learner-centredness as language education*. Cambridge: Cambridge University Press.

Venezky, R. L. (1992). Textbooks in school and society. In P. W. Jackson (ed.). *Handbook of research on curriculum*. New York: Macmillan, pp. 436-61.

Wade, R. C. (1993). Content analysis of social studies textbooks: A review of ten years of research. *Theory & Research in Social Education* 21(3): 232-56.

Wasburn, L. H. (1997). Accounts of slavery: An analysis of United States history textbooks from 1900 to 1992. *Theory & Research in Social Education* 25(4): 470-91.

West, M. (1953). *A general service list of English words*. London: Longman.

West, R. (1994). Needs analysis in language teaching. *Language Teaching* 27(1): 1-19.

Williams, D. (1983). Developing criteria for textbook evaluation. *ELT Journal* 37(3): 251-5.

Williams, M. (1988). Language taught for meetings and language used in meetings: Is there anything in common? *Applied Linguistics* 9(1): 45-58.

Yakhontova, T. (2001). Textbooks, contexts, and learners. *English for Specific Purposes* 20: 397-415.

Young, M. J. (1990).Writing and editing textbooks. In D. L. Elliott & A.Woodward (eds.). *Textbooks and schooling in the United States*. Chicago: National Society for the Study of Education, pp. 71-85.

Zahorik, J. A. (1991). Teaching style and textbooks. *Teaching & Teacher Education* 7(2): 185-196.

PART B

PERSPECTIVES ON MATERIALS

2

Second language acquisition research and language-teaching materials

Rod Ellis

Summary

This chapter considers two ways in which second language acquisition (SLA) research has informed language teaching materials: (1) the design of tasks; and (2) grammar teaching. A "task" can be "unfocused" or "focused" depending on whether the aim is to elicit general samples of language or use of a specific linguistic feature – but in both cases the primary focus must be on meaning and achieving a communicative outcome. SLA research has investigated how different design features impact on the way a task is performed and, thereby, on acquisition. Different SLA theories underlie the use of tasks in "task-supported language teaching," where focused tasks support a structural syllabus, and "task-based language teaching," where the syllabus is specified only in terms of the tasks to be performed. SLA has also led to proposals for specific types of grammar-teaching materials. "Interpretation activities" aim to teach grammar by inducing learners to process the target structure through input rather than by eliciting production. One type of interpretation activity involves input enrichment where the targeted feature is made salient to the learner (e.g., by bolding it in a written text). A second type consists of "structured input activities." These force processing of the targeted feature by requiring a response from the learner (e.g., choosing the picture that correctly matches the sentence they hear). A "consciousness-raising (CR) task" is designed to develop learners' understanding of how a grammatical feature works rather than their actual ability to use it by assisting them to discover how it works for themselves. Again, interpretation activities and CR tasks draw on different theories of second language (L2) acquisition. In this chapter, then, SLA is viewed both as a source of ideas for fine-tuning materials options that have originated from elsewhere and as a source of new ideas for teaching.

Introduction: SLA and language pedagogy

The field of SLA research is a relatively new one, dating from the challenge to behaviorist views of language learning in the 1960s (e.g., Corder 1967) and the first empirical studies of L2 acquisition (e.g., Ravem 1968). It has spawned numerous theories (Larsen-Freeman & Long 1991 counted 40) and a substantial body of empirical research that has investigated both naturalistic and instructed L2 acquisition in "second" and "foreign" contexts. Despite this activity and our growing understanding about what learning an L2 entails, doubts exist as to whether the findings of SLA are sufficiently robust to warrant applications to language pedagogy. Early commentaries (e.g., Hatch 1978; Tarone *et al.* 1976) tended to evince an either "don't apply" or "apply with caution" position. Lightbown (1985) was circumspect in what she thought SLA could offer teachers, pointing out that "language acquisition research can offer no formulas, no recipes" and only "can give teachers appropriate expectations for themselves and their students" (p. 183). Fifteen years later, Lightbown (2000) still felt that it was not possible to "apply" the findings of individual studies although she did consider it feasible to apply "the general principles that they reflect" (p. 454). Teachers, of course, cannot wait until researchers have solved all their problems and ask only that they base their proposals on the best information available. The fact that most teacher education programs include an SLA component is testimony to the conviction that it has relevance to language pedagogy.

"Language pedagogy" is a cover term for a wide-ranging set of practices, including general goal setting and approach, syllabus design, materials development, classroom methodology, and evaluation. It is probably true to say that SLA has had more to say about the general approach to language teaching (e.g., whether language learning can best be promoted by means of a task-based approach or a more traditional structural-based approach) and classroom methodology (e.g., how attention to form can most effectively be achieved in the context of fluency activities) and much less to say about materials development. Nevertheless, there are two aspects of materials development that SLA has addressed: the design of communicative tasks and grammar-teaching activities. My aim in this chapter is to examine what SLA has to say about each of these.

SLA and "tasks"

In this section, I will first define what is meant by a "task," distinguishing tasks and contextualized grammar exercises. I will then briefly expound the rationale that SLA researchers give for using tasks and examine some of the criticisms that have been leveled against this. Finally, I will examine what SLA researchers have had to say about the design features of tasks.

Tasks vs. contextualized grammar activities

In Ellis (2003) I identified a number of criteria that a language-teaching activity must satisfy in order to justify being called a task.[1] The main ones of these are:

1. There is a primary focus on meaning.
2. The students choose the linguistic and nonlinguistic resources needed to complete the task.
3. The task should lead to real-world processes of language use.
4. Successful performance of the task is determined by examining whether students have achieved the intended communicative outcome.

I will now apply these criteria to two language-teaching activities with a view to clarifying exactly what is and is not a task.

Consider first "Going shopping" (Figure 2.1). At first sight, there may

[1] Long (2005) proposes that "task" should serve as the unit for conducting needs analysis. In this case, "task" has a somewhat different meaning from the one I have given it in this chapter. Long's view is that task-based teaching should be based on an analysis of "target tasks." Target tasks are then converted into "pedagogic tasks" – the focus of this chapter.

seem to be a primary focus on meaning, but closer examination will show that the real objective of this activity is to practice the use of "some" and "any." Students do not choose their own linguistic resources; they are given a model to follow and merely substitute items in the model. The activity is unlikely to lead to real-world processes of language use – there is unlikely to be any negotiation of meaning, for example, as there is no information or opinion gap involved. Finally, there is no communicative outcome. The activity will be evaluated in terms of whether learners use "some" and "any" correctly. That is, the outcome is simply the display of correct language. This activity is an "exercise," albeit one of the "situational" kind. It is an example of what is commonly called a "contextualized grammar activity." Such activities are not to be confused with tasks.

Going shopping

Look at Mary's shopping list. Then look at the list of items in Abdullah's store.

Mary's shopping list

1. oranges	4. powdered milk
2. eggs	5. biscuits
3. flour	6. jam

Abdullah's store

1. bread	7. mealie meal flour
2. salt	8. sugar
3. apples	9. curry powder
4. tins of fish	10. biscuits
5. coca cola	11. powdered milk
6. flour	12. dried beans

Work with a partner. One person is Mary and the other person is Mr. Abdullah.

Make conversations like this:

Mary: Good morning. Do you have any flour?

Abdullah: Yes, I have some.

Figure 2.1 A contextualized grammar activity

Now consider "What can you buy?" (Figure 2.2). This activity is a redesigned version of "Going shopping." There is now a clear focus on meaning. There is no attempt to specify the language that the students should use while they perform this activity. Student A, for example, could ask questions like "Do you have any oranges?" but could equally well say "I want to buy some oranges" or even "Oranges – you have?" Real-world processes of language use are likely to arise because the students will need to ensure that they understand each other and deal with breakdowns in understanding. There is a clear communicative outcome; in the case of Student A, a list of the items s/he could buy and in the case of Student B, a list of the items that Student A wanted but that were not stocked in the store. This activity is clearly a task.

What can you buy?

Student A:

You are going shopping at Student B's store. Here is your shopping list. Find out which items on your list you can buy.

1. oranges	4. powdered milk
2. eggs	5. biscuits
3. flour	6. jam

Student B:

You own a store. Here is a list of items for sale in your store. Make a list of the items that Student A asks for that you do not stock.

1. bread	7. mealie meal flour
2. salt	8. sugar
3. apples	9. curry powder
4. tins of fish	10. biscuits
5. coca cola	11. powdered milk
6. flour	12. dried beans

Figure 2.2 An information-gap task

Unfocused and focused tasks

Two general types of tasks can be distinguished. Unfocused tasks are intended to elicit general samples of learner language; that is, they are not designed with a specific linguistic feature in mind, although it may be possible to predict a cluster of features that learners are likely to need when they perform the task. Focused tasks, on the other hand, are designed to elicit use of a specific linguistic feature (typically a grammatical structure). However, focused tasks can still be distinguished from contextualized grammar exercises. Whereas a contextualized grammar exercise explicitly identifies the target feature to be used (as in the activity in Figure 2.1), a focused task does not. In accordance with criterion (2) on page 38, learners are still free to choose the linguistic resources for performing the task. Therefore, the target feature cannot be specified in the rubric of the task or provided in a model. Focused tasks, then, have two aims: One is to stimulate communicative language use (as with unfocused tasks); the other is to target the use of a particular, predetermined target feature and provide an opportunity to practice this in a communicative context.

The ideal focused task is one where the performance of the task makes the use of the target structure "essential." However, as Loschky and Bley-Vroman (1993) point out, this is difficult to achieve because learners can always use communication strategies to get around using the targeted feature. For this reason, task designers often have to settle for tasks where the use of the target structure is "useful" or perhaps just "natural" – that is, the task may predispose learners to use the target structure but does not require it. In Ellis (2003), I reviewed a number of studies that have investigated whether learners actually do use the grammatical structure targeted in focused tasks, noting that success depended on whether the target structure was one that the students were already in the process of acquiring. Students cannot be expected to use a structure that is not yet part of their linguistic repertoire!

One type of focused task that has attracted interest from SLA researchers and teachers is "dictogloss" (Wajnryb 1990). This makes use of a short text that has been selected or devised to have a structural focus. The text is read at normal speed, sentence by sentence, while the learners note down key words and phrases (i.e., the content words). The learners then work in groups to try to reconstruct the text collaboratively. Wajnryb emphasizes that the aim is not to generate an exact replica of the original text but rather to reproduce its content.

The "focus" comes from the "seeding" of the original text. In the example in Figure 2.3, the text has been seeded with a number of examples of relative clauses using "where" and "when."

1. The teacher reads the following passage aloud at normal speed. Students take notes.

   Are you looking for a wedding with a difference? How about Hawaii? Hawaii is a place where thousands of couples get married each year. You can get married in a zoological garden, where there is a chapel by the sea. Or you can choose a volcanic crater, where the service is held in a helicopter. Or you can do it on a tennis court, where the minister calls out "Love-all." Or you can choose underwater in a submarine, where you are surrounded by tropical fish. Or you can get married in the sky, where the service is held with everyone in parachutes. And there are different times when you can get married. You can get married at dawn, when the sun rises over the mountains, or at midday when the sun beats down on the beaches, or in the evening when the sun sets over the ocean. Hawaii offers a wedding that you will never forget.

2. The teacher reads the passage a second time while students amplify their notes.
3. Students work in groups to reconstruct the passage.
4. Students compare their reconstructed passage with the original passage.

Figure 2.3 A dictogloss task

The theoretical rationale for tasks

A number of SLA researchers (myself included) have argued that tasks constitute an important pedagogic tool for promoting L2 acquisition. There are two principal reasons given for basing language teaching on tasks. The first is that learners will only succeed in developing full control over their linguistic knowledge if they experience trying to use it under real operating conditions.

The second is that true interlanguage development (i.e., the process of acquiring new linguistic knowledge and restructuring existing knowledge) can only take place when acquisition happens incidentally, as a product of the effort to communicate. It is important to distinguish these two reasons as they support very different ways of employing tasks in language pedagogy, with obvious implications for materials development.

Task-supported language teaching

The idea of using tasks to promote automatization of existing L2 knowledge is compatible with task-supported language teaching. In this form of teaching, tasks constitute the final step in a traditional present-practice-produce (PPP) sequence. That is, a language item is first presented to the learners by means of examples, with or without an explanation. This item is then practiced in a controlled manner using "exercises." Finally, tasks provide opportunities for using the item in free language production. Implicit in PPP is the idea that it is possible to lead learners from controlled to automatic use of new language features by means of text-manipulation exercises that structure language for the learner, followed by text-creation tasks in which learners structure language for themselves (see Batstone 1994). It is probably true to say that this is how tasks figure in the majority of existing course books.

The rationale for task-supported language teaching comes from skill-learning theory (DeKeyser 1998; Johnson 1996). DeKeyser proposes that grammar is first taught explicitly to develop declarative knowledge and this is then proceduralized by means of exercises that require some conscious thought. Finally, tasks are used to provide the opportunity to automatize the new knowledge by engaging learners in real-life communicative behavior. This is essential if learners are to achieve full control over their knowledge. Task-supported teaching, however, has been rejected by other SLA theorists (e.g., Skehan 1996). It is argued that it is problematic because it is premised on a structural syllabus that treats language acquisition as the sequential learning of "accumulated entities" (Rutherford 1987) and ignores research that shows learners pass through a series of transitional stages in acquiring a specific grammatical feature, often taking months or even years before they arrive at the target form of the rule. Another problem is that the PPP sequence will encourage learners to focus primarily on form rather than on meaning as they perform the task. As a result, the task ceases to be a task, as I have defined it, and becomes a contextualized grammar activity. These challenges to PPP have themselves been challenged. Swan (2005), for example, argues that "evidence for inbuilt acquisition sequences currently lacks generality" and, even if they do exist, "there seems to be no good evidence that they cannot be interfered with" (p. 379). Swan also points to "the experience of countless people who have apparently learnt languages successfully by 'traditional' methods" (i.e., PPP).

Task-based language teaching

In task-based language teaching, tasks serve as the organizing principle for a course. That is, the course consists of a series of tasks sequenced according to difficulty. However, it is important to recognize that this does not eliminate the possibility of attention to form. As we have already noted, focused tasks can be used to practice specific linguistic forms while learners are engaged in the effort to communicate. Also, attention to form while students are performing a task can occur preemptively and reactively. Preemptive attention to form occurs when students (or the teacher) elect to ask questions about form, whereas reactive attention to form occurs through corrective feedback. Ellis, Basturkmen, and Loewen (2001) showed that such attention to form can be very common in task-based lessons. Finally, attention to form can occur in a posttask activity that addresses the linguistic problems that the teacher observed while the students were performing the task. What distinguishes task-supported and task-based teaching, therefore, is not attention to form *per se* but the context in which this occurs and how it is accomplished.

Task-based teaching can take a number of different forms – a point ignored by critics such as Swan (2005). One of the earliest proposals for task-based teaching involved humanistic language teaching. Moskowitz (1977) gives examples of what she calls "humanistic exercises" for language learning, which, in fact, have all the characteristics of tasks as these have been defined here. For example, "Identity Cards" asks students to pin on cards that give some personal information about themselves (e.g., "three adjectives that describe you"). The students circulate while the teacher plays some music. When the music stops, they choose a partner and talk about the information written on their cards. A very different approach to task-based teaching is that embodied in the "procedural syllabus" proposed by Prabhu (1987). Prabhu devised a series of meaning-focused activities consisting of pretasks, that the teacher completed with the whole class, followed by tasks where the students worked on similar activities on their own. For example, in one task the students were asked to find, name, and describe specific locations on a map. Tasks can also be designed with a metacognitive focus for learner-training purposes. This can be achieved by constructing tasks that help learners to become aware of, reflect on, and evaluate their own learning styles and the strategies they use to learn. Ellis and Sinclair (1989) offer a number of tasks aimed at making learners more effective and self-directed in their approach to learning an L2. For example, in one task learners fill in a questionnaire designed to help them understand what kind of language learners they are.

Task-based teaching draws on a number of constructs and theories about the nature of L2 learning – teachability, implicit knowledge, emergentism, focus-on-form, and noticing. According to Pienemann's (1985) Teachability Hypothesis, "instruction can only promote language acquisition if the interlanguage is close to the point when the structure to be taught is acquired in the natural setting (so that sufficient processing prerequisites are developed)" (p. 37). The difficulty of ensuring that all the students are "ready" for whatever is the target structure of the day means that an approach based on a structural syllabus is problematic and perhaps not feasible. The alternative is to allow learners to follow their own "internal syllabus" by engaging with the L2 through performing a series of tasks. Linked to the idea of teachability is another key construct, "implicit knowledge" (i.e., linguistic knowledge that is intuitive, unconscious, and proceduralized). According to emergentist SLA theories (Ellis 1998), implicit knowledge is not acquired intentionally but rather incidentally as a response to the frequency of sequences of sounds, syllables, and words in the input that learners are exposed to – that is, it involves associative rather than rule learning. Finally, there is "focus-on-form." Long (1991) has argued that in order to acquire the form-function mappings of the target language, learners need to attend to form *while* they are engaged in trying to communicate. This can be achieved in a variety of ways (e.g., proactively by seeding the input of tasks with numerous exemplars of the target structure, or reactively by means of corrective feedback when learners make an error). Focus-on-form draws on Schmidt's (1994) Noticing Hypothesis which claims that acquisition takes place when learners pay conscious attention to exemplars of a linguistic form in the input. Thus, although the end product is implicit knowledge (which is unconscious), the processes by which this is acquired are in part conscious. In short, the view of L2 acquisition embodied in these constructs precludes the possibility of intervening directly in interlanguage development and supports indirect intervention by means of task-based teaching.

The challenges to task-based teaching are on three fronts. Seedhouse (2005) has argued that there is no necessary relationship between task-as-workplan and task-as-process; thus, there is no guarantee that students will perform a task in the manner that was intended by the designer of the task. If this is correct – and there is some research (e.g., Coughlan & Duff 1994) to suggest that it is – then clearly it will be very difficult to design a coherent course based on tasks, as what transpires when learners perform a task may not correspond to what is intended by the course designer. However, as we will see below, there are grounds for disputing Seedhouse's position. That is, to some degree at least, it is possible to predict the language samples that result from particular tasks. Swan (2005) has mounted an extensive critique of the theoretical bases of task-based teaching, arguing that there is insufficient evidence to support either the Teachability or the Noticing Hypotheses. Sheen (2003) claims that the relative merits of a task-based approach incorporating focus-on-form and a more traditional approach based on a structural syllabus and some version of PPP have not been systematically investigated, and that, this being so, it is premature for SLA researchers such as myself to promote task-based teaching.

The controversy surrounding task-based as opposed to task-supported language teaching should not detract from the importance attached to "task" as a pedagogic tool. There is widespread acceptance of the value of tasks in language pedagogy even if there is no consensus on how they can best be utilized.

In the following section we will examine task design from an SLA perspective.

Task design

In Ellis (2003), I proposed a framework for distinguishing the design features of tasks. Figure 2.4 illustrates the use of this framework by describing the design features of the "What can you buy?" task shown in Figure 2.2. The input to this task consists of two lists of grocery items, so the medium is "written." The organization of this input can be considered "tight" in so far as it structures the interaction that the learners will engage in (i.e., the shopper can simply go through the list from top to bottom). The task conditions involve split information (i.e., the shopper and storekeeper have different information), two-way interaction (i.e., both the shopper and the shopkeeper will be involved in talking), required interaction (i.e., the task cannot be performed successfully unless both students speak), and the orientation is "convergent" (i.e., the aim is for the students to agree on a solution to the task). The processes which the task will instigate are the exchange of information by means of dialogic discourse. The outcome is a written list of items and, as there is only one correct answer, the task is a closed one.

Design features	**"What can you buy?"**
Input	1. Medium – verbal (written) 2. Organization – tight structure
Conditions	1. Information configuration – split 2. Interactant relationship – two-way 3. Interaction requirement – required 4. Orientation – convergent
Processes	1. Cognitive – exchanging information 2. Discourse mode – dialogic
Outcomes	1. Medium – written 2. Discourse mode – list 3. Scope – closed

Figure 2.4 Task design features

The question arises as to which design features are likely to be effective in promoting L2 acquisition. SLA researchers have addressed this question theoretically and empirically. That is, they have advanced claims about what kinds of tasks will work best for acquisition on the basis of some theory, and they have investigated the kinds of language use that result from performing tasks with specific design features. For example, Pica, Kanagy, and Falodun (1993) drew on Long's Interaction Hypothesis (1996), which claims that when learners engage in the effort to negotiate meaning as a result of a breakdown in communication, their attention will be directed to linguistic forms in a way that promotes acquisition. They suggested that tasks that induce lots of negotiation of meaning will work best for acquisition. They then reviewed a number of task-based studies, concluding that "jigsaw tasks" (of which "What can you buy?" is an example) have the greatest psycholinguistic validity. Skehan (2001) drew on his own Cognitive Approach to Language Learning to suggest that tasks need to be varied so that they induce learners to attend to different aspects of language use at different times. For example, tasks that have a tight structure assist the development of fluency, tasks that have complex outcomes contribute to the development of complexity, whereas dialogic (as opposed to monologic) tasks promote greater accuracy. These claims were based on Skehan's theory of language representation; he saw linguistic knowledge as partly exemplar-based (i.e., consisting of formulaic chunks) and partly rule-based. Skehan (in conjunction with Foster) demonstrated in a series of studies that the way tasks are designed can induce learners to draw differently on these two types of knowledge. It should be noted, however, that, to date, SLA researchers have only been able to show the relationship between the design features of tasks and language use. There have been very few studies that have examined the relationship between design features and acquisition.

In a very different approach to investigating the design of tasks, Johnson (2000) studied how task designers designed tasks. He asked them to verbalize their thoughts as they set about their work. Johnson identified three general ways in which the designers viewed tasks – in terms of task function (e.g., "describing a person"), task genre (e.g., information gap) or task frame (i.e., giving consideration to a cluster of factors such as the participatory organization, skills to be practiced, timing, and teacher roles). In an analysis of the designers' control procedures, Johnson found that the less experienced designers utilized task frames as a starting point for design, whereas the experienced designers opted predominantly for task genre and to a lesser extent for task function. Johnson's study illuminates the procedures that experienced task designers were found to follow. Interestingly, these procedures do not agree with those recommended in handbooks for teachers (e.g., Estaire & Zanon 1994; Lee 2000). For example, whereas the recommended procedures propose "thematic content" as the starting point, Johnson's experienced designers generally preferred to begin by selecting a "task genre."

SLA and grammar teaching

Much of the work in SLA has focused on the acquisition of grammar, and a number of proposals relating to the kinds of activities likely to promote the acquisition of L2 grammar have been forthcoming. One of these is the use of "focused tasks" as a means of providing opportunities for learners to practice specific grammatical features within a communicative context. These were considered in the preceding section. I will now look at two further proposals: (1) interpretation activities; and (2) consciousness-raising tasks. I will describe each of these, offer some illustrative materials, and outline the theoretical rationale in support of each.

Interpretation activities[2]

Interpretation activities aim to teach grammar by inducing learners to process the target structure through input rather than by eliciting production of the structure. That is, they constitute a type of comprehension activity. Traditional comprehension activities, however, are intended to practice listening or reading comprehension (i.e., they require learners to process a text for meaning).

---

[2] I have elected to use the term "activity" as a superordinate term that covers both "tasks" and "exercises." I have preferred to refer to interpretation activities rather than interpretation tasks because they do not conform entirely to the criteria I specified for defining a task. Interpretation tasks do focus on meaning, but *semantic* meaning at the level of sentence, rather than *pragmatic* meaning at the level of utterance. Also, they do not really involve real-world processes of language use (i.e., we do not go around saying whether sentences express definiteness or possibility). Finally, there is generally no clearly defined nonlinguistic outcome by which to measure whether the activity has been accomplished successfully. Interpretation activities are perhaps more exercise-like than task-like.

Interpretation activities, on the other hand, require learners to process the target structure in order to arrive at the meaning of the text. They aim to enable the learner to relate the target form to the meaning it realizes – to create a form-function mapping. Interpretation activities can be viewed as a kind of focused task. However, whereas learners often avoid the use of the target structure in production-based focused tasks, this is not possible in an interpretation activity; they have to process the target structure in order to perform the task. Two kinds of interpretation activities can be distinguished: input-enrichment activities and structured-input activities.

Input-enrichment activities

Input enrichment involves designing activities in such a way that the targeted feature is (1) frequent; and/or (2) salient in the input provided. Enriched input of this kind can take many forms. It can consist of oral/written texts that learners simply listen to/read, or written texts in which the target structure has been graphologically highlighted in some way (e.g., through the use of underscoring or bold print), or oral/written texts with follow-up activities designed to focus attention on the structure (e.g., questions that can only be answered if the learners have successfully processed the target structure). Figure 2.5 provides an example of an input-enrichment activity designed to teach subject-verb inversion with negative adverbs. Clearly, learners will need to read a number of such texts in order for any effect on their acquisition of the target structure to become evident. That is, input enrichment must provide them with an "input flood" so that, through sheer frequency, the target structure becomes salient, and there is a gradual impact on their interlanguage systems. Reinders (2005) conducted a study that showed that having learners listen to a number of texts such as that in Figure 2.5 had a measurable effect on their acquisition of this structure. However, other studies (e.g., Alanen 1995; Trahey & White 1993) have found that, for some structures at least, input flooding is not effective.

The rationale for input-enrichment tasks is that L2 acquisition can proceed incidentally. That is, learners do not need to be intentionally focused on the target structure with a view to learning it. However, they do need to notice it.

Read the following text.

I first came to New Zealand nine years ago. **No sooner had I arrived** than I knew I loved the place. **Not only was the weather** beautiful but the people were also very friendly. I think I am very lucky to live here now. **Seldom do people** get such a chance. I hope to stay here the rest of my life.

Figure 2.5 An input-enrichment task (from Reinders 2005: 406)

Enriched-input tasks aim to assist noticing by increasing the salience of the target structure in the input. This raises the interesting question as to whether tasks where the target input has been enhanced in some way are more effective than seeded tasks without any enhancement. White (1998) investigated this in a study that compared the effects of three types of enriched input: (1) a typographically enhanced input flood plus extensive listening and reading; (2) a typographically enhanced input flood by itself; and (3) a typographically unenhanced input flood. White found no differences in the three groups' acquisition of the target structure (possessive determiners "his" and "her"). She concluded that the target structure was probably equally salient in all three types of input. It is likely, however, that some structures (e.g., redundant features such as third person *-s*) will only become noticeable if they are enhanced in some way.

Of course, traditional grammar activities that call for intentional learning are likely to be more effective in promoting acquisition (Norris & Ortega 2000), but they may result in explicit knowledge rather than the implicit knowledge needed to use the target structure easily and naturally in communication. One use of input-enrichment activities is as a means of exposing learners to continuous input containing the target structure. That is, the activities can be used to reinforce the learning that results from a more traditional, explicitly instructional approach. Such exposure may be essential if the effects of the grammar instruction are to be consolidated (Lightbown 1991).

Structured-input activities

Structured-input activities are comprehension-based grammar activities that go beyond simply presenting learners with enriched input containing the target structure (the stimulus) by means of some instruction that forces them to process it (the response). In Ellis (1995: 98-9), I listed some general principles for designing structured-input activities, the main ones being:

1. The stimulus can take the form of spoken or written input.
2. The response can take various forms (e.g., indicate true-false, check a box, select the correct picture, draw a diagram, perform an action), but in each case the response will be completely nonverbal or minimally verbal.
3. The activities in the task can be sequenced to require first attention to meaning, then noticing the form and function of the grammatical structure, and finally error identification.
4. Learners should have the opportunity to make some kind of personal response (i.e., relate the input to their own lives).
5. Learners need to be made aware of common errors involving the target structure as well as correct usage.
6. Structured-input tasks require the provision of immediate and explicit feedback on learners' responses to the input.

Figure 2.6 gives an example of a structured-input activity designed to encourage learners to notice the difference between the present simple tense to refer to definite actions and modal verbs such as "may," "might," and "can" to express possibility. Thus the activity aims to enable learners to make the connection between the form of the modal verbs and their semantic function (possibility).

Structured-input activities are an integral part of an approach to grammar teaching known as Processing Instruction. VanPatten (1996) defined this as "a type of grammar instruction whose purpose is to affect the ways in which learners attend to input data. It is input-based rather than output-based" (p. 2). What is distinctive about it is the theoretical basis for identifying instructional targets. This consists of a set of principles that is hypothesized to govern the way learners process input. For example, the "first noun principle" states that learners will automatically assume that the first noun in a sentence is the agent of the verb. In the case of an active sentence such as "The dog bit Mary," this

Listen to the sentences about people who have Alzheimer's disease. Indicate whether each sentence describes something that is DEFINITE (write D) or just POSSIBLE (write P).

1. People with Alzheimer's disease **forget** things all the time.
2. For example, they **may forget** even very simple words.
3. They **might prepare** a meal and then forget they cooked it.
4. They **can** even **get** lost on their own street.
5. They **put** things down and forget where they have put them.
6. For example, they **could put** a wristwatch in the sugar bowl and then wonder where it is.
7. They **behave** calmly one minute and angrily the next.
8. For example, they **might** suddenly **say** you have stolen something from them.
9. They **do** very strange things.
10. For example, someone with Alzheimer's disease **might put** an iron in the freezer.

Figure 2.6 A structured-input activity

strategy results in the correct interpretation. However, in the case of passive sentences such as "The dog was bitten by Mary," it does not. In such cases, learners need to have their attention drawn to the linguistic markers that signal that "The dog" in this sentence is the patient, not agent (i.e., "was," the past participle and the preposition "by"). This can be achieved by means of a structured-input activity that presents learners with active and passive sentences and asks them to match each sentence to a picture to show its meaning. VanPatten and his co-researchers (see, for example, the collection of papers in VanPatten 2004) have carried out a number of studies that indicate that Processing Instruction incorporating structured-input activities is effective in enabling learners to acquire grammatical structures that do not accord with their natural processing strategies. VanPatten has argued that Processing Instruction is more effective than traditional production-based instruction, but some studies (e.g., Allen 2000; Erlam 2003) have shown that production-based instruction that helps learners map forms onto their functions (i.e., is meaning-based rather than mechanical) may be just as effective. Nevertheless, structured-input activities clearly constitute a useful addition to the materials writer's armory.

Consciousness-raising tasks

A consciousness-raising (CR) task is designed to cater primarily to explicit learning – that is, it is intended to develop awareness at the level of "understanding" rather than awareness at the level of "noticing" (Schmidt 1994). A CR task makes language itself the content by inviting learners to discover how a grammatical feature works for them. A CR activity constitutes a "task," as defined earlier in this chapter, in the sense that learners are required to talk meaningfully about a language point using their own linguistic resources, that is, grammar becomes a topic to communicate about. Thus, the "taskness" of a CR activity lies not in the linguistic point that is the focus, but rather in the talk in which learners must engage to achieve the outcome of the task.

In Ellis (1991: 234), I listed the main characteristics of CR tasks as follows:

1. There is an attempt to *isolate* a specific linguistic feature for focused attention.
2. The learners are provided with *data* that illustrate the targeted feature and they may also be provided with an *explicit rule* describing or explaining the feature.
3. The learners are expected to utilize *intellectual effort* to understand the targeted feature.
4. Learners may be optionally required to verbalize a rule describing the grammatical structure.

A CR task consists of (1) data containing exemplars of the targeted feature and (2) instructions requiring the learners to operate on the data in some way. In Ellis (1997) I listed the different data options and types of operations that are possible. The data options were (1) authentic versus contrived; (2) oral versus written; (3) discrete sentences versus continuous test; (4) well-formed vesus deviant sentences; and (5) gap versus non-gap. The types of operations were:

(1) identification (e.g., learners underline the target structure in the data);
(2) judgment (i.e., they respond to the correctness or appropriateness of the data);
(3) completion (i.e., they are invited to complete a text);
(4) modification (i.e., they are invited to modify a text in some way, for example, by replacing one item with another);
(5) sorting (i.e., they classify the data by sorting it into defined categories);
(6) matching (i.e., they are invited to match two sets of data in accordance with a stated principle); and
(7) rule provision (i.e., they may be asked to state the rule they have discovered).

By permuting data options and types of operations, a considerable variety of CR tasks can be designed. A CR task constitutes a kind of puzzle that, when solved, enables learners to discover how a linguistic feature works.

Figure 2.7 provides an example of a CR task. This task addresses the form and meaning of possessive relative pronouns. The options here are (1) contrived; (2) written; (3) discrete sentences; (4) well-formed; and (5) nongap. The operations are (1) noticing; (2) analyzing the sentences; and (3) verbalizing a rule. It would be possible to redesign this task with a gap if the sentences were divided into two groups (those with "who" and those with "whose"), with one group being given to one student and the other to another group. In this case, the first part of this task would simply be to ask the student to "notice the difference" in their sentences.

The rationale for the use of CR tasks draws on two theoretical claims. The first is that explicit knowledge functions as a facilitator of implicit knowledge by helping learners to notice grammatical features in input and to notice the gap between the input and their own interlanguage. Explicit knowledge is also needed by the "monitor," which is activated when learners wish to fine-tune formulations derived from their implicit knowledge or edit their own production. The second claim is that learning is more significant if it involves

A. Listen carefully to these book reviews. Write in the missing word ("who" or "whose") as you listen.

1. *The Color Purple*: This novel is about an African woman ____ life is made miserable by her husband.
2. *The Day of the Jackal*: This thriller tells the story of an assassin ____ tries to kill General de Gaulle.
3. *The Invisible Man*: This novel tells the story of an African American man ____ journey through the United States reveals the chronic racism in that country.
4. *The Remains of the Day*: This is the strange story of an English butler ____ is devoted to his master.
5. *The Ginger Tree*: This novel tells the story of a young Scottish woman ____ marriage to a young English officer in China is a failure.
6. *The Passion*: This historical romance tells the story of Henri, Napoleon's cook, ____ becomes happily married to the daughter of a Venetian boatman.
7. *The Murder*: This is the story of a man ____ murder leads to the resignation of the president of the United States.
8. *Sad Ending*: This bittersweet comedy tells the story of two teenagers ____ marriage is nearly destroyed by their parents.

B. Divide each book review into separate sentences. The first two are done for you.

1. This novel is about an African woman. Her life is made miserable by her husband.
2. This thriller tells the story of an assassin. He tries to kill General de Gaulle.

C. Now explain when to use "who" and when to use "whose."

Figure 2.7 A consciousness-raising task

greater depth of processing (e.g., Craik & Lockhart 1972). CR tasks cater to discovery learning through problem solving (Bourke 1996) in accordance with the general principle that what learners can find out for themselves is better remembered than what they are simply told.

A number of studies have investigated whether CR tasks are effective in developing explicit knowledge of the L2. For example, Mohamed (2001) compared direct consciousness-raising (i.e., the teacher provided the grammatical explanation) with indirect consciousness-raising through a CR task (i.e., the learners work out the grammatical explanation for themselves). She found that the CR task worked better than direct consciousness-raising with groups of high-intermediate ESL learners from mixed L1 backgrounds but not with a group of low-intermediate learners. This study suggests that the effectiveness of CR tasks may depend on the proficiency of learners. Clearly, learners need sufficient proficiency to talk metalinguistically about the target feature and, if they lack this, they may not be able to benefit to the same degree from a CR task. Mohamed also reported that the students enjoyed doing the CR tasks.

The value of CR tasks lies not just in whether they are effective in developing explicit knowledge and subsequently promoting noticing, but also in the opportunities they provide for learners to communicate. A key question, then, is the extent to which CR tasks do promote communicative behavior and also its quality. One way of answering this question is by examining whether CR tasks lead to the negotiation of meaning. Fotos (1994) compared the amount and quality of negotiation in unfocused tasks and CR tasks that shared the same design features, and found no significant differences.

CR tasks, as Ellis (1991) and Sheen (1992) have pointed out, have their limitations. They may not be well suited to young learners, who view language as a tool for "doing" rather than as an object for "studying." Beginner learners will need to use their L1 to talk about language, although the product of their discussion (e.g., the answers to parts B and C in the task in Figure 2.7) should be in the L2. Learners lacking in metalanguage may also find it difficult to talk about language problems. Because CR tasks are problem solving in nature, they are "essentially intelligence-related" (Sheen 1992) and thus may not appeal to learners who are less skilled at forming and testing conscious hypotheses about language. Nevertheless, CR tasks offer a valuable alternative to direct explicit instruction. They can be used by themselves or as a follow-up in the posttask phase of task-based teaching to address a grammatical problem that the students have manifested. CR tasks have become increasingly common in grammar-teaching materials in the last decade or so.

Conclusion

The relationship between SLA and language pedagogy has always been a close one. Many SLA researchers were originally motivated to explore how learners learn an L2 by their desire to identify activities that are effective in promoting acquisition. I have examined two areas where SLA has informed language pedagogy (i.e., task-based teaching and grammar teaching) and pointed to ways in which this can assist the development of teaching materials.

SLA researchers have helped to produce a more rigorous definition of "task" (although the term continues to be used loosely in language pedagogy); they have demonstrated that focused tasks can be used to provide opportunities for the practice of specific grammatical structures; they have shown how "tasks" can serve as the organizing principle in task-based teaching; and they have explored how tasks can be designed to promote different kinds of language use and, possibly, acquisition. However, it would be a mistake to look to SLA for a definitive account of the role that tasks should play in language pedagogy if only because there is, as yet, no agreed theory of how an L2 is acquired. The real value of SLA task-based research is in the wealth of ideas, theoretical and practical, about tasks that it has generated. These are undoubtedly of value to the materials developer.

SLA has had much to say about the teaching of grammar. I have examined two ways in which SLA has sought to modify the dominant approach to grammar teaching (i.e., present-practice-produce). Interpretation activities seek to affect change in learners' interlanguage by inducing noticing of grammatical forms in the input and identifying the meanings that these forms realize. They are comprehension-based rather than production-based. Enriched-input activities cater to the incidental learning of grammar. Structured-input activities guide learners to form-meaning mapping. Consciousness-raising tasks aim to develop learners' explicit understanding of grammatical structures by making grammar a topic to communicate about and by turning the students into mini-grammarians capable of building their own explicit grammar.

I began this chapter by noting the reservations SLA researchers have voiced about the applicability of their theories and research to language pedagogy. I noted also that, despite the reservations, applications are needed and desirable. The question is what form the applications should take. The approach that I favor is of viewing SLA as a source of ideas for fine-tuning materials options that have originated from elsewhere (tasks being a good example) and, also, as a source of new ideas for teaching grammar (e.g., interpretation activities and consciousness-raising tasks).

The proposals for materials development that emanate from SLA are research- and theory-based, as I have tried to show. That is their strength. But it does not obviate the need for teachers to test them out in their own classrooms and reach a decision about their suitability and effectiveness. What has been shown to work in one classroom may not work in another as a result of cultural factors and individual differences. In this respect, of course, the proposals emanating from SLA are no different from the proposals that originate from any other source.

Discussion questions and tasks

1. Which of these activities is an "exercise" and which a "task"? Use the criteria listed on page 38 to help you decide.

   Activity 1: Dialog

   Students are paired and given a script of a dialog. Each student is allocated a part in the dialog and asked to memorize the lines for this part. The students then act out the dialog.

   Activity 2: Spot the difference

   Students are placed in pairs. Each student is given a picture and told that the two pictures are basically the same, but there are five small differences. Without looking at each other's picture, they talk together to locate and write down the five differences.
2. Outline a focused task you could use to elicit the use of the following grammatical structures:
   a. epistemic modals (i.e., the use of verbs like "must," "might," and "could" to express degrees of probability)

b. prepositions of location (e.g., “on,” “in,” “under”)

c. “when” questions

3. a. Write definitions of “task-supported” and of “task-based” language teaching.

   b. Review the theoretical bases for each approach.

   c. Which approach do you favor? Why?

4. Explain the difference between “input enrichment” and “structured-input activities.”

5. Why do some SLA researchers argue for an input-based approach to teaching grammar? What are your own views about such an approach? Do you also see value in providing opportunities for learners to practice producing the targeted feature?

6. Explain the rationale for “consciousness-raising tasks.” How convincing do you find this rationale?

7. Work through the following consciousness-raising task. Then consider these questions:

   a. Did you find this task interesting to do? Give a reason for your answer.

   b. Did you find it easy or difficult to do?

   c. Which type of learner do you think this activity is best suited to?

   d. Are there any changes you would like to make to this task?

A. What is the difference between verbs like “give” and “explain”?

She gave a book to her father. (= grammatical)

She gave her father a book. (= grammatical)

The policeman explained the law to Mary. (= grammatical)

The policeman explained Mary the law. (= ungrammatical)

B. Indicate whether the following sentences are grammatical or ungrammatical.

1. They saved Mark a seat.
2. His father read Kim a story.
3. She donated the hospital some money.
4. They suggested Mary a trip on the river.
5. They reported the police the accident.

(to be continued)

(continued)

6. They threw Mary a party.
7. The bank lent Mr. Thatcher some money.
8. He indicated Mary the right turning.
9. The festival generated the college a lot of money.
10. He cooked his girlfriend a cake.

C. Work out a rule for verbs like "give" and "explain."
   1. List the verbs in B that are like "give" (i.e., permit both sentence patterns) and those that are like "explain" (i.e., allow only one sentence pattern).
   2. What is the difference between the verbs in your two lists?

8. From your reading of this chapter, is there any support in SLA for mechanical grammar practice exercises (e.g., substitution exercises)? What are your own views about such exercises?
9. This chapter concludes by saying that any proposal emanating from SLA needs to be tested out by teachers in their own classrooms. Which of the activities described in this chapter would you personally like to try out? Why?

References

Alanen, R. (1995). Input enhancement and rule presentation in second language acquisition. In R. Schmidt (ed.). *Attention and awareness in foreign language learning*. Honolulu: University of Hawai'i, Second Language Teaching and Curriculum Center, pp. 259-302.

Allen, L. (2000). Form-meaning connections and the French causative: An experiment in input processing. *Studies in Second Language Acquisition* 22: 69-84.

Batstone, R. (1994). *A scheme for teacher education: Grammar*. Oxford: Oxford University Press.

Bourke, J. (1996). In praise of problem solving. *RELC Journal* 27: 12-29.

Corder, S. P. (1967). The significance of learners' errors. *International Review of Applied Linguistics* 5: 161-69.

Coughlan, P., & Duff, P. A. (1994). Same task, different activities: Analysis of a SLA task from an activity theory perspective. In J. Lantolf & G. Appel (eds.). *Vygotskian approaches to second language research*. Westport, CT: Ablex, pp. 173-94.

Craik, F., & Lockhart, R. (1972). Levels of processing: A framework for memory research. *Journal of Verbal Learning and Verbal Behavior* 11: 671-84.

DeKeyser, R. (1998). Beyond focus-on-form: Cognitive perspectives on learning and practicing second language grammar. In C. Doughty & J.Williams (eds.). *Focus-on-form in classroom second language acquisition.* Cambridge: Cambridge University Press, pp. 42-63.

Ellis, G., & Sinclair, B. (1989). *Learning to learn English.* Cambridge: Cambridge University Press.

Ellis, N. (1998). Emergentism, connectionism and language learning. *Language Learning* 48: 631-64.

Ellis, R. (1991). Grammar teaching – Practice or consciousness-raising? In R. Ellis. *Second language acquisition and second language pedagogy.* Clevedon, UK: Multilingual Matters.

Ellis, R. (1995). Interpretation tasks for grammar teaching. *TESOL Quarterly* 29: 87-105.

Ellis, R. (1997). *SLA research and language teaching.* Oxford: Oxford University Press.

Ellis, R. (2003). *Task-based language learning and teaching.* Oxford: Oxford University Press.

Ellis, R., Basturkmen, H., & Loewen S. (2001). Learner uptake in communicative ESL lessons. *Language Learning* 51: 281-318.

Erlam, R. (2003). Evaluating the relative effectiveness of structured-input and output-based instruction in foreign language learning: Results from an experimental study. *Studies in Second Language Acquisition* 25: 559-82.

Estaire, S., & Zanon, J. (1994). *Planning classwork: A task based approach.* Oxford: Heinemann.

Fotos, S. (1994). Integrating grammar instruction and communicative language use through grammar consciousness-raising tasks. *TESOL Quarterly* 28: 323-51.

Hatch, E. (1978). Apply with caution. *Studies in Second Language Acquisition* 2: 123-43.

Johnson, K. (1996). *Language teaching and skill learning.* Oxford: Blackwell.

Johnson, K. (2000). What task designers do. *Language Teaching Research* 4: 301-21.

Larsen-Freeman, D., & Long, M. (1991). *An introduction to second language acquisition research.* London: Longman.

Lee, J. (2000). *Tasks and communicating in language classrooms.* Boston: McGraw-Hill.

Lightbown, P. (1985). Great expectations: Second language acquisition research and classroom teaching. *Applied Linguistics* 6: 173-89.

Lightbown, P. (1991). Getting quality input in the second/foreign language classroom. In C. Kramsch & S. McConnell-Ginet (eds.). *Text and Context: cross-disciplinary perspectives on language study*. Lexington, MA: D. C. Heath and Company.

Lightbown, P. (2000). Anniversary article: Classroom SLA research and second language teaching. *Applied Linguistics* 21: 431-62.

Long, M. (1991). Focus on form: A design feature in language teaching methodology. In K. de Bot, R. Ginsberg, & C. Kramsch (eds.). *Foreign language research in cross-cultural perspective.* Amsterdam: John Benjamins, pp. 39-52.

Long, M. H. (1996). The role of the linguistic environment in second language acquisition. In W. C. Ritchie & T. K. Bahtia (eds.). *Handbook of second language acquisition.* New York: Academic Press, pp. 413-68.

Long, M. (2005). Methodological issues in learner needs analysis. In M. Long (ed.). *Second language needs analysis*. Cambridge: Cambridge University Press.

Loschky, L., & Bley-Vroman, R. (1993). Grammar and task-based methodology. In G. Crookes & S. Gass (eds.). *Tasks in a pedagogical context: Integrating theory and practice.* Clevedon, UK: Multilingual Matters, pp. 123-67.

Mohamed, N. (2001). Teaching grammar through consciousness-raising tasks: Learning outcomes, learner preferences and task performance. MA thesis, Department of Applied Language Studies and Linguistics, University of Auckland, Auckland, New Zealand.

Moskowitz, G. (1977). *Caring and sharing in the foreign language class*. Rowley, MA: Newbury House.

Norris, J., & Ortega, L. (2000). Effectiveness of L2 instruction: A research synthesis and quantitative meta-analysis. *Language Learning* 50: 417-528.

Pica, R., Kanagy, R., & Falodun, J. (1993). Choosing and using communication tasks for second language research and instruction. In. S. Gass & G. Crookes (eds.). *Task-based learning in a second language.* Clevedon, UK: Multilingual Matters, pp. 9-34.

Pienemann, M. (1985). Learnability and syllabus construction. In K. Hyltenstam & M. Pienemann (eds.). *Modelling and assessing second language acquisition.* Clevedon, UK: Multilingual Matters, pp. 23-75.

Prabhu, N. S. (1987). *Second language pedagogy*. Oxford: Oxford University Press.

Ravem, R. (1968). Language acquisition in a second language environment. *International Review of Applied Linguistics* 6: 165-85.

Reinders, H. (2005). The effects of different task types on L2 learners' intake and acquisition of two grammatical structures. Unpublished PhD thesis, University of Auckland, Auckland, New Zealand. Available from: www.hayo.nl.

Rutherford, W. E. (1987). *Second language grammar: Learning and teaching.* London: Longman.

Schmidt, R. (1994). Deconstructing consciousness in search of useful definitions for applied linguistics. *AILA Review* 11: 11-26.

Seedhouse, P. (2005). "Task" as a research construct. *Language Learning* 55: 533-70.

Sheen, R. (1992). Problem solving brought to task. *RELC Journal* 23: 44-59.

Sheen, R. (2003). Focus on form: Myth in the making. *ELT Journal* 57: 225-33.

Skehan, P. (1996). Second language acquisition research and task-based instruction. In J. Willis & D. Willis (eds.). *Challenge and change in language teaching.* Oxford: Heinemann, pp. 17-31.

Skehan, P. (2001). Tasks and language performance assessment. In M. Bygate, P. Skehan, & M. Swain (eds.). *Researching pedagogic tasks, second language learning, teaching and testing.* Harlow: Longman.

Swan, M. (2005). Legislation by hypothesis: The case of task-based instruction. *Applied Linguistics* 26: 376-401.

Tarone, E., Cohen, A., & Dumas, G. (1976). A closer look at some interlanguage terminology: A framework for communication strategies. *Working Papers on Bilingualism* 9: 76-90.

Trahey, M., & White, L. (1993). Positive evidence and preemption in the second language classroom. *Studies in Second Language Acquisition* 15: 181-204.

VanPatten, B. (1996). *Input processing and grammar instruction in second language acquisition.* Norwood, NJ: Ablex.

VanPatten, B. (2004). *Processing instruction: Theory, research, and commentary.* Mahwah, NJ: Erlbaum.

Wajnryb, R. (1990). *Grammar dictation.* Oxford: Oxford University Press.

White, J. (1998). Getting learners' attention: A typographical input enhancement study. In C. Doughty & J.Williams (eds.). *Focus-on-form in classroom second language acquisition.* Cambridge: Cambridge University Press, pp. 85-113.

3

The theory and practice of technology in materials development and task design

Hayo Reinders and Cynthia White

Summary

Technology nowadays plays a prominent role in the development of language-learning materials, both as a tool in support of their creation and as a means of delivering content. Increasingly, technology is also used to support the individual's language-learning process and to extend language-learning opportunities outside the classroom. The development of materials is still largely a practitioner-led practice, not always clearly informed by theories of learning (Chapelle 2001). In this chapter, we aim to first identify the distinctive features of computer-assisted language-learning (CALL) materials versus traditional non-CALL materials, and how these features affect their development. Theoretical principles for task design in CALL are then reviewed, followed by examples of current practice in CALL materials development discussed from a practical, pedagogical, and theoretical perspective. We conclude by identifying a number of issues that are likely to affect future developments in this area.

Introduction

A decade ago, Tomlinson's (1998) edited collection, entitled *Materials development in language teaching*, made little reference to the contribution of computers, apart from a discussion of corpus data and concordances and Maley's (1998) observation that we stand on the threshold of a new generation of computerized materials for language teaching. The absence of a focus on computer-assisted language-learning (CALL) materials in that collection was remarked on (see, for example, Johnson 1999; Levy & Stockwell 2006) as an indicator of the divide between CALL and the wider field of language teaching. In the decade since Tomlinson's book, opportunities for language learning and teaching have been further transformed by the rapid development of a wide range of technology-mediated resources, materials, tasks, and learning environments. The place of these developments in the field of language teaching has been the subject of debate. Coleman (2005), for example, argues that current research and practice in CALL has the potential to enhance our understanding of language learning and teaching, but that it remains in a relatively marginal position. Chapelle (2001) maintains that anyone concerned with language teaching in the twenty-first century "needs to grasp the nature of the unique technology-mediated tasks learners can engage in" (p. 2). The key challenge according to Gruba (2004) is to think of ways to construct tasks to make effective use of the vast computer networks available, noting that earlier attempts to migrate classroom-based tasks to online environments have not always been successful, largely due to a poor understanding of task design within the affordances of the new environments. And Levy and Stockwell (2006) propose that CALL can bring important insights, such as understanding the language teacher's role as a designer in CALL, not only of materials but of whole learning environments. Innovations in technology and practice have clearly outstripped theory development in technology-mediated language teaching (White 2006), yet important contributions have been made to the development of principles for the design of CALL materials, which we review in this chapter. First, however, we need to define what is meant by CALL materials, and explore the central notion of design in technology-mediated language teaching.

Technology, materials, and design in language teaching

CALL materials – that is, artifacts produced for language teaching (Levy

& Stockwell 2006) – can be taken to include tasks, Web sites, software, courseware, online courses, and virtual learning environments. So, clearly, language-teaching materials conceptualized in this way may include rather more than may be the case for materials conceptualized in face-to-face classroom settings. However, Levy and Stockwell (2006) identify earlier precedents for this view, drawing on the work of Breen, Candlin, and Waters (1979) who distinguish between *content* materials as sources of information and data and *process* materials that act as frameworks within which learners can use their communicative abilities. CALL products then encompass both content and process dimensions of materials. Although CALL materials can be seen as sharing many of the features of non-CALL materials, they also have a number of unique features, largely due to the materiality of the medium. We review these features in the next section, but first consider the concept of design.

The centrality of design to the theory and practice of CALL identified by Levy (1997, 1999, 2002) has emerged as a recurrent theme in the literature on technology-mediated language teaching (Gonzalez-Lloret 2003; Gruba 2004; Hampel 2006; Rosell-Aguilar 2005; Salaberry 2001; Wang 2006; Yutdhana 2005). Levy and Stockwell (2006) note that design, including, for example, materials design, screen design, task design, and software design, "enters into the discourse of CALL in many forms and at a variety of levels, from the scale of an institution down to the level of an exercise" (p. 10). Furthermore, the design process is extremely complex, endeavoring to draw on elements of theory, research, and practice in an optimal way given the affordances of particular technologies and the opportunities and constraints of individual contexts, not the least of which are the needs and resources of teachers and learners. As such, design procedures and practices have been closely examined.

A number of principled theoretical approaches to design have been proposed in CALL and are reviewed later in the chapter, but the challenge remains one of closing the distance and bridging the gap between theory and practice. The nature of the gap and the relationship between theory and practice of design in CALL is also the subject of much debate. Levy (1997) argues that requiring CALL instructional design to be theory-driven is unnecessarily restrictive, noting too that many of the theories suggested for CALL have been created and applied in non-CALL contexts; rather, what matters is the fit between the capabilities of technology and the demands of the learning objective. Following Richards and Rodgers (1986), it is argued that the design of pedagogical activities may begin at any of their three levels: theoretical approach, pedagogical design, or teaching procedure. More recently, Hampel (2006) has applied the framework to computer-mediated communication (CMC) and online tasks, presenting a nonlinear, nonhierarchical, three-level model for task development in virtual classrooms, which is represented in Lamy and Hampel (2007) in Table 3.1.

Table 3.1 A model for online task development

Approach	Scrutinizing theoretical frameworks and concepts for their ability to inform task design appropriately (e.g., ensuring that cognitive theories inform conversation-based tasks or that community-building concepts inform simulation tasks).
Design	Examining the triangular relationship between task type, tutor or student role, and the affordances of the medium based on its materiality. For example, what can we say about the effectiveness of tasks designed for audiographic versus videoconferencing environments?
Procedure	Thinking about how tasks can be orchestrated in the virtual classroom in order to foster interaction between learners and improve their communicative competence; taking account of research to ensure more frequent participation, release more control to the students, enable collaborative work and a problem-solving approach, and negotiate certain pitfalls (e.g., issues of power online).

(Lamy & Hampel 2007: 71)

The model is intended to represent dynamic, iterative processes of design and implementation, with each stage exerting an influence on the development and progression of other stages, and cyclical relationships between the stages.

A key point here is that design and development processes for technology in language teaching have diverse points of departure, with a broad concern for the relationship between theory, research – including teacher research – and practice, and include matching the affordances of the technologies with the complexities of the teaching context in a pedagogically optimal way.

The distinctive features of CALL materials

CALL materials are similar in many ways to traditional materials in that they function as tools in aiding the development of L2 acquisition and are therefore subject to the same pedagogical affordances and constraints. Nonetheless, CALL materials do have certain features that allow educators to draw on potential affordances and deal with constraints in different ways. Many discussions of new software or CALL in general point out advantages of their use. Summarizing some of these in relation to "new" technologies such as peer-to-peer networking, gaming, and messaging, Godwin-Jones (2005) suggests that CALL materials help with (1) computer literacy development (which some have pointed out creates a circular argument); (2) communicative skills development; (3) community building; (4) identity creation; (5) collaborative learning; and (6) mentoring. Although none of these are specific to language learning *per se*, they help facilitate using and learning the social aspects of language or aid learning indirectly.

Zhao (2005) suggests several advantages that are more directly related to language learning and teaching. According to Zhao, CALL materials help (1) by enhancing access efficiency through digital multimedia technologies; (2) by enhancing authenticity using video and the Internet; (3) by enhancing comprehensibility through learner control and multimedia annotations; (4) by providing opportunities for communication (through interactions with the computer and through interactions with remote audiences through the computer); (5) by providing feedback; (6) by offering computer-based grammar checkers and spell checkers; (7) through automatic speech recognition technology; and (8) by tracking and analyzing student errors and behaviors. Although this list combines technical (e.g., speech recognition) and pedagogical advantages (e.g., authenticity), it is clear that there is a broad range of potential areas where CALL materials can make a contribution. Below we offer an alternative selection, divided into organizational and pedagogical advantages.

Organizational advantages of CALL materials

Access

CALL materials can be offered to learners independent of time and place. This is a frequently cited advantage, especially in relation to Internet-based materials. For materials developers, this means opportunities to provide materials to learners for use outside the classroom and to learners who are otherwise unable to attend classes. Although this has offered many practical opportunities, it is not yet clear what the effects of access to materials are on second language acquisition. Recent studies have especially shown the importance of support where learners access materials without the direct intervention of a teacher, whether in a self-access context (Reinders 2005; Ulitsky 2000) or in distance education (Hampel 2006; Wang 2007; White 2006). Without such support, learners tend to use fewer or inefficient learning strategies, motivation levels tend to be low, and dropout rates high.

Recent studies in Mobile-Assisted Language Learning (MALL) offer a similar picture. Thornton and Houser (2005; see also Levy & Kennedy 2005) offered a vocabulary-learning program based on principles of distributed learning. Text messages were used to present vocabulary items along with regular options for review. They found that the participants in their study did not necessarily access materials more often than when they did not have mobile access. At this point, it is not yet clear what the effects of "anytime/anywhere" material access are on second language behavior and acquisition.

Storage and retrieval of learning behavior records and outcomes

Learner progress and test results can be stored electronically (and potentially automatically) and retrieved at any time, which is not only an organizational benefit for teachers and administrators but also potentially a pedagogical benefit for students. And recently, considerable progress has been made in the area of automatic essay scoring and evaluation (see, for example, Warschauer & Ware 2006).

Sharing and recycling of materials

CALL materials can easily be shared and updated. For materials developers, learning *objects* that meet certain international standards, such as the shareable courseware object reference model (www.scorm.com), are interoperable and can reduce development time, as they can be employed in different contexts. Changes to online resources are immediately available to users, and learners can thus be given new materials without having to return to class.

Cost efficiency

CALL materials are sometimes said to result in cost reduction, for example, by providing learners with electronic instead of print materials or by having students study independently rather than with a teacher. However, the provision of hardware and software and their maintenance has proven costly. Also, as mentioned above, learners need considerable guidance and a reduction in staffing has not always proven possible. In the future, Mobile-Assisted Language Learning may reduce the need to provide dedicated facilities and thus reduce associated costs. Text messaging, for example, is already being used as a cost-effective way to bypass unavailable or unreliable infrastructure in developing countries to deliver education (cf. www.kiwanja.net). Increasing interoperability of technologies and the use of *open-source* technologies and content may also make it possible to reduce the overall costs of developing language-learning materials.

Pedagogical advantages of CALL materials

Authenticity

There are two aspects to the potential advantage given by authenticity: CALL materials aid in the development of more authentic materials (computer-based or not) by allowing the selection of content based on actual language use. Examples are the application of corpora in the creation of dictionaries and the selection of content for textbooks. In addition, corpora are being used with learners in the language classroom, among others, to promote learning by discovery and as a type of consciousness-raising activity (cf. Aston, Bernardini & Stewart 2004).

The second advantage is said to be that CALL materials resemble the types of resources especially younger learners use in everyday life. The use of educational games is an example of ways in which materials developers have attempted to mimic learners' out-of-class activities. Computer games have been shown to be potentially beneficial to learning and literacy development. Gee (2003) identified 36 learning principles in the games he investigated. An example of these is the "active, critical learning principle" (p. 49). This stipulates that "all aspects of the learning environment (including the ways in which the semiotic domain is designed and presented) are set up to encourage active and critical, not passive, learning." In other words, computer games engage learners and get them involved in the tasks at hand. A second principle is the "regime of competence principle" where "the learner gets ample opportunity to operate within, but at the outer edge of, his or her resources, so that at those points things are felt as challenging but not 'undoable.'" Despite their potential, early attempts at designing games for language learning have not been entirely successful. One reason for this is that developers have not yet adapted to the (open and interactive) characteristics of the game environment but instead have attempted to copy existing content into a game (Prensky 2001).

Perhaps more important is the claim that the use of computers can help learners engage in inherently more authentic forms of language use, for example, through a language exchange, where two or more students with different language backgrounds communicate in each language for some of the time, or through a Web quest, where learners have to interact with authentic materials. This claim raises similar questions as with traditional materials: What is our definition of "authentic"? Are authentic materials always necessarily better than nonauthentic materials? And if the answer is no, then what would be the ideal balance? Claims that CALL materials are "authentic" are only useful to the extent that this concept is operationalized and has been shown to be beneficial to learning.

Interaction

A major advantage of CALL materials is said to be that they facilitate interaction and language *use*. Chapelle (2005) refers to "interaction" as "any two-way exchanges." This can be between two people, or between a person and the computer, as well as within the person's mind.

Swain's output hypothesis (2005) claims that, by producing the language, learners can become aware of gaps in their interlanguage, and others (e.g., Ellis 1996) have argued that language production can act as a form of practice, thereby strengthening existing connections in the mind. Sociocultural theory emphasizes the importance of interaction in a meaningful context (Lantolf 2000), and various popular CALL programs aim to create this context and opportunities for language use through e-mail or chat communication, or through language exchanges between learners (where a learner with a specific L1 is partnered with someone who wants to learn that language as a second language). Some researchers, however, have pointed out that the comprehensible input from the interaction alone is not sufficient to result in the development of accuracy and that some type of attention to form is necessary. In computer-mediated communication (CMC), materials and instructions would thus have to include some direction as to what learners are expected to do and what aspects of the language they are required to use.

The accompanying instructions can affect whether the interaction focuses predominantly on meaning, on form, or on both. In a study of the effects of peer feedback in online communication, Ware and O'Dowd (2008) assigned students to either an e-tutoring group (where they were asked to correct their partners' mistakes), or an e-partnering group (where they were not asked to do so). Even though participants in the e-tutoring group provided more corrections, it was clear that many participants were not well equipped to give feedback:

> We speculate that, from a student's perspective, online exchanges are likely "forward-oriented" toward the next message containing new information, unlike, perhaps, teacher-directed class assignments that can be iterative products that are revised multiple times for accuracy (and a grade). Therefore, we would suggest that teachers structure carefully sequenced tasks so that they build on the previous interaction. (Ware & O'Dowd 2008: 54)

Situated learning

Mention has already been made of the importance of providing learners with the opportunity to use the language in a socioculturally meaningful context. Mobile technologies may make it easier to provide materials and support tailored to a particular situation. Ogata and Yano (2004), for example, developed a system that used PDAs to provide information on which Japanese forms of address to use in which situations. As participants moved from room (situation) to room, and from interlocutor (more status) to interlocutor (less status), the information changed. Developing materials for such situations requires knowledge of the entire domain (participants, situations, language used) and may prove to be very challenging, unless learners can actively tap into a larger database or access support from teachers when faced with difficulties in using the language. A more open-ended and somewhat less ambitious approach was used by Reinders (2007b; Reinders & Lewis 2009), who created exercises for use on iPods and gave students tasks to complete for which they had to go out, talk to people, find and share information, and answer questions. The ability to have access to guidance and support, to record progress (using a microphone plugged into the iPod), and to complete real-world activities with other learners seemed to have a positive effect on students' motivation and their ability to speak. However, more research is needed to investigate how situated language learning can be structured and its effects on language acquisition.

Multimedia

The ability to integrate different modes of presentation is an improvement over traditional materials. Different modalities have been shown to result in vastly different processing on the part of the learner (Leow 1995), and the ability for the teacher to "repackage" materials to emphasize one modality over the other can be of benefit. Learners, too, can choose on the basis of their preferences or to request more help (for example, by turning on or off the subtitles on a DVD). The ability to use multimedia thus results in an enriched learning environment. Simulations are an example of a multimodal environment that has the potential to mimic real-world processes. In practice, however, CALL simulations have been built on very specific domains and are therefore limited in scope. This is largely due to technical challenges.

New types of activities

CALL materials can include activities that are difficult or impossible to achieve using other learning materials, such as moving objects across the screen (matching), recording one's voice, and so on. Of course, the effects of each of these activity types needs to be investigated for what it aims to measure or teach, and this has not always happened yet.

Feedback

Immediate feedback is possible with CALL materials, dependent on the user's input and a whole range of other factors (past input, timing, etc.). Different forms of feedback can also be given, such as those using sound, movement, text, or a combination of these. Also, it is possible to implement forms of feedback such as modeling, coaching, and scaffolding that are hard or impossible to implement in traditional learning environments. Natural language processing and parser-based CALL can potentially provide feedback based on participants' prior language-learning progress and their specific needs (Heift & Schulze 2007).

Nonlinearity

A long-recognized benefit of hypermedia is its ability to display information in a nonlinear way and for students to access information as and how they want to, rather than in a predetermined sequence. This is a benefit only if students know how to find the information they need and have strategies to learn with hypermedia. Of course, and first and foremost, this is also only an advantage if the quality of linked resources is of a sufficiently high standard.

Monitoring and recording of learning behavior and progress

CALL programs can record and monitor learners' behavior and progress, and dynamically alter input – or make suggestions to the learner. They can also compare learners' progress with their own goals and against that of other learners' (Reinders 2007b). The records can be made accessible to the student to encourage reflection on the learning process. Part of the rationale behind initiatives, such as the European Union's e-portfolio project, that encourage the keeping of personal records to support ongoing study and planning, is to develop learners' metacognitive awareness and to engage their metacognitive strategies. Metacognitive awareness helps learners to prioritize their learning and to select the most appropriate study plan and learning strategies. This, in turn, gives learners a sense of control over their learning and may help them to self-motivate (Ushioda 1996). Metacognitive strategies also help learners develop autonomy by allowing them to self-monitor and self-assess. In practice, however, it has proven to be particularly difficult to encourage learners to keep records or to plan their learning. Reinders (2006) found, for example, that many learners did not respond to computer prompts to create or revise learning plans and concluded that more training and staff intervention was necessary.

Control

Beyond monitoring, learners potentially have more control over how they use CALL materials, as these can often be accessed randomly or adapted to suit individual needs in the level of difficulty of the input or in the amount of support available (e.g., with or without glossaries, spell checkers, etc.).

Empowerment

An important benefit of the characteristics of CALL materials discussed above is that together they have the potential to *empower* learners by offering easier access to materials, greater control to learners, and more opportunities for the development of metacognitive skills and learner autonomy (cf. Shetzer & Warschauer 2000). On the other hand, people have worried about the "digital divide" or the potential for new technologies to leave disadvantaged groups even further behind. Yet, people (including ourselves) have argued that technology can actually help close that gap, and numerous examples exist of the technology bringing access to resources and opportunities that before did not exist, especially in the area of mobile technology (see also Warschauer 2004).

Conclusion

Many differences exist between CALL and traditional materials; however, the above brief review makes it clear that whether or not these differences translate into improved learning and teaching depends entirely on how the technology is implemented. It is also clear from the above that considerably more research is needed to establish how the differences do or do not impact our learners and how we can best take advantage of this. In the remainder of the chapter, we look at two sets of theoretical principles for task design in CALL and then describe two approaches to the design of CALL materials, one in distance language teaching, the other in self-access.

CALL in theory

A recurrent theme in CALL is the need for more explicit links between materials development and SLA theory. Here we review two influential frameworks of principles for task design, proposed by Chapelle (2001, Table 3.2), and Doughty and Long (2003). Drawing on interactionist second language acquisition theory, the aim of Chapelle's (2001) framework of criteria for CALL task appropriateness is to provide "ideal cognitive and social affective conditions for instructed SLA" (p. 45). The first of these criteria, and arguably the most critical, language-learning potential is based on general processes for SLA, referring to the degree to which the task promotes focus on form; it is this focus that distinguishes language-learning activities from an opportunity purely for language use. The requirement for focus on form is closely aligned to the requirement for meaning focus, referring to the need for learners' attention to be directed toward the meaning of the language required to complete the task: Both a focus on form and meaning focus need to be present in the completion of a meaning-focused task. The importance of the individual learner is captured in the criteria of learner fit, including characteristics which need to be considered in designing CALL activities such as learning style, age, and willingness to communicate. Authenticity in CALL, as discussed above, is based around the links between classroom and real-world language use, centering on texts and tasks that learners can find relevant in their language use beyond the classroom. Positive impact refers to effects beyond language-learning potential, including engaging learners' interest and the development of literacy skills, learner autonomy, and metacognitive awareness, for example. The final criterion, practicality, is an important one, in that CALL activities should not impose too much of a burden on teachers and learners in terms of accessibility and use; the resourcing of CALL is a key dimension to this criteria.

Table 3.2 Criteria for CALL task appropriateness

Language-learning potential	The degree of opportunity present for beneficial focus on form.
Learner fit	The amount of opportunity for engagement with language under appropriate conditions given learner characteristics.
Meaning focus	The extent to which learners' attention is directed toward the meaning of the language.
Authenticity	The degree of correspondence between the CALL activity and target language activities of interest to learners out of the classroom.
Positive impact	The positive effects of the CALL activity on those who participate in it.
Practicality	The adequacy of resources to support the use of the CALL activity.

(Chapelle 2001: 55)

Another example of such an explicit formulation of design principles, based on cognitive and interactionist SLA theory, is offered by Doughty and Long (2003). Specifically, 10 methodological principles (or MPs, see Table 3.3) of task-based learning are proposed:

1. Use tasks, not texts, as the unit of analysis.
2. Promote learning by doing.
3. Elaborate input (do not simplify; do not rely solely on "authentic" texts).
4. Provide rich (not impoverished) input.
5. Encourage inductive (chunk) learning.
6. Focus on form.
7. Provide negative feedback.
8. Respect "learner syllabuses"/developmental processes.
9. Promote cooperative/collaborative learning.

10. Individualize instruction (according to communicative needs and psycholinguistically). (Doughty & Long 2003: 52)

Table 3.3 Doughty and Long's design principles

	Principles	L2 implementation	CALL implementation
Activities			
MP1	Use tasks, not texts, as the unit of analysis.	task-based language teaching (TBLT; target tasks, pedagogical tasks, task sequencing)	simulations; tutorials; worldware
MP2	Promote learning by doing.		
Input			
MP3	Elaborate input (do not simplify; do not rely solely on "authentic" texts).	negotiation of meaning; interactional modification; elaboration	computer-mediated communication/ discussion; authoring
MP4	Provide rich (not impoverished) input.	exposure to varied input sources	corpora; concordancing
Learning processes			
MP5	Encourage inductive ("chunk") learning.	implicit instruction	design and coding features
MP6	Focus on form.	attention; form-function mapping	design and coding features
MP7	Provide negative feedback.	feedback on error (e.g., recasts); error "correction"	response feedback

(to be continued)

(continued)

	Principles	L2 implementation	CALL implementation
MP8	Respect "learner syllabuses"/ developmental processes.	timing of pedagogical intervention to developmental readiness	adaptivity
MP9	Promote cooperative/collaborative learning.	negotiation of meaning; interactional modification	problem solving; computer-mediated communication/discussion
Learners			
MP10	Individualize instruction (according to communicative needs and psycholinguistically).	needs analysis; consideration of individual differences (e.g., memory and aptitude) and learning strategies	branching; adaptivity; autonomous learning

(Doughty & Long 2003: 52)

Distance foreign-language learning is the specific technology-mediated context Doughty and Long have in mind, and much of their discussion is based around the constraints of that context. For example, they identify the practicalities of developing an understanding of learners and emerging learner needs in the distance context as key issues in adopting a task-based approach in distance language learning. Doughty and Long's (2003) work informs many of the most significant contributions to task design in distance foreign-language teaching, including research on task design for desktop videoconferencing (Wang 2006) and for audiographic conferencing (Hampel 2006; Rosell-Aguilar 2005). The relative weight given to theoretical and practical issues is interesting in Doughty and Long's (2003) framework: Chapelle (2005) comments that the guidelines for instructional materials given by Doughty and Long (2003) rely strongly on a theoretical view of how language is acquired through interaction and that this is "a defensible course of action for materials development" (p. 57). From another perspective, referring to Doughty and Long's (2003) contribution, White (2006) argues that there remains an important gap in the research literature, since no one has yet extended and elaborated such a synthesis, putting it into practice not only for course design but also for sustained course delivery, and then identifying implications for theory, research, and practice.

CALL in practice

In the next section, we discuss two projects in terms of their unique CALL features and the theoretical/pedagogical considerations reviewed above. The first project concerns a distance-education environment, the second an online self-access program.

Task design in online distance foreign-language teaching

The challenges in materials design for the distance context, including the fact that the teacher-designer is at times distant from the learners and the sites of learning, have been well documented (see, for example, White 2003). One result of this challenge has been that a number of researcher-practitioners have articulated rich accounts of the design processes they have undertaken. Here we explore one such account and relate it to our previous discussion.

Hampel's (2006) exploration of task design centers on the fact that, although the computer medium differs from the kinds of resources generally used in face-to-face language-learning settings in terms of its materiality, the field has been slow to appreciate and accommodate the particular features of technology-mediated learning environments, relying instead on transferring face-to-face tasks to the new settings. In the process of "rethinking task design," Hampel (2006), explores how tasks can be devised that are appropriate for a multimodal virtual environment. A fascinating contribution made by her research is the sustained comparison between task design and task implementation with different groups of learners and different tutors – that is, exploring what happens to tasks in audiographic conferencing (see Table 3.4).

Table 3.4 Outline of tasks

Step	Sequence	Activity	Resources	Skills
1	In advance of tutorial (voluntary)	reading preparation document (tutorial summary)	course Web site	reading
2	In advance of tutorial (voluntary)	preparatory activity: finding information about the topic	course materials; www (via selected links on course Web site)	reading; processing information from different sources
3	Tutorial (plenary)	sound check; warm-up activity	Lyceum (audio, images, text)	listening; speaking
4	Tutorial (plenary)	introduction of the topic through brainstorming or preliminary discussion; instructions for group work (e.g., allocation of roles)	Lyceum (audio, images, text)	listening; speaking
5	Tutorial (group work)	preparation for final activity (e.g., preparing roles, arguments, presentation, or written text)	Lyceum (audio, images, text)	summarizing information; negotiating positions; collaboration; preparing presentation or discussion
6	Tutorial (plenary)	final activity (e.g., discussion, presentation)	Lyceum (audio, images, text)	taking part in presentation or discussion
7	After plenary	feedback on task, error correction	Lyceum or e-mail	reflection on learning
8	After the tutorial (voluntary)	additional group activity: expanding the task	Lyceum and/or e-mail	writing; collaboration

(Hampel 2006: 114)

The learning environment named Lyceum, developed by the Open University UK, is an Internet-based application that allows learners to interact synchronously using a range of modes: The modes include audio, writing, and graphics, and the environment includes a voicebox, whiteboard, a concept map, a document facility, and text chat. The key point is that whereas multimodal environments offer seemingly similar modes of communication to those of conventional classrooms, they have very different affordances, which in turn impacts on how the environment, and tasks, are used by learners. (For a detailed description of audiographic environments, see Hampel & Baber 2003.)

In discussing task development, Hampel (2006) draws on the three-level approach discussed earlier, with approach, design, and procedure stages, noting that the approach influences not just the design and implementation stages, but also that the evaluation during implementation feeds back into how the approach is understood in online environments. The theoretical approaches Hampel draws on are primarily interactionist SLA theory, sociocultural theory, and theories of medium, mode, and affordances, all of which are needed to understand and inform the design of sociocollaborative tasks in multimodal environments.

The tasks designed by Hampel (2006) aim to address one of the key challenges of the distance-learning context, that is, providing opportunities for learners to develop the kinds of real-time interactive competence that is required to use language in interpersonal social processes (Kötter 2001; White 2003). They have been designed to be part of online tutorials, and are just one learning source within the course. Hampel (2006) notes that the tasks "show a number of criteria which Chapelle [...] has summarized for CALL and CMC" (p. 113); she does not indicate whether the criteria were used implicitly or explicitly at different stages of the development process. What is clear, however, is that learner fit is critical for distance students in a technology-mediated mode, and that, addressing Doughty and Long's (2003) concerns, detailed, practical knowledge of learners was drawn on in identifying the kinds of experiences they were likely to bring to tasks that would facilitate interaction and participation. Beneficial focus on form and meaning focus were also considered, as was authenticity, focusing on current issues in German-speaking countries using predominantly authentic texts. Hampel notes that although the scenarios and participant roles were not of themselves authentic, they simulated authenticity and the authentic texts were seen as having a positive impact – another of Chapelle's (2003) features – on student interest. Practicality, that is, having resources to support the CALL activities, was a key concern, as learners were mostly located in their home environments, and careful planning – including online socialization – were directed at supporting this aspect of the process. Finally, and critically, positive impact was central to the tutorial tasks, as learner motivation is often vulnerable at key points in distance-learning processes, and opportunities for interaction and support have been found to impact very positively on persistence and progression. Below are the sequences of activities available in Lyceum, including the online resources used and the skills practiced.

The second part of Hampel's (2006) study moves from theory and design to implementation, identifying significant differences between tasks as conceptualized and tasks as realized. First, Hampel (2006) notes how tutors adapted the tasks largely for practical reasons, such as fluctuating student numbers; for unforeseen issues of learner fit, particularly in terms of learner needs and interests; and finally, because of timing, with different stages of tasks taking much longer than anticipated to complete. Although positive impact was carefully considered at the design phase, Hampel (2006) notes that not all students found the tasks engaging or motivating: In some cases this was due to the actions of peers who were linguistically or technologically more proficient; in other cases, it was due to the lack of assessment awarded to this part of the course, pointing to wider issues of curricular articulation for technology-mediated tasks (White 2006). In addition, the complexity of the multimodal environment was found, certainly in the initial stages, to overwhelm some students, having a somewhat inhibiting effect on communication, as did the absence of visual cues. Thus the mediating role of what can be broadly defined as learner interpretation of tasks (Batstone 2005) was key to understanding task enactment in synchronous online environments. Hampel (2006) concludes by underlining the importance of context-dependent features noted by Chapelle (2003) that must be taken into account when designing and implementing tasks: In this case, the materiality of the multimodal environment and the ways in which learners and teachers responded to those features had a dramatic effect on what happened to tasks in audiographic conferencing.

An online self-access environment

In a rather different project carried out at the University of Auckland, the development of an online self-access environment (called English Language Self-Access Centre, or ELSAC) was initiated as a response to the large numbers of students needing English support. Studies done at the University estimated as many as 10,000 students could be in need of improving, especially, their academic English skills. The online self-access environment was designed as a practical solution to supporting this many students from all different backgrounds and faculties, and also as a way to foster learner autonomy and to allow students to develop skills to continue improving their English on their own (see Schwienhorst 2003, 2007, for a discussion of the relationship between autonomy and CALL). In terms of the unique features of CALL materials discussed above, especially the organizational advantages of anytime/anywhere *access*, the automatic *storage and retrieval of learner records*, and the hopes of *cost efficiency* were important drivers. Pedagogically speaking, the key aim was to offer students *control* and to *empower* them through allowing *nonlinear* access to a wide range of *multimedia* resources that cater to a wide range of learner differences, and to offer *feedback* and support through the *monitoring* of learning behavior and progress.

To this end, the online environment was developed consisting of two elements: (1) a large database of electronic resources, some commercially published, some developed in-house, to cater to all learner needs and interests; and (2) several tools to support the students' learning *process*. Examples of the latter included a needs analysis, a learning plan, a learning record, and learning strategies worksheets. In addition to these tools, there were several mechanisms that monitored student learning and gave feedback at key points in the learning process. An example of these was a process for comparing students' needs (as identified in their needs analysis) with their learning plans and their actual learning. It was not uncommon, for example, for students to establish, say, writing expository essays as one of the priority skills for improvement, but then to continue using grammar resources. At this point the computer would prompt the students to revise their plans and/or materials use.

Studies into the effects of these tools and mechanisms on student learning (Reinders 2006, 2007a) made a number of interesting findings. In general, both questionnaires and interviews showed that students were extremely satisfied with the program. Usage records showed that many students had accessed the resources and had done so frequently and over longer periods of time. Many students reported using more resources and more often than they normally did or would have done without the program; in this sense, the program's access features were a clear advantage. Staff, too, were satisfied because they could look up students' progress and did not have to spend much time on administration – an advantage of the automatic *storage* and *retrieval* of learners' work. However, SQL queries (queries of information stored in the records of a SQL database) of 1,200 student database records collected over one year gave a somewhat less positive picture. Despite numerous suggestions, many students did not complete their initial needs analysis, and very few updated their learning plans as a result. Similarly, the prompts made by the computer were seldom heeded; when participants had set their minds on learning with particular materials or in a particular way, it was clearly difficult to encourage them to change.

The results of these studies were interpreted as showing a need for more learner training and more staff support. Students obviously needed more information about the rationale behind the program and how to respond to its prompts. As a result of these studies, additional support structures were put in place. These included language advisory sessions where students met face-to-face with a language advisor to discuss their learning needs and progress. Although the advisors made extensive use of the electronic records of the program, obviously the cost-efficiency factor of the software turned out to be lower than expected. In addition, a range of workshops was implemented to help students develop independent learning skills.

Taking the above findings into account, a more recent incarnation of ELSAC, called *My English*, was developed for King Mongkut University of

Technology in Bangkok. Developed in a similar context (albeit in an EFL setting) and for similar reasons, this differed from the above program by including additional support mechanisms so that students could contact staff more easily to get help, as well as several elements to encourage communication in English, such as chat rooms and online communication activities.

As with ELSAC, the program is a shell in which teachers can place language-learning materials, and so its main intended advantages are at the level of the learning process (containing both *process* and *content* materials) rather than individual tasks. Nonetheless, the inclusion of interaction-oriented modules is in line with Doughty and Long's recommendations. An important difference between ELSAC and *My English* is that the latter is not designed to be mainly used by students independently, but rather as an integral part of and complement to the existing language courses; the aim is to encourage ongoing study during and after those courses finish. In this way, it is hoped that over time students engage in more language use and receive more input than they would without such support programs.

Conclusion

In the preceding sections, we have tried to identify some of the features that make CALL materials unique and have discussed relevant theories and pedagogical approaches. We then reviewed several examples of CALL materials and programs. Although it is paramount to consider language-learning materials from a pedagogical perspective, it is important to remember that, even more so than with non-CALL materials, issues of practicality play an important role. Organizational and practical advantages offered by the use of technology can sometimes be sufficient reasons to adopt a new technology, even outweighing any pedagogic advantages. Among the many important questions arising during the process of the development of CALL materials, a key one is how to reconceptualize language tasks in ways that enable us to provide the best opportunities for language learning. And a key way to meet this challenge suggested by Gruba (2004) can be found in our collective attempts to define tasks, write them, and try them out with students; equally importantly, there is a need to strengthen the links between theory, research, and practice, and to acknowledge that the divide between CALL and non-CALL materials is disappearing.We hope that this will lead to a new understanding of materials development.

Discussion questions and tasks

Reflection

1. Note how CALL materials are defined in this chapter – how does it relate to the way you think about language teaching materials?
2. Think about a CALL program that you have used. Which of the benefits in Table 3.2 do you think it offers? Are there any missing in the table that you would add?
3. How useful is the idea of the role of a language teacher as designer? What are some of the strengths and limitations of this as a perspective on what language teachers do?
4. Think about a teaching context you are familiar with. Which organizational and pedagogical advantages of CALL materials are the most evident?
5. What do you think can be the effect of providing students with nonlinear access to CALL materials?
6. Can you identify the kinds of differences that may occur between task design and task implementation in the kinds of synchronous online environments described by Hampel (2006)?

Evaluation

7. Look at some CALL materials in terms of Breen *et al.*'s (1979) distinction between content materials and process materials. Do you find this distinction helpful? How would you evaluate materials in terms of content and in terms of process?

Adaptation/Design

8. Choose a set of language-teaching materials designed to fit a particular learning need. How would you need to adapt them to take account of the opportunities and constraints of a particular technology-mediated environment and pedagogical context?

References

Aston, G., Bernardini, S., & Stewart, D. (2004). *Corpora and language learners*. Amsterdam: Benjamins.

Batstone, R. (2005). Planning as discourse activity: A sociocognitive view. In R. Ellis (ed.). *Planning and task performance in a second language*. Amsterdam: John Benjamins, pp. 277-95.

Breen, M., Candlin, C., & Waters, A. (1979). Communicative materials design: Some basic principles. *RELC Journal* 10: 1-13.

Chapelle, C. A. (2001). *Computer applications in second language acquisition*. Cambridge: Cambridge University Press.

Chapelle, C. A. (2003). *English language learning and technology*. Amsterdam/ Philadelphia: John Benjamins.

Chapelle, C. A. (2005). Interactionist SLA theory in CALL research. In J. Egbert & G. Petrie (eds.). *Research perspectives on CALL*. Mahwah: Lawrence Erlbaum, pp. 53-64.

Coleman, J. (2005). CALL from the margins: Towards effective dissemination of CALL research and good practices. *ReCALL* 17: 18-31.

Doughty, C., & Long, M. H. (2003). Optimal psycholinguistic environments for distance foreign language learning. *Language Learning & Technology* 7: 50-80.

Ellis, N. C. (1996). Sequencing in SLA. Phonological memory, chunking, and points of order. *Studies in Second Language Acquisition* 18: 91-126.

Gee, J. P. (2003). *What video games have to teach us about learning and literacy*. Basingstoke, UK: Palgrave Macmillan.

Godwin-Jones, B. (2005). Emerging technologies. Messaging, gaming, peer-to-peer sharing: Language learning strategies and tools for the millennial generation. *Language Learning & Technology* 9: 17-22.

Gonzalez-Lloret, M. (2003). Designing task-based CALL to promote interaction: En Busca De Esmeraldas. *Language Learning & Technology* 7: 86-104.

Gruba, P. (2004). Designing tasks for online collaborative language learning. *Prospect* 19(2): 72-81.

Hampel, R. (2006). Rethinking task design for the digital age: A framework for language teaching and learning in a synchronous online environment. *ReCALL* 18: 105-121.

Hampel, R., & Baber, E. (2003).Using Internet-based audio-graphic and video conferencing for language teaching and learning. In U. Felix (ed.). *Language learning on-line: Towards best practice*. Lisse, Netherlands: Swets & Zeitlinger, pp. 171-91.

Heift, T., & Schulze, M. (2007). *Errors and intelligence in computer-assisted language learning: Parsers and pedagogues*. New York: Routledge.

Johnson, M. (1999). Review of B. Tomlinson (ed.). Materials development in language teaching, Cambridge University Press. *New Zealand Studies in Applied Linguistics* 5: 93-7.

Kötter, M. (2001).Developing distance learners' interactive competence – Can synchronous audio do the trick? *International Journal of Educational Telecommunication* 7: 327-53.

Lamy, M.-N., & Hampel, R. (2007). *Online communication in language learning and teaching*. Basingstoke, UK: Palgrave Macmillan.

Lantolf, J. P. (2000). Introducing sociocultural theory. In J. P. Lantolf (ed.). *Sociocultural theory and second language learning*. Oxford: Oxford University Press.

Leow, R. P. (1995). Modality and intake in second language acquisition. *Studies in Second Language Acquisition* 17: 79-89.

Levy, M. (1997). *Computer-assisted language learning: Context and conceptualization*. Oxford: Clarendon Press.

Levy, M. (1999). Design processes in CALL: Integrating theory, research and evaluation. In K. C. Cameron (ed.). *CALL: Media, design and applications*. Lisse, Netherlands: Swets & Zeitlinger, pp. 85-109.

Levy, M. (2002). CALL by design: Products, processes and methods. *ReCALL* 14: 129-42.

Levy, M., & Kennedy, C. (2005). Learning Italian via mobile SMS. In A. Kukulska-Hulme, & J. Traxler (eds.). *Mobile learning. A handbook for educators and trainers*. London: Routledge, pp. 76-83.

Levy, M., & Stockwell, G. (2006). *CALL dimensions: Options and issues in computer assisted language learning*. Mahwah, NJ: Lawrence Erlbaum Associates.

Maley, A. (1998). Squaring the circle – Reconciling materials as constraint with materials as empowerment. In B. Tomlinson (ed.). *Materials development in language teaching*. Cambridge: Cambridge University Press, pp. 279-94.

Ogata, H., & Yano, Y. (2004). Context-aware support for computer-supported ubiquitous learning. In *BT IEEE International workshop on wireless and mobile technologies in education*. Alamitos: IEEE Computer Society, pp. 27-34.

Prensky, M. (2001). *Digital game-based learning.* New York: McGraw-Hill.

Reinders, H. (2005). Non-participation in a university language programme. *JALT Journal* 27: 209-26.

Reinders, H. (2006). Supporting self-directed learning through an electronic learning environment. In T. Lamb & H. Reinders (eds.). *Supporting independent learning: Issues and interventions.* Frankfurt: Peter Lang, pp. 219-38.

Reinders, H. (2007a). Big brother is helping you. Supporting self-access language learning with a student monitoring system. *System* 35: 93-111.

Reinders, H. (2007b). Podquests. Language learning on the move. *ESL Magazine* 58.

Reinders, H., & Lewis, M. (2009). Podquests. Language games on the go. In M. Andreade (ed.). *Language games.* Alexandria: TESOL. (Series: Classroom Practice).

Richards, J., & Rodgers, T. (1986). *Approaches and methods in language teaching. A description and analysis.* Cambridge: Cambridge University Press.

Rosell-Aguilar, F. (2005). Task design for audiographic conferencing: Promoting beginner oral interaction in distance language learning. *Computer Assisted Language Learning* 18: 417-42.

Salaberry, M. (2001). The use of technology for second language learning and teaching: A retrospective. *The Modern Language Journal* 85: 39-56.

Schwienhorst, K. (2003). Neither here nor there? Learner autonomy and intercultural factors in CALL environments. In D. Palfreyman & R. Smith. (eds.). *Learner autonomy across cultures: Language education perspectives.* Houndmills, UK: Palgrave Macmillan, pp. 164-81.

Schwienhorst, K. (2007). *Learner autonomy and virtual environments in CALL.* London: Routledge.

Shetzer, H., & Warschauer, M. (2000). An electronic literacy approach to network-based language teaching. In M. Warschauer & R. Kern (eds.). *Network-based language teaching: Concepts and practice.* New York: Cambridge University Press, pp. 171-85.

Swain, M. (2005). The output hypothesis: Theory and research. In E. Hinkel (ed.). *Handbook on research in second language teaching and learning.* Mahwah, NJ: Lawrence Erlbaum, pp. 471-84.

Thornton, P., & Houser, C. (2005). Using mobile phones in English education in Japan. *Journal of Computer Assisted Learning* 21: 217-28.

Tomlinson, B. (ed.). (1998). *Materials development in language teaching.* Cambridge: Cambridge University Press.

Ulitsky, H. (2000). Language learner strategies with technology. *Educational Computing Research* 22: 285-322.

Ushioda, E. (1996). *Learner autonomy 5: The role of motivation.* Dublin: Authentik.

Wang, Y. (2006). Negotiation of meaning in desktop videoconferencing-supported distance language learning. *ReCALL* 18: 122-46.

Wang, Y. (2007). Task design in videoconferencing-supported distance language learning. *CALICO Journal* 24: 657-73.

Ware, P., & O'Dowd, R. (2008). Peer feedback on language form in telecollaboration. *Language Learning & Technology* 12: 43-63.

Warschauer, M. (2004). *Technology and social inclusion: Rethinking the digital divide.* Cambridge, MA: MIT.

Warschauer, M., & Ware, P. (2006). Automated writing evaluation: Defining the classroom research agenda. *Language Teaching Research* 10: 1-24.

White,C. (2003). *Language learning in distance education.* Cambridge: Cambridge University Press.

White, C. (2006). State of the art article: The distance learning of foreign languages. *Language teaching* 39: 247-64.

Yutdhana, S. (2005). Design-based research in CALL. In J. Egbert & G. Petrie. (eds.). *CALL research perspectives*. Mahwah, NJ: Lawrence Erlbaum Associates.

Zhao, Y. (2005). *Research in technology and second language education. Developments and directions*. Greenwich, CT: Information Age Publishing.

4

Principles of effective materials development

Brian Tomlinson

Summary

This paper takes the position that language-learning materials should ideally be driven by learning and teaching principles rather than be developed ad hoc or in imitation of best-selling coursebooks. It reviews the literature which contributes positively toward the principled development of ELT materials and comments on its implications for materials writing. It then presents six principles of language acquisition and four principles of language teaching that the author thinks should be given a lot more attention in materials development. It outlines and justifies each principle and then derives from it materials development principles and procedures to be applied to the actual development of materials. Using the proposed principles as criteria, typical current ELT materials are evaluated, a characterization of the typical ELT coursebook is made, and the author makes suggestions for improvement. The paper concludes by arguing that what is needed are principled frameworks to help materials writers achieve principled coherence in their contextualized application of theory to effective practice.

Introduction

In recent years there have been a number of insightful publications which have concerned themselves with how authors typically write ELT materials. For example, Hidalgo *et al.* (1995) and Prowse (1998) asked numerous authors to detail the typical procedures they follow, Bell and Gower (1998) reflected on their own procedures for writing a coursebook, Johnson (2003) gave a group of expert writers a materials development task and researched the procedures they used to write their materials, and Tomlinson (2003e) reviewed the literature on developing ELT materials. This literature reveals that many experienced authors rely on their intuitions about what "works" and make frequent use of activities in their repertoire that seem to fit with their objectives. Very few authors are actually guided by learning principles or considerations of coherence, and many seem to make the assumption that clear presentation and active, relevant practice are sufficient to lead to acquisition.

My position is that materials should not be random recreations from repertoire nor crafty clones of previously successful materials. Instead they should be coherent and principled applications of:

i) Theories of language acquisition and development.
ii) Principles of teaching.
iii) Our current knowledge of how the target language is actually used.
iv) The results of systematic observation and evaluation of materials in use.

This is the position that drives this chapter. In it, I will focus in particular on (i) and (ii) above.

Review of the literature

In this section I will review some of the literature that I think contributes positively toward the principled development of ELT materials.

In Hidalgo *et al.* (1995), some writers articulate principled approaches to materials development. Flores (1995: 58-9) lists five assumptions and principles that drove the writing of a textbook in the Philippines; Penaflorida (1995: 172-9) reports her use of six principles of materials design specified by Nunan (1988); Fortez (1995: 26-7), Luzares (1995: 26-7), and Rozul (1995: 210) advocate needs analysis as a starting point; and Flores (1995: 60-5), Fortez (1995: 74), Richards (1995: 102-3), and Rozul (1995: 213) describe lesson and/or unit frameworks that they use. Maley (1995: 221) says that materials development is "best seen as a form of operationalised tacit knowledge" that involves "trusting our intuitions and beliefs," and Hall (1995: 8) insists that the crucial question we need to ask is, "How do we think people learn languages?" Hall goes on to discuss the following principles, which he thinks should "underpin everything we do in planning and writing our materials" (ibid):

- The need to communicate.
- The need for long-term goals.
- The need for authenticity.
- The need for student-centeredness.

I would completely agree with Hall, as I would with the principle, which many of the authors in Hidalgo *et al.* (1995) advocate, that ELT materials should stimulate interaction.

Tomlinson (1998b: 5-22) proposes 15 principles for materials development that derive from second language acquisition research and experience. Of these, I would now stress the following six as those that should drive ELT materials development. The materials should:

- Expose the learners to language in authentic use.
- Help learners to pay attention to features of authentic input.
- Provide the learners with opportunities to use the target language to achieve communicative purposes.
- Provide opportunities for outcome feedback.
- Achieve impact in the sense that they arouse and sustain the learners' curiosity and attention.
- Stimulate intellectual, aesthetic, and emotional involvement.

A number of other writers outline principled approaches to developing ELT materials in Tomlinson (1998a). For example, Bell and Gower (1998: 122-5) discuss the need for authors to make principled compromises to meet the practical needs of teachers and learners and to match the realities of publishing materials, and they articulate 11 principles that guide their writing. Of these, I would particularly agree with the importance of:

- Flexibility – so as to help teachers to make their own decisions.
- Moving from text to language (e.g., focusing on the meaning of a text first before returning to it to pay attention to a language feature).
- Providing engaging content.
- Learner development (in the sense of helping learners to further develop their skills as language learners through, for example, analyzing grammar for themselves and starting their own personalized vocabulary and grammar books).

The principles I have mentioned so far could be proceduralized in a unit of materials that provided the teacher (and possibly the learners) with opportunities to change the sequence of (or even select from) a range of texts and tasks. In this way, the learners can gain opportunities for language acquisition from motivated exposure to language in use and gain opportunities for language awareness from a subsequent focus on a linguistic feature of a text just enjoyed.

Also in Tomlinson (1998a), Edge and Wharton (1998: 299-300) talk about the "coursebook as ELT theory" and as a "genre whose goal is a dialogue about principle via suggestions about practice," and they stress the need to design coursebooks for flexible use so as to capitalize on "teachers' capacity for creativity." In the same volume, Maley (1998: 283-7) provides practical suggestions for "providing greater flexibility in decisions about content, order, pace and procedures" (p. 280), and Jolly and Bolitho (1998: 97-8) advocate the following principled framework:

- Identification of the need for materials.
- Exploration of need.
- Contextual realization of materials (e.g., the teacher makes a decision to provide practice in communicating hypothetical meaning in contexts familiar to the students).
- Pedagogical realization of materials (e.g., the teacher develops a

worksheet focusing on the distinction between fact and hypothesis and the verb forms involved in making this distinction).

- Production of materials (e.g., the teacher types out the worksheet and photocopies it for distribution to the learners).
- Student use of materials.
- Evaluation of materials against agreed objectives.

A usefully detailed review of the literature on advice and principles for materials developers is provided by McGrath (2002: 152-61). This ranges from Methold (1972), who stressed the importance of recycling and of localization, via Hutchinson and Waters (1987) and their focus on the intended effect of the materials, to Rossner (1988) and his focus on the quality and authenticity of the experience offered, and to Tomlinson (1998a) and his focus on learning principles. As well as reporting on recommended procedures for materials development, McGrath also reports the literature on principled frameworks and procedures for units of materials, and he focuses, in particular, on the theme- or topic-based approach, the text-based approach (Tomlinson 2003d), and the storyline (Nunan 1991).

Tan (2002a) is concerned with the role that corpus-based approaches can and should play in language teaching and contains chapters in which contributors from around the world report and discuss the contribution that corpora have made in, for example, the teaching of vocabulary, the teaching of fixed expressions, the conversation class, the teaching of writing, and the teaching of collocation. Tan (2002b: 5-6) stresses how corpus-based materials can achieve the important criterion of providing "real contextualised examples of written and spoken language" and she states that these should be designed to help language learners to:

a. Be consciously aware of the unfamiliar usages of language they have heard or read in native speaker contexts.
b. Investigate how these unfamiliar usages are employed in natural authentic communication.
c. Experiment with these usages in spoken or written communication, so that they become familiar.

Other writers who have stressed the role that corpora can play in developing principled materials by exposing learners to authentic samples of language use are Carter (1998), Carter and McCarthy (1997), Fox (1998), Hoey (2000), McCarthy (1998), Tribble and Jones (1997), and Willis (1998). See also Tomlinson (2009) for discussion of some of the limitations of corpora and for suggestions on how to supplement them with author, teacher, and learner research.

Perhaps the publication that gives most attention to principles and procedures of materials development is Tomlinson (2003b). This volume contains, for example, chapters on:

- Materials evaluation (Tomlinson 2003c) – this proposes a process of articulating beliefs about language learning, turning the beliefs into universal criteria, specifying a profile of the target context of learning, deriving local criteria from the profile and then using both the universal and the local criteria for both developing and evaluating the materials.
- Writing a coursebook (Mares 2003) – this describes and discusses a principled process for writing a coursebook.
- Developing principled frameworks for materials development (Tomlinson 2003d) – this reviews the literature on principled frameworks and then outlines and exemplifies a text-driven flexible framework that has been used successfully on materials development projects in Namibia, Norway, and Turkey (and that is currently being used on projects in Ethiopia and Oman).
- Creative approaches to writing materials (Maley 2003) – this offers a framework for generating creative materials.
- Humanizing the coursebook (i.e., giving it more personal relevance and value for the people using it) (Tomlinson 2003e) – this proposes ways of humanizing language learning without a coursebook, of humanizing it with a coursebook, and of developing humanistic coursebooks.
- Simulations in materials development (Tomlinson & Masuhara 2003) – this explores the principles and procedures of using materials development simulations for teacher development.

Other publications with valuable contributions to the subject of principled materials development include Byrd (1995), Fenner and Newby (2000), McDonough and Shaw (1993), Mishan (2005), Mukundan (2006a), Ribe (2000), Richards (2001), and Tomlinson and Masuhara (2004). Tomlinson (2007a) deals with language acquisition and development, but many of the chapters propose applications of the research to materials development for language learning. Tomlinson (2008a) provides critical reviews of ELT materials currently being used around the world and most of its chapters make reference to principles and procedures of materials development. It also contains an introductory chapter on "Language acquisition and language learning materials" (Tomlinson 2008b), which proposes ways of applying commonly agreed theories of language acquisition to materials development.

As yet, there is very little literature reporting research results of projects investigating the actual effectiveness of language-learning materials. However, Tomlinson and Masuhara (forthcoming 2010) will publish the results of research projects from around the world that are attempting to discover how effective certain materials actually are in the learning contexts in which they are being used.

Proposals for principled approaches to the development of ELT materials

In this section, I am going to present my own proposals for principled approaches based on my 40 years' experience of teaching English, developing language-learning materials, observing materials in use, and researching language acquisition and development. In the absence of empirical data to substantiate my claims and to support my proposals, I can only offer my convictions in order to stimulate thought, debate, and (hopefully) research. Other materials writers would no doubt suggest different (and equally valid) principled approaches.

One of the things materials writers need is an inventory of flexible frameworks to help them develop effective materials for target learners in principled and coherent ways. But before such frameworks are developed, we must first determine what the principles are that should drive the procedures.

Each principle of materials development needs to be derived from principles of language acquisition and should then be used to develop frameworks that link together procedures in an organic and coherent way. Each principle of language acquisition should also be used to develop universal criteria that act as criteria for both the development and evaluation of materials in conjunction. In the process of developing materials for specified target learners, the universal criteria need to be combined with local criteria derived from what is known about the learners, their teachers, and their context of learning (Tomlinson 2003c).

Below I list the main principles of language acquisition that I follow when developing materials, and some of the principles for materials development that I derive from them. As you read them, you might like to evaluate their validity and usefulness and to think of other principles of your own.

Principle of language acquisition No. 1

A prerequisite for language acquisition is that the learners are exposed to a rich, meaningful, and comprehensible input of language in use (Krashen 1985, 1993, 1999; Long 1985). In order to acquire the ability to use the language effectively, the learners need a lot of experience of the language being used in a variety of different ways for a variety of purposes. They need to be able to understand enough of this input to gain positive access to it, and it needs to be meaningful to them. They also need to experience particular language items and features many times in meaningful and comprehensible input in order to eventually acquire them. This is a point made by Nation and Wang (1999), whose research endorses the value of extensive reading (providing the learners read at least one graded reader per week) because of the benefit gained from the many times new vocabulary items are repeated in controlled graded readers. The point is also made by Nation (2005: 587), who stresses the importance of repetitions in extensive reading "with an optimal space between the repetitions so that previous knowledge is still retained and yet there is some degree of novelty to the repetition," ideally with the word occurring each time "in a new context." Nation (2003) also stresses the importance of the elaboration that takes place when meeting a known word again in a way that stretches its meaning for the learner.

Principles of materials development

1. Make sure that the materials contain plentiful spoken and written texts, which provide extensive experience of language being used to achieve outcomes in a variety of text types and genres in relation to topics, themes, events, and locations likely to be meaningful to the target learners.
2. Make sure that the language the learners are exposed to is authentic in the sense that it represents how the language is typically used. If the language is inauthentic because it has been written or reduced to exemplify a particular language feature, then the learners will not acquire the ability to use the language typically or effectively.

   Much has been written on the issue of authenticity, and some experts consider that it is useful to focus attention on a feature of a language by removing distracting difficulties and complexities from sample texts. My position is that such contrived focus might be of some value as an additional aid to help the learner to focus on salient features, but that prior and subsequent exposure to those features in authentic use is essential. For other recent thoughts on the value of authentic materials, see Day (2003), Gilmore (2007), Mishan (2005), and Tomlinson (2001a).

   Of course, in order to ensure authenticity of input, we need to know how the language is typically used. Recently a number of very large corpora of language use have been developed, and we now know a lot more about language use than we did 30 years ago. However, there are still gaps between what we do and what we know and between what we know and what we "tell" our learners (Tomlinson 2009).
3. Make sure that the language input is contextualized. Language use is determined and interpreted in relation to its context of use. Decontextualized examples do not contain enough information about the user, the addressee(s), the relationships between the interactants, the setting, the intentions, or the outcomes for them to be of value

to the language learner. I can, for example, think of at least three different interpretations of "Give him the keys. Let him drive it." But I do not know what it really means, nor why the speaker has used the imperative, until I know who is saying it, who they are saying it to, what the relationship between them is, where they are, what has happened before, and what the objectives of the conversation are. Only extended samples of language in contextualized use can provide the learner with the "information" they need to develop awareness of how the target language is actually used.

4. Make sure that the learners are exposed to sufficient samples of language in authentic use to provide natural recycling of language items and features that might be useful for the learners to acquire.

Principle of language acquisition No. 2

In order for the learners to maximize their exposure to language in use, they need to be engaged both affectively and cognitively in the language experience (Arnold 1999; Tomlinson 1998b, 1998d). If the learners do not think and feel while experiencing the language, they are unlikely to acquire any elements of it. Thinking while experiencing language in use helps to achieve the deep processing required for effective and durable learning (Craik & Lockhart 1972), and it helps learners to transfer high-level skills such as predicting, connecting, interpreting, and evaluating (Tomlinson 2007a) to second language use. If the learners do not feel any emotion while exposed to language in use, they are unlikely to acquire anything from their experience. Feeling enjoyment, pleasure, and happiness, feeling empathy, being amused, being excited, and being stimulated are most likely to influence acquisition positively, but feeling annoyance, anger, fear, opposition, and sadness is more useful than feeling nothing at all (Tomlinson 2003e). Ideally, though, the learner should be experiencing positive affect in the sense of being confident, motivated, and willingly engaged even when experiencing "negative" emotions. There is a substantial amount of literature on the value of affective and cognitive engagement while engaged in responding to language in use. For example, Braten (2006) reports on research into the role of emotion in language learning and use; Damasio (1994) reports research on the important role of emotion in memory; Mathewson (1994) refers to the many articles on the importance of affect in *The Reading Teacher from 1948-1991*; Pavlenko (2005) investigates the role of emotion in second language learning; and both Schumann (1999) and Stevick (1999) report research on the value of affective engagement while learning a language. Anderson (1990, 1993) shows the benefits of cognitive engagement during language experience; Byrnes (2000) focuses on the value of using higher-level cognitive skills in second language learning; Green (1993) picks out cognitive engagement as one of the main drives of second language acquisition; and Robinson (2002) contains a number of chapters reporting research on cognitive engagement.

Principles of materials development

1. Prioritize the potential for engagement by, for example, basing a unit on a text or a task that is likely to achieve affective and cognitive engagement rather than on a teaching point selected from a syllabus.
2. Make use of activities that make the learners think about what they are reading or listening to and respond to it personally.
3. Make use of activities that make the learners think and feel before, during, and after using the target language for communication.

Principle of language acquisition No. 3

Language learners who achieve positive affect are much more likely to achieve communicative competence than those who do not (Arnold 1999; Tomlinson 1998d). Language learners need to be positive about the target language, about their learning environment, about their teachers, about their fellow learners, and about their learning materials. They also need to achieve positive self-esteem and to feel that they are achieving something worthwhile. Above all, they need to be emotionally involved in the learning process and to respond by laughing, getting angry, feeling sympathy, feeling happy, feeling sad, and so on. Positive emotions seem to be the most useful in relation to language acquisition, but it is much better to feel angry than to feel nothing at all. The value of positive affect has been attested to, for example, by de Andres (1999), who reports research on the value of positive self-esteem in language learning; by Arnold and Fonseca (2007), who report research on how teachers can positively influence affective involvement; by Dörnyei (2002), who offers 35 strategies for how teachers might enhance their students' motivation, and who also stresses the importance of positive motivation; by Rost (2005), who reports research on the value of positive affective involvement; and by Schumann (1997, 1999), who focuses on the benefits of positive appraisal.

Principles of materials development

1. Make sure the texts and tasks are as interesting, relevant, and enjoyable as possible so as to exert a positive influence on the learners' attitudes to the language and to the process of learning it.
2. Set achievable challenges, which help to raise the learners' self-esteem when success is accomplished.
3. Stimulate emotive responses through the use of music, song, literature, art, and so on, through making use of controversial and provocative texts, through personalization, and through inviting learners to articulate their feelings about a text before asking them to analyze it.

Principle of language acquisition No. 4

L2 language learners can benefit from using those mental resources that they typically utilize when acquiring and using their L1. In particular, they can gain from multidimensional representation of both the language they experience and the language they intend to produce (see Masuhara 1998, 2006, 2007; Tomlinson 1998c, 2000a, 2000b, 2001b, 2001c, 2003a; and Tomlinson & Avila 2007a, 2007b for principled suggestions as to how making use of multidimensional mental representation can help L2 learners). In L1 learning and use, learners typically employ mental imaging (e.g., seeing pictures in their mind), inner speech, emotional responses, connections with their own lives, evaluations, predictions, and personal interpretations. In L2 learning and use, learners typically focus narrowly on linguistic decoding and encoding. Multidimensional representation of language that is experienced and used can enrich the learning process in ways that promote durable acquisition, the transfer from learning activities to real-life use, the development of the ability to use the language effectively in a variety of situations for a variety of uses, and the self-esteem that derives from performing in the L2 in ways as complex as they typically do in the L1.

There is a considerable literature on the vital use of the inner voice in L1 and the infrequency of use of the inner voice in the L2. For example:

- Akhutina (2003), Steels (2003), and de Bleser and Marshall (2005) demonstrate how effective inner speech is vital for effective outer speech.
- Appel and Lantolf (1994) and Masuhara (1998) report on the use of inner speech by advanced L2 learners.
- Blonsky (1964) demonstrates that the inner voice reproduces the speech of the speaker you are listening to, and Anderson (1995), Klein (1981), and Sokolov (1972) report the vital role of the inner voice during silent reading.
- Jenkin *et al.* (1993), Masuhara (1998), and Tomlinson (1998e) report on the rarity of use of the L2 inner voice by L2 learners.
- Johnson (1994) researched the role of inner speech in defining and guiding the self.
- Korba (1986, 1990) researched the speed of inner speech and found it to be ten times faster than outer speech.
- Sokolov (1972) reports research demonstrating the characteristics and functions of the inner voice.
- Vygotsky (1986) reports research on the roles of the inner voice and stresses the importance of these roles.

What the literature demonstrates is that in the L1 we use the inner voice to give our own voice to what we hear and read, to make plans, to make decisions, to solve problems, to evaluate, to understand and "control" our environment, and to prepare outer voice utterances before saying or writing them. When talking to ourselves, we use a restricted code that consists of short elliptical utterances expressed in simple tenses with the focus on the comment rather than the topic, on the predicate rather than the subject. It is cotext and context dependent, implicit, partial, vague, novel, and salient to ourselves. However, L2 users rarely use an L2 inner voice until they reach an advanced level – though there is evidence that the use of an L2 inner voice at lower levels can enhance L2 performance and can be facilitated by teachers and materials (de Guerro 2004; Tomlinson 2000b). For further details of the characteristics and roles of the inner voice, see Archer (2003), de Guerro (2005), and Tomlinson and Avila (2007a, 2007b).

There is also a considerable body of literature on the role of visual imaging in language use and acquisition. For example:

- Barnett (1989), Tomlinson (1998a), and Avila (2005) report that L2 learners do not typically use visual imaging when using the L2.
- Eysenk and Keane (1990) show how visual imaging is used to make inferences about what is not explicitly stated.
- Paivio (1979) and Sadoski (1985) demonstrate how we represent linguistic utterances by combining images from relevant prior experience with images generated by text.
- Sadoski and Paivio (1994) report the importance of visual imaging in the development of the ability to read and understand text.
- Sadoski and Quast (1990) and Esrock (1994) stress the value of visual imaging in deep processing (demonstrated by Craik & Lockhart 1972 to be vital for long-term learning).
- Tomlinson (1996, 1998a) presents research on the role of visual imaging in retention and recall and in preparation of what you want to say or write.
- Tomlinson (1998a) and Avila (2005) report research demonstrating the potential effectiveness of training L2 learners to use visual imaging in their learning and use of the L2.

Basically, what the literature demonstrates is that visual imaging plays a very important role in L1 learning and use, that it tends not to be used by L2 learners, and that L2 learners can be trained to use visual imaging to improve their learning and use of the L2.

Ideally the inner voice and mental imaging should be used concurrently (Collins 2009; Leontiev & Ryabova 1981; Sadoski & Paivio 1994), and also in conjunction with affective connections and motor imagery. This is what happens in L1 use and what could happen in L2 use, too.

For details of research on mental imaging and on inner speech and its application to materials development, see in particular Tomlinson and Avila (2007a, 2007b).

Principles of materials development

1. Make use of activities that encourage learners to visualize and/or use inner speech before, during, and after experiencing a written or spoken text.
2. Make use of activities that encourage learners to visualize and/or use inner speech before, during, and after using language themselves.
3. Make use of activities that help the learners to reflect on their mental activity during a task and then to try to make more use of mental strategies in a similar task.

Principle of language acquisition No. 5

Language learners can benefit from noticing salient features of the input. If learners notice for themselves how a particular language item or feature is used (Ellis, this volume; Schmidt & Frota 1986; Tomlinson 2007b), they are more likely to develop their language awareness (Bolitho *et al.* 2003; Bolitho & Tomlinson 1995; Tomlinson 1994). They are also more likely to achieve readiness for acquisition (Pienemann 1985). Such noticing is most salient when a learner has been engaged in a text affectively and cognitively and then returns to it to investigate its language use. This is likely to lead to the learner paying more attention to similar uses of that item or feature in subsequent inputs and to increase its potential for eventual acquisition.

Principles of materials development

1. Use an experiential approach (Kolb 1984) in which the learners are first of all provided with an experience that engages them holistically. From this experience, they learn implicitly without focusing conscious attention on any particular features of the experience. Later, they revisit and reflect on the experience and pay conscious attention to its features in order to achieve explicit learning. For example, L2 learners could first of all be helped to respond multidimensionally to a text as

a whole, to articulate personal responses to it, and then to revisit it to focus more narrowly on particular features of the text. This enables the learners to apprehend before they comprehend and to intuit before they explore. And it means that when they focus narrowly on a specific feature of the text they are able to develop their discoveries in relation to their awareness of the full context of use (Tomlinson 1994).

2. Rather than drawing the learners' attention to a particular feature of a text and then providing explicit information about its use, it is much more powerful to help the learners (preferably in collaboration) to make discoveries for themselves.

Principle of language acquisition No. 6

Learners need opportunities to use language to try to achieve communicative purposes. In doing so, they are gaining feedback on the hypotheses they have developed as a result of generalizing on the language in their intake and on their ability to make use of them effectively. If they are participating in interaction, they are also being pushed to clarify and elaborate (Swain 2005), and they are also likely to elicit meaningful and comprehensible input from their interlocutors.

Principles of materials development

1. Provide many opportunities for the learners to produce language in order to achieve intended outcomes.
2. Make sure that these output activities are designed so that the learners are using language rather than just practicing specified features of it.
3. Design output activities so that they help learners to develop their ability to communicate fluently, accurately, appropriately, and effectively.
4. Make sure that the output activities are fully contextualized in that the learners are responding to an authentic stimulus (e.g., a text, a need, a viewpoint, an event), that they have specific addressees, and that they have a clear intended outcome in mind.
5. Try to ensure that opportunities for feedback are built into output activities and are provided for the learners afterwards.

There are many other principles of language acquisition that should ideally inform materials development. Among these are the proposals that the materials should:

- Have the potential to facilitate transfer of learning by replicating features of real-life activities in which the learners are likely to need to function after their course (James [2006] presents research supporting this and van den Branden [2006] reports the results of classroom research investigating the effects of replicating future workplace realities in classes for Dutch as an L2).
- Help learners to monitor themselves before, during, and after language production (Krashen 1985).

When developing classroom materials we should also, of course, consider principles of language teaching. Below is a list of the principles of language teaching that I follow when developing materials and the principles for materials development that I derive from them.

Principle of language teaching No. 1
The content and methodology of the teaching should be consistent with the objectives of the course and should meet the needs and wants of the learners.

Principles of materials development

1. For any course in which the main objective is to help the learners to improve their communicative competence in English, it is important that the English the learners are exposed to is used in ways that either represent or replicate the reality of language use in typical English discourse. This implies that most of the texts and tasks should be authentic in the sense that they have not been contrived for language-teaching purposes (Gilmore 2007; Mishan 2005) and that they are "as similar as possible to future applications of learning" (James 2006: 153). It also implies that any explicit exemplification should be informed by corpus data (Tan 2002a) or by systematic observation by the materials developers (Tomlinson 2009).

2. The materials need to be written in such a way that the teacher can make use of them as a resource and not have to follow them as a script. There must be a built-in flexibility to the course that helps teachers and learners to make principled decisions about texts, tasks, learning points, approaches, and routes in relation to learner needs and wants.

Principle of language teaching No. 2

The teaching should be designed to help learners to achieve language development and not just language acquisition (Tomlinson 2007a). In other words, the teachers should not restrict their objectives to the achievement of basic communicative competence, but should aim to help their learners to develop the ability to use language fluently, accurately, appropriately, and effectively in numerous genres and for numerous purposes. This not only prepares the learners for the reality of language use (van den Branden 2006), but can also positively affect their self-esteem (de Andres 1999) and help them to develop communicative competence (Canale & Swain 1980), cognitive academic language proficiency (Cummins 2000; Duff 2006), and functional literacy (Wiley 2005).

Principles of materials development

1. The activities should, from the earliest levels onward, involve and encourage the use of such high-level skills as imaging, using inner speech, making connections, predicting, interpreting, evaluating, and applying (see Principle of Language Acquisition No. 4 above for supporting references). This not only helps to prepare learners to become effective communicators, but it can also help them achieve the deep processing required for long-term learning.
2. The activities should not be restricted to the practice of language forms and functions, but should provide opportunities to use the target language to achieve intended outcomes in a range of genres and text types for a range of objectives.
3. The materials should help the teacher to assess the learners and to give constructive feedback in relation to achievement of intended outcomes.

Principle of language teaching No. 3
The teaching should be designed so as to provide the learners with learning opportunities that will help them to develop educationally in the sense that they become more mature, more critically astute, more creative, more constructive, more collaborative, more capable, and more confident as a result of the course.

Principles of materials development

1. The materials should be cross-curricular in that they relate to other subject areas and are not narrowly focused on language learning.
2. The materials should include some element of content-based teaching (Snow 2005) so that the learners learn more about an area of knowledge that is of particular interest or value to them.
3. The activities should help learners to develop skills, which can transfer to other subjects of study or to professional and/or leisure pursuits (e.g., creative, analytical, evaluative, organizational, coordination, and leadership skills).

Principle of language teaching No. 4
The teacher needs to be able to personalize and localize the materials (McKay 1992; Tomlinson 2006) **and to relate them in different ways to the needs, wants, and learning-style preferences of individual learners** (Anderson 2006). This can help to achieve the relevance and connectivity found to promote language acquisition, to help learners to relate the materials to previous experience (Tomlinson 2007b), and to facilitate the use of mental imaging and inner speech (Tomlinson & Avila 2007a).

Principles of materials development

1. The materials should provide the teacher with ideas (and maybe even banks of materials) for localizing and personalizing generic activities.
2. The materials should help the teacher to suggest ways in which individuals can make their own choices and work at their own level and speed.

Obviously, there are many other principles of language teaching, and there are also language-teaching realities to cater to in designing materials. The ability to cater to variations in class size, course duration, course intensity, lesson duration, teacher experience, teacher skills, teacher personality, teacher communicative competence, learner access to the target language in use and learner motivation should obviously be a consideration when designing principled language-learning materials.

Principled approaches to the development of ELT materials

Most global coursebooks these days seem to be clones of other commercially successful coursebooks, driven mainly by the need to appear attractive, to provide comprehensive coverage, to achieve face validity as typical coursebooks, to prepare learners for examinations, to help teachers by reducing their preparation time, to help administrators to allocate lessons to teachers, to standardize teaching, and to provide teaching that would be useful to any learner anywhere at a specified language level. This does not mean, of course, that such books are not principled, but any analysis of current global coursebooks will reveal the following common approach that I have just uncovered from an analysis of seven recently published global coursebooks:

i) Presentation of a language-teaching point through contrived examples and/or a short text.
ii) Questions on the examples focusing on the teaching point.
iii) Practice of the teaching point through matching, transformation, completion, rewriting, and sentence-construction exercises.
iv) Reading or listening to a short text providing further exemplification of the teaching point.
v) Comprehension questions testing understanding of the text.
vi) Speaking and writing activities related to the theme or topic of the unit and to the grammar and vocabulary points presented and practiced earlier.

This might be a reassuringly familiar approach to administrators, teachers, and learners, but its adherence to the presentation-practice-production format that has been much criticized for not matching what is known about language acquisition (Tomlinson *et al.* 2001;Willis 1996) is hardly likely to lead to success in facilitating language acquisition and development. The materials generated from this format sometimes do achieve a topic and/or language point coherence, which connects each activity to the others, but they rarely achieve coherence in the sense that each activity gains from the previous ones and is a preparation for the subsequent ones. These materials seem to be based on a very dubious principle that what is taught will be learned and to disregard most of the commonly agreed principles of language acquisition outlined above. Interestingly, I cannot find anybody in the literature actually recommending, supporting, or justifying this commonly used framework.

There are numerous exceptions to the generalization above about the typical framework for published coursebooks. Some of these can be found in global coursebooks, but most of them are to be found in local coursebooks, which do not have to compete in the marketplace. Such books can afford to be more principled (and therefore different from the norm), especially if they have been commissioned by a Ministry of Education or an institution and will be given to all teachers to use. I know of examples of local coursebooks driven by principles of language acquisition in Bulgaria, Japan, Morocco, Namibia, Norway, Rumania, Russia, Singapore, and Turkey, and of such a coursebook currently being developed in Oman. The most principled of the books already published are a low-budget, basic, black-and-white publication in Namibia (*On Target*) and a glossy, full-color publication in Norway (Fenner & Nordal-Pedersen 1999). Both follow the flexible, principled, text-driven framework outlined in Tomlinson (2003d), both follow a principle of moving from personal to local to international, and both match the six principles of language acquisition outlined above.

For more detailed accounts of principled local coursebooks, see Bolitho (2008), Popovici and Bolitho (2003), and Tomlinson (1995). For evaluations of coursebooks in relation to principles of language acquisition, see Masuhara *et al.* (2009), Tomlinson (2008), and Tomlinson *et al.* (2001).

Conclusions

It seems that most current global coursebooks and many local and localized coursebooks are not driven or even informed by principles of language acquisition and development. Some of them manage to help learners to acquire language because their writers have been effective teachers and are intuitively applying principles of teaching. Most of them could be a lot more effective if they had been driven by the principles of learning and teaching outlined above. What is needed are principled frameworks to help future materials writers to manage to achieve principled coherence in their contextualized application of theory to effective practice.

Discussion questions and tasks

Reflection

1. In the literature, there is frequent reference as to whether materials work or not. Which of the following do you think are the most important criteria for deciding whether certain materials work or not?
   i) Do the materials help learners to understand and remember grammar rules?
   ii) Do the materials help learners to remember definitions of vocabulary items?
   iii) Do the learners enjoy using the materials?
   iv) Does the teacher find the materials easy to use?
   v) Do the materials eventually help to facilitate successful language acquisition and development? Can you think of any other important criteria?
2. i) Which of the six principles of language acquisition outlined in this paper do you think should be made more use of by materials writers?
   ii) Are there any of the six principles that you don't think should be followed by materials writers?
   iii) Can you think of any other principles of language acquisition that you think materials writers should pay more attention to?
3. i) Which of the four principles of language teaching outlined in this paper do you think should be made more use of by materials writers?

ii) Are there any of the four principles that you don't think should be followed by materials writers?

iii) Can you think of any other principles of language teaching that you think materials writers should pay more attention to?

4. Do you know of any coursebook that differs from the typical approach outlined in Principle of Language Teaching No. 4 (pp. 111-2)? Do you think this coursebook is potentially more effective than the others or not?

Evaluation

5. Take any one of the six principles of language acquisition outlined above and use it to evaluate a coursebook you know. As a result of your evaluation, suggest adaptations that could be made to the coursebook so that it becomes potentially more effective for a particular learning context which you are familiar with.

Adaptation/Design

6. Decide on a target group of learners and then write a unit of material for them that is driven by those learning and teaching principles that you agree with.

   If possible:

   - Teach your unit.
   - Evaluate it in relation to the principles that drove it.
   - Adapt your unit in order to make it even more principled and effective.

References

Akhutina, T. V. (2003). The role of inner speech in the construction of an utterance. *Journal of Russian and East European Psychology* 41(3/4): 49-74.

Anderson, J. R. (1990). *Cognitive psychology and its implications* (3rd ed.). New York: W. H. Freeman.

Anderson, J. R. (1993). Problem solving and learning. *American Psychologist* 48: 35-44.

Anderson, J. R. (1995). *Learning and memory: An integrated approach.* NewYork: John Wiley and Sons, Inc.

Anderson, N. J. (2006). L2 learning strategies. In E. Hinkel (ed.). *Handbook of research in second language teaching and learning*. Mahwah, NJ: Erlbaum, pp. 757-71.

Appel, G., & Lantolf, J. P. (1994). Speaking as mediation: A study of L1 and L2 text recall tasks. *The Modern Language Journal* 78(4): 437-52.

Archer, M. S. (2003). *Structure, agency and the internal conversation*. Cambridge: Cambridge University Press.

Arnold, J. (ed.). (1999). *Affect in language learning*. Cambridge: Cambridge University Press.

Arnold, J., & Fonseca, C. (2007). Affect in teacher talk. In B. Tomlinson (ed.). *Language acquisition and development: Studies of learners of first and other languages*. London: Continuum, pp. 107-21.

Avila, F. J. (2005). *El uso de la imagen mental en la lectura en el proceso de la adquisición de una secunda lengua*. PhD thesis. University of Seville.

Barnett, M. (1989). *More than meets the eye: Foreign language reading*. Englewood Cliffs, NJ: Prentice Hall Regents.

Bell, J., & Gower, R. (1998). Writing course materials for the world: A great compromise. In B. Tomlinson (ed.). *Materials development in language teaching*. Cambridge: Cambridge University Press, pp. 116-29.

Blonsky, P. P. I. (1964). *Izbrannye psihologiceskie proizvedenija* [*Selected psychological works*]. Moscow: Prosvescenie.

Bolitho, R. (2008). Materials used in Central and Eastern Europe and the former Soviet Union. In B. Tomlinson (ed.). *English language learning materials: A critical review*. London: Continuum, pp. 213-22.

Bolitho, R., & Tomlinson, B. (1995). *Discover English*. Oxford: Heinemann.

Bolitho, R., Carter, R., Hughes, R., Ivanič, R., Masuhara, H., & Tomlinson, B. (2003). Ten questions about language awareness. *ELT Journal* 57(3): 251-9.

Braten, S. (ed.). (2006). *Intersubjective communication and emotion in early ontogeny*. Cambridge: Cambridge University Press.

Byrd, P. (1995). *Materials writer's guide*. Rowley, MA: Newbury House.

Byrnes, H. (2000). Language across the curriculum: Interdepartmental curriculum construction. In M.-R. Kecht & K. von Hammerstein (eds.). *Languages across the curriculum: Interdisciplinary structures and internationalized education*. Columbus: National East Asian Resource Center, Ohio State University.

Canale, M., & Swain, M. (1980). Theoretical bases of communicative approaches to second language teaching and testing. *Applied Linguistics* 1: 1-47.

Carter, R. (1998). Orders of reality: CANCODE, communication and culture. *ELT Journal* 52(1): 43-56.

Carter, R., & McCarthy, M. (1997). *Exploring spoken English.* Cambridge: Cambridge University Press.

Collins, R. (2009). *Internalized symbols and the social process of thinking. Interaction ritual chains.* Princeton: Princeton University Press.

Craik, F. I. M., & Lockhart, R. S. (1972). Levels of processing: A framework for memory research. *Journal of Verbal Learning and Verbal Behaviour* 11: 671-84.

Cummins, J. (2000). *Language, power and pedagogy.* Clevedon, UK: Multilingual Matters.

Damasio, A. (1994). *Descartes' error: Emotion, reason, and the human brain.* New York: Avon.

Day, R. (2003). Authenticity in the design and development of materials. In W. A. Renandya (ed.). *Methodology and materials design in language teaching.* Singapore: SEAMEO Regional Language Centre, pp. 1-11.

de Andres, V. (1999). Self-esteem in the classroom or the metamorphosis of butterflies. In J. Arnold (ed.). *Affect in language learning.* Cambridge: Cambridge University Press, pp. 87-102.

de Bleser, R., & Marshall, J. C. (2005). Egon Weigl and the concept of inner speech. *Cortex* 41(2): 249-57.

de Guerro, M. C. M. (2004). Early stages of L2 inner speech development: What verbal reports suggest. *International Journal of Applied Linguistics* 14 (1): 90-113.

de Guerro, M. C. M. (ed.). (2005). *Inner speech: Thinking words in a second language.* New York: Springer Verlag.

Dörnyei, Z. (2002). The motivational basis of language learning tasks. In P. Robinson (ed.). *Individual differences and instructed language learning.* Amsterdam: John Benjamins, pp. 137-58.

Duff, P. (2006). ESL in secondary schools: Programs, problematics, and possibilities. In E. Hinkel (ed.). *Handbook of research in second language teaching and learning.* Mahwah, NJ: Erlbaum, pp. 45-64.

Edge, J., &Wharton, S. (1998). Autonomy and development: Living in the materials world. In B. Tomlinson (ed.). *Materials development in language teaching.* Cambridge: Cambridge University Press, pp. 295-310.

Esrock, E. (1994). *The reader's eye.* Baltimore: The John Hopkins University Press.

Eysenk, N.W., & Keane, M. T. (1990). *Cognitive psychology. A student's handbook.* Hillsdale, NJ: Lawrence Erlbaum.

Fenner, A., & Newby, D. (2000). *Approaches to materials design in European textbooks: Implementing principles of authenticity, learner autonomy, cultural awareness.* Strasbourg: European Centre for Modern Languages.

Fenner, A. N., & Nordal-Pedersen, G. (1999). *Search 10.* Oslo: Gyldendal.

Flores, M. M. (1995). Materials development: A creative process. In A. C. Hidalgo, D. Hall, & G. M. Jacobs (eds.). *Getting started: Materials writers on materials writing.* Singapore: SEAMEO Language Centre, pp. 57-66.

Fortez, G. E. (1995). Developing materials for tertiary level expository writing. In A. C. Hidalgo, D. Hall, & G. M. Jacobs (eds.). *Getting started: Materials writers on materials writing.* Singapore: SEAMEO Language Centre, pp. 67-81.

Fox, G. (1998).Using corpus data in the classroom. In B. Tomlinson (ed.). *Materials development in language teaching.* Cambridge: Cambridge University Press, pp. 25-43.

Gilmore, A. (2007). Authentic materials and authenticity in foreign language learning. *Language Teaching* 40: 97-118.

Green, C. P. (1993). Learner-drivers in second language acquisition. *Forum* 31: 2.

Hall, D. (1995). In A. C. Hidalgo, D. Hall, & G. M. Jacobs (eds.). *Getting started: Materials writers on materials writing.* Singapore: SEAMEO Regional Language Centre, pp. 8-24.

Hidalgo, A. C., Hall, D., & Jacobs, G. M. (eds.). (1995). *Getting started: Materials writers on materials writing.* Singapore: SEAMEO Language Centre.

Hoey, M. (2000). A world beyond collocation: New perspectives on vocabulary teaching. In M. Lewis (ed.). *Teaching collocation: Further developments in the lexical approach.* Hove: LTP, pp. 224-5.

Hutchinson, T., & Waters, A. (1987). *English for specific purposes: A learning-centred approach.* Cambridge: Cambridge University Press.

James, M. A. (2006). Teaching for transfer in ELT. *ELT Journal* 60(2): 151-59.

Jenkin, H., Prior, S., Rinaldo, R., Wainwright-Sharp, A., & Bialystok, E. (1993). Understanding text in a second language: A psychological approach to an SLA problem. *Second Language Research* 9(2): 118-39.

Johnson, J. R. (1994). Intrapersonal spoken language: An attribute of extrapersonal competency. In D. R. Vocate (ed.). *Intrapersonal communication: Different voices, different minds.* Hillsdale, NJ: Lawrence Erlbaum, pp. 169-92.

Johnson, K. (2003). *Designing language teaching tasks*. Basingstoke, UK: Palgrave Macmillan.

Jolly, D., & Bolitho, R. (1998). A framework for materials writing. In B. Tomlinson (ed.). *Materials development for language teaching*. Cambridge: Cambridge University Press, pp. 90-115.

Klein, E. S. (1981). *Inner speech cue preference in reading disabled and normal children*. Ann Arbor, MI: University Microfilms International.

Kolb, D. (1984). *Experiential learning: Experience as the source of learning and development*. Englewood Cliffs, NJ: Prentice Hall.

Korba, R. J. (1986). *The rate of inner speech*. Unpublished PhD thesis. University of Denver.

Korba, R. J. (1990). The rate of inner speech. *Perceptual and Motor Skills* 71: 1043-52.

Krashen, S. (1985). *The input hypothesis*. London: Longman.

Krashen, S. (1993). *The power of reading*. Englewood, NJ: Libraries Unlimited.

Krashen, S. (1999). *Three arguments against whole language & why they are wrong*. Portsmouth, NH: Heinemann.

Leontiev, A. A., & Ryabova, T. V. (1981). *Psychology and the language learning process*. Oxford: Pergamon Press.

Long, M. (1985). Input and second language acquisition theory. In S. Gass & C. Madden (eds.). *Input in second language acquisition*. Rowley, MA: Newbury House, pp. 377-93.

Luzares, C. E. (1995). Scientific writing: Developing materials without reinventing the wheel. In A. C. Hidalgo, D. Hall, & G. M. Jacobs (eds.). *Getting started: Materials writers on materials writing*. Singapore: SEAMEO Language Centre, pp. 25-30.

Maley, A. (1995). Materials writing and tacit knowledge. In A. C. Hidalgo, D. Hall, & G. M. Jacobs (eds.). *Getting started:Materials writers on materials writing*. Singapore: SEAMEO Language Centre, pp. 22-39.

Maley, A. (1998). Squaring the circle: Reconciling materials as constraint with materials as empowerment. In B. Tomlinson (ed.). *Materials development for language teaching*. Cambridge: Cambridge University Press, pp. 279-94.

Maley, A. (2003). Creative approaches to writing materials. In B. Tomlinson (ed.). *Developing materials for language teaching*. London: Continuum, pp. 183-98.

Mares, C. (2003). Writing a coursebook. In B. Tomlinson (ed.). *Materials development in language teaching*. Cambridge: Cambridge University Press, pp. 130-40.

Masuhara, H. (1998). *Factors influencing the reading difficulties of advanced learners of English as a foreign language when reading authentic texts*. Unpublished PhD thesis. University of Luton.

Masuhara, H. (2006). The multi-dimensional awareness approach to content teaching. In J. Mukundan (ed.). *Focus on ELT materials*. Petaling Jaya, Malaysia: Pearson/ Longman, pp. 1-11.

Masuhara, H. (2007). The role of proto-reading activities in the acquisition and development of effective reading skills. In B. Tomlinson (ed.). *Language acquisition and development: Studies of learners of first and other languages*. London: Continuum, pp. 15-31.

Masuhara, H., Tomlinson, B., Haan, M., & Yong, Y. (2009). Adult EFL Coursebooks. *ELT Journal* 62(3): 294-312.

Mathewson, G. C. (1994). Model of attitude influence upon reading and learning to read. In R. B. Ruddell, M. R. Ruddell, & H. Singer (eds.). *Theoretical models and processes of reading*. Newark, DE: International Reading Association, pp. 1131-61.

McCarthy, M. (1998). *Spoken language and applied linguistics*. Cambridge: Cambridge University Press.

McDonough, J., & Shaw, C. (1993). *Materials and methods in ELT: A teachers' guide*. London: Blackwell.

McGrath, I. (2002). *Materials evaluation and design for language teaching*. Edinburgh: Edinburgh University Press.

McKay, S. (1992). *Teaching English overseas*. Oxford: Oxford University Press.

Methold, K. (1972). The practical aspects of instructional materials preparation. *RELC Journal* 3 (1/32): 88-97.

Mishan, F. (2005). *Designing authenticity into language learning materials*. Bristol: Intellect.

Mukundan, J. (ed.). (2006). *Readings on ELT material II*. Petaling Jaya, Malaysia: Pearson/Longman.

Nation, P. (2003). Materials for teaching vocabulary. In B. Tomlinson (ed.). *Developing materials for language teaching*. London: Continuum Press, pp. 394-405.

Nation, P. (2005). Teaching and learning vocabulary. In E. Hinkel (ed.). *Handbook of research in second language teaching and learning*. Mahwah, NJ: Erlbaum, pp. 581-96.

Nation, P., & Wang, K. (1999). Graded readers and vocabulary. *Reading in a Foreign Language* 12: 355-80.

Nunan, D. (1988). Principles for designing language teaching materials. *Guidelines* 10: 1-24.

Nunan, D. (1991). *Language teaching methodology*. Hemel Hempstead: Prentice Hall.

On target. (1995). Windhoek: Gamsberg Macmillan.

Paivio, A. (1979). *Imagery and verbal processes*. Hillsdale, NJ: Lawrence Erlbaum.

Pavlenko, A. (2005). *Emotions and multilingualism*. Cambridge: Cambridge University Press.

Penaflorida, A. H. (1995). The process of materials development: A personal experience. In A. C. Hidalgo, D. Hall, & G. M. Jacobs (eds.). *Getting started: Materials writers on materials writing*. Singapore: SEAMEO Language Centre, pp. 172-86.

Pienemann, M. (1985). Learnability and syllabus construction. In K. Hyltenstam & M. Pienemann (eds.). *Modelling and assessing second language acquisition*. Clevedon, UK: Multilingual Matters, pp. 23-75.

Popovici, R., & Bolitho, R. (2003). Personal and professional development through writing: The Romanian textbook project. In B. Tomlinson (ed.). *Developing materials for language teaching*. London: Continuum, pp. 505-17.

Prowse, P. (1998). How writers write: Testimony from authors. In B. Tomlinson (ed.). *Materials development in language teaching*. Cambridge: Cambridge University Press, pp. 130-45.

Ribé, R. (2000). Introducing negotiation processes: An experiment with creative project work. In M. P. Breen & A. Littlejohn (eds.). *Classroom decision making: Negotiation and process syllabuses in practice*. Cambridge: Cambridge University Press, pp. 63-82.

Richards, J. C. (1995). Easier said than done: An insider's account of a textbook project. In A. C. Hidalgo, D. Hall, & G. M. Jacobs (eds.). *Getting started: Materials writers on materials writing*. Singapore: SEAMEO Language Centre, pp. 95-135.

Richards, J. C. (2001). *Curriculum development in language education*. Cambridge: Cambridge University Press.

Robinson, P. (ed.). (2002). *Cognition and second language instruction*. Cambridge: Cambridge University Press.

Rossner, R. (1988). Materials for communicative language teaching and learning. In C. Brumfit (ed.). *Annual Review of Applied Linguistics* 8. Cambridge: Cambridge University Press, pp. 140-63.

Rost, M. (2005). L2 listening. In E. Hinkel (ed.). *Handbook of research in second language teaching and learning*. Mahwah, NJ: Erlbaum, pp. 503-28.

Rozul, R. H. (1995). ESP materials: The writing process. In A. C. Hidalgo, D. Hall,

& G. M. Jacobs (eds.). *Getting started: Materials writers on materials writing*. Singapore: SEAMEO Language Centre, 209-18.

Sadoski, M. (1985). The natural use of imagery in story comprehension and recall: Replication and extension. *Reading Research Quarterly* 20: 658-67.

Sadoski, M., & Paivio, A. (1994). A dual coding view of imagery and verbal processes in reading comprehension. In R. B. Ruddell, M. R. Ruddell, & H. Singer (eds.). *Theoretical models and processes of reading*. Newark, DE: International Reading Association, pp. 582-60.

Sadoski, M., & Quast, Z. (1990). Reader response and long term recall for journalistic text: The roles of imagery, affect, and importance. *Reading Research Quarterly* 26: 463-84.

Schmidt, R., & Frota, S. (1986). Developing basic conversational ability in a second language: A case study of an adult learner of Portuguese. In R. Day (ed.). *Talking to learn: Conversation in second language acquisition*. Rowley, MA: Newbury House, pp. 237-326.

Schumann, J. H. (1997). *The neurobiology of affect in language*. Boston: Blackwell.

Schumann, J. H. (1999). A neurobiological perspective on affect and methodology in second language learning. In J. Arnold (ed.). *Affect in language learning*. Cambridge: Cambridge University Press, pp. 28-42.

Snow, A. M. (2005). A model of academic literacy for integrated language and content instruction. In E. Hinkel (ed.). *Handbook of research in second language teaching and learning*. Mahwah, NJ: Erlbaum Associates, pp. 693-712.

Sokolov, A. N. (1972). *Inner speech and thought*. New York: Plenum Press.

Steels, L. (2003). Language re-entrance and the "inner voice." *Journal of Consciousness Studies* 10 (4/5): 173-85.

Stevick, E. W. (1999). Affect in learning and memory: From alchemy to chemistry. In J. Arnold (ed.). *Affect in language learning*. Cambridge: Cambridge University Press, pp. 43-57.

Swain, M. (2005). The output hypothesis: Theory and research. In E. Hinkel (ed.). *Handbook of research in second language teaching and learning*. Mahwah, NJ: Erlbaum Associates, pp. 471-84.

Tan, M. (ed.). (2002a). *Corpus studies in language education*. Bangkok: IELE Press.

Tan, M. (2002b). Introduction. In M. Tan (ed.). *Corpus studies in language education*. Bangkok: IELE Press, pp. 1-14.

Tomlinson, B. (1994). Pragmatic awareness activities. *Language Awareness* 3 (3 & 4): 119-29.

Tomlinson, B. (1995). Work in progress: Textbook projects. *Folio* 2 (2): 26-31.

Tomlinson, B. (1996). Helping L2 learners to see. In T. Hickey & J. Williams (eds.). *Language, education and society in a changing world.* Clevedon, UK: Multilingual Matters, pp. 253-62.

Tomlinson, B. (ed.). (1998a). *Materials development in language teaching.* Cambridge: Cambridge University Press.

Tomlinson, B. (1998b). Introduction. In B. Tomlinson (ed.). *Materials development in language teaching.* Cambridge: Cambridge University Press, pp. 1-24.

Tomlinson, B. (1998c). Seeing what they mean: Helping L2 readers to visualise. In B. Tomlinson (ed.). *Materials development in language teaching.* Cambridge: Cambridge University Press, pp. 265-78.

Tomlinson, B. (1998d). Affect and the coursebook. *IATEFL Issues* 145: 20-1.

Tomlinson, B. (1998e). And now for something not completely different: An approach to language through literature. *Reading in a Foreign Language* 11(2): 177-89.

Tomlinson, B. (2000a). Talking to yourself: The role of the inner voice in language learning. *Applied Language Learning* 11(1): 123-54.

Tomlinson, B. (2000b). A multi-dimensional approach. *The Language Teacher Online,* July 24 (www.alt-publications.org/tlt/articles/2000/07/index).

Tomlinson, B. (2001a). Materials development. In R. Carter & D. Nunan (eds.). *The Cambridge guide to Teaching English to Speakers of Other Languages.* Cambridge: Cambridge University Press, pp. 66-71 .

Tomlinson, B. (2001b). The inner voice: A critical factor in language learning. *Journal of the Imagination in L2 Learning* vol. VI: 26-33.

Tomlinson, B. (2001c). Connecting the mind: A multi-dimensional approach to teaching language through literature. *The English Teacher* 4(2): 104-15.

Tomlinson, B. (2003a). The role of the inner voice in language learning: A personal view. *RELC Journal* 34: 178-94.

Tomlinson, B. (ed.). (2003b). *Developing materials for language teaching.* London: Continuum Press.

Tomlinson, B. (2003c). Materials evaluation. In B. Tomlinson (ed.). *Developing materials for language teaching.* London: Continuum Press, pp. 15-36.

Tomlinson, B. (2003d). Developing principled frameworks for materials development. In B. Tomlinson (ed.). *Developing materials for language teaching.* London: Continuum Press, pp. 107-29.

Tomlinson, B. (2003e). Humanizing the coursebook. In B. Tomlinson (ed.). *Developing materials for language teaching*. London: Continuum Press, pp. 162-73.

Tomlinson, B. (2006). Localising the global: Matching materials to the context of learning. In J. Mukundan (ed.). *Readings on ELT materials II*. Petaling Jaya, Malaysia: Pearson Malaysia, pp. 1-16.

Tomlinson, B. (ed.). (2007a). *Language acquisition and development: Studies of learners of first and other languages*. London: Continuum.

Tomlinson, B. (2007b). Teachers' responses to form-focused discovery approaches. In S. Fotos & H. Nassaji (eds.). *Form focused instruction and teacher education: Studies in honour of Rod Ellis*. Oxford: Oxford University Press, pp. 179-94.

Tomlinson, B. (ed.). (2008a). *English language teaching materials*. London: Continuum.

Tomlinson, B. (2008b). Language acquisition and language learning materials. In B. Tomlinson (ed.). *English language teaching materials*. London: Continuum, pp. 3-14.

Tomlinson, B. (2009). What do we actually do in English? In J. Mukundan (ed.). *Readings on ELT materials*. Petaling Jaya, Malaysia: Pearson Longman, pp. 20-41.

Tomlinson, B., & Avila, J. (2007a). Seeing and saying for yourself: The roles of audio-visual mental aids in language learning and use. In B. Tomlinson (ed.). *Language acquisition and development: Studies of learners of first and other languages*. London: Continuum, pp. 61-81.

Tomlinson, B., & Avila, J. (2007b). Applications of the research into the roles of audio-visual mental aids for language teaching pedagogy. In B. Tomlinson (ed.). *Language acquisition and development: Studies of learners of first and other languages*. London: Continuum, pp. 82-9.

Tomlinson, B., & Masuhara, H. (2003). Simulations in materials development. In B. Tomlinson (ed.). *Developing materials for language teaching*. London: Continuum Press, pp. 462-78.

Tomlinson, B., & Masuhara, H. (2004). *Developing language course materials*. Singapore: RELC Portfolio Series.

Tomlinson, B., & Masuhara, M. (eds.). (2010). *Research for materials development: Evidence for best practice*. London: Continuum.

Tomlinson, B., Dat, B., Masuhara, H., & Rubdy, R. (2001). Survey review. EFL courses for adults. *ELT Journal* 55: 80-101.

Tribble, C., & Jones, G. (1997). *Concordances in the classroom: A resource book for teachers*. Houston, TX: Athelstan.

van den Branden, K. (ed.). (2006). *Task-based language education*. Cambridge: Cambridge University Press.

Vygotsky, L. S. (1986). *Thought and language*. Cambridge: MIT Press.

Wiley, T. G. (2005). Second language literacy and biliteracy. In E. Hinkel (ed.). *Handbook of research in second language teaching and learning*. Mahwah, NJ: Erlbaum, pp. 529-45.

Willis, J. (1996). *A framework for task-based learning*. Harlow, UK: Longman.

Willis, J. (1998). Concordances in the classroom without a computer: Assembling and exploiting concordances of common words. In B. Tomlinson (ed.). *Materials development in language teaching*. Cambridge: Cambridge University Press, pp. 44-66.

5

Critical praxis as materials development: Responding to military recruitment on a US campus

Sarah Benesch

Summary

This chapter explores the influence of critical theory on materials development, focusing on *situatedness*, *dialogue*, *praxis*, *hope*, and *reflexivity*. These theoretical constructs are exemplified through a discussion of classroom materials and activities developed in response to a particular sociopolitical context: military recruitment on a US college campus. To demonstrate the dialogic character of critical teaching, students' responses to the materials and subsequent modification of *praxis* are examined. The chapter also raises questions about balancing materials that challenge the status quo with ones that support it so that students may engage with a range of positions. In addition, questions about appropriateness and effectiveness of critical materials are taken up: Which ones belong in the classroom, and which are more suitable for public posting, such as on an office door? These inquiries demonstrate the reflexivity demanded of critical teachers who must simultaneously present a variety of views, in the interest of *hope* and *possibilities*, while avoiding imposition of any particular ones. This self-questioning stance acknowledges the limitations of classrooms as arenas of social change while encouraging *hope* for a better world.

Introduction

In 1995, Congress passed the first Solomon Amendment, denying schools that barred military recruiters from campus any funds from the Department of Defense. The next year, Congress extended the law's reach to include funds from the Departments of Education, Labor, and Health & Human Services .... In 2005, Congress amended the law to explicitly state that military recruiters must be given equal access to that provided other recruiters. (www.law.georgetown.edu/solomon/ solomon.html)

> For Specialist James Garrovillas, enlisting in the Army meant more than just joining the military. It meant joining the United States .... Specialist Garrovillas is among 20,000 military service members who have become American citizens since July 2002, many of whom applied under a fast-track process approved by President Bush .... The new citizenship laws have offered a powerful tool to recruiters at a time when the military is struggling to meet its monthly enlistment quotas.
>
> (*New York Times*, Aug. 9, 2005; A11)
>
> The Army National Guard, which has suffered a severe three-year recruiting slump, has begun to reel in soldiers in record numbers, aided in part by a new initiative that pays Guard members $2,000 for each person they enlist.
>
> (*Washington Post*, Mar. 12, 2006; A01)

The activities and materials described in this chapter are grounded in a particular sociopolitical context: attempts by the US armed forces to enlist new recruits in the face of growing opposition to the US occupation of Iraq. Given the public's disenchantment with the war, various recruitment tools were developed, illustrated by the quotes above. Signing bonuses, fast-track citizenship,[1] and the Solomon Amendment – legislation requiring high schools

1 On July 3, 2002, George Bush signed Executive Order 13269 declaring that: "Those persons serving honorably in active-duty status in the Armed Forces of the United States, during the period beginning on September 11, 2001, and terminating on the date to be so designated, are eligible for naturalization in accordance with the statutory exception to the naturalization requirements .... For the purpose of determining qualification for the exception from the usual requirements for naturalization, I designate as a period in which the Armed Forces of the United States were engaged in armed conflict with a hostile foreign force the period beginning on September 11, 2001. Such period will be deemed to terminate on a date designated by future Executive Order" (www.fas.org/irp/offdocs/eo/eo-13269.htm).

and colleges to permit military recruiters on their campuses – aimed to bolster enlistment. Viewed together, these recruitment tools point to the targeting of high school and college students, including immigrant youth, as potential recruits.

Also part of the context is the publicly funded postsecondary institution in New York City where I teach. Military recruiters maintained a consistent presence during the 2004–2006 period and approached students on a regular basis. Given my position as a teacher of immigrants at this institution I, too, am part of this context. As a critical teacher, with an interest in power, inequality, and resistance, I choose to address military recruitment in my ESL classes. The students are immigrants of diverse linguistic and cultural backgrounds (Chinese, Korean, Pakistani, Egyptian, Albanian, Polish, Russian, Sri Lankan, Nigerian, among others), the vast majority of whom attended secondary and, in some cases, middle school in the United States. Due to their financial difficulties, these students are vulnerable to military recruitment, with its promises of job training, money, and citizenship.

The materials described in this chapter include those I used to introduce the topic of military recruitment on US college campuses to an ESL class. Students' responses to the introductory materials are also described as course materials, to demonstrate how both the students and I contributed to dialogic inquiry of the subject matter. In addition, the pedagogical decisions I made in response to students' talk and writing are also regarded as materials. That is, in critical pedagogies, teachers' and students' responses are joint contributions to a mutually informing dialogue, with unpredictable outcomes.

Theoretical assumptions about language and pedagogy in critical applied linguistics

Critical applied linguistics (CAL) has emerged over the last 15 years as a response to the complexities of language use, learning, teaching, and translation in a globalizing world. Influenced by postmodern theories, critical applied linguists address relationships between language and power, seeking to connect aspects of applied linguistics to broad social, cultural, and political domains. In their research and teaching, critical applied linguists examine and critique prevailing assumptions about language and language use, moving from positivism, and viewing language as an autonomous object, toward a socially constructed paradigm (Reagan 2004). Theoretical assumptions about language and pedagogy informing this critical paradigm are discussed next.

Language as discourse(s)

The pedagogy and materials described in this chapter are grounded in critical theory, based on the assumption that language is not simply a biological instinct nor a neutral medium of communication, but, rather, discourse(s) "embedded in social institutions and practices" (Pennycook 1994: 32). The "social practice of language use," according to Pennycook, "is always an act situated within some discourse" (p. 32). That is, there is no language outside of discourse. Nor is discourse associated solely with language. Rather, "[d]iscourses are ways of being in the world, or forms of life which integrate words, acts, values, beliefs, attitudes, and social identities, as well as gestures, glances, body positions, and clothes" (Gee 1996: 127). Discourses signal membership in social groups and networks, "people who associate with each other around a common set of interests, goals, and activities" (p. 128).

Power is central to the concept of discourses, an acknowledgment of hierarchical arrangements favoring some discourses and devaluing others in social contexts. Power, as a theoretical tool, highlights the dominance of certain discursive practices and the subordination of others, in texts, institutions, and social interactions. Attending to power allows for an understanding of the "ordering and dominance relations between practices *and* how people select from amongst available practices on specific occasions" (Fairclough 1995: 12). In other words, who is entitled to speak, to act, to participate in various contexts, and who is silenced and excluded?

Yet, language-as-discourse in critical applied linguistics does not conceptualize power as indomitable, but instead theorizes agency, the Foucauldian notion of resistance to power. Rather than viewing power as deterministic and all-encompassing, Foucault (1980) theorized the interplay of power and resistance, that is, humans actively engaging in the mechanisms of power rather than surrendering to their control. Power "signifies a level of conflict and struggle that plays itself out around the exchange of discourse" (Giroux 1997: 121). On the other hand, acknowledging resistance to power does not deny that humans are susceptible to regulation and, when external restrictions have been internalized, self-regulation. Rather, language-as-discourse constructs the self as "a terrain of conflict and struggle, and subjectivity ... a site of both liberation and subjugation" (Giroux 1997: 203).

The relationship between power and resistance is examined by studying discourses critically, "to call up for scrutiny, whether through embodied action or discourse practice, the rules of exchange within a field" (Luke 2004: 26). This critical stance requires dissociation from normative discursive practices, that is, ways of walking, talking, gesturing, interacting, thinking, appearing, and so on, to enable analysis of the status quo. To consider alternatives to the status quo requires "[o]thering of the self from dominant text and discourse ... a sense of being beside oneself or outside oneself in another epistemological, discourse, and political space" (Luke 2004: 26). Self-othering in critical pedagogies is a process through which students can imagine better choices than the ones currently offered to them, what Simon (1992) called "possibilities" and Freire (1994, 1998a, 1998b) called "hope."

Hope

Critical teachers facilitate examination of the relationship between power and resistance in various discourses so that students may determine whether current conditions are acceptable to them or not. If conditions are deemed unacceptable, strategies for challenging the status quo may be developed. That is, critical teaching goes beyond a "language of critique" to promote "a language of possibility" (Giroux 1997: 122). Critique is necessary for an understanding of power relations, but it is insufficient. Critique alone leads to cynicism. A language of possibility offers hope and, perhaps, strategies for challenging the way things are.

Freire theorizes hope as an "indispensable" aspect of human life, without which "we would have pure determinism" (Freire 1998b: 69). Education without hope, for Freire, is a process of despair and inaction. Distinguishing "training" and "education" (Freire 1994: 91), he posits the former as preparation for a predetermined future to which students must resign themselves. Education, on the other hand, engages students in "the problematization of the future rather than its inexorability" (Freire 1998a: 42). So, for example, my choice of military recruitment as a topic of study invited students to consider a range of possible responses to being approached by a recruiter, from enlisting to resisting.

Dialogue

When concerns are raised about critical pedagogies, they often focus on the role of the critical teacher, seen as someone eager to impose a political agenda on students. Santos (1998), for example, expressed her belief that "critical pedagogy ... advocates and attempts to implement overt in-your-face ideological activism in the classroom" (p. 182). She promoted, instead, "traditional teaching," claiming that it "prevents classrooms from becoming open political training grounds and students from being used by their teachers for the purpose of political proselytizing, on the left or right" (p. 182).

I aim to show in this chapter that critical teachers can be scrupulous about the dialogic nature of their praxis, avoiding undemocratic practices, such as, "overt in-your-face ideological activism" or "political proselytizing." According to Freire (1998b), in critical classrooms, students "know that their teachers are continuously in the process of acquiring new knowledge and that this new knowledge cannot simply be transferred to them" (p. 33). Students are "engaged in a continuous transformation through which they become authentic subjects of the construction of what is being taught, side by side with the teacher who is equally subject to the same process" (p. 33).

As I show in my discussion of the materials, instead of proselytizing, I facilitated a dialogue about military recruitment on college campuses in which opinions seemed to be freely expressed and elaborated. In fact, proselytizing would have been impossible because, rather than possessing a fixed ideological position on the issue, I allowed my opinion to be informed by the rich, multilayered classroom discussions. This is not to say that I had no opinion at the outset. Rather, I was initially opposed to military recruiters on college campuses, wanting to shield students from their intimidating presence. However, as students expressed and elaborated their responses to the issue, my views changed. I was convinced by their arguments that the presence of recruiters could provoke students to formulate various responses to these representatives of the military, from approval to opposition, leading to open discussion and informed decision making, both in and outside of class. Had I had a fixed position on the issue before the discussions began, such a modification in my thinking would have been impossible.

Praxis

Pennycook (2001) posits praxis, "a constant reciprocal relationship between theory and practice" (p. 3), as a central concern of critical applied linguistics. Yet, there continues to be a shortage of examples of the practice side of praxis, some exceptions being Goldstein (2003), Lin (2004), Morgan (1998), and Rivera (1999). My support for more examples of critical teaching is not to oppose theory building, but, rather, to argue for theorized accounts of messy classroom interactions, including their unpredictable responses and constant modifications in light of those responses. Examples of classroom interaction are needed to demonstrate the critical scrutiny of discourses and dialogic teaching. These examples show that students do not passively absorb material, but, rather, respond in a variety of ways, including opposition, insights, boredom, and humor. How these varied responses are taken up is an essential aspect of critical pedagogy, one that needs to be documented more fully. This chapter aims to reveal the texture of a critical dialogue between students and teacher working together on a complex and pressing issue.

Situatedness

Though my response to concerns about proselytizing in previous paragraphs focused in part on the centrality of dialogue, it is important to distance critical pedagogies from student-centered process pedagogy with its promotion of students' individual voices. Critical pedagogies are concerned, above all, with collective solutions to social inequality, encouraging ways to achieve social justice. This is the reason for self-othering and for scrutinizing topics not normally discussed in college classrooms, such as military recruitment. That is, critical pedagogies introduce material that has generally been ignored because of its political nature, and push inquiry beyond the safe and comfortable terrain of abstract ideas, definitions, and testable fact(oid)s. However, the topics and materials are not pulled from a list of teacher interests, but are, instead, situated in students' lives. Thus, military recruitment, as an increasingly widespread phenomenon on US college campuses, was an aspect of students' experience that they may not have been equipped to respond to and was therefore an important area to explore critically.

Reflexivity

Critical teachers must be sensitive to the demands of self-othering, of analyzing the status quo. Students who are unaccustomed to positioning themselves outside of normative discourses can find the process challenging. They may resist critical scrutiny because it seems to threaten their routine ways of thinking and behaving. However, resistance on the part of some students does not require abandoning critical work (Benesch 2001, 2006). Furthermore, there may be other students who have already adopted a critical stance to social norms, but from a cynical perspective leading to alienation and hopelessness. These varied reactions point to the need for critical teachers to tread lightly and thoughtfully, taking into account those who identify with the status quo, those who already stand outside of it, and those who have not yet considered their position. Critical teachers attend to this range while being mindful of the limitations of classroom curricula in enacting social change.

Humility about limitations, what Pennycook (2001) calls *self-reflexivity*, avoids grand and self-aggrandizing claims about what can be accomplished in a classroom to correct social ills and injustice. Humility is not just reflected in pedagogy, but also in the discourse used to report critical classroom activities and research results. Rather than adopting definitive language, the reports are tentative and speculative, an acknowledgment of the complexity of teaching and learning and the difficulty of effecting change.

Reflexivity is also seen in how materials are gathered and presented. For example, while working with students on military recruitment, I asked myself the following questions at various points: Should I push them beyond their initial understandings? How do I do this without giving the impression that I want them to take a particular position? How do I make room for a variety of opinions? These and other questions are taken up in the next section on the materials and responses to them.

In the spirit of reflexivity, in the section following the next one, I will discuss what I might have done differently and might do in the future with the same topic.

Critical praxis: Responding to military recruitment

Various antiwar, civil liberties, religious, and student groups have developed counter-recruitment materials as a response to the presence of military recruiters on US high school and college campuses. These materials serve to inform parents and students of their rights and, more generally, to offset the impact of the more widely available, and more expensively produced, recruitment materials. However, my aim in this section is not to describe certain pro- or counter-recruitment materials. Rather, I will discuss how I introduced the topic, how students responded to it, and how I modified my teaching according to students' responses. That is, in critical teaching, there is reciprocity between the materials and praxis, or, to put it another way, critical praxis can be seen as materials development.

Introducing the topic

I introduced the topic of military recruitment on campus in an ESL reading class during the spring 2006 semester by distributing a reading that debated the question, "Should colleges be allowed to bar military recruiters?" (*On Campus*, November 2005). It included two short essays, one arguing for and the other against barring recruiters. Though the debate format of the reading seemed to offer balance, the question itself was problematic for several reasons. First, the Solomon Amendment requires colleges receiving any type of federal funding to permit military recruiters on campus; therefore, the question is moot. However, of greater concern was that the question naturalized the power of the military, positioning colleges in the weaker position of needing permission to bar recruiters ("Should colleges *be allowed* ...").

Another concern about this particular article was that the title of the essay articulating the "no" position, "Students must choose for themselves," is an appealing proposition to young people. I therefore anticipated that most students would side with this position. The "yes" essay, on the other hand, was titled, "Campuses deserve the right to choose," a more abstract formulation requiring students to imagine what it might mean for a campus to make a choice.

Despite my reservations, however, I included the debate because I expected the dialogic process to engage students deeply with the question, no matter how flawed the materials might be. Even if the structure of the article seemed slanted toward favoring the presence of military recruiters, the classroom discussion and subsequent readings might provide greater balance.

Before students read the article, I wrote the debate question, "Should colleges be allowed to bar military recruiters?" on the chalkboard and asked students to argue one side of the issue or the other in a short essay. Only 9 out of 15 students turned in this initial writing. Of those 9, 6 said that colleges should not be allowed to bar recruiters; 3 said they should.

Students' initial written responses

I have grouped six "no" answers according to three themes: (1) choosing for ourselves; (2) recruiters provide useful information to students; and, (3) protecting the country is our duty. The three responses with the theme *choosing for ourselves* express opposition to barring recruiters, based on the belief that students are equipped to make a decision about joining the military and do not, therefore, need to be shielded from encounters with recruiters. Though other "no" responses included variations on this theme, the following three responses make it their main focus. I have added italics to emphasize that focus (R = response):

> **R1:** No, I think they shouldn't bar the military recruiter because I think that *verybody have our own opinion about that.* So if somebody want to go to the military *this is his choice.* It doesn't mean that somebody push him to do that. Some people just want to work in a military. And if somebody doesn't, *nobody can make him to do that.* For example, I know that I don't want to go to the military and nobody can change my mind.

> **R2:** I think colleges should allow military recruiters because some of the students might be insecure about their career and maybe the information they provide will be useful for them, they will finally find what they want to do, while others can *just say "no" and stick with their believes and choices*. As example, is I went to the cafeteria and one of the military recruiters approached to me, he gave me his information, but he didn't convinced me, because that is not what I will like to do in the future.
>
> **R3:** No, because *students have their own mind, they are decide for themselves*. If they are not interesting, military recruiters can do nothing to them. Also we could get military information from these people. So I disagree with allows to bar military recruiters.

It is interesting to note that though R1, written by a young woman born in Poland, and R2, by a young woman born in Colombia, argue for allowing students to choose whether or not to join the military, both had strong convictions about not joining themselves. They would therefore most likely be impervious to recruiters' appeals. R3, on the other hand, does not state whether the writer, a young man born in China, would join the military. However, like the others he, too, does not believe that recruiters persuade people who do not want to join the military to do so.

In addition, R3 includes an observation found in the response of the next group of "no" responses: Recruiters provide useful information to students. This theme assumes that recruiters are no different from other job recruiters. Their role, according to this position, is to offer helpful information students might use in making a career choice. Not surprisingly, this is the argument made by supporters of the Solomon Amendment who claimed that the military is equivalent to any company seeking employees and that it, like other employers, should be permitted access to college students to distribute its information.

I note that though R4 focuses on information provided by recruiters in a general way, R5 goes beyond, expressing the opinion that the US military pays college tuition for students who enlist. This claim can be found in recruitment materials, belying the fact the goal is to sign up soldiers, not support students financially while they are earning degrees:

> **R4:** My opinion is college should allowed to military recruiters. In my view college *student can get more information about job, benefit program* that when they start military in college. For example, in the college students learn different opinion about job. They can get *idea from military recruiter.*
>
> **R5:** No, I disagree and college students should not be allowed to bar military recruiters. The college students still need to go to school, and they have a right to join the military or not. Many people said that *military gives benefits and offer students many things.* Like *the military pay money for college students, and they will pay the students if they join the military.* But I think that college students have their own decision to make a choice.

Finally, one "no" response agrees with others that "everyone has a right to make their own decision," but includes a new theme, "protecting the country is our duty":

> **R6:** No, the colleges should not be allowed to bar military recruiters. Because everyone should has a right to make their own decision. I think that *everyone should guard their own country which is duty*. The military recruiters are related our country or our community.

To summarize the "no" responses, five out of six state that students should choose for themselves whether or not to join the military and that colleges should therefore not ban recruiters. However, as I will show next, this viewpoint was interrogated during the class discussion of the initial written responses. What informed that discussion was not so much what students had written, but, instead, a testimonial from a student about being approached by a recruiter on campus.

Before turning to that discussion, I will briefly summarize the three "yes" responses. In contrast to the "no" responses, they focus on possible effects on students of being recruited. That is, the stance is more personal, as if the students were imagining themselves, or friends, being approached by recruiters whose seductive promises of benefits might prove difficult to resist:

> **R7:** Yes, because the *military recruiters will effect college students, destroy his education.* Most military *benefit are very interest to them.* Also his family will lose their children by the accident or war.
>
> **R8:** I think that colleges should be allowed to bar military recruiters because we *don't want other unknown people in our city colleges who want to talk for 30 minutes and take our time.* I think if people want to join the military they'll go to the military department and ask them about benefits and other information. Also, I think that they shouldn't tell young people to join the military. People are free and they don't want to be bother by others.
>
> **R9:** Yes, military recruiters should not be allowed in colleges. The amount of student willing to leave school and join the army is more than the students who are willing to stay. *Contracts, grants, benefits and social status tempt the people to quit.* Army recruiters must be able *to explain their real reason* in these business.

As I will show next, the author of R9, Isaac, a young man born in Nigeria, was writing from his experience, and those of his friends, of being recruited.

Discussion of initial written responses

After students had written their responses to the debate question, I asked if anyone wanted to read or summarize what they had written. Isaac did not want to read. Instead, he wanted to speak about his recruitment experience. According to Isaac, he had been approached on campus by a recruiter who persisted, even after Isaac had expressed his lack of interest in the military. Rather than accepting Isaac's demurral, the recruiter continued talking to him for another 15 minutes, trying to change his mind. Isaac had felt cornered, unsure if he was permitted to simply walk away from this man wearing a military uniform.

The experience had upset Isaac, particularly because he thought he had been racially targeted. To test his hypothesis, I asked the class how many of them had been recruited, either on campus, in high school, or by phone. As it turned out, only Isaac and Diana (R2), the young woman from Colombia, had been recruited. We noted that none of the Russian or Polish students had been approached and that of seven Chinese students, only one had been telephoned. She, however, had gone voluntarily to the military recruitment table at a high school job fair the year before and had offered contact information, a move she regretted after receiving numerous calls at her home. One young Chinese man joked, "They know Chinese will fail boot camp." Despite the laughs his comment elicited, there seemed to be an uncomfortable awareness that Isaac's hypothesis was upheld, at least from this small sample. The only two students who had been approached on campus were of South American and African origins.

It may seem surprising that Isaac claims in his written response that more students are willing to leave school for the army than stay in school. However, his comment supports the observation that Nigerian-born students seemed to have been enlisting in disproportionate numbers. In addition, of five students from the university killed in Iraq at that time, two were Nigerian-born.

To sum up the findings of the initial responses, most striking is that while the "no" responses seem to view military recruiters as a benign presence and a source of useful information, the "yes" responses perceive them as a possible threat. From a critical perspective, it might be said that the second group has conceptualized power, either explicitly or implicitly. They acknowledge the power of uniformed military people over them and would rather not have to deal with the intrusion, perhaps feeling ill-prepared to respond. This concern was raised during the following class period as part of a discussion of the homework assignment.

Follow-up discussion

The homework was to write two response papers,[2] one about the "yes" essay and one about the "no" essay. Students met in groups to share their response papers and choose questions or reactions to a quote to share with the class by

[2] The four-part response paper consists of a brief summary of the reading, two questions, a reaction to a word, phrase, or sentence from the article, chosen by the student, and vocabulary.

writing them on the chalkboard. The class discussion began by focusing on a quote from the "no" essay written by one of the groups on the board: "As members of the academic community, we have a responsibility to educate our nation's youth by preparing them to effectively decide complex issues through civil debate." To launch the discussion of that quote, I asked the student who had written about it for homework to read her reaction: "I could not agree more with this quote; my mother always tells me that she will not be with me forever, therefore the best she can do is provide me with the knowledge to conduct myself successfully in life. The same is true in this case, college's obligation is to prepare us for the real world, they don't need to defend us instead they need to teach us to defend ourselves."

Students mainly agreed with this proposition. Those who spoke up disagreed with barring recruiters because they felt infantilized by that proposition. Yet, they acknowledged needing tools for dealing directly with recruiters and for making the decision about whether or not to enlist.

Looking over what else students had written on the board, I noticed this question: "What should students do if they are not interested in military, but recruiters are keep talking about it?" This seemed to be a good focus for addressing "teach us to defend ourselves." So, I asked what might be possible ways to deal with a recruiter who would not take "no" for an answer, but, instead, kept talking, as had happened to Isaac. The students came up with a variety of strategies, including telling the recruiter they were late for class or pretending they didn't understand English. Then I asked whether they would feel comfortable simply walking away without offering an excuse. Though at first they seemed dubious, they began to consider this as a possible response.

Because this was the first time I had worked with students on the topic of recruitment, I wasn't sure whether I should pursue related issues. Should I interrogate the power of the military, displayed in the uniform worn by recruiters? Should I distribute some counter-recruitment literature? Should I tell them about students from the university who had been killed in Iraq?

Rather than raising these issues, I decided to end the second class by sharing my opinion, one that had been changed by their responses. I told them that before discussing the issue with them, I had been opposed to the presence of military recruiters on campus. However, after reading their responses and hearing their opinions, I began to consider the possibility that having recruiters on campus allowed for the type of discussions in which we had been engaged during the last two class periods.

Self-reflexivity: What I might have done differently

In the spirit of self-reflexivity, I asked myself questions while selecting and presenting materials and after the lessons were over. The focus of these questions was not so much the materials themselves, but, rather, whether the dialogue facilitated thoughtful responses, ones that allowed students to consider their positions and deepen their understanding of the issues.

In retrospect, I believe I could have done more to highlight the centrality of power in interactions between young immigrants and representatives of the military. Though power was discussed implicitly when students sought strategies for avoiding or deflecting recruiters' pitches, it was not foregrounded in those discussions. Having had time to think about the lessons, I realize that there might have been ways to raise awareness of power differentials between students and recruiters, in terms of age, status, and other social factors, including gender, in cases where young women are being recruited by men. Such a discussion would allow students to examine the assumption expressed in R2 that students can "just say no" to recruiters. It might lead them to consider why it is hard for some to just walk away.

Another approach to issues of power would have been to pose the following question: If students can choose for themselves whether or not to join the military, why are recruiters necessary? I believe that this question would get at the actual physical power of recruiters (their size and experience as fighters) and their symbolic power (their uniform and social status). Once these issues were engaged, I could ask the following questions, related to class, race, and gender: Are some students more vulnerable than others to military recruitment? How does your financial situation affect your response? What about your family life? What about your immigration status?

Another issue worth exploring is that, despite the awesome power of the military, the US armed forces were desperate for recruits at that time. That is, although this branch of government appears to be a mighty force, achieving recruitment goals was a struggle, especially given the absence of a military draft. The military's lack of appeal during an unpopular war led them to offer incentives, such as fast-track citizenship. To get at this issue, I might have attended to micro-level discursive features by introducing terms such as "fast-track citizenship" and "posthumous citizenship," the granting of citizenship to soldiers who die in war zones. Students could have read news articles and/or military documents about these ways of gaining citizenship and written responses to them.

Though my focus in this section has been more on dialogue than materials, I want to add that I might experiment in the future with pro- and antirecruitment materials in tandem. For example, I could have students carry out critical discourse analyses of recruitment ads produced by the military as well as counter-recruitment materials produced by peace groups. Offering both types of materials might allow students who support recruitment on campus to voice their opinions more freely. Given that most of my students responded favorably to military recruitment in their initial writing, it is important to encourage greater discussion of this viewpoint. In addition, the contrast between the glossy military ads and the cheaply produced counter-recruitment materials would lend itself to a discussion of power relations.

Despite the benefits of self-reflexivity, I'm not suggesting that, having introduced military recruitment and having considered additional ways to pursue the issue, I now have ready-made lessons to use next time. I may have more pedagogical tools, but I would be guided by students' responses to the introductory materials rather than the tools themselves. That is, as I've mentioned several times in this chapter, critical teaching is an exploratory dialogue of unknown outcomes, through which teachers and students learn from each other, not a transfer of knowledge from teacher to student through materials.

Critical materials beyond the classroom: I'm a counter-recruiter

During the semester the ESL reading class was working on military recruitment, I collected counter-recruitment materials. Yet, I was unsure about how to present them to students without short-circuiting open discussion of their varying views. On the other hand, I was not comfortable about withholding counter-recruitment information, especially because on-campus military recruitment was not regularly counter-balanced with recruitment toward other career paths. I considered posting some counter-recruitment materials on my office door, but continued to hesitate about airing my views, especially while students were working on the topic in the reading class. However, toward the end of the semester I saw a film, discussed next, that urged me to be more public about my views, outside the classroom, yet on campus. The day after viewing the film, I posted a flyer on my office door, "Ten Points to Consider Before You Sign a Military Enlistment Agreement," published by the American Friends Service, a Quaker organization (www.afsc.org/resources/documents/10pts-english.pdf). The points include: "Do not make a hasty decision by enlisting the first time you see a recruiter or when you are upset"; "Take a witness with you when you speak with a recruiter," and so on.

The film, *Das kurze Leben des José Antonio Gutierrez* (*The Short Life of José Antonio Gutierrez*), tells the story of the first US soldier killed in Iraq, an immigrant from Guatemala. The director, Heidi Specogna, traces Gutierrez's life back to an impoverished childhood in the mountains of Guatemala, his life on the streets of Guatemala City as an orphan, and his eventual flight to the United States, riding dangerously on top of trains that took him through Mexico to the US border and then to Los Angeles. Gutierrez was assigned a foster family, earned a high school degree, and attended community college briefly. He then joined the US Marines. After completing boot camp, Gutierrez was sent to Kuwait and then to Iraq where, on the first day of the US invasion, he was killed, apparently by "friendly fire."

"Ten Points to Consider Before You Sign a Military Enlistment Agreement" had been on my office door all summer, when, one day in the fall 2006 semester walking toward my office, I saw a young man reading it intently. As I approached the door, I introduced myself to the young man, he introduced himself, and I invited him into my office. I asked "Angel" (pseudonym) what had made him stop to read the list. He told me that he wanted to join the US Army, but was only 17 years old and needed his mother's permission. She was opposed. When I asked why his mother refused to sign the necessary papers, he told me that she always worried about him. Next I asked whether he was a student at the college. He was and, according to what he told me, in good standing. Then I asked why he wanted to join the military. He told me it had always been a dream. Yet, it became clear as we continued talking that he knew almost nothing about the war or what his life might be like once he joined.

Next, I asked whether he had been recruited. As it turns out, he had been approached in high school by a recruiter who continued to pursue him on a regular basis, through phone calls and visits. It seemed from the way Angel spoke about his recruiter that he considered him a trusted friend. At that moment, I decided to call myself a "counter-recruiter," a term I had not previously applied to myself. I told Angel that just as there are military recruiters who encourage young people to join the military, there are counter-recruiters who urge them to stay in college. The main difference, I told him, was that military recruiters can get signing bonuses for each recruit they enlist. This was news to Angel. Yes, I explained, your recruiter might be offered a bonus if you enlist. On the other hand, counter-recruiters receive no bonuses. I don't know you, I told him, so I'm not worried about you like your mother. However, I think you should stay in school and get a degree, I said, because right now you seem confused about what to do, referring him to the first item on the "Ten Points to Consider ..." list. Next I gave Angel "The New Yorker's Guide to Military Recruitment," a booklet published by an antiwar group, Friends of William Blake (www.counterrecruitmentguide.org), containing advice for students who are being recruited. Angel was surprised that such materials existed. He asked about the group and then, to my surprise, asked how he could join it. Though I never saw Angel again and don't know whether or not he chose to join the US military, I had, at least, introduced him to materials that could help him make an informed decision.

As a self-declared counter-recruiter, I'm left with the question of whether to present counter-recruitment materials in the classroom, perhaps in conjunction with recruitment materials. Or, should I instead continue to present an open-ended question, leading to debate in the classroom and leave counter-recruitment outside the classroom where I am more comfortable expressing my antiwar views? Or, perhaps I will attempt both a debate and a presentation of competing materials, though these activities could lead to spending more time on the topic than students will want to. These questions are characteristic of critical pedagogy with its constant reflection on assumptions and praxis.

Conclusion

Materials and the way they are presented and explored reflect teachers' theories, whether or not those theories are explicit and conscious. My choice of military recruitment as a topic expressed my concern, as a critical teacher, about the unequal power of the military whose presence on college campuses forces students to confront a choice they may not be sufficiently informed to make. Armed with glossy materials, psychological knowledge, well-rehearsed pitches, and the promise of financial rewards and citizenship, recruiters have abundant social capital. Immigrant students, on the other hand, have little. Confronted by recruiters, they may not have the knowledge required to make an intelligent and appropriate choice. My goal in introducing recruitment in an ESL reading class was to equip students with a variety of ways to respond. And, of course, as they worked on the materials, they were reading, speaking, listening, and writing in academic English. Because the materials were situated in their daily lives, students had the chance to think deeply about matters affecting their daily lives, an important foundation for acquiring academic skills.

The pedagogy described in this chapter is situated in a particular time and place, during the US occupation of Iraq and at a publicly funded US college. I'm therefore not recommending that others adopt or even adapt the materials. Rather, I hope that the description of students' responses to the materials in one class offers an example of critical praxis. Readers of this chapter might find equally pressing issues confronting their students as topics for critical academic engagement.

Discussion questions and tasks

Reflection

1. Which aspects of critical theory did you find most accessible? Which did you find more difficult to grasp?

2. How easy or difficult do you think it would be to apply critical theory to selecting and developing materials?
3. What might be some advantages for language learners of a critical approach to materials and teaching, in terms of skills development?
4. What challenges might students face when using materials grounded in critical theory? How could you try to address these challenges as (i) a teacher; and (ii) a materials designer?
5. The materials described in this chapter were designed for learners in a postsecondary setting in the United States. To what extent could a similar approach be taken when designing materials for the context in which you are or will be teaching?

Evaluation

6. Look at some textbook materials you have used with a class in the past. In light of this chapter, how might you modify these materials to experiment with teaching critically?

Adaptation/Design

7. Using what you have learned in this chapter, choose one issue affecting the lives of students you teach or will teach. Prepare a reading/writing task on this issue. Explain the rationale behind your approach.
8. Applying what you have learned about critical praxis in this chapter, adapt or design some materials. Then try these materials out on the students in your group. Discuss their views on your materials/teaching.

References

Benesch, S. (2001). *Critical English for academic purposes: Theory, politics, and practice*. Mahwah, NJ: Erlbaum.

Benesch, S. (2006). Critical media awareness: Teaching resistance to interpellation. In J. Edge (ed.). *(Re)locating TESOL in an age of empire*. Houndsmill, Basingstoke, UK: Palgrave Macmillan, pp. 49-64.

Das kurze Leben des José Antonio Gutierrez (2006), dir. Heidi Specogna, New York: The Cinema Guild.

Fairclough, N. (1995). *Critical discourse analysis: The critical study of language*. London: Longman.

Foucault, M. (1980). Power and strategies. In C. Gordon (ed.). *Power/knowledge: Selected interviews and other writings, 1972-77*. New York: Pantheon Books, pp. 134-45.

Freire, P. (1994). *Pedagogy of hope*. New York: Continuum.

Freire, P. (1998a). *Pedagogy of the heart*. New York: Continuum.

Freire, P. (1998b). *Pedagogy of freedom: Ethics, democracy, and civic courage*. Lanham, MD: Rowman & Littlefield Publishers, Inc.

Giroux, H. (1997). *Pedagogy and the politics of hope: Theory, culture, and schooling*. Boulder, CO: Westview Press.

Gee, J. P. (1996). *Social linguistics and literacies: Ideology in discourses* (2nd ed.). London: Taylor & Francis.

Goldstein, T. (2003). *Teaching and learning in a multilingual school: Choices, risks, and dilemmas*. Mahwah, NJ: Erlbaum.

Lin, A. M. Y. (2004). Introducing a critical pedagogical curriculum: A feminist reflexive account. In B. Norton & K. Toohey (eds.). *Critical pedagogies and language learning*. Cambridge: Cambridge University Press, pp. 271-90.

Luke, A. (2004). Two takes on the critical. In B. Norton & K. Toohey (eds.). *Critical pedagogies and language learning*. Cambridge: Cambridge University Press, pp. 21-9.

Morgan, B. (1998). *The ESL classroom: Teaching, critical practice, and community development*. Toronto: University of Toronto Press.

New York Times (2005). Swift road for US citizen soldiers already fighting in Iraq. August 9, A11.

On Campus (2005). Should colleges be allowed to bar military recruiters? November.

Pennycook, A. (1994). *The cultural politics of English as an international language*. London: Longman.

Pennycook, A. (2001). *Critical applied linguistics: A critical introduction*. Mahwah, NJ: Erlbaum.

Reagan, T. (2004). Objectification, positivism, and language studies: A reconsideration. *Critical Inquiry in Language Studies* 1(1): 41-60.

Rivera, K. (1999). Popular research and social transformation: A community-based approach to critical pedagogy. *TESOL Quarterly* 33(3): 485-500.

Santos. T. (1998). The place of politics in second language writing. In T. Silva & P. K. Matsuda (eds.). *On second language writing*. Mahwah, NJ: Erlbaum, pp. 173-90.

Simon, R. I. (1992). *Teaching against the grain: Texts for a pedagogy of possibility.* New York: Bergin & Garvey.

Washington Post (2006). Army guard refilling its ranks: Members get bonus for new recruits. March 12, A01.

www.afsc.org/resources/documents/10pts-english.pdf

www.counterrecruitmentguide.org

www.law.georgetown.edu/solomon/solomon.htm

PART C

MATERIALS FOR THE LANGUAGE SYLLABUS

6

A principled approach to content-based materials development for reading

Norman W. Evans, K. James Hartshorn, and Neil J. Anderson

Summary

Effective reading involves complex processes that vary with specific contexts including proficiency level, age, motivation, and reading purposes, such as content mastery, general language development, or the improvement of specific reading skills. Therefore, those who develop reading materials for ELT practitioners must understand these processes and the appropriate teaching and learning contexts in which their materials will be used. In addition, the work of effective ELT materials developers is guided by sound theory and principles. The innovation we illustrate in this chapter is in how the development of ELT reading materials can be anchored to such principles and contexts. We emphasize the three curriculum principles of responsiveness, cohesion, and stability in guiding the development process. Though these principles would be beneficial and applicable in many different settings, we have chosen one specific context to illustrate how they might be used.

Moreover, we have selected a context that might include inherent challenges for the less experienced materials developer. Therefore, the contextual framework for developing ELT reading materials in this chapter centers on a group of low-advanced, university-bound learners studying biology in an intensive English program. The form and focus of these materials grows out of this context and emphasizes fluency, linking language and content, and reading online versus printed materials. Following a discussion of theory and relevant literature, we provide a model of how ELT reading materials can be prepared and illustrate this with specific samples. Throughout the chapter we continue to address the dynamic balance between the curriculum principles of responsiveness, cohesion, and stability.

Introduction

Reading is a complex process that requires the use of multiple skills. Readers must be able to draw upon background knowledge and relate it to the new material that they are reading. They must also be able to access the meaning of vocabulary quickly and accurately. This involves identifying the individual letters that make up a word and stringing them together to form a comprehensive unit. Additionally, good readers have strong phonological skills that assist them in saying a particular word correctly. While reading, they must also access their knowledge of English grammar. Effective readers are aware of a variety of reading strategies that they can draw upon to successfully accomplish their purpose. And they do read with a purpose! This entire process happens fluently. Embedded in the reading process is an evaluation of comprehension, or, in other words, the reader makes sense of the material that he or she is reading.

English language teaching (ELT) educators face the challenge of teaching second language readers the skills needed to successfully comprehend reading materials. Especially, they need to develop appropriate materials to explicitly teach second language readers how to foster these many skills. The process of developing materials should be anchored to principles that balance both theory and practice. This balance is often difficult to achieve, but it is essential for the development of effective materials.

Research on reading has greatly influenced the development of reading materials. One important concept that we want to emphasize in this chapter is that of reading with a purpose. For example, Ediger (2006) points out that while reading purpose is addressed in research on reading, "few go the next step to spell out *how* to focus reading toward accomplishing the purpose that one has set" (p. 312, italics in original). One underlying principle that guides the development of appropriate reading materials is understanding the reading purpose. Appropriate materials provide both a purpose and an opportunity for readers to practice the skills that will enhance their ability to read with a purpose.

In this chapter, we address major principles that can inform the development of reading materials. These principles are important since all teachers must be aware of ways to adapt required textbooks or develop new texts and materials to meet the needs of individual readers. The three principles discussed in this chapter are responsiveness, cohesion, and stability.

Though reading contexts and readers' needs differ in proficiency in various places around the world, we will limit our discussion to the development of ELT materials for teaching reading skills to low-advanced learners who are preparing to enter a university setting where English is the language of instruction. However, the underlying principles will have broad applications in a variety of contexts and at varying levels of proficiency. Primarily, we will identify how to prepare appropriate materials in a content-based instructional reading program. Teachers using these materials would be teaching in an intensive English context where students have access to classroom reading instruction for at least four hours per week. We describe a process that we use at the English Language Center (ELC) at Brigham Young University, Provo, Utah, in the United States.

The majority of the low-advanced learners that we work with are undergraduate students at a university when they complete their English studies at the ELC. Because undergraduate programs at most universities in the United States are based on a general-education approach to learning, we anticipate that our students are going to have to take courses in biology, American history, sociology, and humanities, as well as a variety of other content classes. Our goal is to provide opportunities for students to use materials that will enhance their language proficiency as well as prepare them to successfully deal with academic content.

Although teaching contexts differ widely from one locale to another, the processes of developing an effective curriculum and materials, as well as the principles implemented in this chapter, are applicable in a variety of reading contexts. Here, we first discuss the theory and review appropriate literature that influences the development of the reading materials. We then address three major principles of curriculum development, as well as specific evidence from reading research that guides the development of the materials. Finally, we provide a model for how these principles can be used in preparing effective reading materials.

Theory and literature review

Research and theory in second language teaching have moved us from a reliance on methodologies to a "post-method era," in which principles guide our language-teaching decisions (Brown 2001; Ellis 2005; Kumaravadivelu 1994, 2006; Nunan 1999; Richards 2001). Many of these language-teaching principles have emerged from what Shulman calls the "wisdom of practice" (Shulman 2004). Years of experience, trial and error, and substantial research have provided us with valuable principles on which to base both our language-teaching practices and our materials. As stated before, the reading materials presented in this chapter have been developed based on three such curriculum development principles: responsiveness, cohesion, and stability.

In the sections that follow, each of these principles is defined in detail and illustrated by examples. In order to understand how materials can be responsive, cohesive, and stable, we must first consider the individual and collective meanings of these terms in the framework of a program curriculum and then in the context of content-based reading materials development.

Curricular principles: Responsiveness, cohesion, and stability

Responsiveness, from a curriculum developer's perspective, is critical and central. The chief component of any curriculum development is a thorough needs analysis, which identifies what content needs to be taught to whom and why (Brown 1995; Richards 2001). The point of such an analysis is to make the curriculum responsive to stakeholders, program expectations, an ever-changing environment, and, most importantly, the learners. Similarly, a language program's curriculum ought to be responsive to quality research, which has been generated within a specific program as well as the language-teaching profession in general. As our understanding of language learning and teaching increases, a vibrant curriculum must respond and adapt to research insights. Without this responsive component, the development and subsequent success of the curriculum would be uneven and stagnant at best (Richards 2001; Stark & Lattuca 1997).

Cohesion in a curriculum suggests that logical links exist within and between curricular elements. Depending on a program's structure, this may happen in a number of ways. A curriculum can be cohesive *within* levels, classes, skills, and materials. Typically, cohesion within a level occurs in a horizontal syllabus (Reid 1993; Richards 2001), where students are placed at the same level in all language skills. Such cohesion is characterized by materials and lessons in one class that contribute to and build upon what is taught in another class at the same level. Cohesion within a class is most effectively achieved through carefully planned course outlines or syllabi. For example, lessons and activities occurring in any given week should be linked to what happened in the preceding weeks, as well as to the lessons yet to come. Cohesion within materials suggests that lessons, chapters, and activities will contain internal links. What is taught in one chapter should logically prepare learners for subsequent chapters (Stoller & Grabe 1997).

Cohesion is also possible *between* levels, classes, skills, and materials. What students are taught in level 3, for instance, should build on the foundation of levels 1 and 2. It should also prepare them for subsequent language needs in future levels, university studies, employment, and so on. Links between skills or skill integration should in like manner connect what students do in reading class with what they are studying in writing, listening, and speaking classes. (The strength such cohesion or integration brings to a language class is well documented: see Brown 2001; Kumaravadivelu 1994; Selinker & Tomlin 1986.)

Stability and responsiveness may at first seem to be contradictory principles, but they are, in fact, complementary. Stability in a curriculum is based on the idea that change involves deliberate and careful review of needs, research, and resources. Most important of all, a stable curriculum is built on sound language-teaching and -learning principles. A curriculum that seems to be in a constant state of change may lead to frustration for both educators and students alike (Markee 2001). Contrarily, a stable program has a deliberate, principled, and systematic procedure for managing curricular change. It is in this respect that responsiveness becomes a complementary rather than conflicting principle to stability.

The complementary aspect of these three principles is the final point to consider before applying this model to the development of content-based reading materials. Any one of these principles applied in isolation may result in unfavorable consequences. A program director who strives to establish a stable curriculum without building in a mechanism for change (responsiveness) will run the risk of curriculum and program stagnation. At the same time, a program that institutes every new idea presented at conferences or in materials catalogs may have to deal with program instability. Similarly, a cohesive curriculum would be impossible without the advantage of stability and responsiveness operating in dynamic balance with each other. Perhaps the best way to view these three principles is as overlapping circles, each drawing strength and meaning from the other (see Figure 6.1). It is a case of the whole being greater than the sum of the parts.

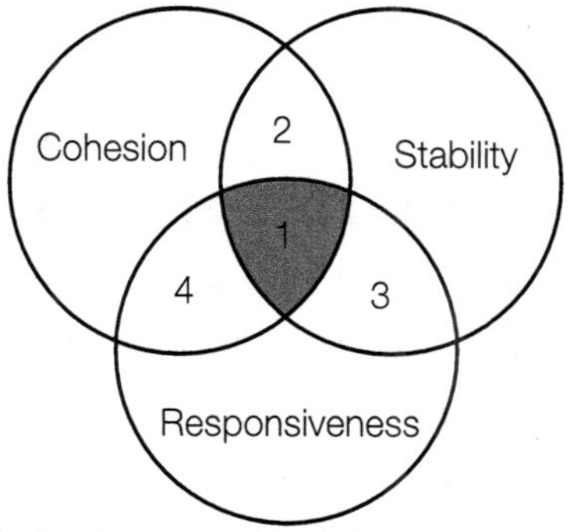

Figure 6.1 Materials development principles: Responsiveness, cohesion, and stability

Note that in Figure 6.1, the shaded area labeled "1" falls in the area of overlap of all three principles: responsiveness, cohesion, and stability. A balance of these three principles is the goal for anyone developing a curriculum and materials for teaching reading. One principle is not more important than the other two principles. The area labeled "2" illustrates the overlap between cohesion and stability. A curriculum that is cohesive and stable is one that is well organized in terms of meeting the needs of learners within a level, as well as across levels within a program. It also changes based on guidance of principles, rather than changing whenever a teacher or a textbook changes. The area labeled "3" represents the overlap between stability and responsiveness. This overlap suggests a curriculum where change is not impulsive, but when changes are necessary, they are responsive to the needs of learners. Finally, the area labeled "4" illustrates the overlap between responsiveness and cohesion. This overlap suggests a curriculum that responds to learner needs, but is also cohesive in terms of focusing on course objectives and programmatic goals within and across proficiency levels.

One effective way to achieve responsiveness, cohesion, and stability in a curriculum is to use the principles as filters when developing or selecting the materials. Responsiveness, for instance, is a valuable filter for developing language-teaching materials that meet the needs of the students in the program. Cohesion ensures that materials build on what students have learned and that it is linked to what they will be learning in the future. Finally, applying tried and tested techniques and procedures to teaching those materials will bring stability to the language-learning process.

Table 6.1 outlines how we have used responsiveness, cohesion, and stability as filtering principles for the development of our content-based reading materials. The lists in Column 1 demonstrate how these three principles are related to general curriculum development theory (Richards 2001; Stark & Lattuca 1997). For instance, an effective curriculum must be responsive to stakeholders' needs, market demands, and current ongoing research. Cohesion in a curriculum accounts for linkage between and within curricular elements like lessons, levels, classes, and skills. Stability in a curriculum helps to maintain consistency while allowing for purposeful, principled, planned change.

Column 2 includes a few specific examples of how the theoretical principles in Column 1 can be put into practice in content-based instruction (CBI). For instance, in theory, a curriculum should be responsive to environmental changes. A practical example of this is the advent of the Internet. In practice, therefore, students need to learn the differences between reading online and in-print materials and the strategies that will help them be efficient, effective

Table 6.1 Curriculum development principles in theory and practice

	Curriculum principles in theory		**Curriculum principles in practice**
RESPONSIVENESS	**Responds to:** • students' needs • program needs • program requirements • market demands • research findings • environmental changes		• reading online versus print strategies* • activation of background knowledge • using context to get meaning of specialized vocabulary • comprehension checks • pre-/while/postreading activities • online reading passages • reading large quantities of material for main ideas
COHESION	**Within** • materials • classes • levels • skills	**Between** • materials • classes • levels • skill	• linking language and content activities* • skill integration (reading, writing, speaking) • focus on language aspects of content • pre-/while/postreading activities
STABILITY	• Curriculum is consistent. • Change is planned, purposeful, and carefully reviewed. • Holds to "tried and true" practices. • Anchored to sound language learning/teaching principles.		• fluency development activities* • reading with a purpose • vocabulary within the content • reading authentic materials

* Materials of focus in this chapter

readers of electronic materials. As space constraints in this chapter will not allow us to develop all the items listed in Column 2, the materials of focus in this chapter are marked with an asterisk (*).

Three concepts of focus for materials development

The items in Table 6.1 represent many different types of reading materials that might be developed. Depending on the teaching and learning objectives of a course, any given reading lesson may include one or many of these types. To indicate how reading materials can be developed using the principles of responsiveness, cohesion, and stability, we examine three concepts from Table 6.1: (1) reading online versus printed texts; (2) linking language and content activities; and (3) fluency development activities. After considering these concepts in theory, we demonstrate how they can be put into practice (see sample materials at the end of the chapter).

Responsiveness: Strategies for reading online versus print

Computers and the Internet play an increasingly important role in the lives of L2 readers around the world. Online reading serves as the primary source of input for thousands of L2 readers. Leu (2002) points out that "the Internet has entered our classrooms faster than books, television, computers, the telephone, or any other technology for information and communication" (p. 311). With the increased use of computers comes the increased need to train language learners how to read online. Coiro (2003) stresses that "electronic texts introduce new supports as well as new challenges that can have a great impact on an individual's ability to comprehend what he or she reads" (p. 458). More and more L2 classrooms are engaging learners in online learning tasks (Bikowski & Kessler 2002; Ioannou-Georgiou 2002; Sutherland-Smith 2002; Warschauer 1997, 1999, 2002). To date, however, very little research has addressed the similarities and differences between reading online and reading traditional print materials.

According to Murray (2005), "there has been an assumption that the literacies of print texts will necessarily transfer to the new media without intervention," but based on research that she and a colleague conducted in

Australia, "print literacy does not necessarily transfer to digital literacy" (p. viii).

One aspect of reading that has been addressed with first language readers in the online-versus-print reading environments is reading speed. Kurniawan and Zaphiris (2001) report on their study in which they tested reader preferences for reading online or printed texts with one, two, or three columns. They also investigated reading speeds in both contexts to determine if there is a difference in reading speed in the two reading contexts. Their data suggest that reading on paper was 10-30 percent faster than reading online in the one- and two-column formats. No differences were found between the two contexts with three-column readings. Kurniawan and Zaphiris conclude that designers of online materials should be aware that reading will be slower in the online context, and therefore designers should do all they can to enhance online reading materials.

Online materials can be enhanced in a number of ways. The focus should be on how to make online reading more accessible to readers, especially second language readers. Teachers can explain that many online sources provide technical glosses of vocabulary. The reader can move the mouse over an unknown word and receive a definition and, in some cases, a translation. Likewise, educators can inform their students of the various layouts of Web pages and online reading materials and how they differ from print materials. (See Murray & McPherson [2005] for additional insights on ways teachers can enhance online reading materials.)

In his study, Anderson (2003) addresses two research questions: (1) What are the online reading strategies used by second language readers? and (2) Do the online reading strategies of English as a second language readers (ESL) differ those of English as a foreign language readers (EFL)?

Participants in this study consisted of 247 L2 readers. Of those, 131 (or 53 percent) of the learners studied English as a foreign language at the Centro Cultural Costarricense Norteamericano (CCCN) in San José, Costa Rica. The remaining 116 (47%) studied in an ESL environment at the ELC at Brigham Young University in Provo, Utah. The *Survey of Reading Strategies* (SORS) (Sheorey & Mokhtari 2001) was adapted for use in this research project. The adapted Online SORS (OSORS) consists of 38 items that measure metacognitive reading strategies. The 38 items are subdivided into three categories: global reading strategies (18 items), problem-solving strategies (11 items), and support strategies (9 items).

Perhaps the most significant outcome of this research is a greater awareness of the importance of metacognitive online reading strategies for second language learners. This strategy plays a more important role in L2 reading instruction than perhaps we have previously considered. When classroom teachers engage their learners in online learning tasks, a strategy awareness and training component is essential. L2 reading teachers can focus learner attention on the metacognitive reading strategies identified in the OSORS to help learners improve their online reading skills.

Tindale (2005) outlines various issues that teachers should take into consideration when engaging learners in reading electronic texts. She lists specific questions in four areas: breaking the code, participating in understanding texts, using texts, and analyzing texts. One key question from each of these four areas illustrates the challenges teachers face when working with print and online texts:

> What physical characteristics of electronic texts have an impact on learners' ability to read them (for example screen characteristics, text characteristics, and the use of different fonts and colours)? ... What do learners need to know about navigational elements of webpages (for example navigation bars, pull-down or pop-up menus, and "back" buttons)? ... How is the structure and organization of a web text linked to the meaning and purpose of the text? ... What teaching and learning activities will help learners develop an understanding of what the Web excludes as well as what it includes? (Tindale 2005: 10-1)

It is evident that materials developers need to incorporate online reading tasks into newly developed materials and at the same time teach L2 readers how to navigate them. This is a major task in the development of reading materials and one that requires our attention.

Cohesion: Linking language and content

Content-based instruction (CBI) has become a significant part of second and foreign language teaching over the past three decades (Celce-Murcia 2001; Met 1999). In fact, the most common trend in ESL curriculum development over the past 10 years has been to build language-teaching materials around a common theme. This trend can be attributed to various factors, not the least of which has been to make language learning meaningful (Brown 2001; Celce-Murcia 2001; Ellis 2005; Kumaravadivelu 1994). The need to teach language in a meaningful context, especially in English for academic purposes, is buttressed by the work of Cummins (1980, 1981, 1996), which suggests that it takes ESL students five to seven years to become proficient in English at the level required of university students. This is known as *cognitive academic language proficiency* (CALP).

Anyone who has studied at a university in a second language understands the enormity of the task. Survival and success become synonymous as students find themselves reading and rereading late into the night to grasp the material required for classes. The more unfamiliar the content, the greater the task becomes. That being the case, language teachers of university-bound students have a responsibility to introduce students to the language and content they are likely to encounter in university work. Current theory and practice suggest that CBI is an effective means of introducing students to these challenges.

The manner in which content and language are presented to students depends on the CBI approach that is used. Some of the more popular approaches and methods associated with CBI include English for specific purposes (ESP), theme-based, task-based, adjunct, and sheltered CB-ESL (Oxford 1992; see also Met 1998; Stoller & Grabe 1997). These various models are not all equivalent in scope or intent (Brinton 1997; Met 1999; Oxford 1992; Snow 2001; Snow & Brinton 1997; Stoller & Grabe 1997). Despite their differences, as Snow (2001) and others point out, CBI models all share "a common point of departure – the integration of language teaching aims with subject matter instruction" (p. 303). Stoller and Grabe (1997) suggest that, regardless of the philosophical or practical orientations the various CBI models take, they all "view language as a medium of learning content and content as a resource for learning language" (p. 78).

Although the objective of CBI seems to be generally accepted, ironically, one of its most perplexing problems is creating an appropriate balance (or a cohesive link) between language and content. A tendency in CBI courses is to teach the content at the expense of language focus. How much a CBI model focuses on content and language is a matter of great importance when it comes to such fundamental issues as assessment, course objectives, and materials development.

Interestingly, one feature that differentiates the various CBI models from each other is the degree of attention given to language and content (Brinton, Snow, & Wesche 2003; Met 1998, 1999). This is of particular importance to our discussion of materials development. Met (1999; also cited in Snow 2001) sees the various CBI models' focus on language as a continuum. On the extreme content end of the continuum – total immersion – are programs that give no attention at all to language. Instead, the content is the priority, and language learning is largely coincidental. On the opposite end of the continuum are language programs that make frequent use of content for language practice. In this case, language learning is the priority and content learning is primarily incidental. CBI models that tend toward the middle of the range, such as sheltered, adjunct, and theme-based courses, are faced with the particularly perplexing task of balancing appropriate attention to both language and content. Building cohesion between language and content is not something that happens automatically; it requires planning.

One effective way to link language study to content study is to ensure that materials have clear teaching objectives that emphasize that balance (Brinton 1997; Met 1998; Oxford 1992; Snow 2001). A second and related way to effectively link language study and content study is to design materials with the objective of linking language and content clearly in mind. This is precisely the approach taken in the materials we present in this chapter. The materials were designed with clear content and language-learning objectives in mind.

Stability: Fluency

The development of reading fluency has received increased attention in recent years. The National Reading Panel (2000) emphasizes that reading fluency can be taught and that reading comprehension increases as fluency increases. Field (2006) identifies reading fluency as an essential element for any program designed to meet the needs of advanced level readers. Additionally, Grabe (1991) states that "fluent reading is rapid; the reader needs to maintain the flow of information at a sufficient rate to make connections and inferences vital to comprehension" (p. 378).

Anderson (1999, 2007/2008, 2008), one of the few researchers who examines reading fluency from the perspective of both reading rate and comprehension, defines *reading fluency* as reading at an adequate rate with adequate comprehension. He specifically uses the term *rate* as opposed to *speed.* He emphasizes that teachers should not be engaged in developing speed readers but rather developing readers who know how to adjust their reading rate according to the purpose for reading.

The next question to ask is: "What is an appropriate rate and what is appropriate comprehension?" It is clear from reading research that one's reading purpose will determine the rate. Carver's research (1990) points out that reading speed will change depending on the reading process that one is engaged in. Table 6.2 summarizes five different reading processes (scanning, skimming, rauding, learning, and memorizing) along with the targeted words per minute (wpm) that native English speakers typically use during reading. (Note that *rauding* is a term invented by Carver. It is a blend of the words *reading* and *auditory.* Rauding is the process of reading or listening to text at a "normal" rate.)

Table 6.2 Carver's reading processes and targeted words per minute

Reading process	Processing components	Target wpm
Scanning	lexical accessing	600
Skimming	semantic encoding	450
Rauding	sentence integrating	300
Learning	idea remembering	200
Memorizing	fact rehearsing	138

In Anderson's definition of reading fluency (1999, 2007/2008, 2008), he emphasizes that there is a threshold rate that second language readers should target as a goal. That threshold rate is identified as 200 wpm, and adequate comprehension is defined as 80 percent. He stresses that we cannot discuss reading rate without also discussing reading comprehension.

Field (2006) identifies eight critical elements in a program for developing reading fluency. She suggests that these eight elements are "crucial" for the success of fluent reading. These include time, motivation, metacognitive materials, appropriate materials, approach to vocabulary study, willingness to change, confidence in the program, and reading.

Learners need a pedagogical plan that regularly focuses on fluency development. Field (2006) explains how the eight critical elements can be integrated into such a plan. *Time*: A minimum of four months is needed to develop reading fluency, though six months is preferable. *Motivation*: Both intrinsic and extrinsic motivation play a role in the development of fluency – learners need to see external rewards as well as internal ones. *Metacognitive materials*: Awareness of reading strategies facilitates reading fluency. *Appropriate materials*: A wide variety of reading materials should be used in class so that readers have practice with different genres. *Four-pronged approach to vocabulary study*: This comprises (a) bottom-up strategy training; (b) reading at students' language level; (c) collocation study; and (d) narrow-reading exercises. *Willingness to change*: These four strategies help build a more solid program for vocabulary study, but both teachers and learners need to be willing to adapt to this new program, since fluency instruction is new to both. *Confidence in the program*: Once the change has been made, both teachers and their students will have greater confidence in their potential for success. *Reading*: Ultimately, the best way to improve reading skills is through actual reading. Teachers should engage the learners in as many reading opportunities as possible.

Sample materials

Using the principles outlined above, we now illustrate the development of appropriate reading materials for a content-based language-learning class in which biology is the content subject. Though the following materials will not illustrate all of the principles discussed above, those principles appropriate to the accompanying lesson will be included and will demonstrate how such principles might be utilized in materials development.

Three program reading purposes will be accomplished in this lesson. Students will read texts that are academic and scientific and that describe complex processes.We will also meet five specific objectives in this reading lesson: (a) compare and contrast two elements of photosynthesis; (b) compare and contrast two articles on photosynthesis; (c) learn about compound adjectives in English; (d) practice summarizing information from two reading passages; and (e) practice online reading skills and identify how online-reading strategies compare with print-reading strategies. Each of these five objectives will help achieve the broader reading goals of the program.

The value of what we present here is that the development of reading materials can be anchored to the three principles we have suggested in this chapter: responsiveness, cohesion, and stability. Many people can develop innovative materials for the reading classroom, but we believe that the materials must be affixed to these three principles. The innovation of materials development for the reading classroom comes in the application of these three principles in each individual context. As good as published textbooks may be, unless teachers or curriculum coordinators make local decisions guided by the principles of responsiveness, cohesion, and stability, those texts may not best help learners make appropriate progress. As you are guided by these three principles, you can help your students make improvements in language learning.

In order to support the innovative nature of these reading materials, we present them in two columns below. The left-hand column is the actual material and the right-hand column is a brief discussion of the applicable materials development principle. Not all materials exemplify *responsiveness, cohesion*, and *stability*. Furthermore, space limitations prevent us from presenting all of the materials developed for the accompanying reading lesson, though the samples should adequately illustrate the principles emphasized in this chapter.

Photosynthesis

Prereading activities

Describe the following equation.

light + $6CO_2 + 6H_2O \rightarrow C_6H_{12}O_6 + 6O_2$

Write your explanation below:

____

____

____

____

____

____

Share your description with a partner.

In preparation for reading the passage on photosynthesis, look at the following graphic. Can you fill in the ovals? We will return to this graphic following the reading.

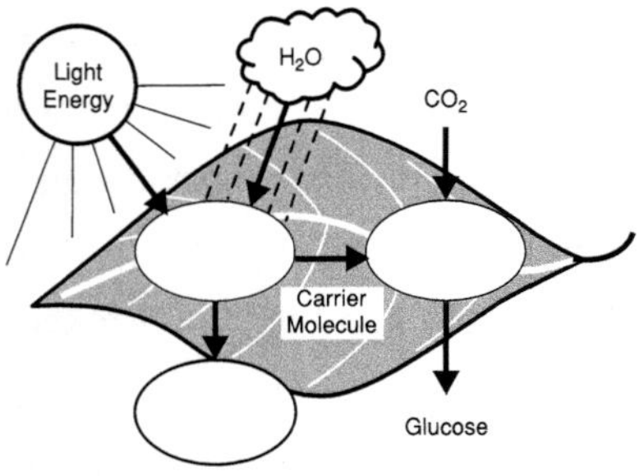

Figure 6.2 Photosynthesis

Description

The prereading activities are designed to prepare students for the reading of two passages on photosynthesis: one print text and one online text. These activities can be used to determine students' prior knowledge about photosynthesis and help them be more successful in reading the two texts.

Stability

Although reading purposes can vary, establishing a purpose for reading specific materials helps students focus on learning. The objectives remain stable in the reading program, but content can change to respond to readers' needs. The topic of photosynthesis is stable and will not be outdated with the passing of time.

Responsiveness

Teachers will know what knowledge the reader brings to the passage through this prereading activity. This allows the teacher to make adjustments if necessary.

Language focus:
Compound adjectives

Adjectives are words that modify or describe a noun. One special type of adjective, a compound adjective, is formed by joining two or more words together with a hyphen. A compound adjective typically consists of words that are not normally used together. Here are some examples of compound adjectives: rain-soaked, fast-growing, electron-charged, light-driven, and temperature-dependent.

Description

The distinction between language and content focus is not always obvious. The exercises in this section were developed to draw students' attention to specific language features – compound adjectives and specialized biology vocabulary. The objectives are (1) to teach students what compound adjectives are, how they are formed, and what they mean, and (2) to help students learn specialized vocabulary by using contextual clues.

Make a list of all the compound adjectives you find in the photosynthesis article.

Specialized vocabulary

Rate your knowledge of each of the vocabulary words below according to the following scale: 1 = I can use this word correctly; 2 = I know the meaning of this word but can't use it; 3 = I think I know the meaning of this word, but I'm not sure; 4 = I don't know this word.

You can find the following specialized vocabulary on the line number indicated before each word. Read the word in the context. Write a definition of the word in the space provided.

24	Photosynthesis	1 2 3 4	________
29	Biological	1 2 3 4	________
33	Greek	1 2 3 4	________
44	Glucose	1 2 3 4	________
55	Carbon dioxide	1 2 3 4	________
56	H_2O	1 2 3 4	________
54	Molecule	1 2 3 4	________
57	$C_6H_{12}O_6$	1 2 3 4	________
57	O_2	1 2 3 4	________
57	Oxygen	1 2 3 4	________
70	Cells	1 2 3 4	________
72	Chlorophyll	1 2 3 4	________
97	Electrons	1 2 3 4	________
98	Atoms	1 2 3 4	________
114	Hydrogen	1 2 3 4	________

...

Reading activities

Fluency development: Repeated reading

To develop your reading fluency, we will practice using an exercise called *Repeated Reading*. Read Section 1 (the first two paragraphs) three times in four minutes. If you are able to do this, you will be reading 196 words per minute.

Stability

A principle of sound language learning is that vocabulary can be used in many different readings and thus is a stable component (Hatch & Brown 1995; Nation 1990, 2001). Reading fluency should be consistent and thus stable. Working toward 200 wpm with 80 percent comprehension should be the target.

Cohesion

Exercises focused on language aspects of the content material help students keep a language-learning focus while still learning content.

Responsiveness

Using the context to get the meaning of specialized vocabulary is an effective reading strategy that provides a responsive aspect to the materials. This strategy responds to individual student needs and abilities. It also helps the reader respond to the text by using the context instead of a dictionary. Note that many of the sentences from the text provide the definition of these words.

Description

This is a 750-word reading passage on the key biological concept of photosynthesis. This passage was developed by the teacher, but similar passages of a general nature can be found in textbooks, magazines, or online.

Photosynthesis – Section 1

How would you respond if someone asked, "What is the most valuable commodity on earth?" Though we could identify various things that are highly valued by society, many biologists would probably answer, "Water." Water is essential to sustaining life. Virtually every internal process in the human body depends on water to function; without it, life could not continue. Most of us know that we need to drink plenty of water every day to maintain good health. However, some of us may not realize the critical role of water in helping produce the food that we need. Water is an essential part of the most important chemical process on earth, and without it there would be no food. This vital chemical process takes place inside most green plants and is called *photosynthesis*.

Virtually all life on earth relies on photosynthesis, directly or indirectly, for the production of food. Like so many other biological processes, however, photosynthesis could not occur without water. The word *photosynthesis* comes from Greek and has two parts: *photo*, which means "light," and *synthesis*, which means "to bring things together." In other words, photosynthesis means to put something together using light. But what does photosynthesis put together, and why is it so important? Just as all living things need water, all living things need food. Photosynthesis is important because it makes glucose, a special sugar that is used by living

Stability

A passage such as this builds stability in various ways. The most obvious is that students are reading authentic material related to a topic that is central to any biology course. Also, one of the main uses of this passage is to build students' fluency in reading. Fluency, as noted in this chapter, is a critical core skill that every good reader must have.

Responsiveness

Checking comprehension, as suggested at the end of Section 1 of the reading, verifies that the readers have understood what they have read. In this way, teachers are responsive to individual student abilities and knowledge. This is one of the language objectives for the lesson – verify that learners can write a summary.

Stability

This reading fluency activity provides a stability factor to these materials. It is anchored in sound principles of teaching reading fluency. The principle being taught with the reading fluency exercise is that repetition builds automaticity. This exercise implements the eight critical elements in a fluent reading program outlined by Field (2006) and discussed earlier in this chapter.

things as the primary source of energy. Without the energy stored in glucose, plants could not grow, and animals could not move, breathe, or even think.

Reading fluency development
Turn to a partner and identify the main ideas from what you read above.

Fluency development: Repeated reading
Read Section 2 three times in five minutes. If you are able to do this, you will be reading 203 words per minute.

Photosynthesis – Section 2

How does photosynthesis make glucose? Glucose is the product of a series of chemical reactions that begins with molecules of carbon dioxide (CO_2) and water (H_2O) and results in glucose ($C_6H_{12}O_6$) and oxygen (O_2). Interestingly, whenever you breathe out, you probably exhale enough carbon dioxide and water vapor to form at least some glucose. Yet no glucose is formed because there are additional requirements that need to be met. The first requirement is a source of energy able to activate the necessary chemical reactions. In photosynthesis, the energy to activate these processes comes from light. Green plants have cells that include a special substance called *chlorophyll*. The chlorophyll is very effective at absorbing most visible light except for some shades of green and blue. These are reflected back, thus explaining why most plants appear to be green. The light that is absorbed is used to power the needed chemical reactions involved in photosynthesis.

Description
A vocabulary analysis was conducted for those words that were included in the photosynthesis passage. The following is a brief description of our analysis and how such an analysis might be useful.

Responsiveness, stability, and cohesion
Analyzing the vocabulary you intend to use in your reading materials can help ensure related aspects of responsiveness, cohesion, and stability. For example, vocabulary analysis can help you identify whether your passage responds to student needs by exposing them to the right words at the right frequency. Vocabulary analyses not only help the materials developers respond to student needs, but they can also help ensure cohesion with other materials or vocabulary that may precede or follow. In addition, they may also help ensure stability as particular vocabulary or word lists are targeted for review.

A sample of our analysis shows:

- 80 percent of the vocabulary appears in the list of the 2,000 most common English words.
- 11 percent appears in the Academic Word List.
- 6 percent are specialized vocabulary.
- 3 percent of the words in the passage were new to our students, on average.

Vocabulary mastery will vary by reader, as was the case with our students.

To make glucose, however, there are actually two related but separate processes. One process is called *light-dependent* because it needs light to power the process, and the other process is called *light-independent* because it does not use light energy. The two external requirements for the light-dependent reaction are water and light. The water enters the plant through the roots and is carried to the leaves, which are capable of photosynthesis. As light is absorbed by chlorophyll, it excites electrons, the smallest, negatively charged part of atoms. This process helps create special molecules that can safely carry the energy that will be needed in light-independent reactions, where glucose is made. Water is essential in the light-dependent reaction because it is broken apart and used to provide a continuous supply of electrons that allows the process to continue. As this process occurs, the O_2 from the water is released into the air as breathable oxygen through special openings on the surface of the plant. The remaining hydrogen (H) from the water becomes part of the molecule that carries the energy needed to make glucose in the light-independent reaction.

Reading fluency development
Turn to a partner and identify the main ideas from what you read above.

Postreading activities
Comprehension check
Respond to the following reading comprehension questions without referring to the passage.

(For more information on the 2,000 most common words in English, see West [1953] and Coxhead [2000]. For more information on the Academic Word List, see Coxhead [2000].)

Description
The postreading activities focus on content, concepts, and language and are designed to assess and assist student mastery of the material they have read.

1. The article suggests that the reader may not know that water is:
   A. essential for good health.
   B. necessary for food production.
   C. useful to biologists.
   D. important to all living things.
2. What is the most likely meaning of the word *phototropism*?
   A. the process by which plants drop seeds onto the soil
   B. the practice of eating leafy green plants to gain energy
   C. the tendency for plants to grow toward a source of light
   D. the act of a carnivorous plant feeding off flies or other insects

Responsiveness
This check provides immediate feedback about comprehension to both the student and the teacher. Thus, specific adjustments can be made in the quality of instruction, the pacing of classroom activities, and the nature of the reading tasks in order to maximize the learning experience.

Note: Though 8-10 questions may be ideal for a passage this size, due to space constraints, we have only included the first two questions here. ***Answers***: 1 (B), 2 (C).

Concept mapping
Based on what you have read, write the missing information in the three ovals in the graph below:

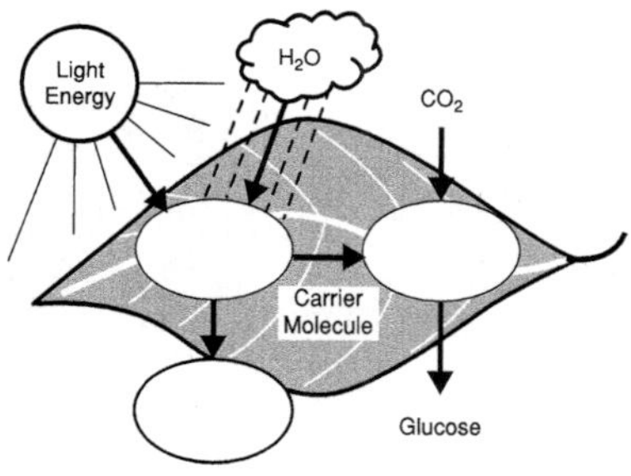

Figure 6.3 Photosynthesis

Responsiveness
The accompanying concept map, used previously as a prereading tool, is now used to assess student understanding of the complex and interrelated processes involved in photosynthesis. Such activities not only allow teachers to determine whether or not objectives have been met, but they also allow teachers to reexamine students' needs and make appropriate adjustments for future activities.

Answers

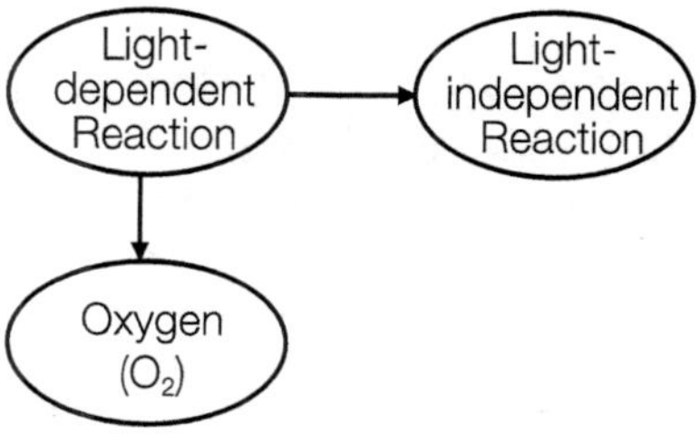

Figure 6.4 Answers

Practice summarizing
Summarize the passage on photosynthesis, using the following guidelines:

1. *Comprehensive* – Make sure your summary conveys all the important information in the reading.
2. *Brief* – Make sure your summary conveys the information concisely.
3. *Accurate* – Make sure your summary correctly conveys the author's ideas, findings, or arguments.
4. *Neutral* – Make sure your summary

Cohesion
Learning how to summarize is an essential academic skill. This summarizing activity provides a cohesive element to the materials by focusing on the development of that language skill. Rather than assuming that students know *how* to summarize, this

avoids judgments concerning the topic or style.

5. *Independent* – Make sure your summary makes sense to someone who has not read the source text.

Compare your summary with a classmate.

Online reading
Read more about photosynthesis online at this address: <http://en.wikipedia.org/wiki/Photosynthesis#Overview>

Compound adjectives
Identify each of the compound adjectives in the Wikipedia article. Can you define them? Are any of them also found in the article you read earlier? If so, identify them.

Language focus: Organizational pattern
What similarities and differences do you see between the passage on photosynthesis above and the Wikipedia entry? Use the table below to compare and contrast the two articles you have read on photosynthesis. Add your own ideas to what is already written below:

Compare (similarities)	Contrast (differences)
Both articles discuss the basic concepts of photosynthesis.	The Wikipedia article is more detailed than the photosynthesis article.

Reading printed materials versus reading online
How was reading the printed material different from reading online? Identify specific reading strategies that might help you be successful when reading printed material and when reading online. Share these with a classmate.

activity provides explicit direction on what teachers are looking for in the summary (Wilhoit 2004).

Responsiveness
The online and the printed materials respond to students' needs to be better prepared to read in both environments. By engaging students in reading the printed materials first, they will be better prepared to read the online content.

This activity lends itself well to explicit instruction of reading strategies to discuss the similarities and differences in the strategies used while reading the printed text versus the online text.

Summarizing
Summarize the passage on photosynthesis from Wikipedia, repeating the process followed above. Compare your summary with a classmate.

Content focus
Based on what you have read in the two articles, draw a table like the one used above to compare and contrast the light-dependent and light-independent reactions. Compare your table with a classmate's table.

Content focus: Applying photosynthesis principles
As you read the following situations, consider how photosynthesis is related to each. Respond to the questions at the end of each passage.

A. Volcanoes and photosynthesis
Corn is an essential crop in many parts of the world because it is an important source of both food and fuel. It is a fast-growing plant – usually needing only 75 days to go from seed to harvest. Because corn requires a lot of warm weather, water, and sunshine to thrive, a subtropical climate provides ideal growing conditions.

A major volcanic eruption has sent out thick clouds of volcanic ash hundreds of miles in every direction in a very productive subtropical farming region. Nearly 70 percent of the region's corn is grown within several hundred miles of the volcano. As the volcanic ash settles to the ground, it clings to the wet, rain-soaked leaves of trees and plants. Thousands of acres of corn were planted 30 days prior to the eruption. The plants are growing quickly and will be blossoming in about two weeks.

1. Discuss this situation in terms of light-dependent and light-independent reactions in photosynthesis.
2. What will probably happen to the corn crop? Be sure to include the photosynthesis processes in your answer.

Note: Whereas this activity may be rich in language use, such an activity could also be used as a content-focused activity that develops or assesses content mastery.

Description
Most CBI reading teachers see the need to make sure students understand key principles of the content being studied. The desired level of content mastery varies from program to program. This application exercise focuses on content and a student's ability to articulate (by speaking or writing about) key photosynthesis principles found in case studies.

Cohesion
No study of content can be language free, and all language has content associated with it. Although this activity is designed to assess student understanding of photosynthesis principles, students will certainly also be building language skills in the process.

Note: Additional content-based activities could be included here depending on the available time and the objectives of the specific lesson.

Conclusion

ELT practitioners understand that reading requires complex processes and that the specific contexts for reading may differ widely among individuals or classes. Such contexts could involve variations in proficiency level, age, motivation, learning ability, and reading purpose, including mastery of a particular content, general language development, or improvement of specific reading skills.

In this chapter, we have presented a theoretical framework for the development of ELT reading materials and have highlighted the essential roles of responsiveness, cohesion, and stability in guiding the development process. To illustrate these principles, we presented a specific set of materials designed for low-advanced learners that emphasizes fluency, linking language and content, and reading online versus printed materials. Though we limited the focus of our discussion and our materials to one specific context, these guiding principles may be applied successfully to a variety of circumstances and learning environments.

First, an effective reading curriculum and its accompanying materials must be responsive. In addition to responding to new insights gleaned from research and practice, materials must be able to respond to student needs and expectations within the context of programmatic goals and course objectives. Such awareness helps shape the development of materials, the reading purpose, the pacing of lessons, and the nature of prereading, reading, and postreading activities.

Second, learners benefit from materials and activities that are linked together in a cohesive curriculum. Where possible, reading materials should be linked to other courses or authentic language activities to help reinforce learning. This can be done with linguistic or thematic threads that weave themselves through multiple courses, thereby building students' skills, perspectives, and schemata. Students may also benefit from reading activities designed to prepare them for additional listening, speaking, and writing activities on the same topics, or complex tasks that require an integration of all language skills. In addition, reading materials should be carefully sequenced so they build upon each other, moving students toward texts that are increasingly more complex.

Third, an effective reading curriculum is one that is stable. In addition to a balanced and principled approach to improvement, reading materials that grow out of a stable curriculum are consistent in their use of sound principles of language teaching and learning. Such materials are associated with clearly articulated learning outcomes and successfully move students toward those ends using the most appropriate methods, given the unique needs of the learners and the specific requirements of the program.

Although most of our discussion has addressed these guidelines separately for illustrative purposes, they are actually closely interrelated. Rather than acting in isolation, the principles of responsiveness, cohesion, and stability complement each other and provide ELT educators with insight, perspective, and balance that ultimately strengthen the reading materials they develop.

Discussion questions and tasks

Reflection

1. What is a *principled curriculum*?
2. Review Figure 6.1 on page 155. *Stability, cohesion*, and *responsiveness* are key curriculum principles outlined in this chapter. How are these elements applicable to the development of materials for a reading class? What strength is added to a curriculum by integrating all three of the principles?
3. Identify possible factors that could bring instability to the materials in a reading curriculum.
4. Identify those factors that are likely to strengthen cohesion in a reading curriculum.
5. In what ways can the materials in a reading curriculum be more responsive?
6. This chapter provides a model for linking language and content in content-based instruction materials. Can you think of other ways to link language and content that are not discussed here?

Evaluation

7. Look at some reading texts with which you are familiar. In light of this chapter, what changes would you make to these materials now? Why?

Adaptation/Design

8. Table 6.1 on page 157 illustrates curriculum development principles in theory and practice. Can you identify additional theoretical principles that could be added to our list? How would those principles be applied in the development of reading materials?

References

Anderson, N. J. (1999). *Exploring second language reading: Issues and strategies*. Boston: Heinle and Heinle.

Anderson, N. J. (2003). Scrolling, clicking, and reading English: Online reading strategies in a second/foreign language. *The Reading Matrix* 3(3).

Anderson, N. J. (2007/2008). *ACTIVE skills for reading, Intro, Books 1-4* (2nd ed.). Boston: Heinle/Cengage.

Anderson, N. J. (2008). *Practical English language teaching: Reading*. New York: McGraw Hill.

Bikowski, D., & Kessler, G. (2002). Making the most of the discussion boards in the ESL classroom. *TESOL Journal* 11(3): 27-29.

Brinton, D. (1997). The challenges of administering content-based programs. In M. A. Snow and D. M. Brinton (eds.). *The content-based classroom: Perspectives on integrating language and content*. New York: Longman, pp. 340-6.

Brinton, D. M., Snow, M. A., & Wesche, M. B. (2003). *Content-based second language instruction* (*Michigan Classics* edition). Ann Arbor: University of Michigan Press.

Brown, H. D. (2001). *Teaching by principle: An interactive approach to language pedagogy* (2nd ed.). New York: Longman.

Brown, J. D. (1995). *The elements of language curriculum*. New York: Newbury House.

Carver, R. P. (1990). *Reading rate: A review of research and theory*. San Diego, CA: Academic Press.

Celce-Murcia, M. (2001). *Teaching English as a second or foreign language* (3rd ed.). Boston: Heinle/Thomson.

Coiro, J. (2003). Reading comprehension on the Internet: Expanding our understanding of reading comprehension to encompass new literacies. *The Reading Teacher* 56: 458-64.

Coxhead, A. (2000). A new academic word list. *TESOL Quarterly* 34: 213-38.

Cummins, J. (1980). Psychological assessment of immigrant children: Logic or institution? *Journal of Multilingual and Multicultural Development* 1: 97-111.

Cummins, J. (1981). Age on arrival and immigrant second language learning in Canada: A reassessment. *Applied Linguistics* 11: 132-49.

Cummins, J. (1996). *Negotiating identities: Education for empowerment in a diverse society*. Ontario, CA: California Association for Bilingual Education.

Ediger, A. M. (2006). Developing strategic L2 readers ... by reading for authentic purposes. In E. Uso-Juan & A. Martinez-Flor (eds.). *Current trends in the development and teaching of the four language skills*. New York: Mouton de Gruyter, pp. 303-28.

Ellis, R. (2005). Principles of instructed language learning. *System* 33: 209-24.

Field, M. L. (2006). Finding a path to fluent academic and workplace reading. In E. Uso-Juan & A. Martinez-Flor (eds.). *Current trends in the development and teaching of the four language skills*. New York: Mouton de Gruyter, pp. 329-53.

Grabe, W. (1991). Current developments in second language reading research. *TESOL Quarterly* 25: 375-406.

Hatch, E., & Brown, C. (1995). *Vocabulary, semantics, and language education*. New York: Cambridge University Press.

Ioannou-Georgiou, S. (2002). Constructing meaning with virtual reality. *TESOL Journal* 11(3): 21-26.

Kumaravadivelu, B. (1994). The post-method condition: (E)merging strategies for second/foreign language teaching. *TESOL Quarterly* 28: 27-48.

Kumaravadivelu, B. (2006). *Understanding language teaching: From method to postmethod*. Mahwah, NJ: Lawrence Erlbaum Associates.

Kurniawan, S. H., & Zaphiris, P. (2001). Reading online or on paper: Which is faster? In *Proceedings of the 9th International Conference on Human Computer Interaction, August 5-10*. New Orleans, LA. Available at: http:// users.soe.ucsc.edu/~srikur/year.html.

Leu, D. J., Jr. (2002). The new literacies: Research on reading instruction with the Internet. In A. E. Farstrup & S. J. Samuels (eds.). *What research has to say about reading instruction* (3rd ed.). Newark, DE: International Reading Association, pp. 310-36.

Markee, N. (2001). The diffusion of innovation in language teaching. In D. R. Hall & A. Hewings (eds.). *Innovation in English language teaching*. New York: Routledge, pp. 118-26.

Met, M. (1998). Curriculum decision-making in content-based second language teaching. In J. Cenoz & F. Genesee (eds.). *Beyond bilingualism: Multilingualism and multilingual education*. Clevedon, UK: Multilingual Matters, pp. 35-63.

Met, M. (1999). *Content-based instruction: Defining terms, making decisions*. (NFLC Report, January.) Washington DC: National Foreign Language Center.

Murray, D. E. (2005). Introduction. In D. E. Murray & P. McPherson (eds.). *Navigating to read – reading to navigate*. Sydney: National Centre for English Language Teaching and Research, Macquarie University, pp. viii-xiv.

Murray, D. E., & McPherson, P. (eds.). (2005). *Navigating to read – reading to navigate*. Sydney: National Centre for English Language Teaching and Research, Macquarie University.

Nation, I. S. P. (1990). *Teaching and learning vocabulary*. New York: Newbury House.

Nation, I. S. P. (2001). *Learning vocabulary in another language*. New York: Cambridge University Press.

National Reading Panel. (2000). *Teaching children to read: An evidence-based assessment of the scientific research literature on reading and its implications for reading instruction* (National Institute of Health Pub. No. 00-4769). Washington, DC: National Institute of Child Health and Human Development.

Nunan, D. (1999). *Second language teaching and learning*. Boston: Heinle.

Oxford, R. L. (1992). Progress in tertiary content-based ESL instruction. *TESL Canada Journal* 11: 53-61.

Reid, J. (1993). *Teaching ESL writing*. Englewood Cliffs, NJ: PrenticeHall Regents.

Richards, J. C. (2001). *Curriculum development in language teaching*. Cambridge: Cambridge University Press.

Selinker, L., & Tomlin, R. S. (1986). An empirical look at the integration and separation of skills in ELT. *ELT Journal* 40: 227-35.

Sheorey, R., & Mokhtari, K. (2001). Differences in the metacognitive awareness of reading strategies among native and non-native readers. *System* 29: 431-49.

Shulman, L. (2004). *The wisdom of practice: Essays on teaching, learning, and learning to teach*. San Francisco: Jossey-Bass.

Snow, M. (2001). Content-based and immersion models for second and foreign language teaching. In M. Celce-Murcia (ed.). *Teaching English as a second or foreign language* (3rd ed.). Boston: Heinle/Thomson, pp. 303-18.

Snow, M. A., & Brinton, D. M. (eds.). (1997). *The content-based classroom: Perspectives on integrating language and content*. NewYork: AddisonWesley.

Stark, J. S., & Lattuca, L. R. (1997). *Shaping the college curriculum: Academic plans in action*. Boston: Allyn and Bacon.

Stoller, F., & Grabe, W. (1997). A six-T's approach to content-based instruction. In M. A. Snow & D. M. Brinton (eds.). *The content-based classroom:Perspectives on integrating language and content*. New York: Longman, pp. 78-94.

Sutherland-Smith, W. (2002). Integrating online discussion in an Australian intensive English language course. *TESOL Journal* 11(3): 31-5.

Tindale, J. (2005). Reading print and electronic texts. In E. Murray & P. McPherson (eds.). *Navigating to read – reading to navigate*. Sydney: National Centre for English Language Teaching and Research, Macquarie University, pp. 2-15.

Warschauer, M. (1997). Computer-mediated collaborative learning: Theory and practice. *Modern Language Journal* 81: 470-81.

Warschauer, M. (1999). *Electronic literacies: Language, culture, and power in online education*. Mahwah, NJ: Lawrence Erlbaum Associates.

Warschauer, M. (2002). Networking into academic discourse. *Journal of English for Academic Purposes* 1: 45-58.

West, M. (1953). *A general service list of English words*. London: Longman, Green.

Wilhoit, S. W. (2004). *A brief guide to writing from readings* (3rd. ed.). New York: Pearson Longman.

7

A genre-based approach to developing materials for writing

Christopher Tribble

Summary

This chapter has six main sections. In the first, I review a number of theoretical issues that are central to any program that attempts to develop L2 writing skills. These include the linguistic differences between speaking and writing, the role of writing in society, and the specific needs of L2 writers. In the next section, I discuss the needs of students and the needs of teachers and how these needs have to be taken into account when developing teaching materials. I then go on to show how sets of relevant materials can be developed to support the kind of teaching/learning cycle that is common in contemporary, genre-informed approaches to writing instruction.

In order to exemplify this approach to materials development, in the section on developing materials for writing instruction at FCE level, I focus on the discursive essay, an L2 task that is common in many educational cultures and widely used in language examinations. I stress the value of learner texts as a classroom resource, and also show how language corpora, or other resources, such as those now readily available on the World Wide Web, can be drawn on to provide input. I then show how these resources can be used both at the beginning of a writing task and at later points as resources to support vocabulary development and grammar awareness.

Some theoretical issues

Linguistic contrasts between speaking and writing

Whatever the level of the students we are working with, there are some fundamental language facts that teachers have to take into account when preparing materials to support EFL writing development. The most important of these is the difference between spoken and written language[1]. Over time, these two modes have changed as a response to their contrasting social purposes. The writing system has become our preferred medium for recording permanent accounts of what people own, what is legal, what is held to be scientifically true. Speaking, in contrast, has been at the heart of our human relationships, our need to persuade, to move, to entertain. Because of these differing social purposes, writing and speaking display different characteristics:

> Talking and writing, then, are different ways of saying. They are different modes for expressing linguistic meanings .... Speech and writing are in practice used in different contexts, for different purposes – though obviously with a certain amount of overlap. (Halliday 1989: 92-3)

Because of the role of written texts in the efficient recording or reporting of facts, writers in English have tended to concentrate information into noun phrases, and to put important information at the beginnings of clauses and sentences. In written communication, the noun phrase, therefore, tends to be where the action takes place in text development, and this grammatical unit has become the most highly elaborated aspect of written texts. Halliday refers to this phenomenon when he discusses the *lexical density* of written communication. In contrast, because spoken communication is primarily oriented toward establishing and maintaining relationships, speakers make extensive use of the verb system in order to establish how "I" and "you" relate to one another. This results in the *syntactic intricacy* and relative *lexical sparseness* of spoken communication (Halliday 1989: 87).

These differences are easily seen in the brief examples given in Figures 7.1 and 7.2:

---

[1] Biber *et al.* (2000) is an excellent resource for information on many aspects of this contrast.

Written communication

"Data integration is one of the fundamental GIS operations (Burrough 1986). It involves transformation of data so that they are reported at a comparable geographical scale, projection and set of geographical units. The need for data integration arises because many of the questions which scientists and social scientists investigate require data from a wide range of sources which are only reported on disparate spatial bases. Data integration is especially a problem for geographers because information synthesis is at the very heart of the discipline."

(Langford *et al.* 1991. *The areal interpolation problem: Estimating population using remote sensing in a GIS framework.* Harlow, UK: Longman Scientific & Technical, Source: British National Corpus: file ref B1G – Written Academic Data)

Figure 7.1 Written communication

Spoken communication

PS1A9: How's it gone today?
PS1AA: Not bad.
PS1A9: Good. Good.
PS1AA: That's all?
PS1A9: Good. But now he
PS1AA: I've been watching videos most of the day.
PS1A9: Have you? Why?
PS1AA: Did this this morning watching a video. It was on evacuation.
PS1A9: Oh! Was it?
PS1AA: It was really good, especially for schools.
PS1A9: Yes.
PS1AA: You know, I mean, why teach with chalk and talk. Why not just put a video on?
PS1A9: Well fancy that!
PS1AA: Cos it's all there, you know. Er, it was really good. Er and it's only half an hour.
PS1A9: Was it all about evacuees?
PS1AA: About half an hour, you know. Well, German evacu evacuees, but it's all condensed so that you got a lot of information. (Source: British National Corpus: file ref KBC – Spoken Demographic Data)[2]

Figure 7.2 Spoken communication

---

[2] The British National Corpus, Version 2 (BNC World). 2001. Distributed by Oxford University Computing Services on behalf of the BNC Consortium. URL: www.natcorp.ox.ac.uk.
(Examples of usage taken from the British National Corpus (BNC) were obtained under the terms of the BNC End User Licence. Copyright in the individual texts cited resides with the original IPR holders. For information and licensing conditions relating to the BNC, please see the website at www.natcorp.ox.ac.uk.)

Kress summarizes this contrast when he comments:

> ... the textual structuring of speech and that of writing proceed from two distinctly different starting points. The structure of speech starts from the question: "What can I assume as common and shared knowledge for my addressee and myself?" This question, and its answer, are at the basis of the structure of speech. Writing starts with the question: "What is most important, topically, to me, in this sentence which I am about to write?" This question and its answer, are at the basis of the structure of writing. (Kress 1993: 27)

Learning how to achieve this shift in emphasis can be a major challenge for learners – especially for those whose main reason for engaging in language learning has been spoken fluency. For their part, teachers need both to be aware of these contrasts and also to be able to integrate this understanding into the materials that they prepare. In this way, they can help learners extend their capacity to write effectively for relevant audiences.

The role of written language in society

We have already noted some of the ways in which written language has developed special characteristics as a result of the uses to which it is put. We also need to be aware that learning to write in the first or additional language has an impact on the writers themselves. Kress observes:

> Command of writing gives access to certain cognitive, conceptual, social and political arenas. The person who commands both the forms of writing and speech is therefore constructed in an entirely different way from the person who commands the forms of speech alone. (Kress 1989: 46)

Kress draws attention to the personal and social construction that is implicit in the acquisition of literacy. Stubbs makes the point even more forcibly:

> Written language makes a radical difference to the complexity of organisation that humans can manage, since it changes the relation between memory and classification, and it allows many forms of

> referencing, cataloguing, indexing, recording and transmitting information .... The mere fact that something is written conveys its own message, for example of permanence and authority. Certain people write, and certain kinds of things get written. (Stubbs 1987: 20-1)

If it is the case that "certain people write and certain kinds of things get written," as teachers of writing, we need to be aware of what exactly we are asking of our students. We may be (a) asking learners to take on roles that they do not normally have access to in their first language (this can be particularly the case in courses where English is being taught as an additional language); or (b) asking learners to engage with literacy practices that they consider to be largely superfluous to their primary need to engage with the target language as a medium for spoken interaction. In English for Academic Purposes programs, writing is, of necessity, a central plank in the curriculum. In general EFL programs, getting learners to engage with the roles that are implicit in extending literacy in the target language can be a significant problem.

The challenge of teaching writing in EFL

A second challenge for the writing teacher is that of balancing learners' expectations of their real-world literacy needs with the literacy practices that are required of them in the educational settings of the language classroom or the examination.

Tribble (1996: 68-9) has discussed the contrast between *learning to write* and *writing to learn*. In the former, an apprentice writer is learning how to extend his or her textual knowledge, cognitive capacities, and rhetorical skills in order to take on (usually prestigious) social roles, which require the production of certain kinds of text. In the latter, language learners are using the writing system to practice new *language* knowledge, or are using writing to demonstrate this knowledge in the context of assessment.

One of the problems facing the writing instructor is the fact that all too often, learners' main experience of EFL writing has been in *writing* to learn, and that they have had few opportunities to extend their literacy in the target language – and that they feel little or no motivation to climb this particular learning curve.

An additional problem is that literacy skills established in their first language may clash with or otherwise impede their development of writing skills in the target language. Hyland comments:

> ... L2 writers are unique because of their bilingual, bicultural, and biliterate experiences, and these can facilitate or impede writing in various ways ....
> L2 learners' cultural schemata can impact on the ways they write and the writing they produce.
> Effective L2 writing instruction can make schemata differences explicit to students, encouraging consideration of audience and providing patterns of unfamiliar rhetorical forms. (Hyland 2003: 50)

This last point – the need to make "schemata differences explicit to students" – will be stressed in the practical section of this chapter. Learning to write is not a single-stage process. Students may be able to write a perfectly adequate summary of a text, but can still have no idea of how to go about writing argumentatively. They may be able to describe a personal experience in a conversational style, but have no idea of how to write a report that summarizes the results of a survey. This goes back to my earlier comment on the socially constructed nature of language. My position here is that when we teach writing in EFL, we are not simply giving students access to the mechanics of writing in English. To help learners develop as writers, we also have to help them understand that in the world outside the classroom, each text has a job to do, and that each job requires the effective exploitation of different linguistic resources. We are not only helping students to write in the foreign language, we are helping them to engage with new roles and purposes.

> To think of text structure not in terms of the structure of each individual text as a separate entity, but as a general statement about a genre as a whole, is to imply that there exists a close relation between text and context .... The value of this approach lies ultimately in the recognition of the functional nature of language .... [T]here cannot be just one right way of either speaking or writing. What is

> appropriate in one environment may not be quite so appropriate in another.
> Further, there is the implication that an ability to write an excellent essay on the causes of the Second World War does not establish that one can produce a passable report on a case in a court of law. This is not because one piece of writing is inherently more difficult or demanding than the other, but because one may have more experience of that particular genre. (Halliday & Hasan 1985: 6)

The challenge that we face as teachers is, then, to help our students gain experience of genres that are relevant to their needs, and to ensure that they are able to draw on the linguistic and cognitive resources that are relevant to the task they need to complete. We also have to be able to recognize where learners have already established the knowledge and skills that will support them in fulfilling a task, where there may be clashes between established ways of working and the requirements of new kinds of writing, and how to help learners – should they have the need – to make the transition from writing "an excellent essay on the causes of the Second World War" to writing a business report, an academic assignment, or a more lowly, but nevertheless important, examination essay.

Developing materials for writing instruction

The needs of learners

As writing teachers, we should have a clear understanding of our students' needs and be able to develop programs that will enhance their capacity to write the texts which matter to them. We also have to recognize the limits to what we can provide. One account of what a writer needs to know is given in Figure 7.3: Content knowledge can present the greatest difficulty to many writing teachers – especially in content-based learning programs in secondary education, or in courses for adults focusing on business or academic writing. A commonly adopted response to this problem is to work cooperatively with experts from within a particular industry or academic discipline and to develop programs that are co-taught, with writing teachers supporting learning

CONTENT KNOWLEDGE knowledge of the concepts involved in the subject area
CONTEXT KNOWLEDGE knowledge of the social context in which the text will be read, including the readers' expectations, and knowledge of the co-texts alongside which this new text will be read
LANGUAGE SYSTEM KNOWLEDGE knowledge of those aspects of the language system (i.e., lexis, syntax) that are necessary to the completion of the task
WRITING PROCESS KNOWLEDGE knowledge of the most appropriate way of approaching the writing task

Figure 7.3 Writers' knowledge (Tribble 1996: 67-8)

development alongside the specialist program taught by subject specialists. (This is especially the case in courses designed to help learners gain access to higher education courses.)

Context, language system, and writing process knowledge fall more obviously into the remit of the writing teacher, and it is these aspects of materials for writing that we will look at in the rest of the chapter. To minimize the issue of content, we will use one of the major international language-testing examinations, the Cambridge First Certificate, as a "case study" in this chapter, to explore how learners' knowledge of context, language system, and writing process can best be supported through the use of appropriate teaching/learning materials.

The needs of teachers

Alongside the complex and sophisticated personal resources that teachers and learners bring to the writing classroom, other materials are needed to stimulate writing and to enable learners to develop contextual, language system, and writing process knowledge. At a general level, these resources "can be classified into texts, libraries/media, realia, student generated resources, activities, and discussions" (Grabe & Kaplan 1996: 256).

Drawing on earlier work by Hutchinson and Waters (1987), Hyland (2003: 101) summarizes the resources that a teacher needs to bring to the classroom as input, content focus, language focus, and task focus. In a writing class, *input* is typically a text, although it may be a dialogue, video, picture, or other realia. This provides:

- A stimulus for new thought, discussion, and writing.
- Opportunities for information processing.
- Opportunities for learners to use and build on prior knowledge.
- New language items or the re-presentation of earlier items.
- A context and a purpose for writing.
- Genre models and exemplar texts.
- Reasons to start using (and to develop) writing process skills such as prewriting, drafting, editing.

The *content focus* of the class will include specifications of topics, situations, information, and other resources, which can lead to communication between students; the *language focus* will create opportunities for students to analyze texts and to draw on new knowledge as they develop a writing task; and the *task focus* should establish the grounds for communicative activities that will enable learners to use the content and language of the unit, and ultimately write an assignment.

Clearly, these materials can be realized as learning resources in many different ways, but the one that we will draw on in this chapter is the teaching-learning cycle proposed by Feez (1998) – a cycle that draws on well-established, genre-informed approaches to writing instruction (Cope & Kalantzis 1993; Grabe & Kaplan 1996; Tribble 1996). Feez's cycle consists of five stages, namely: (1) building the context; (2) modeling and deconstructing the text; (3) joint construction of the text; (4) independent construction of the text; and (5) linking related texts.

This teaching-learning cycle provides a coherent framework in which materials can be developed, and will be the basis for the demonstration of approaches to materials development that I will present in the remaining sections of this chapter.

The Cambridge First Certificate in English Written Paper – Section 2, Discursive Composition: A case study

The examination

The Cambridge First Certificate in English (FCE) is designed for students at Level 2B in the Common European Framework and is one of the suite of examinations offered by the University of Cambridge ESOL Exams. In 2002, these examinations were taken by over 1.2 million students in over 130 countries.[3] The writing exam has two sections. In the first, candidates have to write a "transactional letter" up to 180 words in length. In the second section, candidates have the choice of writing (again with a 120-180 word length) one of the following possible tasks:

- An article.
- A letter.
- A report.
- An essay.
- A short story.

In the rest of this chapter, we will use the discursive composition in the Cambridge FCE examination to exemplify an approach to developing materials for writing instruction. This task type has been selected because it is so commonly used in a wide range of educational cultures. The approach to materials development outlined here could, however, be drawn on to support writing development in a wide range of contexts in which the production of some form of tightly prescribed text is required.

The needs of the learner

The guidance notes for the teacher (available to download from www.cambridgeesol.org) stress that candidates need to be able to:

- Express opinions and suggestions on the subject.
- Agree or disagree with the statement in the task, or discuss both sides.
- Write in a formal or neutral register.

[3] www.cambridgeesol.org/support/dloads/fce/fce_hb_intro.pdf (accessed May 16, 2009).

- Ensure that the flow of ideas in the writing is logical and easy for the reader to follow.
- Not write simple sentences throughout, but to use more complex language.
- Use a variety of linking words.

The challenges we face as teachers lie in finding out how to engage learners in the process of developing these competences and skills. The first issue we have to bear in mind is that four of the six areas summarized above focus on the demonstration of language knowledge – the writing teacher has to remain a language teacher. The second is that we remain educators – helping students to pass an examination is only part of our task. We should also enable them to deal with new kinds of writing once they have finished addressing the immediate needs of the examination.

Developing materials for writing instruction at FCE level

The five stages of the teaching-learning writing cycle can be described as:

- Building the context.
- Modeling and reconstructing the text.
- Joint construction of the text.
- Independent construction of the text.
- Linking related texts.

Each stage requires a range of distinct resources. In the following sections, I will demonstrate how this approach can be realized, and outline the kinds of materials that are best suited to meeting teaching/learning objectives. We will do this by considering an FCE composition topic with the title:

> *"Stricter punishments are the only way of solving a rising level of crime." To what extent do you agree with this statement?*

The process outlined here is one of supporting the learners as they develop their responses to a task (CONTENT knowledge), helping them to understand appropriate textual realizations of this task (CONTEXT and LANGUAGE SYSTEM knowledge), and enabling them independently to write texts that fulfill the requirements of the task (WRITING PROCESS knowledge). This methodology can be applied to a very wide range of educational and real-world genres.

Building the context

Process

Each teacher will have preferred ways of building a set of resources to engage learners' interest and to stimulate discussion before planning writing. These resources will include realia, print materials, audio-visual stimuli for discussions, and the like. Growing access to the World Wide Web has, however, revolutionized the ways in which resources can be identified and exploited. As a simple example, a sequence could be:

a) Identify relevant sections from appropriate Web sites (such as a text about the death penalty taken from the Amnesty International Web site: www.amnesty.org).
b) Use these texts as the starting point for discussion and note-making so that learners can not only establish their positions in relation to the topic, but also have a sense of the evidence they might wish to draw on when planning their compositions.
c) Use revolutionary new resources such as WebCorp (www.webcorp.org.uk) to create a wordlist based on the text in the Web site. Such a list following the examination of a death penalty text will include vocabulary for learners such as:

carried out	convicted	court
crimes	death	executed
execution	Human Rights	murder
offenders	penalty	sentence

d) Use WebCorp again to check on frequent collocates of important words for the assignment: e.g., collocates for *death sentence* include: *mandatory, face, appeal against,* and *given.*

Then bring all this together as a set of resources that will enable learners to begin to engage with the writing task.

Implications for materials developers – Building the context

Learners need access to materials that help them engage with challenging ideas and that provide an evidence base to work with when they start to write. This applies to all factually oriented writing, including academic writing, but is also relevant to the case of more creative and fictional writing. These materials should also have the potential to constitute a source of linguistic information for the learner, enabling them to extend their productive vocabularies and to deepen their appreciation of register variation.

Modeling and reconstructing the text

Process

Alongside the development of materials to support learners' understanding of the context and an evidence base for their argument, it is also essential that learners gain an understanding of how texts are constructed in the genre that they are writing toward. This need is addressed in the modeling and reconstruction phase of a writing learning-teaching cycle.

In the modeling stage, rather than working with an instance of the actual assignment they will have to write, learners typically work with the teacher to build a model of how texts in the genre are organized. This work is done through the study of exemplar texts, which the teacher selects as being different from their assignment yet able to provide an introduction to the structure and main features of the genre that the students are preparing to write. Such texts might be *exemplars* that are relevant to the genre in question, or *analogues* of such texts (Tribble 1997). In many educational settings, it is difficult to get exemplars of the examination scripts that students have to write (for reasons of confidentiality, to avoid plagiarism, etc.). However, there are ways around this. In the case of argumentative writing, for example, it may be possible to use newspaper editorials as analogues. Similarly, in the case of "for or against" compositions, it is possible to find examples in electronic reference works (on DVD or online). The most effective way of overcoming this problem is for teachers or schools systematically to collect graded instances of learner writing (preferably in electronic format) and to build a parallel set of reformulated versions of these texts that can be used as exemplars in teaching (Allwright *et al.* 1988). This is what many coursebook writers do on a regular basis, and there is no reason why a teacher should not be able to do it for his or her own students.

In the modeling phase, assuming that there is an appropriate exemplar text available, learners work with the teacher to understand the move structure of the genre (Dudley-Evans 1994; Swales 1990). In a discursive essay, it is helpful to use a minimum discourse pattern such as Situation > Problem > Response > Solution/Evaluation, Reason > Result, or General > Particular (see Hoey [1983] for a full account of these patterns) or a simple educational genre move structure as a framework for explaining how the text is organized (Hyland [2003: 46] offers a good example).

The example given here is a First Certificate in English level composition with the title: "Continuous assessment or examinations – Which do you prefer?" Assuming that learners have some familiarity with compositions as educational genres, an effective way of getting them to engage with the exemplar text is to present it to them in jumbled format. The example given in Table 7.1 was created simply by alphabetically sorting the paragraphs of the original assignment.

Once they have sequenced the composition appropriately (this is a useful discussion activity), it is then possible to move to the modeling stage. The tabular layout used in Table 7.2 is particularly suitable both for modeling activities and for the later review of learner writing in reformulation. Column 1 contains the original exemplar text, Column 2 the move labels, and Column 3 the commentary that the teacher will share with the class. Table 7.2 is, effectively, the set of notes that the students will take away from the class. The processes whereby moves are analyzed and the commentary elaborated will depend on the level of development of the learners, and on individual teachers' strategies.

Having worked with the teacher on this first example, it can be helpful to consolidate learning through further text reconstruction and editing tasks using more exemplar texts. These activities allow the learners to focus on appropriate argument structure and appropriate language. Editing tasks are best carried out on examples of writing collected from class members, or from the work of learners at a similar level.

Table 7.1 Sequencing task

Task

Read the following paragraphs and organize them into a sequence that makes a logical composition.

a) Written examinations are a good way of testing learners' knowledge and finding out how well they can work without the help of books and other materials. They also reduce the risk of cheating.

b) On balance, I prefer continuous assessment. I like being able to work at my own speed and enjoy having time to complete a task rather than feeling rushed and forced to memorize things. I want teachers to be free to educate learners, and do not want to spend all my time learning facts.

c) Many educationalists, however, claim that written examinations are unfair. They cause high levels of anxiety, and many good students get poor results because they are nervous. These educationalists recommend continuous assessment, saying that it shows the true ability of students, not just their ability to memorize facts. However, many students say that they do not like being under pressure all the time and prefer a formal test or examination.

d) All education systems need to test students and give qualifications, but there is no agreement on the best way of doing this.

Implications for materials developers – Modeling and reconstructing the text

The most important resource for teachers and students at this stage is good-quality sets of exemplar texts. At lower levels, this set of texts is best developed by teachers working cooperatively to collect examples of educational genres that have been written by learners. These learner texts then have to be edited and revised so that they can be used as exemplars. At higher levels, where possible, it is best to build collections of texts that are directly relevant to the needs of learners, or to identify texts that are close analogues of the texts that apprentice writers need to be able to control.

Table 7.2 Move analysis and commentary

Text	Move	Commentary
All education systems need to test students and give qualifications, but *there* is	Situation/Orientation	The composition starts with a strong generalization.
no agreement on the best way of doing this.	Problem	Use a nonhuman grammatical subject to establish a neutral tone. "There" structures are also a very good way of maintaining a neutral tone.
Written examinations are a good way of testing learners' knowledge and finding out how well they can work without the help of books and other materials. They [(1)] also reduce the risk of cheating.	Response 1	Maintain neutral tone by avoiding personal pronouns as grammatical subjects. Claim and supporting statement helps to develop the argument. [(1)] Cohesion maintained by use of pronoun
[(1)] *Many educationalists*, however, claim that written examinations are unfair [(2)]. They cause high levels of anxiety, and many good students get poor results because they are nervous.	Evaluation 1	The negative evaluation of examinations moves from the general [(1)] to the particular [(2)].

(to be continued)

(continued)

Text	Move	Commentary
These (3) *educationalists* recommend continuous assessment, saying that it shows the true ability of students, not just their ability to memorize facts.	Response 2	(3) Cohesion maintained by use of *these*
(4) *However*, many students say that they do not like being under pressure all the time and prefer a formal test or examination.	Evaluation 2	(4) Negative evaluation signaled by *however*
On balance, I (1) prefer continuous assessment. I like being able to work at my own speed and enjoy having time to complete a task rather than feeling rushed and forced to memorize things. (2) I want teachers to be free to *educate* learners, and do not want to spend all my time learning facts.	Final evaluation Reorientation	(1) Appropriate use of personal pronoun in the closing argument (2) Return to the original theme of the composition with the use of *educate*

Access to a *collection* of exemplars is important. To build a full appreciation of what constitutes an allowable contribution to a genre, teachers and students have to be able to work with several exemplars – a single instance can never give a sufficient understanding of what is central and what peripheral in terms of text structure, register, or lexis (see Swales 1990; Tribble 1996). Move analysis and explicit language analysis will be an important part of the process, as well as text reconstruction, register transformation exercises, and text editing.

Joint/independent construction of the text

Process

Once learners are aware of how texts are typically developed in a genre, it is possible to move to joint or independent text construction. In the initial stages of a course – and especially in general education settings, or in preparation for language examinations such as the First Certificate in English – students will often work collaboratively in the planning of texts. They can then go on to write together, or individually, often with the teacher working in parallel.

In such a program, one very useful way of building learner awareness of text structure and register is through *reformulation* (Allwright *et al.* 1988). In a reformulation process, learners are typically asked to complete a written assignment, and then to review the differences between *one* anonymized example of their work and a sympathetic reformulation of the text prepared by an expert writer (in a school context this can be a language teacher; in higher education, it will often need to be an expert informant). After this discussion, they can revise their own texts before getting feedback from their teacher.

Reformulation has the advantage of showing students how texts can be improved – that is, turned into more acceptable contributions – without the learner text having to be edited beyond all recognition. An example reformulation for a composition responding to the "stricter punishment" question is given in Table 7.3. The text is initially given without any markup, the information in the right hand *move* column being withheld until learners have developed their own account of the differences between the learner text and the reformulation.

Discussion of the reformulation usually starts with a review of the differences between the student text and the reformulation on at least three levels: move structure, information structure, and lexico-grammar.

Move structure has been discussed in the previous section. The essential task here is for students to be able to recognize how paragraphing is working, and how more than one move can occur within a paragraph. Once this aspect of the analysis has been completed, the text can be reviewed in terms of **information structure**. A simplified theme/rheme analysis can be very helpful here (Halliday 1994), with learners comparing how sentences are started, and what grammatical themes have been used in the learner text and the reformulation. The last stage of the comparison can consider specific aspects of **lexico-grammar**, including collocation. In the example above, some of the areas on which students might need to concentrate have been highlighted. These range from spelling errors (*endiveduoly*), issues of word choice (*they recognized* vs. *they argue*), through to issues of collocation (*lower committed crime* vs. *the lower crime rate*).

Table 7.3 Original essay and reformulation

"Stricter punishments are the only way of solving a rising level of crime." To what extent do you agree with this statement?

#	Original student text[4]	#	Reformulation	Move
1	In our modern society the **crime level** is **getting higher** and higher *evry* year. This led us to look for the reasons, and try to find a solution for this problem, for safer society.	1	Modern societies are become more affluent every year, but *crime levels are also rising*. This leads us to look for reasons for the problem, and to try to find solutions *which will make society safer*.	*Situation/ Orientation Problem*

(to be continued)

4 FCE Candidate – personal archive.

(continued)

#	Original student text	#	Reformulation	Move
2	Many experts **go for stricter punishment** to eliminate crime. They said if the criminal **would know** that he will be killed if he kills someone then he would not do it. The stricter punishment will **prevent the criminal to commit** their crime. **This** experts take Saudi-Arabia as an example for **lower commited crime** by having "Islamic Law" and the Islamic law is with stricter punishment. We can find even in England many experts *wold* like to restore capital punishment. They believe that capital punishment will prevent crime is fear.	2	Many criminologists *call for* stricter punishments in order to eliminate crime. They say that *if criminals know that **they** will lose their lives* if ***they*** kill someone else, then **they** will not commit such crimes. In other words, stricter punishments will *prevent criminals from committing* crimes.	*Response 1*
			These experts take the lower crime rate in Saudi-Arabia as an example, attributing this to severity of "Islamic Law" and the fact that Islamic laws *impose stricter punishments*. Even in England, many experts would now like to restore	*Example 1*
			capital punishment. They believe that the fear of capital punishment will prevent crime.	*Example 2*

(to be continued)

(continued)

#	Original student text	#	Reformulation	Move
3	**Many others against** capital punishment, said stricter punishment it is not going to eliminate the crime, and the solution for growing crime in the society it is not in killing more people. **They recognized** that there are other countries like Sweden with very low crime rate, but they don't have **a capital punishment**.	3	*Many of those who oppose capital punishment,* say that stricter punishment it is not going to eliminate crime, and that the solution for the growth of crime in society cannot be to kill more people. *They argue* that there are many countries such as Sweden which have very low crime rates, but which do not have capital punishment.	*Evaluation 1*
4	They belive that Sweden **looking well after** each one *endiveduoly*, and the people there *obundant*.		They attribute this to the way in which Swedish society looks after individuals well, *and the affluence of the majority of Swedish people.*	*Response 2*
5	However capital punishment, improving the society standard of living, they might not be an easy task to reach, but the Goverment have to try every possibility for safer society.	4	However, improving a society's standard of living is not an easy task, and government might have to look at all the options, including capital punishment.	*Evaluation 2*

(to be continued)

(continued)

#	Original student text	#	Reformulation	Move
6	**What I wold like to say**, that stricter punishement and providing meaningful and confertable lives for all members of the society will be realy helpful to reduce crime.		*This leads me to conclude* that society has to combine stricter punishment with policies to ensure that all members of a community have more *meaningful and safer* lives if we want to reduce crime.	*Final evaluation/ Recom-mendation*

Although the wide range of commercially available grammar reference materials will help teachers and learners come to terms with issues in lexico-grammar, access to corpus resources can also be useful. For example, the problem with *prevent the criminal to commit* can very easily be resolved by a search in the British National Corpus (BNC) and a review of the collocates of *prevent*. This immediately demonstrates that there is no pattern *prevent X* ***to*** *Y Z*. The pattern is *prevent X* ***from*** *Y-ing Z*.

Similarly, in paragraph 2 in the student text, we find, *Many experts go for stricter punishment to eliminate crime*. A concordance for *go for* using the free search facility for the British National Corpus (BNC – www.natcorp.ox.ac.uk) immediately reveals that *go for* is most frequently used in the sense of "*go for*" + *walk/swim/drink*, with a set including *job* and *interview* coming a close second. It does not include the sense the student has "gone for." This seems to be something between *opt for* and *call for*. A subsequent WebCorp search for *call for* in the context of *stricter* in UK broadsheet newspapers, reveals that *call for* catches the sense we had guessed at – although it actually collocates more positively with *tighter* than it does with *stricter*.

so far tend to lend weight to our call for tighter controls over any case whe
ndustry and the Polish Embassy to call for tighter controls on this furniture.
g-time gun control advocates will call for tighter background checks. Long-tim,
attacking *The New York Times*'s call for tighter gun laws, declaimed that "a

ccasion for some conservatives to call for tighter blasphemy laws. September 1
decry America's "gun culture" and call for tougher gun laws, no guns are allow

Implications for materials developers – Joint/independent production of the text

The materials needed for this stage of the process are student originals and expert reformulations. As with the exemplar bank, in a general EFL setting these reformulations can be carried out by fellow teachers, whereas in more specialist contexts (EAP, ESP) it may be necessary to call on expert informants to carry out this task.

The second resource is access to large corpus resources. Where Internet connection is a problem, then the BNC can be an invaluable asset for language teachers. However, if teachers have access to broadband Internet connections, the tools provided by a resource like WebCorp can be of considerable value.

Linking related texts

The final stage in the writing-learning cycle is to make connections between texts in the genre that has been studied with other texts. This enables learners to see organizational and register parallels and contrasts, and to consolidate their appreciation of the central features of the target genre.

Process

Texts used for linking purposes can either demonstrate shared or contrasting features – either can be useful. The example in Figure 7.4 is taken from a Microsoft Encarta article on capital punishment. When reviewing the text, learners could be asked to do the following tasks:

- Three major arguments against the death penalty are mentioned in the article below. Underline the phrase that the writer uses to introduce the three examples.
- Find and underline the linking phrases/words *for example* and *however*. Why has the author placed them in this position in the different sentences?
- Underline the words that are used to describe those who are in favor of the death penalty, and those who are against it.

> In the United States, the chief objection to capital punishment has been that it was always used unfairly, in at least three major ways: that is, with regard to race, sex, and social status. Women, for example, are rarely sentenced to death and executed, even though 20 per cent of all homicides in the United States in recent years have been committed by women. Defenders of the death penalty, however, have insisted that, because nothing inherent in the laws of capital punishment causes sexist, racist, or class bias in its use, these kinds of discrimination are not a sufficient reason for abolishing the death penalty. Opponents have replied that the death penalty is inherently subject to caprice and mistake in practice and that it is impossible to administer fairly.[5]

Figure 7.4 Encarta essay

Having reviewed some of the features of a text that shares some characteristics of the discursive essay, it can be useful to review a text in which the same topic has been discussed, but where there is a genre contrast. The extract in Figure 7.5 from the British popular newspaper, *The Sun*, provides a good example.

> SHOULD WE HANG THEM?
> It is the issue all Britain is talking about ... should Ian Huntley face the hangman's noose for killing Jessica Chapman and Holly Wells?
> Huntley's mum says he SHOULD be "strung up" for his vile crimes.
> Elsewhere is the grotesque face of paedophile Roy Whiting, caged for life for murdering Sarah Payne.
> The 44-year-old monster's contorted grin and piercing, wild eyes are the personification of evil.
> Yet the little girl's mum Sara argues that NOBODY should face the death penalty. The 34-year-old says the execution of Whiting would "turn her stomach".
> Hanging was abolished for murder in 1965 and since then Governments have ignored calls for its return. As the law stands Parliament cannot bring back the penalty even if public opinion demands it.
> This is because in 1999 the then Home Secretary Jack Straw signed the sixth protocol of the European Convention of Human Rights which formally abolished the death penalty in the UK.
> The Government is unable to reinstate hanging without overturning the entire convention.

Figure 7.5 Article from *The Sun*[6]

Tasks that will help students to understand the contrast between this kind

[5] "Capital Punishment," Microsoft Encarta Online Encyclopedia 2009 http://uk.encarta.msn.com 1997–2009 Microsoft Corporation. All Rights Reserved.

[6] www.thesun.co.uk/sol/homepage/features/life/article162493.ece (accessed November 1, 2009).

of language use and the language of an examination essay include:

- There is a major change approximately halfway through *The Sun* article (Figure 7.5). Underline the sentence where the style changes. What differences can you see between the two sections?
- Underline any typographic, paragraphing, or punctuation features that would not be appropriate in an FCE essay.
- Underline any words or phrases that are less appropriate for use in an FCE essay on the topic of capital punishment.
- Underline any words or phases that could be useful in an FCE essay.

Implications for materials developers – Linking related texts

Alongside collections of exemplars, a bank of texts that can be used when students are investigating links is also invaluable. An essential step in the process of developing a control of different registers is to understand how language use changes depending on audience and genre purpose.

Conclusion

Materials designed to help the development of L2 writing-skills teachers and materials developers have to meet a number of criteria. As a minimum, materials should enable teachers to achieve a small number of essential objectives:

- Materials should **help learners build an appreciation of the context** in which and toward which they are writing. In an examination context, such as the one we have considered in this chapter, this will involve a clear appreciation of what the examiners expect of a successful script. In more real-world settings, it will involve developing an appreciation of the expectations and needs of readers, and ensuring that writers have the evidence base that they need in order to write allowable contributions to specific genres.
- Through **modeling and reconstructing the text**, materials should enable the teacher to ensure that learners understand and can control the textual and lexico-grammatical resources necessary for meeting the register and organizational requirements of readers.

- Once learners have an understanding of the context and the typical organization and wording of texts in the target genre, materials should help them to engage in the **construction of the text** and to see links **between the texts** in the target genre, in related texts, and in contrasting texts.

In other words, materials should help learners gain the contextual knowledge, language system knowledge, and writing process knowledge they require in order to complete a task; in some language-learning contexts, materials may also have to ensure that students have access to the content knowledge that is necessary for task fulfilment.

Although this task remains significant, teachers now have more resources available to them than could have been imagined as recently as the beginning of the 21st century. Even if Internet access is not easily available, the majority of teachers have access to word processors and CD-ROM-based reference materials (although there is still a skills gap when it comes to working with information and communications technology). For those who work in contexts where Internet access is available, the range of resources that can be drawn on for materials development is almost overwhelming. The critical task we now face as a profession is to make appropriate use of all these riches, and to help our students to write appropriately, clearly, and effectively.

Discussion questions and tasks

Reflection

1. Do any of the approaches to teaching writing in this chapter resemble the way you teach? How could you enhance your own approach?
2. At what stages in a writing course could corpus-informed approaches be most helpful? Give one or two examples from your own teaching experience.
3. How easy or difficult do you think it would be to use the genre-based approach outlined in this chapter to select or develop materials?
4. The materials described in this chapter were designed for learners in a general EFL program. To what extent could the same approach

be taken when designing materials for an adult English for Specific Purposes course?

Evaluation

5. Compare the materials focusing on writing in two or more textbooks for learners of the same level. How and why do they differ? If possible, examine the teacher's books for each. Do the materials writers explain and justify their approaches?
6. Look at some textbook materials you have used with a class in the past. In light of this chapter, what changes would you make to these materials now? Why?

Adaptation/Design

7. Look at an activity focusing on writing in a textbook you are familiar with. Make modifications to it on the basis of what you have learned from this chapter to produce appropriate activities for a specific class.
8. Use what you have learned in this chapter to prepare three activities on writing. Explain the rationale behind your approach.

References

Allwright, R. L., Woodley, M. P., & Allwright, J. M. (1988). Investigating Reformulation as a practical strategy for the teaching of academic writing. *Applied Linguistics* 9(3): 237-58.

Biber, D., Johansson, S., Leech, G., Conrad, S., & Finegan, E. (2000). *Longman grammar of spoken and written English*. Harlow, UK: Addison Wesley Longman.

Cope, B., & Kalantzis, M. (1993). *The powers of literacy: A genre approach to teaching writing*. London: The Falmer Press.

Dudley-Evans, T. (1994). Genre analysis: An approach to text analysis for ESP. In M. Coulthard (ed.). *Advances in written discourse*. London and New York: Routledge, pp. 219-28.

FCE Handbook, Cambridge: University of Cambridge ESOL Examinations, pp. 16-18. Accessed online at: www.cambridgeesol.org/support/dloads/fce_ downloads.htm, May 13, 2007.

Feez, S. (1998). *Text-based syllabus design*. New South Wales, Australia: AMES and Macquarie University.

Grabe,W., & Kaplan, R. (1996). *Theory and practice of writing*. London and New York: Longman.

Halliday, M. A. K. (1989). *Spoken and written language*. Oxford: Oxford University Press.

Halliday, M. A. K. (1994). *An introduction to functional grammar* (2nd ed.). London: Edward Arnold.

Halliday, M. A. K., & Hasan, R. (1985). *Language context and text: Aspects of language in a social-semiotic perspective*. Oxford: Oxford University Press.

Hoey, M. (1983). *On the surface of discourse*. London: George Allen and Unwin.

Hutchinson, T., & Waters, A. (1987). *English for specific purposes*. Cambridge: Cambridge University Press.

Hyland, K. (2003). *Second language writing*. Cambridge: Cambridge University Press.

Kress, G. (1989). *Linguistic processes in sociocultural practice*. Oxford: Oxford University Press.

Kress, G. (1993). *Learning to write*. London: Routledge.

Stubbs, M. (1987). An educational theory of (written) language. In T. Bloor & J. Norrish (eds.). Papers from the Annual Meeting of the British Association for Applied Linguistics. London: CILT/BAAL.

Swales, J. M. (1990). *Genre analysis*. Cambridge: Cambridge University Press.

Tribble, C. (1996). *Writing*. Oxford: Oxford University Press.

Tribble, C. (1997). Improvising corpora for ELT: Quick-and-dirty ways of developing corpora for language teaching. In J. Melia & B. Lewandowska-Tomaszczyk (eds.). *PALC 97: Practical applications in language corpora*. Lodz: Lodz University Press.

8

Listening as process: Learning activities for self-appraisal and self-regulation

Christine Goh

Summary

The strategy approach is by now familiar to many teachers. While it emphasizes the use of various techniques to facilitate comprehension, strategy training alone does not go far enough in addressing learners' cognitive, affective, and social needs that can influence second language listening development. The aim of this chapter is to provide a theoretical framework that takes account of these needs and to suggest practical ideas for developing learners' ability to facilitate and improve their own listening development. Grounded in the concept of metacognition, which encompasses both knowledge about and control over learning processes, the activity and materials I am proposing can help learners become more aware about themselves as L2 listeners, as well as better understand the cognitive, linguistic, and social demands of L2 listening. The first kind of activities – integrated experiential learning tasks – can be used with existing listening tasks in a language course, whereas the second – guided reflections on listening – can be carried out before or after listening tasks to help direct learners' efforts at planning, monitoring, and evaluating their listening and learning experiences. By using materials based on a principled and systematic metacognitive approach, we are enabling learners to comprehend listening texts more effectively while at the same time guiding them in taking greater control of their listening development.

Introduction

Picture this scene during a listening lesson: A teacher introduces the topic of a listening text and invites students to say what they know about it. She writes their ideas and unfamiliar words on the board. Next, she tells the students to read the instructions for the listening activity carefully to find out what information in the listening text to pay attention to. After this, the teacher plays the recording and the students listen attentively. They complete the activity by giving appropriate written responses (for example, choosing the correct options, filling in the blanks, sequencing information, drawing a diagram, jotting down notes). The teacher plays the recording again and instructs the students to confirm or change their responses. After that, she tells the class what the correct responses are, and the students find out "where they have gone wrong." Does this sound familiar to you? Well, that was what I used to do when delivering listening lessons. My emphasis was on the product or the outcome of my students' listening. What mattered most was how accurate or complete their responses were. In retrospect, even though I did many listening exercises, I was not *teaching* my students how to listen effectively. I was merely *testing* their comprehension without showing them how they could improve their listening.

I found out from my conversations with many language teachers that their listening lessons had the same features as the product-based lesson I have just described. Moreover, listening instruction in many language courses tends to focus almost exclusively on understanding the content of spoken texts, with little time given to teaching about the process of listening and how to listen. While many published materials provide support for listening, this is typically in the form of prelistening activities to generate factual or linguistic knowledge related to the listening texts. Postlistening activities also tend to focus on the product of listening; learners use what they have comprehended to complete another language activity (for example, using the notes they make to write a report or give a talk). Conspicuously absent in the key stages of a listening lesson are learning activities that directly develop learners' capacity to listen beyond the topic. I have argued elsewhere that we should help learners develop metacognitive knowledge and strategies because they need to learn *how* to listen and not just what to listen for (Goh 1997, 2005, 2008). In other words, listening lessons should include activities that teach learners explicitly how to listen effectively as part of their ongoing language development. Every lesson can be an opportunity for them to develop greater awareness about themselves as second language listeners, the nature and demands of listening, and strategies for facilitating comprehension and progress in listening.

I will refer to this type of process-based listening instruction as *metacognitive instruction in listening*, based on the theory of metacognition that is now widely acknowledged to be an indispensable part of human learning. "Metacognition" is often defined as awareness about one's processes in learning, and the appraisal and regulation of these processes. By "metacognitive instruction in listening," I mean pedagogical procedures that enable learners to increase their awareness about the listening process and at the same time develop effective skills for self-appraising and self-regulating listening comprehension and the progress of their overall listening development.

Theoretical principles

The principles of metacognitive instruction and the design of process-based instruction materials I propose are situated within a broad cognitive framework of learning. This framework has four key characteristics: (1) learning is an active, strategic, and constructive process; (2) it follows developmental trajectories in subject-matter domains; (3) it is guided by learners' introspective awareness and control of their mental processes; and (4) it is facilitated by social, collaborative settings that value self-directed student dialogue (Bruer 1998: 681). Metacognitive instruction in listening is based on the premise that learning to listen requires learners to be actively engaged in cognitive, affective, and social domains. Such an involvement will prepare learners to act strategically during listening as well as manage their overall listening development. In addition, by actively engaging in thinking and talking about their own listening, learners construct their understanding of what it takes to succeed as a second language listener. Metacognitive instruction also takes into account the trajectories or the developmental paths that language learners follow when learning to listen. Broadly speaking, listeners develop from controlled to automatized processing of spoken information while they build increasingly sophisticated neural networks for faster parallel processing of text and meaning (Hulstijn 2003; Segalowitz 2003). Although the degree of control and automaticity may vary according to different texts and tasks, it is reasonable to say that for unskilled listeners, even low-level processes such as perception and recognition of spoken input are still very much controlled or "effortful." Whereas perception of spoken input is largely automatized for competent listeners, weaker listeners have to consciously attend to aural signals before interpreting the meaning of the message effectively (Buck 2001; Goh 2000; Rost 2002).

Learners' introspective awareness and control of mental processes are central to metacognitive instruction. An individual's metacognition involves an awareness about mental processes when participating in a learning task and the self-regulation of such processes in order to achieve the goal of the task.

> 'Metacognition' refers to one's knowledge concerning one's own cognitive processes and products or anything related to them. ... Metacognition refers, among other things, to active monitoring and consequent regulation and orchestration of these processes in relation to the cognitive objects or data on which they bear, usually in the service of some concrete goal or objective. (Flavell 1976: 232)

Table 8.1 Types of metacognitive knowledge about listening

Person knowledge
Self-concepts and self-efficacy about listening
Specific listening problems, causes, and possible solutions
Task knowledge
Mental, affective, and social processes involved in listening
Skills (e.g., listening for details, gist) needed for completing listening tasks
Factors that influence listening (e.g., text, speaker)
Ways of improving listening outside class
Strategy knowledge about listening, for example, types of cognitive and metacognitive strategies

(to be continued)

(continued)

General and specific strategies to facilitate comprehension and cope with difficulties
Strategies appropriate for specific types of listening tasks
Ineffective strategies

With respect to awareness, Flavell made a distinction between metacognitive experience and metacognitive knowledge. Metacognitive experience is a feeling we have about our thinking, such as when we know we do not understand what we are listening to; metacognitive knowledge consists of our beliefs and knowledge about learning. Some metacognitive experiences are fleeting and do not invoke any particular knowledge pertaining to learning. For example, when we hear something, we may feel a momentary sense of puzzlement that we subsequently ignore.

Flavell distinguished three dimensions of this knowledge: person, task, and strategy. *Person* knowledge is knowledge about ourselves as learners, and includes our perceptions of our abilities and factors that affect the success or failure in our learning (for example age, aptitude, personality, gender, and learning style). Person knowledge also includes beliefs about oneself as a learner. *Task* knowledge is knowledge about the purpose, the demands, and the nature of learning tasks. It includes knowledge of the procedures involved in accomplishing these tasks. *Strategy* knowledge is knowledge about which strategies are useful for achieving learning goals. It also includes knowing which strategies that are currently being used should be avoided and eventually abandoned. Table 8.1 gives examples of how the three dimensions of metacognitive knowledge are applied to listening.

Metacognitive knowledge can lead an individual to select, evaluate, revise, or even abandon tasks, goals, and strategies; in other words, to self-regulate their learning and thinking. This executive aspect of cognition was elaborated upon by Brown (1978), who further distinguished three processes: planning, monitoring, and evaluating one's thinking. Table 8.2 shows how this is applied to learner listening at the levels of general listening development and specific listening tasks.

Table 8.2 Metacognitive strategies for self-regulation in learner listening

Planning	**A strategy for determining learning objectives and deciding the means by which the objectives can be achieved**
General listening development	Identify learning objectives for listening development Determine ways to achieve these objectives Set realistic short-term and long-term goals Seek opportunities for listening practice
Specific listening task	Preview main ideas before listening Rehearse language (e.g., pronunciation) necessary for the task Decide in advance which aspects of the text to concentrate on
Monitoring	**A strategy for checking the progress in the course of learning or carrying out a learning task**
General listening development	Consider progress against a set of predetermined criteria Determine how close it is to achieving short-term or long-term goals
Specific listening task	Check and see if the same mistakes are still being made Check understanding during listening Check the appropriateness and the accuracy of what is understood and compare understanding with new information Identify the source of difficulty
Evaluating	**A strategy for determining the success of the outcome of an attempt to learn or complete a learning task**
General listening development	Assess listening progress against a set of predetermined criteria Assess the effectiveness of learning and practice strategies Assess the appropriateness of learning goals and objectives
Specific listening task	Check the appropriateness and the accuracy of what has been understood Determine the effectiveness of strategies used for the task Assess overall comprehension of the text

Most researchers have adopted these twin concepts of metacognition to emphasize "(a) knowledge about cognitive states and processes and (b) control or executive aspects of metacognition" (Paris & Winograd 1990: 17). To use terms that many readers may now be familiar with, I will refer to the former as metacognitive *knowledge* and to the latter as metacognitive *strategy*. The emphasis on knowledge and strategies remains the cornerstone of a unified understanding of metacognition (Veenman *et al.* 2006). Wenden (1998) noted that language learners' metacognitive knowledge can influence their plan and objectives for learning as well as how they choose to evaluate their learning outcomes. With respect to listening, we may say that learners who understand the processes of 184 Christine Goh listening and believe they have the ability to reach their goals will be more willing to handle challenging listening tasks and set demanding goals for their listening development.

The fourth principle underpinning metacognitive instruction is the value of social and collaborative settings for learning. Although some metacognitive tasks require learners to work individually, there are many opportunities for them to cooperate with one another to share their knowledge, beliefs, and skills in learning to listen. Metacognitive instruction places a high premium on the importance of talk among learners and their co-construction of knowledge as they work together evaluating and applying their knowledge and experiences. The tasks also create positive interdependence among learners, leading each learner to play an active role not only in their own learning but also in the learning of their peers (Jacobs *et al.* 2002).

To sum up, the purpose of metacognitive instruction in listening is to help learners develop greater awareness about factors that influence their own listening and learning processes and learn strategies from their teachers and fellow-learners for self-directing these processes. (For a more in-depth discussion of the theoretical basis for metacognitive instruction, see Goh 2008.)

Evidence from research

Metacognitive instruction in listening has been shown to have several achievable goals and is particularly beneficial to weaker learners. First, it improves learner affect (confidence, motivation, and interest) in listening.

Second, it increases learners' knowledge about the listening process and about themselves as second language listeners. Third, it improves listening performance and strategy use for facilitating comprehension. Vandergrift (2003a) provided empirical evidence of the benefits in his study on a group of French as second language learners. The research made use of a lesson sequence that combined metacognitive awareness-raising activities with normal listening activities. The participants were guided in the use of listening strategies through a number of activities that included individual planning, pair discussions, and postlistening reflections. The learners reported that they were highly motivated by the approach and further examination showed an increase in the learners' metacognitive knowledge and engagement with learning to listen. Vandergrift (2003b) found that skilled listeners were "able to systematically orchestrate a cycle of cognitive and metacognitive strategies to arrive at a coherent mental representation of the text in memory" (p. 490).

The use of such closely guided tasks, which Vandergrift referred to as the "metacognitive cycle" (2004), was partially replicated by Liu and Goh (2006) among a group of Chinese tertiary-level ESL students. In addition to experiencing the metacognitive cycle in the main listening activities, the learners also participated in teacher-led process-based discussions (Goh 1997) and self-directed listening tasks (Goh 2002). The participants reported that pair and group discussions had helped them to understand the content better and that they also learned more strategies for tackling listening problems from working collaboratively with other students. Interestingly, positive written comments doubled after they experienced the integrated lesson sequence a second time, strongly suggesting that when the participants became more familiar with the new way of doing listening activities, they also became more convinced of its benefits.

Mareschal (2007) collected self-report data from a group of adult French learners who experienced a similar process-based, self-regulatory approach to listening instruction over nine weeks. The learners participated in a pedagogical cycle that involved writing down their responses and discussing them with one another. All sources of data concurred in indicating that students of different proficiency levels were positive about the instructional approach and at the same time experienced an increase in their metacognitive awareness, strategy use, confidence, and interest in listening. The learners who benefited most from such an approach were the low-proficiency students. In an in-depth study on joint listening activities among Japanese EFL learners, Cross (2009) provided empirical evidence on the positive effects of collaborative dialogue on heightening learners' metacognitive awareness about L2 listening, and specifically in the learners' awareness about features of strategy, comprehension, and text.

Metacognitive instruction can also benefit young learners. As children approach middle childhood and adolescence, they become increasingly adept at monitoring and evaluating their thinking, and acting strategically (Flavell, Miller, & Miller 1993). Vandergrift (2002) showed that when Grade 4 to 6 students completed reflection exercises, they became sensitized to listening processes and developed their metacognitive knowledge. Goh and Taib (2006) also found similar positive results among a group of 11- and 12-year-old ESL learners who experienced listening lessons that combined guided reflection and teacher-led process-based discussions. At the end of the period of metacognitive instruction, the children reported in their diaries a deeper understanding of the nature and the demands of listening, increased confidence in completing listening tasks, and better strategic knowledge for coping with comprehension difficulties. There was also an increase in the scores in the listening examinations of the majority of the students, particularly the weaker listeners, suggesting that metacognitive instruction may have had an impact on listening performance. In another study among 10- and 11-year-olds, Nathan (2008) reported the positive effects of collaborative learning during process-based listening activities. The learners showed an increase in their strategy knowledge with respect to planning and evaluation, and problem solving.

The above studies showed the positive impact metacognitive instruction can have on learners' knowledge and affect. But can metacognitive instruction also lead to better listening performance? Two recent studies investigated whether there was a causal relationship between metacognitive instruction and actual listening performance, and the results are encouraging for anyone considering metacognitive instruction. Zeng (2007) conducted a randomized intervention study among 60 Chinese college-level EFL learners majoring in a subject other than English. Thirty students in the experimental group received training in the use of selected listening strategies and process-based listening activities (discussions and listening diaries). The instruction was incorporated into normal listening-practice activities that the Chinese college students used when preparing for their national-level college listening examinations. At the end of seven weeks, this group of students showed a statistically significant improvement in their listening examination scores compared with the control group, which received the traditional, teacher-centered mode of listening instruction. Vandergrift and Tafaghodtari (in press) investigated the effects of using a lesson sequence that incorporated a "metacognitive cycle" on the listening performance of a group of French learners. The experimental group, which consisted of 60 learners, not only reported a higher degree of metacognitive awareness than the control group, but they also achieved significantly better results in their listening test.

Activities for metacognitive instruction

In this section, I present two types of activities to help learners engage with the process of listening. The first enables learners to experience cognitive and social-affective processes of listening comprehension while working on a listening-related task. I refer to this as *integrated experiential listening tasks*. In these tasks, metacognitive activities are integrated with normal listening activities in coursebooks or prepared by teachers. The second type directs learners' attention to specific aspects of their learning when they reflect on their listening performance and overall progress, and is referred to as *guided reflections on listening*. Figure 8.1 shows the different activities belonging to these two types of metacognitive instruction. Although there are some minor overlaps in some activities, the activities have been differentiated according to their primary instructional objectives and mode of delivery.

These metacognitive instructional activities can be woven into a lesson sequence during formal instruction time. Many of these can be adapted for use with prescribed published materials, to be included at key stages of a listening

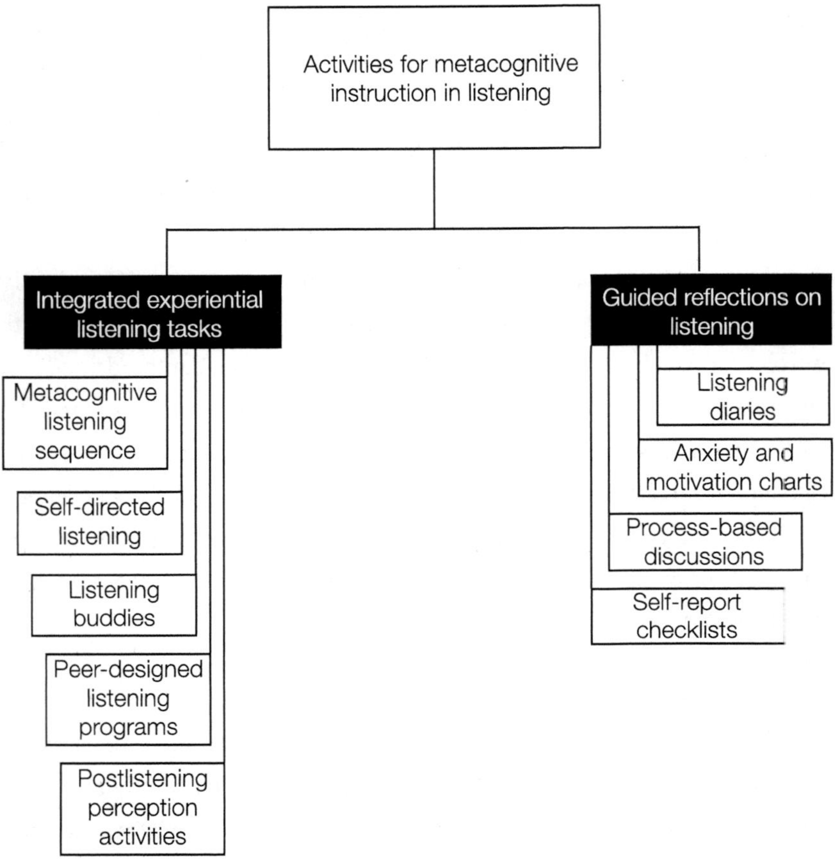

Figure 8.1 Activities for metacognitive instruction in listening

lesson sequence, i.e., prelistening, postlistening, and during listening. Others can be carried out as separate reflection or enrichment activities when learners do extensive listening with recorded or downloaded materials on their own.

Integrated experiential listening tasks

It is true that we cannot manipulate learners' mental processes while they are listening, but there are activities that develop and strengthen their ability to control these processes for themselves. The purpose of integrated experiential tasks is to help learners bring to their conscious attention what these processes are and show them how they can regulate and manage the processes better in order to meet comprehension goals. As the name suggests, the activities are integrated with actual listening input and experience. This is done by weaving awareness-raising and strategy-training tasks into listening lessons, listening practice, and enrichment activities. As learners carry out these activities, they share their observations and comments with one another. Some activities also require learners to cooperate on small listening projects to produce tangible outcomes. The key characteristic of integrated experiential tasks is that they combine the teaching-of-listening-as-product approach with the metacognitive approach of teaching listening as process. In other words, learners are encouraged to arrive at an understanding of what they hear but are at the same time supported by activities that enable them to discover and use listening strategies as well as understand the nature of second language listening. Learners not only become more aware of themselves, the nature and demands of various listening tasks and texts, and effective strategy use; they are also explicitly socialized into the effective mental and social behaviors of skilled listeners. Research has shown that successful listeners use appropriate cognitive, metacognitive, and socio-affective strategies. In particular, skilled listeners use comparatively more metacognitive strategies for monitoring and evaluating their comprehension, and they adopt an approach that orchestrates these processes effectively to achieve comprehension goals.

Metacognitive listening sequence

The metacognitive listening sequence creates a lesson where learners are guided at specific stages to orchestrate metacognitive processes underlying successful listening. It integrates awareness-raising activities with normal listening input and comprehension activities that learners do in class. Each sequence of lessons is aimed at teaching learners how to use listening strategies through teacher scaffolding and modeling, peer collaboration, and individual practice. This procedure is based on the integrated pedagogical model for teaching listening proposed by Vandergrift (2004, 2007). The model provides opportunities for learners to experience three verification phases of a text. In so doing, learners deepen their understanding of the content and become more familiar with the metacognitive processes involved. The model focuses on the use of the following metacognitive strategies: planning, predicting, monitoring, evaluation, directed attention, selective attention, and problem solving. A key feature of Vandergrift's model is the structure it offers for guiding learners through collaborative learning activities. Learners who experience these activities may gradually increase their autonomy and control over their listening processes.

Vandergrift's model was adapted by Mareschal (2007) to include the use of specially designed listening notebooks to support the learners' listening process during various listening stages. The purpose of the listening notebooks is to offer learners visual support (in the form of notes) to aid their listening and memory during the listening exercises, and to provide a written record of some of the processes they engage in during listening. As a result, the learners will have tangible evidence of their listening process, which can allow them to further reflect on and review the strategies they have used. Liu and Goh (2006) also adapted Vandergrift's (2004) model to include peer dialogue in process-based discussions and personal evaluation at the reflection stage. Instead of writing goals for the next listening activity as proposed in the model (thus creating the beginning of a new cycle), students ended the sequence by evaluating the listening lesson and wrote about their perceptions of the task and views on insights gained from the discussions. They also evaluated the strategies they had used to understand the text.

Based on Vandergrift's model and its variations, I describe here a set of integrated sequence-of-lesson procedures that includes further planning activities and active modeling by teachers of some processes:

1. *Planning*: In pairs, students state what their goal is. They discuss what they know about the topic and predict the information and words/phrases that they might hear. They write these down in the target language as well as their first language. They also predict the difficulties they might encounter and select appropriate strategies for coping with these problems.
2. *Listening 1*: As they are listening to the text, students underline or circle words or phrases (including first language equivalents) that they have predicted correctly. They also write down new information they hear.

3. *Pair process-based discussion*: In pairs, students compare what they have understood so far and explain the strategies used for arriving at their understanding. They identify the parts that cause confusion and disagreement and make a note of the parts of the text that require special attention in the second listen. At the same time, the teacher models thinking-aloud of how he/she would listen selectively to problematic parts of the text.
4. *Listening 2*: Students listen to those parts that have caused confusion or disagreement and make notes on any new information they hear.
5. *Whole-class process-based discussion*: The teacher leads a discussion to confirm comprehension before discussing with students the strategies that they reported using. Based on what is discussed, he/she models the use of a selected strategy or strategies for achieving comprehension goals.
6. *Listening 3*: Students who have not used strategies successfully in steps 2 and 4 can now practice the use of a strategy or a combination of strategies (modeled by the teacher) with the same input.
7. *Script-sound recognition*: Students are provided with a transcript of the recording so that they can match sounds to print and vice versa for difficult words or phrases. The teacher elicits these lexical items and demonstrates the pronunciation or phonological modifications found in the listening text.
8. *Personal reflection*: Students make short entries into their listening diaries about the lesson. They note down what they have learned and understood from the listening text. They also reflect on the guided listening process, insights gained from the various discussions, as well as evaluating the effectiveness of strategies they used to understand the listening text.

A distinguishing feature of this set of procedures is the availability of just-in-time input from teachers on strategy use and the opportunity to practice the use of all three types of strategies – cognitive, metacognitive, and social-affective – after the learners have attempted to process the input on their own. It addresses a limitation noted by Chamot (1995) of strategy-training programs that do not take into consideration learners' existing strategy knowledge. As some listening strategies are transferable from first language to second language use (Mendelsohn 1995), learners may not see the need to undergo strategy training. However, when learners are actually listening to different kinds of input, they may experience difficulties in employing strategies, or may fail to achieve their comprehension goals in spite of using certain familiar strategies. The just-in-time strategies modeled by teachers will help learners to explore strategy use in a contextualized manner. Learners who fail to use appropriate strategies in earlier attempts will get another opportunity to practice using these strategies.

Self-directed listening

This technique can be used to help learners use listening strategies when they are practicing listening on their own. Students respond to a set of prompts before and after a listening task to guide them in their prelistening preparation, evaluating their performance and planning their strategy use for future listening (see Figure 8.2). The self-directed listening/viewing guide is based on the three key components of self-regulation: planning, monitoring, and evaluation. An appropriate time to carry out self-directed listening is after the students have received some prior instruction on listening strategies through one of the techniques suggested in this chapter. Liu and Goh (2006) found that when students were asked to direct their own listening after they had learned something about strategy use, their independent use of cognitive strategies, particularly inferencing strategies and contextualization strategies, increased substantially. Learners also reported using confidence-building strategies to overcome anxiety, think positively, and motivate themselves to persist with their listening tasks even though the tasks were challenging. To help learners experience the full benefits of the directed-listening/viewing guide, it may be necessary for the teacher to first model how to use the list of prompts, as Tan (2007) did with her Vietnamese EFL learners, showing them how to self-regulate their listening practice when using Web-based resources.

A. Setting my listening goal
Why am I listening to/viewing this recording?
What do I hope to achieve?
How many times should I listen to/watch this recording? Why?

↓

B. Preparing to listen
What do I know about this topic?
What type of information can I expect to hear (and view)?
What words can I expect to hear? (Use a dictionary, if necessary.)
What difficulties can I expect?
What strategies should I use when I encounter these difficulties?

↓

C. Evaluating my listening
Am I satisfied with what I have understood? Why?
Was I able to make use of my prior knowledge about the topic?
What difficulties did I face? Were my strategies useful?

Figure 8.2 A self-directed listening/viewing guide

She also found that the students demonstrated a significantly higher degree of metacognitive awareness in planning/evaluation and problem solving.

Listening buddies

This activity has some similarities with self-directed listening/viewing in that it encourages learners to carry out guided listening practice. The difference is that learners now work in pairs or with a "buddy" to plan their own listening practice by selecting from their choice of resources: radio/TV broadcasts, videos and movies, podcasts and "live" talks. They are advised to spend 45-60 minutes each time for each session. Here is a simple procedure they follow:

1. Discuss and submit a listening plan outlining schedules, selected listening/viewing programs, equipment (e.g., MP3 player, computer), and strategies for comprehension.
2. Report two listening events each week in writing on a weekly worksheet or as oral summaries in class.

This activity may be carried out biweekly or monthly depending on the program and learner needs. Figure 8.3 outlines the structure for this personalized listening program. Apart from the benefits of improving strategy use and metacognitive knowledge, students also learn to work cooperatively to select programs and ways of practice that suit their interests and learning styles. Because of the freedom of choice, this activity can motivate many learners to carry out extensive listening outside class. By working with a partner, they can also get mutual support and encouragement.

Peer-designed listening tasks

The idea of a group listening project which has a metacognitive dimension was introduced by Liu (2005) in an intensive English program for Chinese ESL learners in Singapore. Here is an outline of the procedure:

1. Students must work in groups of four to develop or select an 8-10-minute audio or video program.
2. They plan listening activities for the whole class based on the program. They have to make a number of important decisions such as the kinds of listening material to use, the types of listening skill they want their classmates to practice, strategies for motivating them to listen and participate, and the problems that they might encounter.

By temporarily taking on the role of a teacher, the learners can develop greater collective metacognitive knowledge about second/foreign-language listening. More importantly, according to Liu (2005), the presentation of the projects can give teachers valuable insights into what learners understand about listening comprehension, and that "listening is more than receiving information and completing exercises" (p. 74).

Our personal listening program

Listening buddies: ____________________ and ____________________
Week ____________________
(Write your responses on separate sheets of paper)

Session 1
Listening material: ____________________
Type of text:
Source:
Equipment:
Date:
Time:
Other considerations, if any:

Our listening goal

1. Why are we listening to/viewing this recording?
2. What do we hope to achieve?
3. How many times should we listen to/watch this recording? Why?

Our listening plan

1. What do we know about this topic?
2. What type of information can we expect to hear (and see)?
3. What words can we expect to hear? (Use a dictionary, if necessary.)
4. What difficulties can we expect?
5. What strategies should we use when we encounter these difficulties?

Our listening report

1. Why did we choose this recording/listening text?
2. What was the most interesting thing about it?
3. Are we satisfied with what we have understood? Why?
4. Were we able to make use of our prior knowledge about the topic?
5. What difficulties did we face? Were our strategies useful?
6. What did we discuss after our listening?
7. What did we agree or disagree about?
8. What have we learned from each other about listening?

Figure 8.3 Outline for a personalized listening program for listening buddies

Postlistening perception activities

Language learners often complain that native speakers speak too fast. Most of the time, this perception of speed is really due to the students' inability to recognize words and phonological modifications in streams of speech. Bottom-up processing, which involves perception of words and lexical segmentation, is an important factor in successful listening, and it is something that all listening lessons should address (Field 2003). A common technique used in the 1960s, which is still found in some classrooms today, is the use of minimal-pair drills or sentence-level perception exercises. These activities, however, can be decontextualized, dry, and repetitive.

To make learning relevant to learners' needs, perception activities are best done after they have completed some listening tasks involving a selected text. Postlistening perception activities enable students to notice sounds in connected speech when they are not under pressure to process what they hear and bearing a heavy cognitive load. One of my former ESL students from China did not recognize the word "hostel" in her listening text. When we carried out the postlistening perception activity, she realized that it was a word she actually knew and that she had not recognized it because of the way she pronounced "hostel" with the same word stress pattern as "hotel." By noticing sounds and phonological rules, learners will increase their task knowledge, namely the nature of spoken English and the demands of listening in another language. This knowledge is particularly important for beginning learners because the perception phase of their comprehension has not been automatized, and many still depend largely on bottom-up processing as a way of "getting into" the message. Through repeated exposure to unfamiliar sounds and noticing how some sounds are changed in speech, they will learn to cope better with these phonological features and improve their perceptual processing.

Features that learners should familiarize themselves with are weak forms, rhythm, word stress, prominence, tone, pauses, and meaning segments. Here are some steps to follow to increase learners' awareness about phonological factors:

1. Select a segment of a recording that your students work with during the listening task. If the text is very short, use the entire text.
2. Identify one or two phonological features that you want to highlight. (This may have to be modified during class depending on the type of problems your students report with their listening.)

3. Play the segment and ask the students to transcribe it or write down prominent words they hear.
4. Give each student a copy of the transcript or project it onto a screen. Highlight phonological features that contributed to listening difficulties.
5. Allow students to listen to the segment a few times, pointing out the way particular sounds or words have been modified in the utterances. An alternative technique is to let your students listen to the entire recording with a transcript. Tell them to notice how certain words are pronounced and listen out for those parts that they cannot hear accurately during the task. Ask them to explain why they have this problem. (It is useful to teach students names of the feature, e.g., word stress, rise in tone, etc.)

Guided reflections on listening

Activities that involve guided reflections encourage learners to attend to implicit processes in listening and help them make their knowledge of listening explicit. They also encourage learners to co-construct some of this knowledge when they share their reflections with one another. There are limitations, however. Learners may find it monotonous if they have to do the same reflection task each week. To help maintain the relevance of reflective tasks, we can vary the reflection guides and the way they are used during the listening course. By doing this, we ensure that learners' insights are fresh, focused, and relevant. Guided reflections are not necessarily retrospective. They can also encourage forward planning, which is an important part of self-regulation and the management of learning. It involves thinking back to learning that has taken place and thinking ahead to how learning can be facilitated. The set of materials presented here can be used at different points of the language course – at the start, during midterm review, and at the end – or used regularly with some variations.

Listening diaries

Listening diaries have been used successfully in helping learners attend to what they implicitly know about their own listening abilities, behaviors, problems, and strengths (Goh 1997; Liu 2005; Sinanu *et al.* 2007). There are different ways in which learners can reflect about their learning in their diaries. They can

a) Focus: Weekly listening activities in and out of class

1. What was the listening event? (for example, TV news broadcasts, radio broadcasts, films, conversations with English speakers, explanations by lecturers)
2. How much of it did you understand?
3. What did you do to understand as much of it as possible?
4. How did you feel about what you did?
5. Are you pleased with the result?
6. What do you plan to do to practice your listening this week?

(based on Goh 2002)

---

b) Focus: Specific lessons in two weeks

(i) *Performance on skills*

Complete the table by using the symbols[1] provided.

√ = Yes, I feel I have learned the skill (Alternative: ☺)

x = No, I have not learned the skill very well (Alternative: ☹)

? = Not sure, I am not sure I have learned the skill (Alternative: 😐)

Skills for weeks 1 & 2	**My performance**
Asking for repetition and explanation/clarification	
Listening for descriptions of past events	
Recognizing words of time order	
Distinguishing styles of requests	
Listening for positive and negative opinions	
Inferring speakers' attitudes from their tone of voice	

(ii) *Specific questions for weeks1 and 2*[2]

1. Describe your previous experiences in learning to listen.
2. Do you think the lessons you've had so far are helpful? Compare them with your previous experiences. (based on Liu 2005)

---

c) Focus: Weekly listening lessons in class

You will be given 10 minutes at the end of the class to write about:

1. the listening comprehension activities done in each class
2. your feelings toward the class today and what makes you feel that way
3. the problems encountered
4. your plans to overcome similar problems in future

(based on Sinanu *et al.* 2007)

Figure 8.4 Variations in focus and prompts of listening diaries

---

[1] This can be done with small children by using smiley icons and simplifying the way skills are described.

[2] The question(s) are changed every two weeks.

respond to a set of generic prompts (see part a in Figure 8.4), evaluate specific listening skills they are taught each week or biweekly (see part b in Figure 8.4), or write about some specific points about the lesson immediately when it is over (see part c in Figure 8.4). All these templates have one thing in common – the guiding questions direct learners' attention to three dimensions of metacognitive knowledge. Learners are invited to reflect on specific listening events: person knowledge (What problems did I experience? How did I respond to the task?), task knowledge (What were the demands of the task?), and strategy knowledge (What special ways of listening did I do to help me understand? Which strategies were useful/not useful? How can I improve my comprehension when I have to listen again in similar situations or to similar kinds of text?).

Another mode of open-ended reflections is the spoken word – learners can talk aloud and record their speech instead of writing about their thoughts.

Anxiety and motivation charts

Besides responding to the mainly task- and strategy-focused prompts, you can also get learners to reflect on specific aspects of their person knowledge, such as motivation and anxiety. Research has shown that anxiety can be a great setback for many second language listeners (Arnold 2000; Lynch 1997; Vogely 1999), and that motivation is also positively correlated with metacognitive awareness about listening (Vandergrift 2005). One way in which language learners have been asked to report on their perceived motivation and anxiety levels is through the drawing of graphs and charts. Diagrams are not only a creative way for learners to reflect and report their person knowledge, but they can also present information in a concise and visually attractive manner for learners who may not enjoy writing. See Figure 8.5 for an example of a listening anxiety graph, which offers a way by which learners can track their changes in anxiety levels according to the type of listening tasks they do in and out of class. To help children explore their feelings of anxiety, you can also use symbols such as smiley faces, which they can attach to a chart.

Process-based discussions

Process-based discussions are discussions that are centered on the theme of learning to listen in another language rather than on the listening text and

Date	What I did
May 3	Watched a movie in class
May 10	Made a telephone call to the department secretary
May 17	Listened to a lecture and took notes in class
May 24	Discussed a listening plan with my listening buddy
May 31	Listened to a lecture and took notes in class
June 7	Had a long chat in the café with classmates
June 14	Did a creative dictation activity in class
June 21	Midterm listening and note-taking exam

Figure 8.5 A listening anxiety graph and a record of listening events

accurate answers for listening tasks (Goh 1997). These discussions can be conducted as separate lessons where learners can share the beliefs or strategies that they mention in their diaries or other postlistening activities. For the former, teachers can use specific discussion questions, such as "What I do to understand spoken English" and "How I practice my listening outside class." When conducted as postlistening activities, the focus can be on specific strategies that the students used during the listening task. One way to do this is to include a short time for individual reflection before the group or class discussion, as Goh and Taib (2006) did in their intervention study with primary school English language learners.

Process-based discussions can also be carried out at the prelistening phase to generate task and strategy knowledge relevant to the particular listening activity. For example, after learners have completed a short prelistening activity based on the contents in the listening materials, you can ask them to identify skills and strategies that are essential for the task they are about to do. In addition, you can guide them in predicting challenges they might face and suggesting ways of dealing with them. You can also explain the reasons for the content-specific prelistening activities you have used. This can help learners notice the planning strategy that you have incorporated into the listening task for them. Some of the prompts presented for self-directed listening can be used for group discussion.

Self-report checklists

A limitation of using open-ended reflection guides such as listening diaries is that some learners may not have learned to observe their learning beyond one or two familiar perspectives. As a result of their limited metacognitive knowledge, the scope of their reflection can be narrow and their comments repetitive. This is where self-report checklists play an important complementary role in guided reflections. A list of carefully preselected items of metacognitive knowledge is a handy tool for directing learners' thinking to specific areas of listening. They can be used for a number of purposes, such as general self-appraisal of listening or focused reflection on specific listening tasks, and are equally useful to adult and young learners.

A set of checklists that has been used both for research and classroom teaching is the Metacognitive Awareness Listening Questionnaire, or MALQ for short (see Vandergrift *et al.* 2006). From a research perspective, it is an instrument with psychometric properties, uncovering perceived use of strategies during listening. As a teaching tool, it can be used as a yardstick for learner self-appraisal to identify current levels of metacognitive awareness and strategy use, or to chart metacognitive development when used at specific points in a listening program. The MALQ can also be used as an awareness-raising tool to influence learners' strategy use in listening. This 21-item questionnaire comprises five distinct factors related to the four listening strategies – planning and evaluation, problem solving, mental translation, and directed attention – and person knowledge. Learners can respond to the items by selecting a point in the Likert scale. (See Goh 2008 for an adapted classroom version of the MALQ.)

It is important to keep checklists relatively simple and short, especially when they are aimed at younger learners. Although having a relatively short checklist may mean that not every item you think is important can be included, it will make the checklist easy to read and respond to. (Some learners may lose interest when they find they have a lot to read!) To allow learners space to include other observations, you can complement checklists with other open-ended reflection activities discussed in this section. Figure 8.6 shows items that can be included in postlistening evaluation checklists and that are suitable to be used even with young learners.

Thinking about what you did during your listening lesson

You have just finished doing a listening comprehension activity. Read the statements below and think about how you listened. Draw a smiley face next to the statements to show what you think.

Yes ☺ No ☹ Only a little 😐

a) Listening to my teacher or a recording

1. Before I began listening, my teacher told me what the listening text was going to be about.
   That helped me to
   - guess what I am going to hear _______
   - listen out for the important words _______
   - understand the meaning of the text better ________
2. While I was listening, I paid very close attention to the passage. _______
3. When I couldn't hear clearly, I wanted to ask my teacher to
   - repeat part(s) of the passage _______
   - speak more slowly ________
   - to explain the word(s) I didn't understand _______

b) Listening to my classmates

1. Before we started the speaking-listening activity, I knew what we had to talk about.
   That helped me to
   - guess what I am going to hear _______
   - listen out for the important words ______
   - understand my classmates' meaning better ________
2. While I was listening, I paid very close attention to what my classmates were saying. ____
3. When I couldn't hear clearly, I asked my classmates to
   - repeat part(s) of the passage _______
   - speak more slowly ______
   - to explain the word(s) I didn't understand _______

My reflection notes: ____

____

____

Figure 8.6 Postlistening evaluation checklist

Principled design of metacognitive instructional materials

The purpose of metacognitive instruction is to provide different kinds of scaffolding so that learners can experience the processes of listening and become aware of factors that influence overall comprehension and listening development. It is important to apply a sound cognitive framework for learning to ensure that activities and materials are designed systematically and in a principled manner. Without a metacognitive framework, process-based listening instruction will at best be intuitive. The framework I have proposed identifies key components of self-appraisal and self-regulation in learning, and when applied to learning materials can help students attend to selected aspects of learning each time. Careful planning and design of materials will ensure that all important aspects of learning are covered. The key items of metacognitive knowledge and strategies are summarized in Figure 8.7, which also gives examples of prompts that can be used in both integrated experiential tasks and guided reflections on listening.

Conclusion

Metacognitive instruction in listening has produced many encouraging results. Not only is an increase in confidence, motivation, and interest consistently reported among learners who have experienced this process-based approach, recent studies have also provided preliminary evidence of its positive effects on improving listening performance. Clearly, more needs to be done by way of research to strengthen the current findings. Nevertheless, verbal reports from participants involved in process-based learning of listening demonstrated the enormous benefits they had derived from it. Informal interviews I conducted with teachers also showed a high level of interest among them. Before they learned about metacognitive instruction, these teachers had been delivering the lessons in much the same way as the scenario I described at the start of this article. Many were encouraged by the way their students had responded to the metacognitive activities they used and were themselves motivated to continue to teach this way, as a result. As one teacher put it, "I never knew there was so much more to teaching listening." Many of them also saw the output of the various metacognitive activities as important materials that students can include

	Examples of prompts
Metacognitive knowledge (self-appraisal)	*Person knowledge* What listening problems do I commonly face? What are my strengths when listening to spoken English? Do I think I'm a good listener? Why do I say that? *Task knowledge* What makes listening to a lecture/conversations difficult? What must I do when trying to understand someone who speaks fast? I did an activity today before listening to the passage. What does it tell me about listening? *Strategy knowledge* What are some good strategies I can use when watching a movie in English? What strategies do I need when making a telephone call?
Metacognitive strategies (self-regulation)	*Planning* What do I plan to do to improve my listening comprehension this term? I am going to listen to a lecture on climate change. What should I do to help me understand the explanations given? *Monitoring* Does what I hear match my knowledge of the topic or the person? Am I making progress in my listening? What are some setbacks I'm facing right now? *Evaluating* I used some strategies to help me understand the listening passage. Are they useful? Should I use them again? Are my goals for developing listening this term realistic?

Figure 8.7 Prompts for raising metacognitive awareness in listening

in their learning portfolios, or more specifically, listening portfolios. Buck (1995) notes that it is not possible for teachers to manipulate learners' listening processes for them. He adds, however, that teachers can facilitate learners' listening development if we understand the nature of listening comprehension and can sensitize learners to important aspects of it, while at the same time providing them with "optimum" practice. In this chapter, I have tried to make a case for metacognitive instruction as a theoretically sound and workable method that can contribute to the type of optimum listening practice that all language teachers aim for.

Discussion questions and tasks

Reflection

1. What do you think is the difference between teaching listening and testing listening?
2. Refer to the examples given in the table on metacognitive knowledge about second language listening. What other examples can you add to each type of knowledge: person, task, and strategy?
3. Listen to a piece of spoken text in a language you are not very familiar with. Describe in writing some of the problems that you face. Compare your notes with another person and suggest what you can do to improve your listening in that language.
4. What do you think are some challenges to using process-based materials as suggested in this chapter? Suggest some possible ways of addressing these challenges.

Evaluation

5. Select three metacognitive listening tasks suggested in the chapter. Discuss their relative strengths and limitations when applied to a group of learners of your choice.

Adaptation/Design

6. Select a listening activity from a published coursebook. Using one of the integrated experiential listening tasks, plan a lesson (or a series of lessons) to improve learners' metacognitive knowledge and/or strategy use.

Acknowledgments

I am grateful to Liu Xuelin for sharing with me her ideas on cooperative listening in Listening Buddies, and to Jasmine Pang for her ideas on the postlistening evaluation checklist for young learners.

References

Arnold, J. (2000). Seeing through listening comprehension exam anxiety. *TESOL Quarterly* 34: 777-86.

Brown, A. L. (1978). Knowing when, where, and how to remember: A problem of metacognition. In R. Glaser (ed.). *Advances in instructional psychology* (Vol. 1). Hillsdale, NJ: Lawrence Erlbaum Associates, pp. 77-165.

Bruer, J. T. (1998). Education. In W. Brechtel & G. Graham (eds.). *A companion to cognitive science*. Malden, MA: Blackwell Publishers Ltd., pp. 681-90.

Buck, G. (1995). How to become a good listening teacher. In D. Mendelsohn & J. Rubin (eds.). *A guide for the teaching of second language listening*. San Diego: Dominie Press, pp. 113-28.

Buck, G. (2001). *Assessing listening*. Cambridge: Cambridge University Press.

Chamot, A. U. (1995). Learning strategies and listening comprehension. In D. Mendelsohn & J. Rubin (eds.). *A guide for the teaching of second language listening*. San Diego: Dominie Press.

Cross, J. (2009). The development of metacognition of L2 listening in joint activity. Unpublished PhD dissertation, University of Melbourne, Australia.

Field, J. (2003). Promoting perception: Lexical segmentation in second language listening. *ELT Journal* 57: 325-34.

Flavell, J. H. (1976). Metacognitive aspects of problem solving. In L. B. Resnick. (ed.). *The nature of intelligence*. Hillsdale, NJ: Lawrence Erlbaum Associates, pp. 231-5.

Flavell, J. H., Miller, P. H., & Miller, S. A. (1993). *Cognitive development* (3rd ed.). Englewood Cliffs, NJ: Prentice Hall.

Goh, C. (1997). Metacognitive awareness and second language listeners. *ELT Journal* 51(4): 361-9.

Goh, C. (2000). A cognitive perspective on language learners' listening comprehension problems. *System* 28: 55-75.

Goh, C. (2002). *Teaching listening in the language classroom*. Singapore: SEAMEO Regional Language Centre.

Goh, C. (2005). Second language listening expertise. In K. Johnson (ed.). *Expertise in second language learning and teaching*. Oxford: Palgrave Macmillan, pp. 64-84.

Goh, C. (2008). Metacognitive instruction for second language listening development: Theory, practice and research implications. *RELC Journal* 40: 2.

Goh, C., & Taib, Y. (2006). Metacognitive instruction in listening for young learners. *ELT Journal* 60(3): 222-32.

Hulstijn, J. H. (2003). Connectionist models of language processing and the training of listening skills with the aid of multimedia software. *Computer Assisted Language Learning* 16: 413-25.

Jacobs, G. M., Power, M. A., & Loh, W. I. (2002). *The teacher's sourcebook for cooperative learning: Practical techniques, basic principles, and frequently asked questions*. Thousand Oaks, CA: Corwin Press.

Liu, X. L. (2005). Teaching academic listening. In P. F. Kwah & M. Vallance (eds.). *Teaching ESL to Chinese learners*. Singapore: Pearson Longman.

Liu, X. L., & Goh, C. (2006). Improving second language listening: Awareness and involvement. In T. S. C. Farrell (ed.). *Language teacher research in Asia*. Alexandria, VA: TESOL, pp. 91-106.

Lynch, T. (1997). Life in the slow lane: Observations of a limited L2 listener. *System* 25(3): 385-98.

Mareschal, C. (2007). Student perceptions of a self-regulatory approach to second language listening comprehension development. Unpublished PhD thesis, University of Ottawa, Canada.

Mendelsohn, D. (1995). Applying learning strategies in the second/foreign language listening comprehension lesson. In D. Mendelsohn & J. Rubin (eds.). *A guide for the teaching of second language listening*. San Diego: Dominie Press, pp. 132-50.

Nathan, P. (2008). Collaboration and metacognitive awareness in second language listening comprehension. Unpublished MA thesis, National Institute of Education, Nanyang Technological University, Singapore.

Paris, S. G., & Winograd, P. (1990). How metacognition can promote academic learning and instruction. In B. F. Jones & L. Idol (eds.). *Dimensions of thinking and cognitive instruction*. Hillsdale, NJ: Lawrence Erlbaum Associates, pp. 15-51.

Rost, M. (2002). *Teaching and researching listening*. London: Longman.

Segalowitz, N. (2003). Automaticity and second language. In C. Doughty & M. Long (eds.). *The handbook of second language acquisition*. Malden, MA: Blackwell Publishing, pp. 382-408.

Sinanu, F. L., Palupi, V. U., Anggraeni, A., & Hastuti, G. (2007). Listening strategies awareness: A diary study in listening comprehension classrooms. Paper presented at the 42nd RELC International Seminar, April 23-25, 2007, Singapore.

Tan, M. H. (2007). Developing metacognitive awareness of listening comprehension using information technology. MMM800 Critical Inquiry paper, National Institute of Education, Singapore.

Vandergrift, L. (2002). It was nice to see that our predictions were right: Developing metacognition in L2 listening comprehension. *Canadian Modern Language Review* 58: 555-75.

Vandergrift, L. (2003a). From prediction through reflection: Guiding students through the process of L2 listening. *Canadian Modern Language Review* 59(3): 425-40.

Vandergrift, L. (2003b). Orchestrating strategy use: Toward a model of the skilled second language listener. *Language Learning* 53: 463-96.

Vandergrift, L. (2004). Learning to listen or listening to learn? *Annual Review of Applied Linguistics* 24: 3-25.

Vandergrift, L. (2005). Relationships among motivation orientations, metacognitive awareness and proficiency in L2 listening. *Applied Linguistics* 26: 70-89.

Vandergrift, L. (2007). Listening comprehension in L2/FL learning. *Language Teaching* 40(3): 191-210.

Vandergrift, L., Goh, C., Mareschal, C., & Tafaghodatari, M. H. (2006). The Metacognitive Awareness Listening Questionnaire (MALQ): Development and validation. *Language Learning* 56: 431-62.

Vandergrift, L., & Tafaghodtari, M. (2010). Teaching L2 learners how to listen does make a difference: An empirical study. *Language Learning* 60(2): 470-97.

Veenman, M. V. J., Van Hout-Wolters, B. H. A. A., & Afflerbach, P. (2006). Metacognition and learning: Conceptual and methodological considerations. *Metacognition Learning* 1: 3-14.

Vogely, A. (1999).Addressing listening comprehension anxiety. In J. D. Young (ed.). *Affect in foreign language and second language learning: A practical guide to creating a low-anxiety classroom atmosphere*. New York: McGraw-Hill.

Wenden, A. (1998). Metacognitive knowledge and language learning. *Applied Linguistics* 19: 515-37.

Zeng, Y. (2007). Metacognitive instruction in listening: A study of Chinese non-English major undergraduates. Unpublished MA thesis, National Institute of Education, Nanyang Technological University, Singapore.

9

Materials to develop the speaking skill

Rebecca Hughes

Summary

This chapter gives an overview of the nature of spoken language and relates this to the processes of choosing or designing materials to develop the speaking skill. The complexities of speech production, how speaking is closely linked to identity, emotional states, and affective factors, and the ways in which it differs from written language, are analyzed. In particular, the difference between simple measures of proficiency in speaking versus the ability to handle spoken language in context are discussed. The reader's attention is brought to key issues in this area: the need to match task aims to realistic fluency and production levels; the ambiguity in some materials as to whether the learning objective is truly appropriate for the spoken form; the need for cultural sensitivity and engaging learner interest in an inclusive way in choosing samples of real speech data to work with; and the need for materials to involve awareness raising about the nature of spoken language. In addition, the status of speech in language theory and approaches to assessment are touched on. The chapter ends with three samples of materials for teaching speaking, which look at awareness raising with a focus on backchannel, understanding speech rhythm, and seminar skills.

Introduction

> The orderly distribution of opportunities to participate in social interaction is one of the most fundamental preconditions for viable social organization. For humans, conversation and other more specialized or context-specific forms of talk-in-interaction ... are species-distinctive embodiments of this primordial site of sociality. (Schegloff 2000: 1)

The most effective way to learn to speak a language is to fall in love with the language, or with a speaker of the language. This comment is not as strange as it may seem, and it is not one I would consider beginning a chapter on materials for teaching the skills of writing, reading, or listening with. Speaking is a unique form of communication which is the basis of all human relationships and the primary channel for the projection and development of individual identity. Particularly in literate societies and cultures, its distinctive characteristics are sometimes overlooked.

First, more than the other language skills, speech production is intimately tied up with questions relating to affect and identity. How you sound, how well you are understood, and how you project yourself in a range of discourse contexts are inextricably linked in ways that do not hold for the written mode. Second, whereas a text can be edited and retracted, reread, analyzed, and objectified from "outside," spontaneous spoken discourse unites speaker and content at the time of production. There is considerably less authorial distance possible in spoken mode. Furthermore, when something has been said, unless it has been recorded mechanically or digitally for posterity, the identical utterance can never be returned to. We can repeat and quote and have conventions of voice and gesture to mark this, but speaking, unlike writing, can only be reformulated. It can never be erased or struck out entirely and a polished final draft presented to the recipient. This makes speaking something of a "high-risk" business for all speakers, and particularly for the second language user. Reluctance to speak out in the new language can be caused by many factors other than abstract language proficiency.

Third, to become a proficient user in spontaneous conversational settings, a second language user needs to acquire an array of cultural and pragmatic skills and knowledge alongside the basic building blocks of vocabulary and grammar, fluency, and pronunciation. Although this is true for all forms of language (indeed, to write well it is assumed that you also need to have awareness of your readers' expectations and cultural norms holding for the genre), it is particularly true of speaking.

Finally, the demands of speech processing in real-time conversational and other speaking contexts place tremendous cognitive load on the second language user as they attempt to draw together the various elements from lexical retrieval to syntactic processing to the motor skills of speech articulation. These demands are high even in contexts where an element of planning is possible, such as lecture format. In the high-speed, high-stakes environment of natural conversational settings, the challenge is particularly great. An excellent overview of the demands of speech processing can be found in Levelt (1993). Materials to teach the skill of speaking, therefore, need to find a balance between several competing demands. These include:

1. Individual speakers' affective needs in private and unpredictable discourse contexts (for instance, how to show interest and emotion or handle criticism or differences of opinion appropriately).
2. Informal day-to-day encounters (the prototypical instance of this domain being spontaneous conversation, but also service encounters or talk-in-action) where there is a high tolerance of grammatical errors, ellipsis, vagueness, and reformulations among native speakers.
3. Public or formal uses of spoken discourse such as presentations, examinations, interviews, or formal meetings where accuracy and lexical range may be more valued and cognitive demands are high.
4. Local and international varieties of spoken English that are, by their nature, more diverse than the written mode and judgment is required as to how to teach a variety or varieties that are not bland and decontextualized, but at the same time meet learners' needs in increasingly internationalized contexts.

And on a practical level, particularly where published materials are concerned, materials for teaching speaking need to synthesize what can be extracted from this immense variety of spoken discourse types and contexts to form the basis of something that can manageably be presented, taught, and assessed.

The above points lead to some fundamental tensions in teaching the skill of speaking, and in creating materials for this purpose. Most significantly, to what extent are materials for the speaking classroom aimed at increasing language proficiency generally (for instance, materials providing a task that generates discussion of probabilities in order to allow a focus on, or practice of, modal verbs through the medium of speech) and to what extent are they meeting much more complex aims such as pragmatic or affective skills building? The tendency has been for the former to be more prevalent as an approach in materials to teach the skill of speaking than the latter.

Broad aims

One of the significant differences between spoken and written discourse is the fact that speaking does not automatically split itself up into neat sentences, and teaching speaking as if it were a matter of placing one accurate sentence after another as in formal writing does not help the learner. Therefore one broad aim of materials to teach the skill of speaking should be to raise awareness of this feature of speech. Often in published materials on the mode there is a sense of "neatness" to what is presented, which is very unlike the reality of spontaneous speech.

A second aim of materials to teach speaking should be to help learners understand that effective speaking skills are based on a collaboration between language users. This can be helpful even at the lowest levels if, for instance, strategies for showing that you are searching for a word are taught and learners can see that this is a natural process in conversational give and take. Similar processes of collaboration can be seen at work in more elaborate ways as more fluent users of the language echo one another, pick up on words used by each other, or finish one another's sentences. McCarthy (1998) provides particular insights about the accommodation that goes on between speakers in spontaneous conversational settings.

A third area that materials to teach the skill of speaking can usefully deal with is the fact that context and user strongly influence language choices and interpretations. Not all cultures and languages handle conversation in the same way. What seems a polite approach in one may be interpreted quite differently in another. This delicate pragmatic element is a difficult, but rewarding, aspect of teaching speaking. How you begin and end a telephone conversation, how you respond to a compliment, how you interrupt, how you lead up to a request for something, or even how much silence you will tolerate before you feel uncomfortable may all be culturally bound and may require adjustment or relearning in interactions with a different language and culture. Pragmatic and cultural interference on speaker interactions is an underresearched area but one that students need to become sensitive to if they are to participate effectively in the second language. Materials that develop this awareness should support the teaching of the skill of speaking rather than assume that there is a single or neutral cultural norm within which it can be approached.

In general, then, since the complexities of the speech situation and the wide range of factors that can influence linguistic behavior are so crucial, materials should generally, and perhaps paradoxically, not be too ambitious in their aims in these areas. It would seem particularly important for learners to focus on two main areas in relation to materials that attempt to introduce actual speech data. The learner needs to become aware of some of the differences between spoken and written mode, the "give and take" of speaking, the greater tolerance of mistakes and lower vocabulary range, and the potential for cultural differences. They also need to build strong language production skills, including confident projection of the voice, pronunciation and fluency, pace, gesture/gaze and so on, without which the other work is wasted. Often, aspects of the spoken form (for instance idioms, or strategies for seeking clarification) are taught in isolation from these fundamental productive skills. If we ignore them, it is as if we imagine that a student can write without a pen and paper, or computer, screen, and printer.

What particular learners and contexts are these materials written for?

The materials presented in this chapter are most suited for upper-intermediate and advanced learners. They lend themselves, however, to being adjusted by experienced teachers to suit lower or higher levels. For instance, the task on speech rhythm later in this chapter could be based on simple sentences from a reading or listening text in a low-intermediate level coursebook where the students have already become familiar with the materials.

The task could be made more challenging by using longer stretches of talk from natural conversational settings for the advanced learner. The approach presented here focuses strongly on the interactive aspects of speaking, and this makes it particularly relevant for challenging interactive contexts for the L2 speaker: academic and work-related seminars, business meetings, negotiations, and socializing with L1 users.

In the case of advanced learners, there is often a gap between their overall proficiency level (for instance, their IELTS score) and their ability to handle speaking in real-world contexts with the demands of real-time speech processing. These materials therefore may seem simple – for instance, the gap-fill exercise on backchanneling in the sample materials below – but are necessary for advanced learners to begin to be aware of the nature of spoken English and put their linguistic knowledge to use in real speech contexts.

Some theory

In theories of language and in theories of language acquisition, the status of speaking is unusual. It is at once highly regarded and yet is generally described and analyzed within the norms of the written form. In language acquisition, it is regarded as fundamental to the communicative approach in both earlier "indirect" and, to a lesser extent, later "direct" conceptualizations, but the ELT curriculum generally focuses on and, in particular, assesses features that are positively unhelpful in terms of natural speech production (Hughes 2004). Such features include the frequent inclusion of wide lexical range or grammatical complexity in assessment criteria. However, research suggests that fluent spontaneous speech will always tend to show a lower type-token ratio (number of different words as a percentage of the total words), and will have a tendency toward simple linking devices, sentence fragments, and juxtaposition of ideas without logical markers. The planning constraints of this form make it difficult to produce a wide variety of vocabulary items and grammatically complex constructions more typical of the written mode "on the go." Expecting second language users to do this in oral examinations is an instance of a mismatch between assessment goals and the nature of the form being assessed. A prior debate about what it is "to speak well," and in what contexts, is needed before we can decide whether a feature such as high lexical density is a good measure for the spoken form.

Within linguistic theory, speech is the primary form of language. All human communication is seen as fundamentally stemming from an inherent capacity for which the human brain and the vocal organs have evolved in tandem to underpin the complex social systems that are carried out via speech communication (Deacon 1998). The human infant brain is "primed" to learn to speak, and it is only later and through many years of explicit training at school that literacy is acquired. Therefore, all linguistic communication is seen as stemming from the spoken mode, and it is in this sense positioned very prominently in language theory.

I have argued elsewhere that there are, however, ambiguities in the status of speech as, on the one hand, it holds this importance as the primary mode, and, on the other hand, is a form that is analyzed and understood for the most part via the "translation" of the written mode and the norms of thinking of a literate culture (Hughes 2002). The literate view of language has powerful effects, which means that, although "primary," many of the distinctive features of the form are underregarded and their effects in terms of applied language theory misunderstood. Whereas all educated people are made explicitly aware of the norms of the written form and, through teaching and assessment criteria of different kinds, what "good" and "poor/incorrect" writing is like, even first language users are rarely introduced to similar concepts in relation to the spoken form. It is not surprising, therefore, that in materials and ELT generally, there is such interest in the insights coming from detailed descriptive analysis of real speech data. An excellent summary of recent advances in the description and application of research on speech is given by McCarthy and O'Keefe (2004), and Thornbury and Slade (2006) provide practical suggestions as to the interface between recent advances in the description of speech and the classroom.

There is a wealth of sources of theoretical and descriptive analysis of the spoken mode, which can nowadays inform the production of materials to teach the skill of speaking, including:

- Study of spoken corpora
- Insights from conversation analysis, discourse, and pragmatics studies
- Work on affect and creativity in language
- Interactional linguistics
- Speech processing and psycholinguistics

Among these areas, "interactional linguistics" may be a term in particular need of expansion. There is a large and growing body of research on the interface between the insights of conversation analysis and specific language features. The work of scholars such as Sandra Thompson, Peter Auer, or Cecilia Ford aims to show the linguistic structures that can be seen in the fabric of spontaneous speech. Taking as a starting point the communicative approach (CA) traditions of very detailed analysis of spoken data in context, interactional linguists challenge and extend some of the "givens" of language description, such as typical clause construction or links between form and function. The work of the Nottingham School, led by Ronald Carter (see, for example, Carter and McCarthy [1995] for what amounted to an early "manifesto" for this work), can also be seen as part of this tradition. It also works at the intersection between speech data in context and insights that emerge from this, rather than assuming speech data will fit neatly any of the existing categories we might take from, for instance, standard pedagogic grammars of English.

Nevertheless, insights from the areas outlined above have been slow to percolate into materials development and, perhaps more importantly, teacher training. It is clearly a shock to many students when they realize that there are no clear boundaries between words in the spoken form that equate to the white space between them in the written form. The "stream" of speech is just like a real stream, and word boundaries, utterance units, and discourse features, such as understanding a topic as given or new, are "overlayed" onto this continuous stream of sounds by the listener. Rather than decode a clear set of unambiguous words presented in black and white, the production and comprehension of speech depends on a speaker's ability to handle, and a listener's ability to interpret, the norms of phonology of the target language, relate these to the lexicon, and use their understanding of syntax, discourse, cultural/pragmatic norms, and the world to interpret meaning. The interpretive aspects of the mode are fundamental to speech perception but are rarely dealt with in approaches and materials to teach speaking.

In terms of language theory, therefore, speaking can be a complex area for language teaching due to something of a "gap" between the realities of speech and what is taught. To sum up, speech is on the one hand the primary locus of input and classroom output in the communicative approaches that have until recently dominated the field of TEFL, and yet, by its nature, as the following sections will suggest, it is often at odds with notions of static, objectified, individual language production, which lend themselves to materials on the page.

One of the biggest challenges in writing materials to support the development of the skill of speaking is deciding what aspects of speaking are to be most prominent in the syllabus. Fundamental to the production of spoken discourse is the ability to handle prosodic and phonemic features in the target language. This is the basic means of delivery on which all other aspects of speech depend. There is little point attempting to introduce more sophisticated points, such as the use of discourse markers, if the surrounding discourse is so badly enunciated that no sense can be made of the speech by a listener. To take a parallel from teaching academic writing, this is similar to the phenomenon familiar to writing tutors around the world when signposting language for argumentation is taught. A text that is basically incoherent cannot be made coherent by scattering linking devices through it. Equally, spoken discourse has to be fundamentally comprehensible for it to be a carrier of meaning, and the more fundamental questions of production need to be dealt with before or in tandem with other aspects of the skill of speaking.

However, coursebooks and materials for teaching speaking generally treat the productive aspects of speech and broader, pragmatic, features of the skill – for example, opening a conversation, making requests, interrupting – as if they are not part of a single skill. Ideally, materials to teach the skill of speaking would acknowledge the need to unify, or at least match, productive competence and task difficulty. A glance at the publication lists of any major ELT publisher will, however, show clear separation of materials to teach pronunciation and fluency from those providing text or coursebooks on speaking. Some integration is necessary in the syllabus, if not in the publishers' lists, as materials introducing broader aspects of speaking will fail to meet their aim if the students lack the basic productive skills.

In the materials shown in this chapter, the two areas that have helped to inform their design most are insights from interactional linguistics and speech processing, together with the notion of the linguistic turn or utterance as a locus of collaborative, real-time, negotiation between speakers.

Sample materials and activities

Materials to raise awareness of the nature of spontaneous speaking

The following example of an extract of real speech and associated set of tasks aims to highlight the potential to raise awareness of how to handle simple, interactive "backchannel" at even a low-intermediate level and build learners' confidence in this area.[1] Those wishing to replicate the tasks with their own stretches of talk should note that the extract has been chosen because it has particular features as follows.

First, the speaker is engaged in telling a story, and this leads to a situation where she is naturally giving background information in quite an explicit way. There can be too much explanation needed if stretches of talk are chosen that are comprehensible only to the people involved in the conversation, however rich it may be in terms of features the conversation analyst or applied linguist might be interested in.

Second, the main speaker is using an international variety of English, which may help the learner to relate to it and also feel that the features being introduced are not simply "inner circle" ones (Kachru 1986). Examples

[1] This extract is from The National Institute of Education Corpus of Spoken Singapore English (NIECSSE) created by David Deterding and Ee Ling Low, to whom I give grateful acknowledgment for its use. The extract can be heard at http://videoweb.nie. edu.sg/phonetic/niecsse/f18/index.htm. (audio file c.)

between speakers of English as a first language may alienate the learner or, particularly in casual conversational exchanges, may make the features seem unrealistic or unnecessary for them to achieve (Higgins 2003).

Third, the story being told has a degree of universality to it, and, although not entirely devoid of cultural references ("Aussie dollars"), the basic elements needed to grasp the story are quite accessible. Being robbed while on vacation is a simple and engaging topic that most people can relate to whatever their cultural background.

SAMPLE MATERIALS 1

Ways of expressing interest when listening

Prelistening activities

A student (S) is telling a story about a time when her husband's credit card was stolen. As she tells the story, the other speaker (I) uses some words to show interest. What do you think he says?

Analysis

Task B1 (omit if advanced students)

Read the transcript of part of the story. Where would you put the following words?

right mmm wow

I - Within half an hour, so how much money did they spend?

S - Er … one of the cards they used about . . . two thousand five Aussie Dollars.

I - …

S - And another about one thousand Aussie dollars.

I - …

S - Yeah.

I - What did they buy, do you know?

S - I don't know (laughs).

I - …

S - And the credit card company didn't er didn't want to reveal to us too.[2]

Task B2

Listen to the extract and check your answers.

Extending understanding

Task C1

With a partner, look at the transcript and decide which word(s) could be used in all three gaps. Give reasons.

Task C2

Which word is the strongest way to show interest? Could you use this word in any of the other gaps?

Implementation task/practice

Task D

Has anything similar ever happened to you? Think of a story about a surprising or difficult thing that happened to you on vacation or when you were staying away from home. Plan your story and think how you will tell it.

Join two other students and tell them the story. Then listen to their stories.

When you are listening, try to use *right*, *wow*, or *mmm* in places to show them that you are interested and listening.

If they finish their story and you have not used any of the words, move to a different group and try again!

[Note for teachers. Two possible round-up activities are:

1. Record a volunteer storyteller and listener and play for the next class to listen to and comment on the use of supportive tokens.
2. Class decides "who told the most interesting story and who was the most encouraging listener?" Story told to larger groups or whole class.]

Version showing full transcript:

I - Within half an hour, so how much money did they spend?

---

2 Teachers should note the need to raise awareness beforehand of the nature of spoken grammar and the fact that the storyteller uses ellipsis ("reveal to us … " in place of "reveal that/it to us") and the nonstandard "too" for emphasis where students may have been taught that "either" would be the choice.

S - Er ... one of the cards they used about ... two thousand five Aussie Dollars.
I - Wow.
S - And another about one thousand Aussie dollars.
I - Right.
S - Yeah.
I - What did they buy, do you know?
S - I don't know (laughs).
I - Mmm.
S - And the credit card company didn't er didn't want to reveal to us too.

An activity on speech rhythm

Here the aims are to help the learner understand the importance of rhythmic "chunking" in English, become aware of the nature of rhythmic patterning, and have practice in hearing and analyzing the regular pattern of strong/long syllables and weak/short syllables, which allow this to be clear.

Although the sentences are simple, the task can be quite demanding even for the advanced learner if they have not had much introduction to the nature of spoken English, and some work on this and the importance of rhythm to producing comprehensible speech would be a good lead-in to these materials.

While this matching task could be created with random sentences, it is far preferable to situate the extracts chosen in a particular domain – here telephone interactions – so that a naturalistic context is provided and also to reduce the potential for this to become merely mechanical oral/aural practice. Using sentences from a scenario allows the teacher to introduce and follow up flexibly, depending on the level of the group. Students also tend to find it more fun and engage more with the task if they are able to imagine a setting in which the language can be used.

SAMPLE MATERIALS 2

Speech rhythm for common phrases in service encounters on the telephone

Prelistening activities

Here are three sentences with three different rhythmic patterns. With a partner, take turns to say the sentences. Make the parts that are underlined louder and longer, and the other words quieter and quicker. (Tip: if you find this hard, try nodding your head as you say the underlined part!)

Pattern 1: – –__ –__

Could you spell that, please?

Pattern 2: –__ –__

I'll go and see.

Pattern 3: –__ – –__ –__

I'm hoping he'll ring us soon.

Extending understanding

Look at the following sentences you might use on the telephone. Mark them pattern 1, 2, 3, or "other" depending on the pattern of loud/long and quiet/quick words they have.

Answering the phone:	Good afternoon.____
Connecting a caller:	I'll put you through.____
	One moment, please.____
Explaining a problem:	I'm sorry, the line's engaged.____
	I'm sorry, there's no reply.____
Offering help:	Would you like to hold?____
Offer a return call:	Could she call you back?____
Checking information:	Could you repeat that, please?____

Answers:

Answering the phone:	Good afternoon. 2
Connecting a caller:	I'll put you through. 2
	One moment, please. 2
Explaining a problem:	I'm sorry, the line's engaged. 3
	I'm sorry, there's no reply. 3
Offering help:	Would you like to hold? 1
Offer a return call:	Could she call you back? 1
Checking information:	Could you repeat that, please? other

An activity to generate discussion and build confidence in interrupting

The aims here are to provide an environment where students can build up their confidence in challenging others and interrupting skillfully during a discussion. The context is that of an academic seminar, but the role cards could be used with a discussion from other domains, such as business proposals being negotiated or very general "EFL" style debate prompts.

SAMPLE MATERIALS 3

Interruption role cards: Cut out when copied, one per student.

Challenge ideas:
You must challenge the ideas of others at least three times during the discussion.

That's all very well, but …	You may be right, but …
Yes, but don't you think …	You have a point, but …
That's OK to some extent, but …	Up to a point, but …
You seem to have forgotten …	How do you account for …?
I don't think it's quite that simple …	That's one way of looking at it …

Interrupt to add to a point:
You must interrupt to add to a point at least three times during the discussion.

Hold on! Wait a minute!	One more thing …
Can I make a point here?	Just a small point.
Can I just add something here?	I'd like to add …

Interrupting to change the subject:
You must interrupt to change the subject at least three times during the discussion.

I just thought of something!	That reminds me of …
I know this is changing the subject, but …	
Oh, while I remember …	Before I forget …

Interrupting generally anytime: **You must interrupt at least three times during the discussion.**	
Can I say something?	By the way ...
That reminds me ...	(I'm) sorry to interrupt, but ...
Sorry to break in.	Excuse me for interrupting.

Clarifying an opinion: **You must interrupt to request clarification at least three times during the discussion.**	
What do you really mean?	Can you be more precise?

Case study: What is your opinion?
Read the case study carefully. Then discuss the questions in your group. Be ready to report your discussion to the class.

"Snake on the Menu"

Eddie is a Canadian journalist currently working in the UK. Both Eddie and his wife Rosanne worked in China for several years in the 1990s. This incident took place in a Beijing restaurant.

> People sometimes say to beware the snake in the grass. In our case, we learned one night in Beijing to beware the snake on the menu. It was fall of 1993 and we were entertaining a visitor from Canada, who had arrived in China to teach English. We decided to go out for an evening meal to a reputable local restaurant, as we often did when we lived in China.
>
> Even though we had a working knowledge of Chinese by then, having lived in China for three years, we were still learning the intricacies of food vocabulary. We ordered some of our usual favorites, like "fish-flavoured eggplant" and "Beijing pork strips," but we also noticed something that included the words "small dragon on a nest of vegetables." It sounded good, so we ordered it from the

waiter. A few minutes later, he arrived back from the kitchen with a long, squirming snake in his hands. "Does this one look good?" he asked. Appalled, as we hadn't realized we had ordered snake, we shook our heads in shock and clearly said "bu yao, bu yao." We tried to tell him we had misunderstood and didn't want the snake. He scurried away. Phew, we thought we had solved a sticky situation. We were surprised when, about 15 minutes later, he arrived back with the snake now dead and well cooked, snuggled up on a plate of vegetables ... and an outrageously large bill.

Zhang, Xiao Ling. (2004). China through Western eyes. Unpublished manuscript.

Discussion questions:

1. What was Eddie's problem?
2. What suggestions would you give Eddie in this situation? Justify your suggestions with reasons.
3. Is it "fair" to charge different customers different prices for the same item? Give reasons to support your point of view.
4. What advice would you give to the restaurant owner to preserve his restaurant's good reputation?
5. How do you think future world food production will affect the restaurant business?

Follow up:

1. Agree on ONE recommendation for action for Eddie.
2. Agree on ONE recommendation for action for the restaurant owner to preserve his restaurant's good reputation.
3. Agree on ONE serious effect future world food production will have on the restaurant business.

Justify your recommendations with reasons.

Discussion and conclusions

Controversially, one might claim that very few materials actually teach speaking skills. Published materials tend to fall into two categories: prompts for talk, and pronunciation/fluency work. Within the former, quite a number of subcategories exist: for example, prompts/tasks for talk generally (icebreakers, warm-up activities), prompts/tasks for specific kinds of talk (seminar skills, discussion and presentation skills), prompts/tasks for specific language features. However, the challenge of dealing with spontaneous speech and the issues of authentic speech data dealt with in this chapter have tended not to be met in many published materials in a systematic way. In assessing materials for the skill of speaking and in light of the insights presented above about the nature of speech and how different it is from writing, teachers may wish to have a mental checklist to use when planning to embark on teaching this skill with anything they have not written themselves.

1. Are the aims of the materials clear?
2. Are these aims compatible with the nature of speech?
3. What aspect of spoken discourse is being taught/presented, exactly?
4. Is the aspect being taught/presented really something particular to speech, or is it using speech as a means of practicing a language feature/function?
5. What level of fluency and ease of pronunciation do these materials assume the student has? Is this at odds with the apparent level of the course or of your class?
6. Are these materials merely prompts for talk, or do they have a clear aim relating to the spoken mode?

There remain, however, a number of complex issues around the creation of materials to support the teaching of the skill of speaking. The three key issues for the applied linguistic community to discuss further in the future development of speaking materials are: (a) the tension between actual speech and theories of language learning; (b) the tension between "real world" or idealistic/humanistic needs and the influential major tests of English such as IELTS or TOEFL; and (c) the need for realism in what nonnative speaker (NNS) teachers can handle and what is a priority in teaching speaking skills for international communication.

Discussion questions and tasks

Reflection

1. This chapter has raised the issue of whether materials are really teaching speaking, or are designed to simply practice or introduce particular linguistic features. Do you agree this is an issue?
2. The task in Sample Materials 1 used a story and explained why this extract was chosen. Remind yourself of these points and consider what else you might need to use as criteria in choosing real extracts to base materials around.
3. The chapter suggested that there is a strong connection between speaker identity and learning to speak a second language well. Do you agree that to be a highly proficient speaker of another language you need to take on board more than grammar and vocabulary? What is your experience?

Evaluation

4. The chapter suggests that published materials sometimes pitch the productive level of speaking tasks above what is realistic in the classroom. Evaluate some published materials to support the development of speaking, preferably ones you are familiar with, and decide whether they reflect this.

Adaptation/Design

5. Could you adapt the materials you evaluated in (4) above in some way to ease the load on the learner, allowing them to focus on speech interaction rather than complex production?
6. Analyze some materials you are familiar with in terms of the issue of lexical range mentioned in the chapter. If you have access to transcripts, do they show the features of simple vocabulary and sentence structure outlined? If the transcript seems authentic, how would you use it in your own materials to persuade a learner that they do not need to construct elaborate, accurate, and lexically dense sentences in speaking?

Acknowledgments

The author wishes to acknowledge the source of SAMPLE MATERIALS 2 (speech rhythm exercise) to Beatrice Szczepek-Reed (materials adapted for inclusion here) and SAMPLE MATERIALS 3 (seminar skills) to Ann Smith (extract of existing materials used), both of the Centre for English Language Education, University of Nottingham, UK, and thanks both for giving permission for their use.

References

Carter, R., & McCarthy, M. (1995). Grammar and the spoken language. *Applied Linguistics* 16(2): 141-58.

Deacon, T. W. (1998). *The symbolic species: The co-evolution of language and the brain*. London: Allen Lane.

Higgins, C. (2003). "Ownership" of English in the outer circle: An alternative to the NS-NNS dichotomy. *TESOL Quarterly* 37(4): 615-44.

Hughes, R. (2002). *Teaching and researching speaking*. London: Longman.

Hughes, R. (2004). Testing the visible: Literate biases in oral language testing. *Journal of Applied Linguistics* 1(2): 295-309.

Kachru, B. B. (1986). The power and politics of English. *World Englishes* 5(2-3): 121-40.

Levelt, W. J. M. (1993). *Speaking: From intention to articulation*. Cambridge, MA: The MIT Press.

McCarthy, M. J. (1998). *Spoken language and applied linguistics*. Cambridge: Cambridge University Press.

McCarthy, M., & O'Keefe, A. (2004). Research in the teaching of speaking. *Annual Review of Applied Linguistics* 24: 26-43. Cambridge: Cambridge University Press.

Schegloff, E. A. (2000). Overlapping talk and the organization of turn-taking for conversation. *Language in Society* 29: 1-63.

Thornbury, S., & Slade, D. (2006). *Conversation: From description to pedagogy*. Cambridge: Cambridge University Press.

10

Developing materials for discipline-specific vocabulary and phrases in academic seminars

Martha Jones and Norbert Schmitt

Summary

This chapter reports on the development and piloting of discipline-specific vocabulary materials on a CD-ROM software program entitled *Sound understanding: Listening and language awareness tasks* (Jones 2003a). The language of academic seminars was focused upon and was explored through needs analysis and corpus analysis techniques. After administering a needs analysis questionnaire and conducting interview surveys among international and home students, as well as members of staff in selected departments at the University of Nottingham, a number of spoken genres were identified as important by the respondents. The survey results prompted the compilation of the Needs-driven Spoken Corpus (NDSC) (Jones 2003b), of which academic seminar data was one element. It was compiled from discourse in three academic departments, and then analyzed quantitatively and qualitatively in order to obtain a list of subject-specific words and phrases frequently used in the seminars. The items on this list were included in the vocabulary section of the CD-ROM program. Three groups of students studying at the Centre for English Language Education (CELE) were subsequently exposed to the academic seminar materials over a three-week period in teacher-led sessions and independent study to ascertain to what extent this exposure would result in the acquisition of the target words and phrases. Posttests demonstrated considerable acquisition of the target words and phrases, indicating that the CD-ROM program was effective in facilitating the students' learning.

Introduction

Several studies on vocabulary development have suggested that a focus on discipline-specific vocabulary and phrases in the EAP classroom can result in learning (Gledhill 2000; Mudraya 2006; Nation 2001; Schmitt 2004; Ward 2007). However, the development of appropriate subject-specific teaching materials is essential for this acquisition to take place. This chapter reports on the process Jones followed in producing such materials for the particular subjects of English Studies, International Law, and Business Studies. The materials were corpus-based and focused on the discipline-specific vocabulary and phrases that occur in academic seminars. The materials were incorporated onto a CD-ROM software program entitled *Sound understanding: Listening and language awareness tasks* (Jones 2003a),[1] and a small-scale exploratory study conducted in order to check the effectiveness of these materials.

Background

A number of research studies have focused on the analysis of academic spoken discourse, based on corpus data with a view to designing materials for the development of speaking skills in an EAP context. Considerable attention has been given to the analysis of initiating acts, components of turns, signaling devices, sequential organization in student-to-student discussion and exchange patterns (Basturkmen 1999, 2002, 2003), seminar structure, and the use of metadiscursive language (Aguilar 2004). Other studies have analyzed language items such as the lexical particle "just" (Lindemann & Mauranen 2001) and hedging devices (Mauranen 2004; Poos & Simpson 2002).

Understanding and mastering the above linguistic features is important for successful communication in an academic setting, but so is the use of precise, discipline-specific vocabulary. Schmitt (2000: 37) argues that in order to

---

[1] The CD-ROM was produced with funding from the Centre for Teaching Enhancement (98 TL/142), and with the technical support of software programmer Suzanne Wright and multimedia graphic designer Coleen McCants at the University of Nottingham.

maintain communication in a specific genre, technical vocabulary for specific fields should be taught and suggests the use of specialized EAP frequency lists to illustrate vocabulary dominant in academic areas. Such an approach requires analysis of this type of language in order to design appropriate materials to meet the lexical needs of international EAP students.

Coxhead and Nation (2001) note that learning academic vocabulary is of great importance to the EAP learner for three reasons. First, it occurs more frequently in a wide range of academic texts than in nonacademic texts. Second, there is evidence that nontechnical academic vocabulary is less known than technical vocabulary. Third, the nonspecialist EAP teacher is more likely to be able to help learners with this type of vocabulary than with technical vocabulary. There are also strong arguments for the teaching of technical vocabulary, especially when the learners' needs center on using the language in a particular discipline. In this case, it is advantageous to learn lists of specific words, which can enable the learner to communicate successfully within one discipline.

Jones and Haywood (2004) conducted an exploratory study of the acquisition of one type of vocabulary – formulaic sequences – in an academic setting. Through the use of awareness-raising reading and writing tasks, they guided EAP students to notice formulaic sequences used in academic discourse first and then produce specific sequences in their essays over a period of ten weeks. By the end of the study, although the students produced only a limited number of sequences accurately and appropriately in their essays, their ability to recognize formulaic sequences in academic texts had improved considerably.

Other studies focusing on specialized vocabulary and collocation in different academic disciplines have been conducted. Gledhill (2000: 115), for example, analyzed the discourse function of collocation in medical research article introductions. He claims that a representative and specialized corpus of research articles can be used to teach languages for specific purposes. Mudraya's study (2006: 235) focused on a combination of data-driven corpus-based methodology and the lexical approach in order to create awareness-raising materials "to help students acquire engineering formulaic multi-word units." Ward (2007) examined collocations that included complex noun-phrase formation found in engineering textbooks aimed at undergraduates.

His corpus-based study revealed that there was a widespread use of technical collocations in the textbooks. He also observed that the collocations in these types of text swere highly specialized and rarely occurred in other subdisciplines. He argued that technicality involves specialization and difficulty, and for this reason it should be tackled by EAP practitioners.

The above research shows that vocabulary is an important component of EAP proficiency, and just as importantly, it is amenable to training. However, it is clear that academic writing is still the focus of many corpus-based studies of specialized vocabulary and phraseology. Although writing will continue to be prominent in EAP pedagogy, it is also important to design materials that reveal the use of disciplinary-specific language in academic spoken genres. Thus, the rest of this report will focus on the spoken vocabulary used in academic contexts.

Analyzing student needs

Since the 1970s, the importance of needs analysis and target situation analysis has been emphasized in order to design EAP materials that address some of the problems students have with academic discourse in general, and with specific disciplinary language in particular (Geoghegan 1983; Hutchinson & Waters 1987; Hyland 2006; Kim 2006; Weir 1983; West 1994). Hyland (2006: 2) defines EAP as "specialized English-language teaching grounded in the social, cognitive and linguistic demands of academic target situations, providing focused instruction informed by an understanding of texts and the constraints of academic contexts." This definition makes clear that any informed EAP teaching must first start with a firm understanding of the EAP context itself, and what students need to know about it.

It is important to enable EAP students to become familiar with features found in both academic written and spoken discourse. Considerable emphasis has been placed on writing, as this is a widespread method for assessment in higher education. However, a growing number of academic departments now assess student participation in academic seminars where discipline-specific topics are discussed, requiring the use of complex vocabulary and phraseology. International students may find this type of activity difficult for three main reasons. They may lack the confidence to take part in academic discussions where there is fast speech, rapid turn-taking, and complex elaboration of arguments. They may also be used to traditional academic contexts where they are only required to listen and take notes. Another reason could be their limited knowledge of disciplinary vocabulary and phrases to discuss issues relevant to their specific subject.

Jones (2003b) conducted a small-scale needs analysis survey to explore the relative importance of the above reasons. She questioned international students attending presessional and insessional EAP programs, as well as home students and staff in selected departments at the University of Nottingham, to identify the perceived difficulties international students had with the language used in different spoken genres at university. She asked about three aspects of the discourse international students found themselves in: (1) the settings where they had to interact with native speakers of English; (2) the types of speakers they often had to speak to either on or off campus (e.g., tutors, other students, departmental administrative staff, shop assistants); and (3) the purposes of the interactions (e.g., asking questions, expressing opinions, complaining). According to the needs analysis survey, a lack of appropriate vocabulary and phrases related to specific disciplines, as well as the use of fast speech and colloquial expressions, seemed to be responsible for the students' inability to communicate successfully with native speakers of English in seminars. The survey results prompted the compilation of the Needs-driven Spoken Corpus (NDSC) (Jones 2003b). Corpus analysis is considered to be an invaluable method for the development of EAP teaching materials, and the corpus does not have to be very large provided that it is well targeted, as is the NDSC (see below). This body of raw data can be adapted to raise awareness of grammatical, lexical, or pragmatic features, which otherwise might be overlooked. Flowerdew (2005: 9) comments on the value of small, specialized corpora of EAP/ESP texts, "where the analyst is probably also the compiler and does have familiarity with the wider socio-cultural context in which the text was created, or else has access to specialist informants in the area." She goes on to add that small corpora, which include features from the students' own sociocultural environment, are very useful for pedagogic purposes, as the teacher can act as a kind of "mediating specialist informant of the raw corpus data."

The NDSC consists of native and nonnative English for EAP use, which includes a combination of academic discourse, the language of service encounters, and casual conversation. This corpus consists of four subcorpora (Table 10.1): academic (seminar discussions and a conversation recorded on an open day in an academic department), community (conversations recorded in various settings on campus), commercial (conversations in various shops), and social (conversations in halls of residence). The spoken genres included in the corpus closely match those mentioned by students in the needs analysis survey.

The materials discussed in this chapter are based on the academic subcorpus only, specifically academic seminar data from three complete seminars recorded in the School of English Studies, the Business School, and the School of Law at the University of Nottingham between 1997 and 1998. These schools were chosen because of the large numbers of international students they attract. The number of words in this subset of the academic subcorpus was 24,119 words.

The participants in the Language and Gender seminar (English Studies) were approximately 12 undergraduate home students and the lecturer. The speakers taking part in the International Law seminar were the lecturer and about 20 postgraduate students (a combination of native and nonnative speakers). In the Business Entrepreneurship seminar, students worked in small groups and the speakers in the data were two native speakers and a nonnative speaker of English with a good command of English.

Table 10.1 Composition of the Needs-driven Spoken Corpus (NDSC)

Spoken contexts in the NDSC	Number of words
Community subcorpus: Library, student life, community / voluntary work	13,948
Commercial subcorpus: Travel agents, restaurants, shops	11,835
Academic subcorpus: Seminar discussions on Language and Gender, International Law, Business, and open day in the Politics Department	26,613

(to be continued)

(continued)

Spoken contexts in the NDSC	Number of words
Social subcorpus:	
Multiparty conversations and a conversation between two students in halls of residence	13,728
Total number of words in the NDSC	66,124

(Jones 2003b)

Identifying key vocabulary in the academic seminar data

After the selection of the academic seminar data for the development of materials for vocabulary practice, it was necessary to identify the vocabulary and phrases to include in the materials on the CD-ROM which our groups of international students would use. The seminar data were POS (part of speech) and were semantically tagged using *Wmatrix* (Rayson 2001) before producing POS and semantic domain frequency lists and concordances. The data were compared with the BNC Spoken Sampler, used as a normative native corpus, to identify key categories that were overrepresented in the academic seminar corpus. Although the academic subcorpus is very different from that of the BNC Spoken Sampler, a statistical comparison between the two corpora could be made by using log-likelihood ratios. Log-likelihood ratios are considered to be the most reliable and accurate statistical method for the comparison of two corpora of a different size. The higher the log figures, the greater the differences between the two corpora. By convention, log-likelihood ratios above 7 indicate real differences, as the threshold of significance equivalent to the chi-square value of $p < 0.01$ is 6.6 (Leech, Rayson, & Wilson 2001: 16-17).

Table 10.2 shows the results of the statistical comparison between the academic subcorpus and BNC Spoken Sampler. Column 1 gives information on the grammatical categories that were overrepresented in the sample corpus, compared with the BNC Spoken Sampler. Columns 2 and 4 show the number of occurrences of such grammatical categories in the sample corpus and the BNC Spoken Sampler, respectively. The percentages of key categories in both corpora are shown in Columns 3 and 5. The POS list was sorted by log-likelihood value in descending order according to the level of overrepresentation of key categories in the sample corpus.

Table 10.2 Results of the statistical comparison between the academic seminar data in the NDSC and the BNC Spoken Sampler

Item	NDSC	%	BNC Spoken Sampler	%	Log-likelihood values
Unit of measurement, e.g., "in," "cc"	94	0.39	159	0.02	375.40
Singular common noun	2,961	12.28	84,446	8.59	326.63
Plural common noun	1,043	4.32	24,407	2.48	261.01
Article	1,492	6.19	38,652	3.93	257.13
-*s* form of lexical verb	405	1.68	6,603	0.67	247.40
General adjective	1,292	5.36	36,947	3.76	140.49
Possessive pronoun, prenominal	433	1.80	10,384	1.06	99.76
that (as conjunction)	302	1.25	6,644	0.68	91.54
of (as preposition)	495	2.05	12,770	1.30	86.78
Plural proper noun	21	0.09	79	0.01	57.77
General preposition	1,213	5.03	40,428	4.11	44.66

We find that a number of grammatical categories occur significantly more often in the academic seminar subcorpus than in general spoken English, as represented by the BNC Sampler. An example is the single common noun, which had a log-likelihood value of 326.63, indicating a very high level of overrepresentation. Each individual academic seminar was also compared with the BNC Spoken Sampler, and the level of overrepresentation of the single common noun was as follows:

Academic seminar on Language and Gender	32.43
Academic seminar on International Law	230.50
Academic seminar on Entrepreneurship	93.74

Research into variation between speech and writing has revealed that specific genres characterized by a high density of nouns followed by complex postmodifying prepositional phrases indicate a high informational content

(Biber 1988; Biber *et al.* 1999). The relatively high density of single common nouns in the Law and the Business seminars, and to a lesser extent the Language and Gender seminar, suggest that the discourse in these seminars did have a relatively high informational content.

We can also learn something about academic collocation from Table 10.2. Among the grammatical categories overrepresented in the academic subcorpus, we find the following:

1. Single common nouns.
2. Plural common nouns.
3. Articles.
4. Adjectives.

All of these are important elements of phrases where the noun is the noun-phrase head. According to Biber *et al.* (1998: 5), "a corpus-based approach allows researchers to identify and analyze complex 'association patterns.'" Single and plural common nouns, as well as articles and adjectives, indicate a high level of "informational" content. Rayson *et al.* (2002) also found that nouns, adjectives, and prepositions, *of* in particular, were very common in informative writing and in the *context-governed* part of the Spoken BNC. In academic seminars, there are likely to be numerous subject-specific phrases where the noun is the noun-phrase head which may be useful for students to understand as chunks and eventually use.

Words and phrases in the academic seminar data where the noun was the noun-phrase head were selected on the basis of the frequency lists as the result of the corpus analysis and also according to their usefulness. The decision on usefulness was initially made intuitively by the lecturers who had delivered the lectures (Language and Gender; International Law). Students discussing the content of their PowerPoint presentation and assignment (Entrepreneurship) were subsequently consulted to ensure the choices made were appropriate. Schmitt (2000: 144) notes that "frequency is not the only criterion for choosing words to teach explicitly. Another is words particularly useful in a specific topic area (e.g., technical vocabulary)." In addition, colloquial words and phrases were chosen, as international students rarely encounter such language in the EAP classroom unless the EAP tutor makes a special effort to teach them. Contrary to what students might expect, colloquial language is also used in academic discussions, as well as general words and phrases.

Based on the corpus statistical analysis and the lecturer and student input, three types of vocabulary and phrases were selected to be included in our material. It is important to note that most, but not all, of these words and phrases have a noun as the head of the phrase. Examples of these are listed in Table 10.3.

Table 10.3 List of words and phrases included in the Sound Understanding: Listening/Language Awareness Tasks CD-ROM

Technical (N = 19)	General (N = 22)	Colloquial (N = 7)
Entrepreneurship	intuitive	gut feeling
Entrepreneurial audit	template	blokey
(to set up) a venture	accomplishment	stuff like that
economic sanction(s)	take the initiative	a hundred grand
coercion	violate	the thing is
acquiescence	recalcitrant	the only thing
economic might	agenda(s)	that's bothering me
a regional body	shift	
in the light of practice	leeway	
peer group	endorse	
single-sex group(s)	tacit consent	
mixed-sex group(s)	at the outset	
peer group(s)	the beauty of the idea	
age group(s)	good point	
hedging device(s)	at the end of the day	
backchanneling device(s)	the problem is	
take the floor	the only problem I've got	
regional arrangement(s)	sell the idea	
imposition of sanctions	run with an idea	
	take a breath	
	state of flux	
	carve out	

(Jones 2003a)

Developing materials for discipline-specific vocabulary derived from corpus data

The vocabulary selected from the above analysis was embedded into learning materials incorporated onto a CD-ROM learning program.

This program consists of a number of audio extracts from seminars on Language and Gender, International Law, and Business Studies, and a series of interactive tasks based on those extracts. It can be used either in guided teacher sessions or independently, as there are clear explanations and feedback throughout the program. These activities are organized in two parts on the CD-ROM.

The features of academic spoken discourse that are portrayed in the program are as follows:

1. The context of academic seminars (Part 1).
2. Types of interaction (Part 1).
3. Speech acts commonly found in academic seminar discussions (Parts 1 and 2).
4. Structure of seminars and patterns of interaction (Part 2).
5. Disciplinary vocabulary (Part 2).
6. Summary of whole seminar (Part 2).

The section devoted to practice of disciplinary vocabulary and phrases includes three activities based on the language used by the lecturer and students in the three seminars: Find the Word, Crossword Puzzle, and Odd One Out. A total of 73 words and phrases were included in these activities, and of these, four were recycled.

The Find the Word activity requires the user of the program to find specific words and phrases horizontally, vertically, or diagonally in a grid. When the student finds and clicks on the correct word or phrase, it is automatically highlighted in light red.

The words and phrases in this task from the seminar on International Law include: *state of flux, deadlocked, agendas, endorse, at the outset, acquiescence, economic might, tacit, carve out, take the initiative, economic sanctions*, and *violate*. From the seminar on Language and Gender: *gut feeling, anecdotally*, and *stuff like that*, and from the seminar on Entrepreneurship: *attributes, template, drive, venture*, and *entrepreneurial audit*.

An example of the Odd One Out activity, based on the seminar on International Law, is provided below. The correct answers are indicated for the reader's convenience by **bold** print, although in the exercise, they appeared in normal font. This task focuses on collocations.

> In this game, you are given four key words or phrases taken directly from the seminars on the CD-ROM. Next to each key word is a list of four words or phrases, only one of which does not fit in well with the context of the key word. This is called "the Odd One Out." See how many you can get right. You have two attempts at each word. NB: The "Odd One Out" may be grammatically correct but you have to judge which word or phrase **best** matches the **context**.

a. impose b. endorse **c. redefine** d. take	sanctions
a. peacekeeping **b. labor** c. Commonwealth d. military	force
a. regional b. inward-looking **c. special interest** d. international	organizations
a. sufficient b. limited **c. professional** d. lots of	practice

Figure 10.1 Example of "Odd One Out" activity on the CD-ROM

A list of target collocations to be included in the Odd One Out task is provided below:

From the International Law seminar: (*impose/endorse/take*) *sanctions*; (*peacekeeping/Commonwealth/military*) *force*; *economic* (*organization/might/measures*); *make* (*a difference/a statement/a decision*); *legal* (*argument/issue/authority*); and *seek* (*authority/approval/advice*).

From the seminar on Language and Gender: (*invite/get/give*) *a response*; (*hedging/backchanneling/softening*) *devices*; *female* (*speaker/conversation/chair*); *mixed sex* (*group/conversations/interaction*); (*create/show/express*) *uncertainty*; and *in a* (*personal/university/social*) *context*.

From the seminar on Entrepreneurship: *entrepreneurial* (*process/audit/idea*); *manufacturing* (*idea(s)/industry/experience*); *land* (*owner/company/titles*); (*set up/own/start*) *a company*; *specific* (*attributes/skills/competencies*); and (*gas/phone/nuclear*) *industry*.

The Crossword Puzzle task requires the user to identify the correct word or phrase based on any of the three seminars included on the CD-ROM. An example of a phrase included in this activity from the International Law seminar is *sanctions were imposed*. The clue for this phrase is "international organization took measures against (a state)." Another example of a phrase in this puzzle from the same seminar is *a regional body*, with the clue for this phrase being "an organization operating in a particular part of the world."

These vocabulary activities were deliberately included toward the end of Part 2 of the CD-ROM to ensure the user of the program had numerous opportunities to encounter the words and phrases in the three seminars before attempting to do such activities.

An exploratory study to check the effectiveness of the vocabulary materials on the CD-ROM

The empirical evaluation of materials effectiveness is something that is often neglected in materials development. In order to explore the effectiveness of our corpus-based CD-ROM materials, we carried out a small-scale study with EAP students.

Participants

Two guided sessions were conducted with students on two different specialized presessional programs: one group of students in Law and Business (August-September 2006), and one group of teachers of English from Japan, who were on an in-service teacher-training program (November 2006) at the Centre for English Language Education (CELE) at the University of Nottingham. The Law and Business group consisted of 29 students[2] (16M, 13F) in their mid-twenties/early thirties. Their proficiency was roughly equivalent to 6.5/7.0 IELTS, and they had offers from the University of Nottingham. All the students were highly motivated and showed great interest in the tasks on the CD-ROM, as the material was relevant to their discipline. The group of Japanese teachers of English consisted of nine students (7M, 2F) in their late thirties/early forties. They were on a teacher development program funded by the Japanese Ministry of Education, Culture, Sports, Science, and Technology, and their proficiency ranged from 5.5 to 6.5 in IELTS. The teachers were all experienced junior or senior high school teachers, and they were also highly motivated.

Instruments

At the end of Part 2 of the CD-ROM program, there is a summary of the main topics covered in each of the three seminars. The texts of these summaries were used to design an adapted C-test, designed to measure whether the participants were able to remember the target words and phrases from the various extracts they had listened to and read in the transcripts and in the glossary. A sample C-test is illustrated in Appendix 10.1. It can be seen that the emphasis was placed on phrases. The scoring scale below was used to assess the accurate use of those phrases:[3]

3 = correct phrase
2 = correct phrase but problems with morphology
1 = some idea of phraseology but could not get the correct phrase
0 = no idea of phraseology

---

[2] Of the 17 students on the specialized Business Presessional Course who had participated in Session 1 using the CD-ROM, only three were able to take part in Session 2, when the C-test was administered.

[3] This scoring approach is the same as was used by Jones and Haywood (2004) for formulaic sequences.

Unfortunately, we were not able to run a pretest to determine the students' previous knowledge of the vocabulary and phrases. However, we were able to test a small group of four students at CELE who were similar to the participants in the study in that they were also studying EAP on a presessional program at CELE. Their results show that, although a few of the phrases in the test were partially produced, on the whole, most were unknown. This provides some evidence that any learning by the students in the study was due to using the program and not to previous knowledge.

Procedure

The learning treatment consisted of two teacher-led sessions with independent study in between. In the first teacher-led session, the students were asked to focus on the tasks in Part 1 that were relevant to their discipline (English, Law, or Business). A sample task worksheet for this session focusing on the language used in the Language and Gender seminar is found in Appendix 10.2. In this session, the students were asked to concentrate on the tasks that focused on the context of seminars, types of interaction, and speech acts, such as eliciting information and replying to questions. At the end of this first teacher-led session, there was a brief discussion on the students' performance and to what extent this type of material had helped them cope with fast speech and specialized vocabulary and phrases. After the initial exposure to this material, the students were advised to use the program independently to consolidate what they had learned. The program was available to them on the desktop of all computers in the IT room at CELE. After approximately two weeks, a second teacher-led session was conducted with each group. Appendix 10.3 includes the worksheet for this session, again based on the Language and Gender seminar. In this session, the students focused on the "Listening for detail" tasks and practiced understanding various speech acts. They also did the vocabulary activities, and at the end of this second session, the discipline-relevant C-test was given to the students to determine to what extent they had learned the vocabulary and phrases to which they had been exposed in the teacher-led sessions and independently.

Results

International law group

The results of the C-test given to the group studying on the specialized Law Presessional Course are presented in Table 10.4. The mean score for the whole group was 2.4 on a scale of 3, which reveals a high level of knowledge of the selected phrases. Students 2, 3, 5, 6, and 10, in particular, were able to achieve very high scores, followed by Students 4, 9, and 11. Even though Students 1, 7, 8, and 12 obtained the lowest scores, they showed a considerable ability to produce the chosen items in the test. As regards the phrases themselves, most were produced without difficulty, as shown by the high mean scores per phrase. *Tacit consent* and *in the light of* were the exceptions, but the mean score of 1.8 for these phrases does show that the students had some idea of phraseology, although they were not able to produce the whole phrase accurately.

Business group

As can be seen in Table 10.5, of the 17 students who had participated in the first session, only three were able to take part in the second session due to a heavy workload in their specialized Business Presessional Course. The group mean score was 2.1, showing a reasonably good knowledge of the terms selected for the C-test on the subject of entrepreneurship. Student 1, who obtained a mean score of 2.8, demonstrated a high level of knowledge of specialized phraseology, while Students 2 and 3 both had a mean score of 1.7. It is interesting to note that both students produced what could be considered, strictly speaking, business-related phrases such as *venture*, *to set up*, *key management skills*, and *sell the idea*, but not phrases of a more general and colloquial nature such as *the only problem I've got*, *the thing is*, or *at the end of the day*.

Group of teachers of English from Japan

Table 10.6 shows the results of the C-test administered to the group of teachers of English from Japan. Like the Law group, the group of teachers obtained a mean score of 2.4. Student 3 was able to produce all phrases accurately and obtained a mean score of 3. This result also matched his performance on the in-service training course. His language level and teaching skills were of a high

Table 10.4 Results of C-test (specialized Law presessional course students)

student	economic sanctions	Security Council	regional arrangements	economic sanctions were imposed against	in the light of	regional body	carve out	impose sanctions against	impose sanctions	tacit consent	economic sanctions	a state of flux	Mean
1	1	3	2	2	0	0	3	3	3	2	2	3	2
2	2	3	2	2	2	3	3	3	3	3	2	3	2.6
3	3	3	2	3	3	3	3	2	3	3	3	2	2.8
4	3	3	2	3	0	3	1	3	3	2	3	3	2.4
5	3	3	2	3	3	3	1	3	3	3	3	3	2.8
6	3	2	3	3	3	3	3	3	3	0	3	3	2.7
7	2	3	2	2	2	3	1	2	2	0	2	0	1.8
8	3	3	2	3	1	1	0	3	3	1	3	2	2.1
9	3	3	2	2	1	2	3	2	3	3	2	3	2.4
10	3	3	3	3	3	2	3	3	3	3	3	3	3
11	3	3	3	3	3	3	1	2	2	1	2	1	2.3
12	3	3	3	2	0	0	1	2	2	1	3	3	2
Mean	2.7	3	2.3	2.6	1.8	2.2	2	2.6	2.8	1.8	2.6	2.4	2.4

Table 10.5 Results of C-test (specialized Business Presessional Course students)

Student	venture	to set up	entrepreneurial audit	key management skills	entrepreneurial audit	the only problem I've got	the thing is	sell the idea	run with the idea	the beauty of the idea	at the end of the day	Mean
1	3	3	2	3	2	3	3	3	3	2	3	2.8
2	3	3	1	3	1	0	0	3	2	3	0	1.7
3	3	3	2	3	2	0	0	2	1	3	0	1.7
Mean	3	3	1.7	3	1.7	1	1	2.7	2	2.7	1	2.1

Table 10.6 Results of C-test (teachers of English from Japan)

Student	gut feeling	single-sex groups	mixed-sex groups	peer groups	age groups	hedging devices	reduce the force	back-channeling devices	checking devices	take the floor	take a breath	Mean
1	3	3	3	0	3	2	3	3	3	3	3	2.6
2	3	2	2	3	3	2	3	3	3	3	3	2.8
3	3	3	3	3	3	3	3	3	3	3	3	3
4	3	3	3	3	3	2	0	3	3	3	3	2.6
5	3	3	2	3	3	3	0	3	0	0	3	2
6	0	3	3	3	3	2	3	3	3	0	0	2
7	3	3	3	3	3	3	2	3	3	0	2	2.5
8	2	3	3	3	2	2	2	3	3	0	3	2.4
9	0	3	0	3	3	2	3	3	3	0	0	1.5
Mean	2.2	2.6	2.4	2.7	2.9	2.3	2.1	3	2.7	1.3	2.2	2.4

standard. Students 1, 2, 4, 7, and 8 obtained high scores, whereas Student 9 had the lowest mean score (1.5). However, he was able to get a score of 3 for those phrases that were closely related to the subject of the type of language used by male and female speakers in the Language and Gender seminar such as *peer groups*, *age groups*, *reduce the force*, *backchanneling devices*, and *checking devices*.

Discussion

The main aim of the two teacher-led sessions focusing on the language used in the three seminars on the *Sound understanding* CD-ROM was to provide the students with numerous opportunities to understand, recognize, and eventually produce key vocabulary and collocations related to the main subject of each seminar in order to ascertain to what extent this kind of language had been acquired by the students. During both guided sessions, the students were able to listen to extracts of the seminars and perform interactive tasks to ensure comprehension of key information and language. Feedback was provided throughout the program and clear explanations were given in the Summary in Parts 1 and 2. In the case of tasks with audio recordings of extracts and transcripts, key vocabulary and collocations were highlighted in dark red, this language was also included in the Glossary, which students could refer to at any time. The tasks in the Vocabulary Check section in Part 2 of the program focused specifically on the target words and phrases that were considered to be most frequent or useful in the seminars and therefore worth learning. Saliency of this type of language in the program may have enabled the students to recall and produce the phrases in the C-test. Studies conducted on the effects of saliency of words and phrases on learning confirm that it is beneficial to draw learners' attention to specific language (Bishop 2004; de Ridder 1999, 2000, 2002). Also, exposure to both the spoken and written word could have helped the students to grasp meaning better rather than relying only on the spoken word.

As expected, not all groups were the same, but all of the three groups did show that they knew quite a bit about discipline-specific vocabulary and phraseology. Read (2000) suggests that there are different ways of interpreting

C-test results. One of these is that, when the test is context-dependent, which was the case with the test used for the present study, "the test score is a measure of the test-takers' knowledge of the deleted words" (p. 114). The test results suggest that after exposure to the material on the CD-ROM, learning was involved, and the students were able to understand text and formulaic language, and that they gained the ability to do the test by filling in the blanks correctly in many cases.

In sum, this exploratory study provides initial evidence that the CD-ROM program was effective to some extent in facilitating the acquisition of academic vocabulary and collocations. However, such a small exploratory study inevitably contains certain limitations.

The study was conducted with a small sample (24 students) and, although the C-test results were encouraging, it is not possible to claim that the same high mean scores can necessarily be replicated with a larger sample. Additionally, the fact that the students were able to produce key vocabulary and phrases in the C-test does not guarantee the same success in a freer situation, i.e., in real seminars in the students' academic departments, as the conditions in the study in question were highly controlled. Furthermore, in the text on International Law, the phrase *economic sanctions* appeared three times and variations of this phrase (*economic sanctions were imposed*, *impose sanctions*, and *impose sanctions against*) were also included in the C-test. This might have led to the students' high mean score of the C-test. Similarly, in the text on Entrepreneurship, the term *entrepreneurial audit* was included twice. However, when the summaries were written during the production of the CD-ROM, these sequences were considered to be key expressions for the students to remember, as they were used extensively during the actual seminars. Therefore, it was important to draw the students' attention to their prominence in the context of the discussions that took place.

Conclusion

This chapter has described part of the needs analysis survey focusing on the problems encountered by international students when interacting with native speakers in formal and less formal academic settings. This survey informed the compilation of the Needs-driven Spoken Corpus (NDSC), from which the academic seminar component was selected for comparison with the BNC Spoken Sampler in order to identify overrepresented key categories. Of these categories, only those which formed noun phrases were chosen for more in-depth analysis in this chapter: single common noun, adjective, and article. Specific discipline-specific words and phrases, as well as colloquial expressions, from the seminars were selected, on the basis of the quantitative analysis, and included in listening and awareness-raising tasks on the *Sound understanding* CD-ROM. Three groups of students at CELE used the program in two guided sessions and independently, as part of an exploratory study. A subsequent C-test suggests that they did acquire some of the discipline-specific lexis taught in the material. However, although the students' mean scores were high on the whole, one has to be cautious and not claim that the high results were necessarily due to exposure to the material on the CD-ROM, as there was no test prior to the use of the program.

Discipline-specific vocabulary and phrases are important in academic spoken discourse, and it would have been hard to develop materials without a principled approach. A needs analysis and corpus analysis can provide good information about what a student needs to know to operate in this discourse environment. The materials developed, described in this chapter, were based on this principled approach and there is some evidence that they were effective. We hope this blueprint of methodology can be useful for EAP teachers to try in their own teaching situations.

Discussion questions and tasks

Reflection

1. Needs analysis surveys informed the compilation of the Needs-driven Spoken Corpus (NDSC), covering three main spoken genres: academic seminars, the language of service encounters, and casual conversation. Why do you think these genres were chosen by the respondents?
2. After conducting the statistical comparison between the academic seminar data in the NDSC and the BNC Spoken Sampler, the authors chose key words and phrases where the noun was the noun-phrase head.

Look at Table 10.2. What other items on this list of overrepresented categories would have generated key words and phrases worth analyzing?

3. Look at the three types of vocabulary and phrases included in the vocabulary activities, listed on page 268. Is there another way in which they can be classified?
4. The authors conducted a small-scale study with EAP students to explore the effectiveness of the corpus-based CD-ROM materials. Do you think that, if a similar study were conducted with a larger student population studying the three same disciplines (Business, International Law, and English Studies) in your teaching environment, similar results would be obtained?

Evaluation

5. Look at the description of the three vocabulary activities included on the CD-ROM: Find the Word, Crossword Puzzle, and Odd One Out on pages 269–71. Evaluate the effectiveness of these activities by making a list of strengths and weaknesses.

Adaptation/Design

6. Look again at the three types of vocabulary and phrases included in the vocabulary activities, listed on page 268. Design a vocabulary activity where these words and phrases could be used in context.

Appendix 10.1

Sample C-test: Seminar on Language and Gender

In the Language and Gender seminar, the lecturer asked the students to look through some data in the form of transcripts of conversations and identify the language features used by male and female speakers. At the beginning of the seminar, the students gave their views, using their *g______ feel______* on the type of language used by speakers within different groups: *sin______ -se ______ groups, mix______ -se______ groups, pe______ groups* and *ag______ groups*.

Before the students started analyzing the language in the conversations, the lecturer reminded them of specific language features in a framework, that they were supposed to identify in the conversations, e.g., *hed______ devices* (devices used to *red______ the for______* of an utterance), *ba______ chan______* devices (devices that show support for the speaker/interest in what they are saying/showing that the speaker is being followed and encouraged) and *chec______* devices (devices used by the speakers to try to check that they are being listened to). The lecturer describes different strategies used in conversation with the word *take*: *take the flo______* (to start speaking in a debate or discussion) and *take a bre______* (to pause to take air in before you continue to speak).

Appendix 10.2

Task worksheet for Guided Session 1: Seminar on Language and Gender

SESSION 1

In your Discussion and Seminar Skills class, you will be covering different aspects of academic discussion, e.g., the difference between a lecture and a seminar, roles of speakers, participation in seminars, interrupting, silence, and so on.

I have developed this program to help international students to observe how different speakers participate in academic seminars.

Aims of this session:

- To learn how to use the program.
- To identify different patterns of interaction in the School of English Studies.
- To become familiar with the topics of the discussion.
- To become familiar with the language used by the speakers.
- To become familiar with the vocabulary relevant to the topic of discussion.
- To become aware of what goes on in a seminar.

Procedure:

It is important that you look at the Introduction – do **not** skip it, as this will guide you so that you are able to use the program appropriately.

Read the instructions carefully.

Also, there is a logical progression of tasks, so please do **not** skip sections.

Reactions/Ideas:

Please spend some time making notes of what you learned through this program today.

Discussion:

Discuss with your partner(s) any aspects of the seminar that you listened to:

- How did you cope with fast speech?
- What subject-specific vocabulary did you learn?
- How would *you* have behaved if you'd been a participant in this seminar?
- How much lecturer intervention was there?

Appendix 10.3

Task worksheet for Guided Session 2: Seminar on Language and Gender

SESSION 2

In Session 1, you had the opportunity to listen to extracts from a seminar on Language and Gender, which took place in this university, and hopefully you were able to become aware of what goes on in seminars as well as the roles that speakers play.

Aims of this session:

- To listen to the extracts from the seminar *in greater detail* (Listening for Specific Information) in Part 2.
- To identify the different expressions (vocabulary, phrases, and grammatical structures) that speakers use to perform different *functions*, e.g., agreeing, disagreeing, and so on.
- To follow the thread of the discussion.

Procedure:

Make sure you finish listening to all extracts in Part 1.

After reading the Introduction to Part 2, do the tasks in the Listening for Specific Information section.

Then do the tasks in the Identifying Functions section. If you get some answers wrong, listen to the extracts again until you think you have identified the correct function(s).

Do the tasks in the Identifying Speakers' Purpose and Feelings section.

Finally do the tasks in the Vocabulary Check.

Reactions/Ideas:

Please spend some time making notes of what you learned through this program today.

Discussion:

Discuss the following with your partner:

- Were you able to understand the detailed information provided in the seminars?
- Were there any useful phrases/structures that you would like to note down so that you can use them yourself when you participate in seminars in your department? If so, which ones did you choose? Compare notes with your partner(s).
- Did you have any difficulties understanding either the content or the language? Why? What can you do *now* so that you are able to perform well in seminars in your department?

References

Aguilar, M. (2004). The peer seminar, a spoken research process genre. *Journal of English for Academic Purposes* 3: 55-72.

Basturkmen, H. (1999). Discourse in MBA seminars: Towards a description for pedagogical purposes. *English for Specific Purposes* 18(1): 63-80.

Basturkmen, H. (2002). Negotiating meaning in seminar-type discussion and EAP. *English for Specific Purposes* 21: 233-42.

Basturkmen, H. (2003). So what happens when the tutor walks in? Some observations on interaction in a university discussion group with and without the tutor. *Journal of English for Academic Purposes* 2: 21-33.

Biber, D. (1988). *Variation across speech and writing*. Cambridge: Cambridge University Press.

Biber, D., Conrad, S., & Reppen, R. (1998). *Corpus linguistics: Investigating language structure and use*. Cambridge: Cambridge University Press.

Biber, D., Johansson, S., Leech, G., Conrad, S., & Finegan, E. (1999). *Longman grammar of spoken and written English*. London: Longman.

Bishop, H. (2004). The effect of typographic salience on the look up and comprehension of unknown formulaic sequences. In Norbert Schmitt (ed.). *Formulaic sequences*. Amsterdam: John Benjamins, pp. 227-44.

Coxhead, A., & Nation, P. (2001). The specialised vocabulary of English for academic purposes. In J. Flowerdew & M. Peacock (eds.). *Perspectives on English for academic purposes*. Cambridge: Cambridge University Press, pp. 252-67.

de Ridder, I. (1999). Are we conditioned to follow links? In K. Cameron (ed.). *CALL and the learning community*. Exeter, UK: ELM Bank Publications, pp. 195-16.

de Ridder, I. (2000). Are we still reading or following the links? Highlights in CALL materials and their impact on the reading process. *Computer-Assisted Language Learning* 13: 183-95.

de Ridder, I. (2002). Visible or invisible links: Does the highlighting of hyperlinks affect incidental vocabulary learning, text comprehension and the reading process? *Language Learning and Technology* 6: 123-46.

Flowerdew, L. (2005). An integration of corpus-based and genre-based approaches to text analysis in EAP/ESP: Countering criticisms against corpus-based methodologies. *English for Specific Purposes* 24: 321-2.

Geoghegan, G. (1983). *Non-native speakers of English at Cambridge University*. Cambridge: The Bell Educational Trust.

Gledhill, C. (2000). The discourse function of collocation in research article introductions. *English for Specific Purposes* 19: 115-35.

Hutchinson, T., & Waters, A. (1987). *English for Specific Purposes*. Cambridge: Cambridge University Press.

Hyland, K. (2006). *English for Academic Purposes: An advanced resource book*. Abingdon, UK: Routledge.

Jones, M. (2003a). *Sound understanding: Listening and language awareness tasks*. CD-ROM focusing on the language of academic seminars, funded by the Centre for Teaching Enhancement, University of Nottingham.

Jones, M. (2003b). The development and exploitation of a Needs-driven Spoken Corpus for students of English for Academic Purposes. PhD thesis, Lancaster University, UK.

Jones, M., & Haywood, S. (2004). Facilitating the acquisition of formulaic sequences. In Norbert Schmitt (ed.). *Formulaic Sequences*. Amsterdam: John Benjamins, pp. 269-300.

Kim, S. (2006). Academic oral communication needs of East Asian international graduate students in non-science and non-engineering fields. *English for Specific Purposes* 25(4): 479-89.

Leech, G., Rayson, P., & Wilson, A. (2001). *Word frequencies in written and spoken English*. London: Longman.

Lindemann, S., & Mauranen, A. (2001). "It's just real messy": The occurrence and function of "just" in a corpus of academic speech. *English for Specific Purposes* 20: 459-75.

Mauranen, A. (2004). "They're a little bit different": Variation in hedging in academic speech. In K. Aijmer & A.-B. Strenström (eds.). *Discourse patterns in spoken and written corpora*. Amsterdam: John Benjamins, pp. 173-97.

Mudraya, O. (2006). Engineering English: A lexical frequency instructional model. *English for Specific Purposes* 25: 235-56.

Nation, P. (2001). *Learning vocabulary in another language*. Cambridge: Cambridge University Press.

Poos, D., & Simpson, R. (2002). Cross-disciplinary comparisons of hedging: Some findings from the Michigan Corpus of Academic Spoken English. In R. Reppen, S. M. Fitzmaurice, & D. Biber (eds.). *Using corpora to explore linguistic variation*. Philadelphia: John Benjamins, pp. 3-21.

Rayson, P. (2001). *Wmatrix: A web-based corpus processing environment*. Computing Department, Lancaster University, UK.

Rayson, P., Wilson, A., & Leech, G. (2002). Grammatical word class variation within the British National Corpus Sampler. In P. Peters, P. Collins, & A. Smith (eds.). *New frontiers of corpus research*. Papers from the Twenty-First International Conference on English Language Research on Computerized Corpora, Sydney 2000, pp. 295-306.

Read, J. (2000). *Assessing vocabulary*. Cambridge: Cambridge University Press.

Schmitt, N. (2000). *Vocabulary in language teaching*. Cambridge: Cambridge University Press.

Schmitt, N. (2004). *Formulaic sequences*. Amsterdam: John Benjamins.

Ward, J. (2007). Collocation and technicality in EAP engineering. *Journal of English for Academic Purposes* 6: 18-35.

Weir, C. (1983). *Identifying the problems of overseas students in tertiary education in the UK*. Unpublished PhD thesis, University of London.

West, R. (1994). Needs analysis in language teaching. *Language Teaching* 27: 1-19.

PART D

MATERIALS FOR SPECIFIC AND ACADEMIC PURPOSES

11

Materials for university essay writing

Martin Hewings

Summary

Although students in higher education are being called on to write an increasing variety of text types, the essay is still a key text, particularly in the arts, humanities, and social sciences, at least in British universities. This paper presents and discusses materials developed to support essay writing by students who have English as an additional language in their Masters in Education program at the University of Birmingham, UK. One of the main problems of teaching "essay writing" is in establishing exactly what an essay is, given that there is considerable variation in what is expected both within and across disciplines. However, there seem to be key features common to most essays: They are short pieces of writing on a single subject that offer an evaluation of claims from either the student writer or published writers, and in which evidence is provided to support or refute these claims. The materials presented here are influenced by the ideas and research of others in the areas of contextualization, writer's "voice," and the analysis of argument and of genre. Starting with a short nonacademic text that presents two sides of a debate, the materials encourage students to explore: the kinds of claims made in essays and the ways in these are expressed; the need for supporting evidence and the types appropriate to an academic essay; the relationship between the organization of essays and their rhetorical purpose; and ways in which student writers can project their own voice into their essays.

Teaching context

I teach in the English for International Students Unit (EISU) at the University of Birmingham, UK. One role of EISU is to offer insessional English language support, focusing primarily on developing writing skills, for groups of students within particular departments. For a number of years, I have worked with Master's students within the School of Education, offering an optional course of 1.5 hours per week for 18 weeks, and additional individual support. The students all have English as an additional language, and there is a wide range of nationalities in the group. There is no assessment of students in the course, and it is impractical to ask students to do written work outside class. Students are required to produce a wide variety of different text types as assessed work for their Master's programs. Some assessments, including reports on school visits, research proposals, introspective diaries of foreign-language learning (in previous years), and a final dissertation, are clearly not what would normally be thought of as "essays." However, many others are "essays" if we take a rather broad view of the term (see next section).

In this paper, I will focus on parts of the course, taught during the middle of Semester 1, that have essay writing as their focus. Other parts, although important for essay writing, have more general relevance to most of the types of academic writing required of students (e.g., writing in an academic style, paraphrasing, referencing conventions) and will not be addressed here.

The materials used for insessional courses at EISU in Birmingham are mainly written in-house and tend to be the products of the teaching staff as a whole. One person may be responsible for teaching a particular course and producing material for that course, usually in the form of a weekly handout. In later years, a different staff member may teach the course and bring their own ideas to the materials, or modify them in response to changes in the needs of students on the course. In this way, in-house materials are in a constant state of development, rarely reaching a "finished," publishable form.

Essays

Recent surveys have shown that students at UK universities are required to produce a wide, and probably increasing, variety of written texts for assessment (Baynham 2000; Nesi & Gardner 2006). However, still at the center of much of the writing done, particularly in the arts, humanities, and social sciences, is the assessed essay. From a survey of writing assignment types undertaken at three British universities, for example, Nesi and Gardner (2006: 113) acknowledge the widespread use of the essay, which, together with the dissertation, book review, and laboratory report, is one of "a set of core assignment types that sit easily with the traditions of university education."

While the notion of an "essay" is a familiar one, its precise characteristics are difficult to pin down, and a number of writers have pointed to the variability in purpose and form of texts that fall under this umbrella term. For example, essays may be framed variously as a critical review, a discussion, a personal response, or an exposition, and this may lead to the inclusion of different elements (Curry & Hewings 2003). Even with the same "framing," the required product may be different. In his work with students of plant biology, Dudley-Evans (1988) noted that essay questions with the instruction "discuss" might require students to present opposing points of view and conclude with their own opinion, describe a theory or process and give some further explanation, or present points in favor of an argument and points against without providing their own opinion.

Further variation might be found across disciplines. Paltridge (2002: 89), for example, reminds his students that "the kind of essay they write for a particular course is not necessarily (or indeed at all) universal across different academic disciplines and needs to be adapted or completely changed for other assignment questions in other areas of study."

Despite this variation, certain key features seem to be common to most texts considered to be essays. They are relatively short pieces of writing on a single subject, which offer an evaluation of ideas or opinions presented as "claims" or "generalizations." These ideas or opinions may be those of other authors and reported by the student, or those of the student himself or herself.

Evidence is presented to provide support (or to show lack of support) for these ideas and opinions.

Reasons for the long-standing popularity of the essay as a text produced for assessment in education can be seen in these key features. Presenting the ideas and opinions (or claims) and evidence of others allows students to display their understanding of a subject gained mainly through reading. Presenting their own ideas, opinions, and evidence (in cases where students include findings from their own research) allows them to contribute to the ongoing discussion of issues within their academic field. Evaluation, which may take such forms as synthesizing, comparing, and contrasting, allows students to demonstrate an intellectual ability to make complex judgments. Further, the very variability of what counts as an essay can be seen as a reason for its popularity. As Nesi and Gardner (2006: 108) note: "The value of the essay would appear to lie in its relatively loosely structured ability to display critical thinking and development of an argument within the context of the cur riculum."

Theoretical influences on the approach to essay writing

The materials to be described in this paper have been influenced by a number of ideas, approaches, and areas of research and debate within applied linguistics and education more generally. Here I wish to focus on the contextualization of academic writing, the writer's "voice," and the analysis of argument and of genre.

The contextualization of academic writing

Bazerman (1981) argues that an author has to establish a "workable balance" between four "contexts" for their text. These contexts are "the object under study, the literature of the field, the anticipated audience, and the author's own self" (p. 362). That is to say: A text will convey information about the objects that are discussed; it will indicate the relationships between the text and previous literature through, for example, citation; it will make certain assumptions about the knowledge and attitudes the readers have, which will be reflected in such things as the structure of the argument; and the authors will present themselves as "individual statement-maker[s]" (p. 363) through reports of their experience, observations, and in the originality of their claims.

What is highlighted in Bazerman's approach to academic writing, and in that of many other influential writers on the subject (e.g., Berkenkotter & Huckin 1995; Gilbert & Mulkay 1984; Hyland 2000; Swales 1990), is that it is a social act that cannot be separated from "the specific local circumstances in which writing takes place nor from the broader institutional and sociohistorical contexts which inform those particular occasions of writing" (Candlin & Hyland 1999: 2). This means that academic texts are shaped by the particular modes of expression that have become accepted both within academia in general and disciplines more specifically and, at an even more local level, that may be required by a particular department. Student writers are expected to acquire the modes of expression relevant to their area of study and to demonstrate their membership in a particular academic community of scholars by implementing them in their own texts.

The writer's "voice"

At the same time, however, it has been suggested that student writers should be encouraged to present their own identity or "voice" in their texts. Starfield, for example, has noted that:

> While academic writing has traditionally been viewed as impersonal, recent research has argued for greater attention to be paid to the significance of identity in academic writing and on the ways in which writers, through the linguistic and discursive resources on which they choose to draw as they write, convey a representation of the self. (Starfield 2004: 68)

Ivanič and Camps (2001) argue that all writers project a personal and cultural identity in the language choices they make. This "self-representation" is manifested in the way they represent the world, in their relative authoritativeness or tentativeness, in the way they represent their relationship with their readers, and their preferences for turning meanings into text. As they go on to point out (p. 6), however, "In settings in which authority is being exercised over writing such as writing academic assignments, the version of self that will be rewarded may be determined by the tutor who will be assessing the work." This suggests that whereas it is important for students to be helped to develop awareness of the linguistic resources available to them to represent themselves, it is also important for them to understand what "voices" are likely to be met with approval in a particular context. They are therefore to be given the means by which they might conform to institutional or disciplinary expectations, or resist them.

Argument

I suggested above that a widely accepted key feature of essays is that they present claims and provide evidence for them. An alternative way of characterizing this is to say that an *argument* is presented, with reasons being given for supporting or opposing claims. Costello and Mitchell (1995: 1) draw a distinction between "argument as a means to put forward a position in preference to others and argument as a means to discover a, perhaps shared, perspective." Arguments, then, may function to report competition between positions, or a consensus. There is a growing body of literature on argument, both in the rhetoric of argument and how the process of argument in written and spoken text can facilitate learning. An important influence has been the work of Toulmin (1958; Toulmin *et al.* 1984). Andrews (2000: 7), for example, offers the model in Figure 11.1, which is a variation on Toulmin, Rieke, and Janik's pattern of analysis of the strength of arguments.

Claims are assertions or propositions; *grounds* are the evidence supporting the claims; *warrants* are the relationship between the claims and grounds; *backing* provides the foundation for war rants, perhaps from the state of knowledge in the discipline; *rebuttals* are conditions in which there are exceptions to claims; and *qualifiers* limit the validity of the warrant, using phrases such as "presumably" and "so far as the evidence goes" (Andrews 2000: 7). This model is valuable for pedagogical purposes in that it provides a clear framework within which weaknesses in written argument can be identified and explained to students (although not necessarily using the same terminology as Andrews or Toulmin *et al.*). So, for example: the evidence (grounds) for a claim might be insufficient or inadequate; it may not be made clear how the claim derives from (backing) or relates to (warrant) the current state of knowledge; or that there is insufficient hedging (qualification) of a link

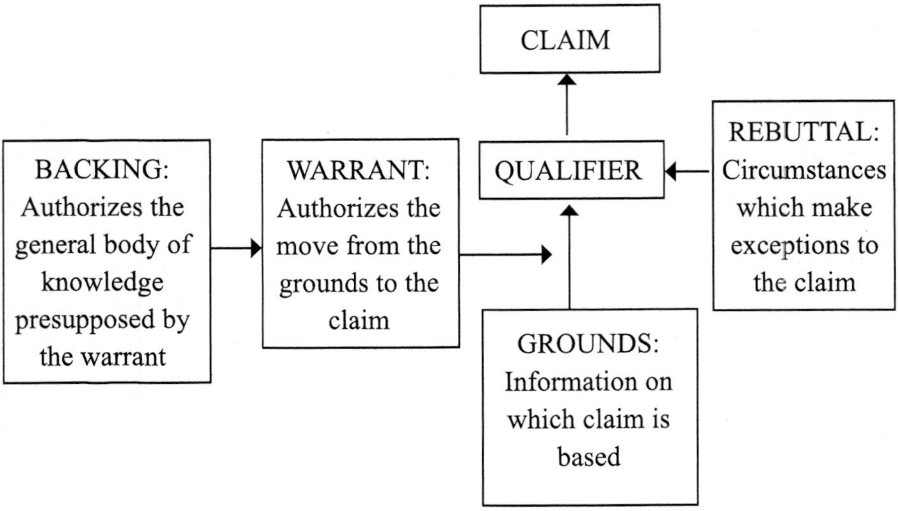

Figure 11.1 A model for analyzing argument

between evidence and claim, or insufficient recognition of limitations on the claim (rebuttal).

Genre analysis

Much of the in-house material for teaching academic writing used in EISU has been heavily influenced by the approach to *genre analysis* developed primarily by Swales (e.g.,1990) and also Dudley-Evans (e.g.,1987). In this approach, functional elements of texts ("steps" that combine into "moves") are identified, with genres having characteristic patterning of these functional elements. However, although a genre-based approach to the teaching of laboratory reports and parts of larger texts, such as dissertation and thesis introductions and discussion sections (e.g., Dudley-Evans 1985; Dudley-Evans & Hopkins 1988) has provided useful insights into their discourse structure, the value of such an approach in the description and teaching of essays is less clear. Dudley-Evans (2002), for example, questions the feasibility of a genre approach, primarily because:

> The genre of the assessed essay ... is much less predictable than the research report and dissertation. (2002: 235)

However, Coffin and Hewings (2003) suggest that different types of essays – "exposition," "discussion," and "challenge" essays – have characteristic structures, determined by their particular rhetorical purpose. These are shown in Table 11.1. Their framework is based on analysis of academic text conducted

Table 11.1 Three ways of structuring an argumentative essay

Argument structure	Exposition	Discussion	Challenge
Rhetorical purpose	To put forward a point of view or argument	To argue the case for two or more points of view about an issue	To argue against a point of view or argument
Functional stages	Background overall position/argument Subarguments and supporting evidence (counter-arguments) Reinforcement of overall position/ argument	Background Issue Subarguments and supporting evidence Overall position/ argument	Background Position challenged Rebuttal of subarguments and supporting evidence Overall position/ argument

mainly during the 1980s and 1990s, intended to improve the understanding and production of academic texts in Australian secondary schools (see, for example, Coffin 1996; Humphrey 1996; Rothery 1994). This work drew on Systemic Functional Linguistic theory, which sees a genre as a "staged, goal-oriented social process" (Martin & Rothery 1980-1981). This perspective emphasizes that:

> 1. any genre pertains to a particular culture and its social institutions (hence "social process");
> 2. social processes are purposeful (hence "goal-oriented");
> 3. it usually takes a number of steps to achieve one's purpose (hence a "staged" process). (Painter 2001: 167-8)

While Coffin and Hewings's "functional stages" are to some extent comparable with "moves" in a Swales-influenced genre analysis, the generality of their stages perhaps makes them more useful in seeking to characterize the organization of essays for pedagogical purposes. However, the limitations of this work should be noted here. As Coffin (2004: 236) points out, "genres emerging from such research do not represent an exhaustive categorisation of argument structures in English" and nor, of course, do they seek to describe the texts other than essays that many students are required to write. Further, whereas my view is that most of the essays my Education students are required to write could be organized using one or other of these general patterns, the relevance of the patterns to the local requirements of the School of Education needs more systematic inquiry (see the section on limitations, p. 319).

The materials

The materials come from those stages of the course that focus on the key features of essays, as identified above.

Stage 1: Making claims

In Stage 1 we explore the claims (or generalizations) presented in support of an argument. The starting point is a short, nonacademic text: a newspaper article entitled "Is it OK ... to have a conservatory?" (see Appendix 11.1). The reason for beginning with a nonacademic text of this type is that it is reasonably simple, is short yet complete, and has certain of the characteristics of an academic essay – primarily, that it presents claims on two sides of an argument and provides evidence to support some of these claims (although in a rather different form from that conventionally found in an academic essay).

After I have introduced the topic of the text, "Conservatories," students read it and then work in pairs or small groups to answer the following questions:

(i) What points does the writer present in favor of/against conservatories?
(ii) What points does the writer present in favor of/against wooden and PVC conservatories?

The most likely answers are summarized in Table 11.2.

Table 11.2 Conservatories – Pros and cons

Conservatories: Points in favor	Conservatories: Points against
• Extra room • A sense of the outdoors when it is too cold to sit outside • A winter home for plants • Relatively low cost • (in theory) Can help reduce domestic emissions of CO_2 *Conservatories: Wood versus PVC* • Wood is a renewable resource versus PVC from nonrenewable oil. • In manufacture, PVC produces hazardous waste and uses energy. • PVC is difficult to recycle.	• (in practice) Increase emissions of CO_2 when they are heated in cold weather or air-conditioned in summer

We then turn to a more academic topic: *Discuss the relative merits of state-funded and private education*. This topic was selected because it has general relevance to students of Education and is something on which they are likely to have an opinion. In order to provide a common focus of interest, I encourage students to consider particularly the situation in the United Kingdom, although I point out that they may wish to bring in information about the debate in their own countries. (See further discussion of this in the section on limitations below.)

First, students work in small groups to brainstorm arguments for private education (and conversely against state-funded education) and against private education (and conversely for state-funded education). They are given two in each category (see Table 11.3) and asked to provide more. At the end of the discussion these are written up on the board.

By the end of Stage 1, I hope that students will see that the "skeleton" of an essay may be a series of claims made about a particular topic, here conservatories and the funding of education.

Table 11.3 Private versus state-funded education

Private education: Arguments for .../State-funded education: Arguments against ... • Educational results are better in private schools than in state schools. • Private schools have greater independence and can respond to the needs of their students. • __________ • __________ • __________
Private education: Arguments against .../State-funded education: Arguments for ... • Private education is socially divisive; power is in the hands of the privately educated. • The existence of private education drives down standards in state-funded education. • __________ • __________ • __________

Stage 2: Providing evidence

Stage 2 focuses on the importance of providing evidence to support claims. I introduce this by making the claim that "The University of Birmingham is one of the best universities in the world." I encourage students to offer challenges to the claim – "How do you know?," "Prove it!" – and then offer pieces of information extracted from the university's Web site. As each one is revealed, students are encouraged to question and challenge the information as evidence supporting my claim. Examples of information from the university's Web site[1] and examples of the kinds of questions and challenges students have made are given in Table 11.4:

---

[1] www.bham.ac.uk (last accessed November 4, 2006).

Table 11.4 The University of Birmingham – Claims and queries

- Birmingham Business School is listed in the global top 50 of the MBA rankings by the Economist Intelligence Unit. In 2004/2005 the University's MBA was ranked the UK's number one Program by *The Economist*. ("Number one in the UK doesn't make it 'one of the best in the world' "; "What has happened to it since 2004/2005?"; "A good business school doesn't mean that the whole university is good.")
- Birmingham is one of the top six universities that major companies target when they are looking for new employees.
  ("What is the source of this information?"; "If this is just information for the UK, it doesn't say much about the standing of the university in the world.")

I conclude this brief introduction by asking students whether I have convinced them of the validity of my claim. Usually, – and quite rightly – the answer is "No!"

We then return to the "Conservatories" text and students identify the evidence the author presents to support each of the claims he makes. The most likely answers are given in Table 11.5.

Students are asked to note not only what evidence is reported, but also where the weight of the evidence lies. They note that the balance is very much in the "points against conservatories" category, which seems to be reflective of the author's point of view. Students at this stage also noted the fact that the evidence for PVC conservatories comes from the British Plastics Federation and, because this organization has a vested interest in promoting PVC conservatories, this is less useful evidence than that taken from a (perhaps more neutral) WWF report. Again, this choice of weaker evidence may reflect the author's position on the subject.

Finally in this stage, we return to the points made in the private versus state-funded education debate. Students are asked to consider the *types* of evidence that would be needed to support these. Suggestions for the four points given to students are listed in Table 11.6.

Table 11.5 Conservatories – Pros and cons: The evidence

Conservatories: Points in favor	Conservatories: Points against
• (in theory) Can help reduce domestic emissions of CO_2 *Evidence*: "This is because, in cold weather, it acts as a buffer zone ... "	• (in practice) Increase emissions of CO_2 when they are heated in cold weather *Evidence*: (i) glass is a poor insulator; (ii) more conservatories are being heated • or air-conditioned in summer *Evidence*: (i) running homes accounts for 28% of CO_2 emissions; (ii) fashion for air-conditioning identified • The more general point that people don't use conservatories in the way intended *Evidence*: statement by an authority
Conservatories: Wood versus PVC	
• Wood is a renewable resource versus PVC from nonrenewable oil. • In manufacture, PVC produces hazardous waste and uses energy. • PVC is difficult to recycle.	*Evidence for wood*: Wood is more sustainable. *Evidence for PVC*: Painting of wood has impact on environment versus PVC lasts longer.

Table 11.6 Private versus state-funded education: The evidence

Private education: Arguments for .../State-funded education: Arguments against ...
• Educational results are better in private schools than in state schools. (*Evidence*: some statistical information comparing educational results in private and state schools) • Private schools have greater independence and can respond to the needs of their students.

(to be continued)

(continued)

Private education: Arguments for .../State-funded education: Arguments against ...
(*Evidence*: examples of how private schools can respond to students' needs more easily)
Private education: Arguments against .../State-funded education: Arguments for ...
• Private education is socially divisive; power is in the hands of the privately educated. (*Evidence*: examples of how private education can be socially divisive; numbers of government ministers [e.g., in the UK] who were privately educated) • The existence of private education drives down standards in state-funded education. (*Evidence*: reasons *why* it may drive down standards in state-funded education; examples of how it does)

Stage 3: Types of evidence

Stage 3 looks in more detail at the type of evidence that is used in essays and the way in which the source of such evidence is presented. First we return to the "Conservatories" text. Students are asked to identify the *sources* of each piece of evidence. Likely answers are given in Table 11.7.

Table 11.7 Conservatories – Claims, evidence, and their sources

Claim	Evidence	Source
• Conservatories (in theory) can help reduce domestic emissions of CO_2.	"This is because, in cold weather, it acts as a buffer zone ... "	None indicated.

(to be continued)

(continued)

Claim	Evidence	Source
• Conservatories (in practice) increase emissions of CO_2 when they are heated in cold weather ...	(i) Glass is a poor insulator. (ii) More conservatories are being heated.	The Building Research Establishment Two studies by the Bartlett School at University College London
• ... or when they are air-conditioned in summer.	(i) Running homes accounts for 28% of CO_2 emissions. (ii) Fashion for air-conditioning identified	Professor Geoff Levermore A study by the Bartlett School at University College London
• People don't use conservatories in the way intended.	Statement by an authority	Professor Geoff Levermore
• Wood is a renewable resource versus PVC from nonrenewable oil.	(i) Wood is more sustainable. (ii) Painting of wood has impact on environment versus PVC lasts longer.	Report from the WWF The British Plastics Federation
• In manufacture, PVC produces hazardous waste and uses energy.		
• PVC is difficult to recycle.		

Students are invited to comment on how reference to sources in the

"Conservatories" text is different from that usually found in essays. For example, we note that:

> The construction of a building, in this case a home, causes pollution and produces CO_2, but a more significant impact comes from the actual running of it, according to Professor Geoff Levermore, a building energy expert and member of the Intergovernmental Panel on Climate Change.

would be more acceptable in an essay if phrased like this:

> The construction of a building, in this case a home, causes pollution and produces CO_2, but a more significant impact comes from the actual running of it (Levermore, date).

It is not necessary in the "author-date" system of referencing required in the School of Education to use title or first name, nor is it normally necessary to establish the author's credentials. (A later class on referencing conventions develops these points, but this is not reported on in this paper.)

Next, students are provided with selected quotations and other information relevant to the bullet points in Table 11.6 in the private versus state-funded school argument. These are given in full in Appendix 11.2. Note that a wide variety of sources is used, including books, papers in edited collections, academic journals, and government and other Web sites. At a later stage in the course, we return to these sources to consider, for example, the relative merits of peer-reviewed publications and nonrefereed Web sites, and also the referencing conventions for these and other documents.

Students are asked to work in pairs to decide how they would use this information in support of the points in the argument. Some choices are relatively straightforward. For example, the information:

H "Despite having only 7% of the school population, independent schools supply 38% of all candidates gaining three A grades or better at A-level. In 2004, 53.5% of GCSE entries from independent schools scored an A* or A, [while] at state schools, this figure was 13.4%." These figures refer to the UK.

would be useful in supporting the claim that:

- Educational results are better in private schools than in state schools.

Similarly, the information that:

E " ... public, or independent, school- and Oxbridge-educated persons continue to be overrepresented in variously defined high-status occupations or élites in British society."

could be used to support the claim that:

- Private education is socially divisive; power is in the hands of the privately educated.

Other pieces of information need to be combined or interpreted in someway to provide support. For example, it is necessary to compare the information in:

J In 2006, the average class size in UK independent schools was 9.87 children per teacher.

with that in the graph in F:

F Chart C: Average size of classes taught by one teacher in maintained primary and secondary schools, England, January 1994 to 2006

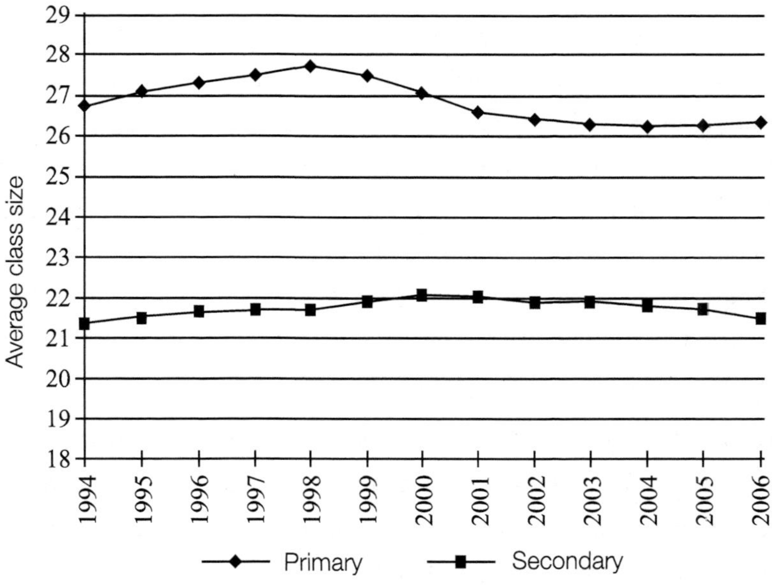

in order to provide support for:

- Private schools have greater independence and can respond to the needs of their students.

It might reasonably be assumed that with substantially smaller average class sizes, teachers in private schools are able more easily to respond to the needs of individual students. Care would need to be taken in comparing the figures in these two sources of information: In J a figure is given for all independent schools (including both primary and secondary), and in F figures are separate for state-funded ("maintained") primary and secondary schools.

Other information might be used to support more than one claim. For example, the information in:

C "Many [private] schools use the main national salary scale as a minimum, often enhancing it by adding an agreed percentage. Larger schools often have their own pay scales, which are likely to be above the standard scales."

could be used to support the claim that:

- Private schools have greater independence and can respond to the needs of their students.

on the basis that by being able to offer higher pay to teachers, they are able to attract specialists in areas where they have particular needs. Alternatively, it might be used in support of the claim that:

- The existence of private education drives down standards in state-funded education.

on the basis that if private schools can afford to pay more for better teachers, these teachers are taken out of state-funded education, lowering overall standards in this sector.

Other information provides contradictory evidence. The information in C above relates to the situation in the UK. However, that in:

I "[P]ublic schools pay higher salaries than non-public schools." This finding was from a survey of teachers conducted in the United States.

suggests that the teacher pay disparities in the UK are not found worldwide.

Students are therefore given the opportunity to build limitations or caveats into their supporting evidence.

The final step in this stage is to ask students to suggest the kinds of evidence they would look for in support of the additional claims they identified in the private versus state-funded debate in Stage 2. Ideally, students would be asked to try to find such supporting information out of class, but this is not practical in this course.

Stage 4: Organizing information for rhetorical purpose

The next stage is to consider the order of presentation of claims and evidence in order to achieve the purpose of the essay. Here we take the now familiar essay title (i), and two variations on the same issue:

(i) *Discuss the relative merits of state-funded and private education.*

(ii) *If you had the money, would you send your children to a private school? Why (not)?*

(iii) *If we genuinely want to improve state-funded education in Britain, private schools should be abolished. Discuss this statement.*

These are examples of titles likely to require, respectively, discussion, exposition, and challenge argument structures (Coffin & Hewings 2003; see above).

The first seems to require arguments to be presented both for state-funded and private education and a judgment on their "relative merits." Coffin and Hewings suggest that the functional stages of this kind of essay are: (i) background; (ii) issue; (iii) subarguments and supporting evidence; and (iv) overall position/argument.

Focusing on the third of these stages, I suggest to students that claims in favor of private/state-funded schools can be organized according to certain criteria: ethics, the quality of the educational experience, examination results, and the wider impact on society. A categorization of relevant claims is presented in the materials, as in Table 11.8.

I then suggest that we might order these claims (together with supporting evidence) either in a "vertical" or a "horizontal" pattern (see Table 11.9). That is to say, in a vertical pattern, we might first put forward all the claims in support of private schools, organized according to the four sets of criteria identified, and follow this with all the claims in support of state-funded schools, organized in a similar way. In a horizontal pattern, on the other hand, we would take each set of criteria in turn, first considering arguments in support of private schools and then arguments in support of state-funded schools.

Table 11.8 Private versus state-funded education – Criteria for evaluation

Criteria	Pro private schools (and anti state-funded schools)	Pro state schools (and anti private schools)
Ethics	• Parents should have the right to choose.	• Morally wrong for educational opportunities to be determined by ability to pay.
Quality of educational experience	• Private schools have greater independence and can respond to needs of students.	• Existence of private education drives down quality of state schools.
Examination results	• Exam results are better in private schools.	• Good exam results are not the only measure of educational achievement.
Wider impact on society	• Private schools can produce people with the qualities needed to become "society's leaders."	• Private schools are socially divisive.

Table 11.9 Patterns of organization for "claims"

Vertical		Horizontal	
1 Pro-private schools	Ethics	1 Ethics	Pro-private schools
2	Educational experience	2 Ethics	Pro-state schools
3	Exam results	3 Educational experience	Pro-private schools

(to be continued)

(continued)

	Vertical	Horizontal	
4	Impact on society	4 Educational experience	Pro-state schools
5 Pro-state schools	Ethics	5 Exam results	Pro-private schools
6	Educational experience	6 Exam results	Pro-state schools
7	Exam results	7 Impact on society	Pro-private schools
8	Impact on society	8 Impact on society	Pro-state schools

Students are then asked to consider how they might organize the information differently in writing essays in response to questions (ii) and (iii) above. In addition, they are asked to consider whether there is any other information they feel it would be necessary to include.

Question (ii), *If you had the money, would you send your children to a private school? Why (not)?*, requires a "yes" or "no" decision and for this decision to be justified. Coffin and Hewings (2003) suggest that the functional stages of this kind of essay are: (i) background; (ii) overall position/argument; (iii) subarguments and supporting evidence (counterarguments); and (iv) reinforcement of overall position/argument.

The differences between this and the suggested functional stages for a discussion essay are that an overall position statement is included prior to the main "claims with evidence" section, and that counterarguments are included. For practical reasons, I usually ask students to assume that in answering this essay they *would* send their children to a private school. The main part of this question then, is the presentation of subarguments (or claims) in favor of private schools, including those in the second column of Table 11.8. There is usually a consensus that the arguments against private schools can be dealt with in a shorter, final section of the main part. The reason given is that these arguments have largely to do with broad concerns of society as a whole, whereas the question focuses on parents' decision to do what is best for their children. Some students have also made the related organizational point that claims related to quality of educational experience and educational results should be highlighted (by being placed first and written about more extensively) over ethical and wider-impact-on-society criteria.

Although a perfectly appropriate response to statement (iii), *If we genuinely want to improve state-funded education in Britain, private schools should be abolished. Discuss this statement*, might be to support the view that private education should be abolished, for practical purposes, I ask students to assume that they will be opposing it. Coffin and Hewings suggest that the functional stages of this kind of essay are: (i) background; (ii) position challenged; (iii) rebuttal of subarguments and supporting evidence; and (iv) overall position/argument.

The main part of this essay, then, is the rebuttal of arguments against private schools, including those listed in third column of Table 11.8. Most students conclude that a horizontal pattern is most appropriate, with each step focusing on one of the sets of criteria. For example:

1. Ethical arguments against private schools (e.g., wrong for opportunities to be determined by pay).
   "However, ..." followed by reasons why these are invalid and/or ethical arguments for private schools (e.g., parents have the right to choose how their children should educated).

Students have suggested other claims that it would be important to introduce in this essay. These include the contention that it would be wrong to abolish private schools, which might provide excellent education, simply in order do away with inequalities produced by parental choice in schooling.

To conclude this section, I should point out (as I do to students) that the aim of Stage 4 is not to provide a "template" for any argumentative essay that the students might be required to write. Rather, it is to help students recognize that although an essay should organize claims in a logical way, there is considerable variation in how claims might be organized within the body of an essay. Students should consider their own purposes in writing the essay – in particular, what position they are trying to persuade their reader to support – and what pattern of organization best achieves this in each case.

Stage 5: The student's position

The question of how opinion is conventionally expressed in academic writing is dealt with at a number of points in the course outside the sessions described here. Some of these are briefly outlined below:

- The use of pronoun "I." We consider when it does appear to be acceptable to use I (in particular, in reporting procedures and choices made in organizing the current text) and when not (including avoiding "I think [etc.]" to preface opinions without special reasons for doing so). (However, see the comment in the next section.)
- The choice of reporting verb in a class on reporting the literature. We consider the implications of choosing verbs that are "less endorsing" (Coffin & Hewings 2003) of the reported writer's work (e.g., claim, contend) and those that are "more endorsing" (e.g., show, prove).
- The indication of the strength of conviction to be attached to a claim. We focus particularly on language resources for making stronger and weaker claims.

In Stage 5, however, we consider just one aspect of expressing opinion, that of providing a statement of the student's own position or stance on the subject of the essay.

The material used at this stage is given in Appendix 11.3. The aim of the activity is to encourage students to consider whether a question requires a statement of the student's own position on the subject – as (i) and (ii) appear to – and how this position might be expressed. Students go on to suggest alternative position statements for these essays, and possible variations on the "In this essay I (will) argue/consider ... " formula.

Limitations and future developments

As I mentioned earlier, most in-house EISU materials are constantly being developed and refined as we understand more about the needs of particular groups of students and the disciplines and departments within which they work. To conclude, I will highlight some of the limitations of the materials presented here (and to some extent of the academic writing course more generally) and suggest in broad terms some ways ahead.

First, the educational debate focused on in the materials is private versus state-funded school education. This was selected because I felt it was such a general educational issue that all students would be able to contribute to it. However, the status of private education varies widely around the world. In some countries, the proportion of students in private education is so small that the existence of private schools is not an issue, whereas in others private education is very much the norm. Consequently, there is often a wide range of views in the class about what exactly the private versus state-funded school debate is, and even whether there is any controversy to discuss. It would therefore be useful to identify an alternative educational issue on which there is a greater consensus among students about the nature of the debate, even though there may be a diversity of opinion on it.

Second, it was noted that the framework provided by Coffin and Hewings (see Table 11.1) does not represent all argument structures and should be taken only as a very useful starting point that requires further development. Coffin (2004), for example, has already presented an extension of the framework, and I hope to explore further its relevance to the essays written in the School of Education. This might be done through: an examination of set topics and essay titles; discussion with staff in the school about the type of texts (in terms of content and organization) these topics and titles are intended to elicit; and further analysis of students' essays themselves.

Third, although the materials take into account to some extent the requirements of writing in the social sciences and education more specifically, local requirements and preferences could be explored further and responded to. To give some indication of the potential value of this, as part of a recent e-mail communication with a member of the academic staff in the School of Education, I received the following message:

> For many assignments in the School of Education, we actively encourage students to reflect on their own experiences as teachers or as learners, and for this anything other than the use of the first person singular becomes very awkward. Additionally, most of us don't

mind students using "I" when expressing their own opinions in essays – as long as they don't overdo it and start to sound like egomaniacal pseudo-experts! So in most cases, students should and do use it.

I noted in the previous section, Stage 5, the kind of information I give to students on the use of "I" in their writing, but clearly the message I received suggests that a wider use of "I" is permitted – or perhaps even expected – by academic staff in the School of Education.

Finally, a weakness of the academic writing program generally, and the materials presented here more specifically, is the lack of a direct link between what is taught in the class and the assessed essays (and other pieces of writing) that students are required to produce. As I mentioned earlier, class time is very limited, and it is impractical to ask students to do writing for the course outside class. Consequently, there is no opportunity directly to assess how students implement in their writing what they have been taught. Clearly, in a more ideal context this would be possible. However, as part of the package of teaching provided to the School of Education, EISU staff, including myself, are available to work individually with students on their assessed writing. This provides some opportunity, although limited in time and not taken up by all students on the course, to examine whether students make use of the information provided in the materials, and to refer students back to the materials where this would help them to improve their writing.

Discussion questions and tasks

Reflection

1. What have you learned in this chapter about the kinds of evidence that can be used to support claims in essays, and how will this influence your teaching?
2. Of the four theoretical approaches discussed in the section on theoretical influences, which, in your view, is the most important in teaching students about essay writing?
3. The materials presented in this chapter began with a short argumentative text taken from a newspaper (see Appendix 11.1). What other kinds of texts would be appropriate for introducing the ideas of claims and

supporting evidence?

4. Have you ever designed materials to teach essay writing? If so, what have you learned from this chapter that would make you do things differently in the future?

Evaluation

5. Look at an EAP textbook that includes materials on essay writing and evaluate these in light of what you have learned in this chapter.

Adaptation/Design

6. The materials described in this chapter were designed to teach essay writing to students doing Education programs. What adaptations would you need to make to them for students in a different discipline? If possible, answer this question with a specific group of students in mind.

Appendix 11.1

Ethical living

Is it OK ... to have a conservatory?

Dominic Murphy's guide to a good life

Dominic Murphy

The Guardian, Tuesday, October 3, 2006

If the domestic must-have of the 1970s was the fitted kitchen, today it is surely the conservatory. More than 200,000 are built each year, and this figure shows no sign of shrinking. You can buy one at DIY stores as easily as a bag of compost and rarely need planning permission.

A conservatory gives you an extra room, a sense of the outdoors when it is too chilly for the real alfresco, and a bijou winter home for your begonias. Not bad for the price of a family car.

But at what cost to the environment? Most conservatories are made of PVC or wood, and there is fierce debate about which version is the most sustainable. Wood is a renewable resource, whereas PVC comes from oil, produces hazardous waste and gobbles energy in manufacture. It is also difficult to recycle, although progress is being made on this. Nevertheless, a report last year for World Wildlife Fund concluded that wood was the more sustainable.

The British Plastics Federation, however, disputes this, claiming that the study "verges on junk science." It points to other reports that seem to plump for plastic-framed windows and says you have to take into account that wood needs painting every so often, which has an impact on the environment. PVC, on the other hand, will last for many years.

This debate, however, distracts from an issue of much more environmental concern: the amount of energy we use in heating – and, more recently, cooling – our conservatories. The construction of a building, in this case a home, causes pollution and produces CO_2, but a more significant impact comes from the actual running of it, according to Professor Geoff Levermore, a building energy expert and member of the Intergovernmental Panel on Climate Change. Cooking, watching TV, keeping warm, and so on at home accounts for 28% of the UK's CO_2 output.

Theoretically, a conservatory can help to reduce our domestic emissions. This is because, in cold weather, it acts as a buffer zone between inside and out, helping to keep the house warm and cutting energy requirements. This principle is taken further in buildings that use "passive solar heating": In winter, a south-facing "conservatory" area not only acts as a draught excluder, but traps the sun's heat, so warming up the interior of the home. For it to work properly, the main part of the house must be separated by doors from the glazed section, and a system of vents and screens is needed so that the building does not overheat in summer.

However, in practice, most conservatories are contributing disproportionate emissions to the atmosphere. These little glass boxes can turn a thermally efficient home into an energy-leaking nightmare. This is not the building's fault, but our own. Conservatories were intended to be used when the temperature permitted, typically between spring and autumn. That is why they are supposed to be separated from the rest of the house by exterior-grade doors, so they would not cool the home in winter. In reality, we want to use them all year round, which means heating them in cold weather.

Glass is a notoriously poor insulator. According to the Building Research Establishment, even good double-glazing loses around seven times more heat than a modern wall. In other words, a heated conservatory is also warming an awful lot of sky. It seems crazy at a time of melting polar ice caps, but the current popularity of outdoor heaters suggests that a lot of people could not care less.

And it is getting worse. According to two studies by the Bartlett School at University College London, domestic conservatories are now being heated more than ever before. In the first study in 1991, when just 50,000 were built a year, researchers found that 91 percent of people used heating in their conservatory, and about half of them did it regularly. The latest findings, to be published in the new year, suggest a more depressing trend, with a greater number heating them for a longer period. The study also identifies a new fashion: air-conditioning units to keep them cool in summer.

This situation is unacceptable, says Levermore. "If people use a conservatory in the way it is intended, then fair enough. But they don't – it's a cheap way of getting an extra room."

But what is to be done? Tighten up planning and building regulations, as Levermore suggests? At the moment, most conservatories can be built as permitted development, and only need planning permission in conservation, heritage or other environmentally sensitive areas. Some small conservatories are even exempt from building regulations, so theoretically you could build one with single-glazing.

Making it harder to get a conservatory might deter some people, but would it break bad habits among the rest? How could you legislate against heating conservatories in winter and switching on the air-con in summer? As we get stuck into autumn, it is one for the politicians to ponder, but as climate scientists keep reminding us, they should pull their fingers out.[2] Those people in glass houses might not be throwing stones this winter, but a lot of them will be turning up the heating.

© Guardian News & Media, Ltd., 2006. http://environment.guardian.co.uk/print/0,,329591357-121571,00.html (accessed October 24, 2006).

Appendix 11.2

A "Many private schools have greater resources than do state schools ... In general, the high fees charged by private schools allow them to provide

[2] "Pull their fingers out" means "hurry up," "stop prevaricating."

relatively well-maintained buildings, smaller classes, better equipment and facilities."

B Private schools "continue to play a dominant role in the self-perpetuation of recruitment to elite positions."

C "Many [private] schools use the main national salary scale as a minimum, often enhancing it by adding an agreed percentage. Larger schools often have their own pay scales, which are likely to be above the standard scales."

D " ... those already occupying high positions,who tend to be drawn from public schools, naturally wish to hire and work with people like themselves – those who went to the same kinds of schools. At the same time, greater social confidence makes those who are privately educated better suited to leadership positions. Demand and supply factors thus reinforce each other, and solidify a class dominance."

E "... public, or independent, school- and Oxbridge-educated persons continue to be overrepresented in variously defined high-status occupations or élites in British society."

F

Chart C: Average size of classes taught by one teacher in maintained primary and secondary schools, England, January 1994 to 2006

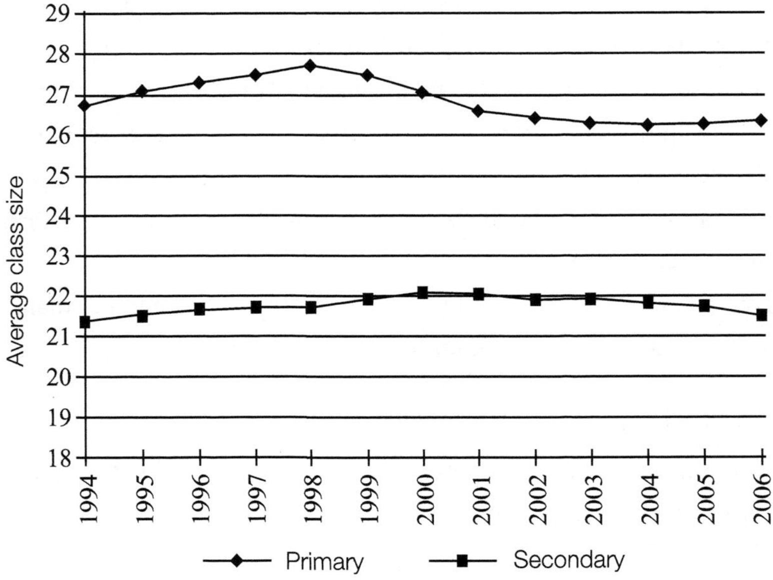

G "[A] system of superior private schools open to the wealthier classes, but out of reach of poorer children however talented and deserving ... much the most flagrant inequality of opportunity, as it is the cause of class inequality generally, in our educational system."

H "Despite having only 7% of the school population, independent schools supply 38% of all candidates gaining three A grades or better at A-level. In 2004, 53.5% of GCSE entries from independent schools scored an A* or A, [while] at state schools, this figure was 13.4%." These figures refer to the UK.

I "[P]ublic schools pay higher salaries than non-public schools." This finding was from a survey of teachers conducted in the United States. (Note: in the United States, public schools = state-funded schools; nonpublic schools = private schools).

J In 2006, the average class size in UK independent schools was 9.87 children per teacher.

K "... from 1997/1998 to 2002/2003, the numbers of state school students admitted each year to our leading universities has risen both in actual numbers – from 16,900 to 22,800 – and as a proportion of the overall intake – from 61% to 68%." These figures refer to the UK.

Sources

A Sullivan, A., & Heath, A. F. (2003). Intakes and examination results at state and private schools. In G. Walford (ed.). *British private schools: Research on policy and practice*. London: Woburn Press, p. 77.

B Giddens, A. (1979). An anatomy of the British ruling class. *New Society*, October 4.

C Web site of the Private Schools Directory, www.privateschools.co.uk/ jobs. htm; last accessed December 4, 2006.

D Prowse, M. (1999). A private problem. *Prospec*t 45, www. rospectmagazine. co.uk/article_details.php?id=3845; last accessed November 30, 2006.

E Reid, I.,Williams, R., & Rayner, M. (1991). The education of the élite. In G. Walford (ed.). *Private schooling: Tradition, change and diversity*. London: Chapman, pp. 14-34.

F UK Government Department for Education and Skills. www.dfes. gov.uk/

trends/index.cfm?fuseaction=home.showChart&cid=3&iid=11& chid=43; last accessed November 30, 2006.

G Crossland, C. A. R. (1956). *The future of socialism*. London: Jonathan Cape.

H Independent Schools Council, www.isc.co.uk/index.php/5; last accessed November 29, 2006.

I Chambers, J. G. (1988). Patterns of compensation of public and private school teachers. In T. James & H. M. Levin (eds.). *Comparing public and private schools*. Philadelphia, PA: The Farmer Press, p. 215.

J BBC Web site, http://news.bbc.co.uk/1/hi/education/4753321.stm; last accessed November 30, 2006.

K Lampl, P. (2005). Foreword to *State school admissions to our learning universities: An update to "The Missing 3000."* Sutton Trust Report. London: Sutton Trust; www.suttontrust.com/annualreports.asp; last accessed November 30, 2006.

Appendix 11.3

Here are the first six sentences in the introduction to an essay on the private versus state school debate. They are jumbled up. What do you think is the best order for them?

Notice that three alternatives are given for sentence (c). Which version of sentence (c) would you choose for each of the following tasks?

(i) Discuss the relative merits of state-funded and private education.

(ii) If you had the money, would you send your children to a private school? Why (not)?

(iii) If we genuinely want to improve state-funded education in Britain, private schools should be abolished. Discuss this statement.

(a) However, there is often considerable debate about their relative effectiveness in providing education, the impact of private schools on state schools, and even whether private schools should be allowed to exist.

(b) State schools, on the other hand, are administered by local or national government, and paid for from government funds.
(c1) In this essay, I will argue that it is perfectly acceptable for parents with the money to do so to send their children to private school, and beneficial for their children.
(c2) In this essay, I will argue that it is possible to raise the quality of education in state schools while, at the same time, maintaining a private sector in education.
(c3) In this essay, I consider the arguments for and against state and private schools.
(d) Private, or independent, schools are those not administered by the state and which are totally or partially funded from the tuition fees paid by students.
(e) The focus will be on the situation in the United Kingdom, although illustrations from other countries will be presented where relevant.
(f) In many countries, private and state schools coexist to provide primary and secondary education.
The most likely answers are –

1 = d   5 = c1 in response to question (ii)
2 = b   5 = c2 in response to question (iii)
3 = f   5 = c3 in response to question (i)
4 = a   6 = e

References

Andrews, R. (2000). Learning to argue in higher education. In S. Mitchell & R. Andrews (eds.). *Learning to argue in higher education.* Portsmouth, NH: Boynton/Cook, pp. 1-14.

Baynham, M. (2000). Academic writing in new and emergent discipline areas. In M. Lea & B. Stierer (eds.). *Student writing in higher education: New contexts.* Buckingham: The Society for Research into Higher Education and Open University Press, pp. 17-31.

Bazerman, C. (1981). What written knowledge does: Three examples of academic discourse. *Philosophy of the Social Sciences* 11: 361-87.

Berkenkotter, C., & Huckin, T. N. (1995). *Genre knowledge in disciplinary communication: Cognition/culture/power.* Hove: Lawrence Erlbaum.

Candlin, C. N., & Hyland, K. (1999). Introduction: Integrating approaches to the study of writing. In C. N. Candlin & K. Hyland (eds.). *Writing: Texts, processes and practices*. Harlow: Longman, pp. 1-17.

Coffin, C. (1996). *Exploring literacy in school history*. Sydney: Metropolitan East Disadvantaged Schools Program, NSW Department of School Education.

Coffin, C. (2004). Arguing about how the world is or how the world should be: The role of argument in IELTS tests. *Journal of English for Academic Purposes* 3(3): 229-46.

Coffin, C., & Hewings, A. (2003). Writing for different disciplines. In C. Coffin, M. J. Curry, S. Goodman, A. Hewings, T. M. Lillis, & J. Swann (eds.). *Teaching academic writing: A toolkit for higher education*. London: Routledge, pp. 45-72.

Costello, P. J. M., & Mitchell, S. (1995). Introduction – Argument: Voices, texts and contexts. In P. J. M. Costello & S. Mitchell (eds.). *Competing and consensual voices: The theory and practice of argument*. Clevedon, UK: Multilingual Matters, pp. 1-9.

Curry, M. J., & Hewings, A. (2003). Approaches to teaching writing. In C. Coffin, M. J. Curry, S. Goodman, A. Hewings, T. M. Lillis, & J. Swann (eds.). *Teaching academic writing: A toolkit for higher education*. London: Routledge, pp. 19-44.

Dudley-Evans, T. (1985). *Writing laboratory reports*. Melbourne: Nelson Wadsworth.

Dudley-Evans, T. (ed.) (1987). Genre analysis and ESP. *ELR Journal* 1. Birmingham: The University of Birmingham.

Dudley-Evans, T. (1988). A consideration of the meaning of "Discuss" in examination questions. In P. Robinson (ed.). *Academic writing: Process and product*. ELT Documents 129. Modern English Publications with the British Council, pp. 47-52.

Dudley-Evans, T. (2002). The teaching of the academic essay: Is a genre approach possible? In A. Johns (ed.). *Genre in the classroom: Multiple perspectives*. Mahwah, NJ: Lawrence Erlbaum, pp. 225-35.

Dudley-Evans, T., & Hopkins, A. (1988). A genre-based investigation of the discussion sections in articles and dissertations. *English for Specific Purposes* 7, 113-21.

Gilbert, G. N., & Mulkay, M. (1984). *Opening Pandora's box: A sociological analysis of scientific discourse*. Cambridge: Cambridge University Press.

Humphrey, S. (1996). *Exploring literacy in school geography*. Sydney: Metropolitan East Disadvantaged Schools Program, NSW Department of School Education.

Hyland, K. (2000). *Disciplinary discourses*. Harlow, UK: Longman.

Ivanič, R., & Camps, D. (2001). I am how I sound: Voice as self-representation in L2 writing. *Journal of Second Language Writing* 10: 3-33.

Martin, J. R., & Rothery, J. (1980-1981). *Writing project reports 1 & 2* (Working Papers in Linguistics). Sydney: Department of Linguistics, University of Sydney.

Nesi, H., & Gardner, S. (2006). Variation in disciplinary culture: University tutors' views on assessed writing tasks. In R. Kiely, P. Rea-Dickins, H. Woodfield & G. Clibbon (eds.). *Language, culture and identity in applied linguistics*. London: BAAL/Equinox, pp. 99-117.

Painter, C. (2001). Understanding genre and register: Implications for language teaching. In A. Burns & C. Coffin (eds.). *Analysing English in a global context*. London: Routledge, pp. 167-80.

Paltridge, B. (2002). Genre, text type, and the English for Academic Purposes (EAP) classroom. In A. Johns (ed.). *Genre in the classroom: Multiple perspectives*. Mahwah, NJ: Lawrence Erlbaum, pp. 73-90.

Rothery, J. (1994). *Exploring literacy in school English*. Sydney: Metropolitan East Disadvantaged Schools Program, NSW Department of School Education.

Starfield, S. (2004). Word power: Negotiating success in a first-year sociology essay. In L. J. Ravelli & R. A. Ellis (eds.). *Analysing academic writing: Contextualized frameworks*. London: Continuum, pp. 66-83.

Swales, J. M. (1990). *Genre analysis: English in academic and research settings*. Cambridge: Cambridge University Press.

Toulmin, S. (1958). *The uses of argument*. Cambridge: Cambridge University Press.

Toulmin, S., Rieke, R., & Janik, A. (1984). *An introduction to reasoning* (2nd ed.). London: Collier Macmillan.

12

Writing for publication: Corpus-informed materials for postdoctoral fellows in perinatology

Christine B. Feak and John M. Swales

Summary

In the first part of this chapter, we discuss how we became involved in a contract to deliver a series of seminars on research writing for a multinational group of specialist medical researchers. We then outline our basic thinking when developing advanced ESP/EAP courses, including a focus on rhetorical consciousness-raising and genre analysis and an appropriate attention to linguistic form. This is followed by a brief section describing how it was possible to create an electronic corpus of 120 research articles in perinatology, which could then be used for analysis and materials preparation.

The main body of the chapter opens with a summary of the syllabus for a 15-hour seminar course. We placed particular stress on the discussion sections of medical research articles, partly because they tend to be the longest and most complex sections, but more importantly because it is this part-genre that receives the most critical attention from manuscript reviewers. Another aspect worth pointing out is that halfway through the course, we took the participants to a computer lab so they could learn how to apply concordance software to the perinatology corpus. The longest section of the chapter is devoted to displays of some of the materials we designed, each of which is followed by a commentary discussing participant reactions and response. After this, we offer a few closing reflections, including the observation that corpus-informed materials have a tendency to emphasize the final textual products rather than the processes that led up to their creation.

Background

Our foray into the teaching of writing in perinatology[1] began quite by chance. The Perinatology Research Branch (PRB) of the US National Institutes of Health in Detroit, Michigan, brings together 35-40 of the best and brightest young perinatologists from around the world to participate in a postdoctoral fellowship program. These fellows come to the PRB to "become productive, independent investigators" in perinatal pathology or ultrasound by participating in efforts to "develop diagnostic and therapeutic strategies to solve clinical problems" (www.med.wayne.edu/prb/home. htm). In addition to conducting research, the PRB also has a very ambitious publication agenda, which is currently aiming at producing 60 papers a year.

The director of the PRB, who is well known in the field of ultrasound, is not a native speaker of English and, perhaps especially for this reason, is keenly aware that to achieve the PRB's publication goals, it is necessary to provide some writing support for the fellows in the form of organized workshops and one-on-one editorial assistance. As a result of this emphasis, an associated goal of the PRB fellowship program is for the fellows to learn to become productive, independent researchers and research writers, especially as many will eventually be returning to their home countries, often in the developing world.

After the PRB had experienced some difficulty in setting up a writing course narrowly focused on the needs and goals of the PRB postdoctoral fellows and staff members, one of the senior PRB administrators decided to try to find the authors of a text that had been used in an earlier workshop. This text was *English in today's research world*, written by us. The director and administrator were surprised – and pleased – to learn that we were working at

[1] Perinatology, also known as maternal-fetal medicine, is a subspecialty of obstetrics that is devoted to managing high-risk pregnancies.

an institution only 40 miles away! After some phone calls and a visit by the administrator and her assistant to Ann Arbor, we found ourselves in what turned out to be an interview with the director to determine whether we could indeed do the job. In the course of the interview, we learned that the director wanted to double the annual number of research papers emanating from the PRB from 30 to 60, an aspiration which we privately thought to be highly ambitious.

Having passed muster, we negotiated a contract for a series of three-hour seminars to be conducted on their premises within the Wayne State University Medical Complex in Detroit. Included in this contract was funding to build a specialized corpus of published writing in perinatology, which we felt would be a major foundation for the teaching materials to be tailored to the needs of our expert group. We also negotiated a fee for some individual editing of manuscripts. Because of the considerable time and effort that would have to go into the preparation of the materials, we arranged for the contract to provide sufficient funds to cover two iterations of the seminar series, one in 2006 and the other in 2007.

Approach to the seminar

In addition to deciding that the course materials would be corpus-informed, we also resolved to draw on an approach that we had developed for advanced graduate writing courses at the University of Michigan (Swales & Feak 2000, 2004), which emphasizes developing rhetorical consciousness via genre analysis, textual explorations of various kinds, as well as the recognition that students bring a considerable amount of expertise into the writing classroom. Something of this approach is captured by this figure:

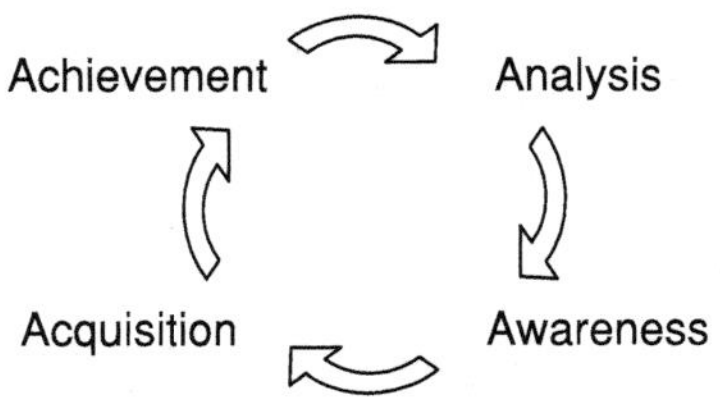

Figure 12.1 Cycle of rhetorical consciousness raising

The figure suggests that the starting point of the cycle depends in part on the writer's previous writing experience and achievement, although in practice it most usually begins with analysis.

A further feature of this seminar series was that we did not want the use of the corpus to be one-sided, that is, simply to function as an aid for producing ELT materials. We therefore arranged for one workshop session to be held in a computer classroom where Wordsmith Tools (Scott 1996) would be introduced. We made sure that the newly created corpus would be available to the PRB for future use so that members could continue exploring the tools of the corpus trade and later make use of the specialized corpus in their own drafting. Our goal here was to help the students acquire a set of skills that could be used in our absence to identify potentially useful patterns of language, examine context "to disambiguate near-synonymous pairs of words" (Lee & Swales 2006), become aware of fixed expressions, and be sensitive to "distributional patterns of language" (Lee & Swales 2006) within perinatology research articles. In taking this approach, we sought to heighten participants' sense of the discoursal world of research in which they were embedded. In sum, this would be a super-specialized English for Specific Academic Purposes (ESAP) activity (Hyland 2006) designed for a group of people who were active researchers, many of whom had several coauthored publications already to their name.

The corpus

We originally selected nine key journals in perinatology from which to build the corpus. These nine journals were chosen because (a) they were the preferred journals to which the PRB fellows were most likely to submit their work; (b) they were highly respected journals in the field; and (c) they were accessible through the University of Michigan Library electronic journals resource. However, according to Gregory Garretson, the skilled corpus compiler we hired, journals varied in the ease with which they could be converted into text files, and in the end we finished up with 140 articles published between 2004 and 2006, with 20 selected from each of seven rather than nine journals (see Appendix for the list of journals). We included only original research articles (RAs), excluding case reports, book reviews, editors' notes, and letters since these appeared to be of less interest to our group. In order to create a suitable electronic corpus, items such as tables and figures, date of acceptance, and author affiliation/contact information were removed, as were all layout features. What remained of each paper was the title, abstract, keywords, section headings, figure/table captions, acknowledgments, and, of course, the body of the text. After excisions, the average length of each RA was about 3,200 words, making a specialized corpus size of approximately 450,000 words. The corpus was designed to be used with Wordsmith Tools, for which the PRB secured a site license, but it will also work with the free Antcorp software which can be downloaded from the Web. Frankly, it surprised us that a corpus of this size and quality could be created by a graduate student in computational linguistics under a contract for only 25 hours work. Obviously, the era of specialized corpora in ESP contexts is upon us (Connor & Upton 2004; Flowerdew 2004; Harwood 2005; Lee & Swales 2006).

The course outline

In designing the course, it was necessary to work around the highly demanding schedules of the fellows and staff and fit our workshops into the work cycle. “Conference season,” generally in mid- to late winter, had to be avoided and, because of our own teaching schedules, the earliest we could begin was April, some eight months after our initial contact with the PRB. At the request of the director of the PRB, we in fact gave two workshop series, one consisting of five three-hour sessions for the fellows and a shorter series of two workshops for the support staff and some administrators who often were involved in the writing and editing of RAs. The latter we do not discuss further. We also had to consider that our course would be attended by both native speakers and nonnative speakers of English, whose proficiency in English ranged from high-intermediate to highly advanced.

The outline of the five-session course is roughly as follows. Sessions took place at two- to three-week intervals.

Session One

- Orientation to research paper discourse
- Article introductions
    - Rationale, organization, phraseology

  - Citations and tense, reporting verbs
- Methods: Describing cohort studies

Session Two

- Writing a discussion section
  - Goals
  - Some possible points of inclusion
  - Summary of the research, connections to previous work
  - Interpretations, limitations, and counterclaims

Session Three

- Discussion sections continued
  - Strength of claims
- Making recommendations
- Establishing a good flow of information
  - Old to new patterns of information
  - The value of repetition
  - *This* + noun
  - Sentence connectors
- An introduction to Wordsmith Tools and the Perinatology RA corpus
  - Using Wordsmith
  - Exploring a specialized corpus

Session Four

- Abstracts
  - Goals
  - Structured versus unstructured abstracts
  - Opening sentences
  - Stating objectives
  - Compressing methods descriptions
  - Main results
  - Concluding an abstract

Session Five

- Corresponding with journal editors
  - Goals
  - Offering a clear response to criticisms

- Standing your ground
- Cover letter analysis
- Wrap-up

Materials development

In essence, the initial stages of materials preparation involved a multilevel analysis of perinatology research articles, notes from our meeting with the director, and reviews of editor and reviewer correspondence from a medical research journal to which we had access (Benfield & Feak 2006). These investigative forays then had to be converted into workshop texts and tasks, and it is the display and discussion of a few of the ensuing handouts that form the central part of this article. Our first series of activities was primarily designed to persuade participants to view texts as discoursal products rather than sources of medical content. Secondly, we wanted their linguistic attention to range from broad research article features to small specific points. Further, we wanted to encourage an approach that stressed a descriptive "let's look and see" attitude as opposed to one relying on prescriptive rubrics from EFL textbooks or teachers. And finally, we were hoping to offer a few surprises – a few new thoughts – and of course to demonstrate our own professionalism.

Despite having received some writing samples from PRB fellows prior to the start of the workshops, we were unsure of their level of rhetorical awareness. Thus, for the opening activity, called "orientation," we designed a series of tasks that would allow participants to reflect on research writing in perinatology. The original seven tasks turned out to be too long; we therefore provide an abbreviated version, followed by some comments.

Writing for publication: The Perinatology Research Branch

Orientation to research writing

Pair or small-group discussion

Task One

The standard research article typically has a four-section Introduction-Method-Results-Discussion structure, usually known as IMRD. Which section would,

(to be continued)

(continued)

on average,

a) have the highest percentages of passives? ________

b) have the highest percentages of present perfect tenses? ________

c) have the least amount of hedging? ________

d) have the most amount of hedging? ________

e) have the most comparisons with other work? ________

f) have the most amount of nonverbal data? ________

g) give the most attention to the future? ________

Task Two

In English, most nouns are either countable (*book/books* – i.e., they can pluralize) or uncountable (*wisdom* – i.e., they can only be singular). However, in research writing ***some*** uncountable nouns can pluralize. In which of the following might this occur?

Put a checkmark (√) next to those nouns for which you think a plural form is possible.

__________ 1. influenza

__________ 2. information

__________ 3. English

__________ 4. training

__________ 5. behavior

__________ 6. equipment

__________ 7. research

__________ 8. heat

Task Three

Medical research papers typically contain nonverbal data of various kinds, often in the form of figures or tables. There are four main options for referring the reader to this nonverbal data:

__________ A. Survival rates were high (see Table 4).
Survival rates were high (Table 4).

__________ B. As shown in Table 4, survival rates were high.

__________ C. The high survival rates are shown in Table 4.

__________ D. Table 4 shows the high survival rates.

(to be continued)

(continued)

In your experience of medical research papers, which is likely to be the most common? In the blanks above, rank the options from 1 to 4, with 1 being the most common.

Figure 12.2 Session One orientation

Commentary

As might be expected with a group of postdoctoral fellows, the first task proved very easy. Lucky it was the first task! The second task was highly successful, giving rise to animated discussion and several (looked for) surprises. None of the group, for instance, thought that *English* could be pluralized, and we were delighted to show them otherwise. For several, we had prepared data from Google™ Scholar, a site we stressed that could be very valuable, especially as a resource for checking native speaker intuition. Below and opposite is some of the data we had prepared.

Table 12.1 Google™ Scholar "hits" for singular and plural forms of typically "uncountable" nouns

Noun	Plural hits	Singular hits	"Type of" singular hits
Influenza	740	443,000	79,000
Information	452,000	7.5 million	4.0 million
Equipment	95,000	4.1 million	1.2 million
Research	256,000	30.0 million	4.2 million

The perinatology staff was right in guessing that *influenza* is rarely pluralized, although we did find a recent example from the highly prestigious *New England Journal of Medicine*:

> The incubation period of avian influenza A (H5N1) may be longer than other known *influenzas*. (The Writing Committee 2005: 1377)

The other three items listed in the table gave rise to much discussion, and we realized it would have been helpful to have had a laptop with an LCD screen so that we could discuss whether, for example, many of the instances of *informations* came from nonnative speaker authors or were translations. We ourselves were surprised by the results of the last two nouns in the table. It turned out that *equipments* looked quite respectable when embedded in patents, engineering, or management articles. On the last, here is an example from a well-cited RA published as far back as 1965:

> The block replacement policy is similar to the periodic policy in that *equipments* are replaced as they fail. (McCall 1965: 493-524)

As the screenshot from Google™ Scholar below shows, *research* in the plural has a venerable history, as a number of the book titles below illustrate. Our guess is that *research* could easily pluralize in the nineteenth and early twentieth centuries – after all, there is a volume by no less a luminary than Charles Darwin with *researches* in its title – but fell out of favor until recently, and it may be starting to make a comeback, perhaps as a result of nonnative speaker preference for the plural, particularly among speakers of Romance languages.

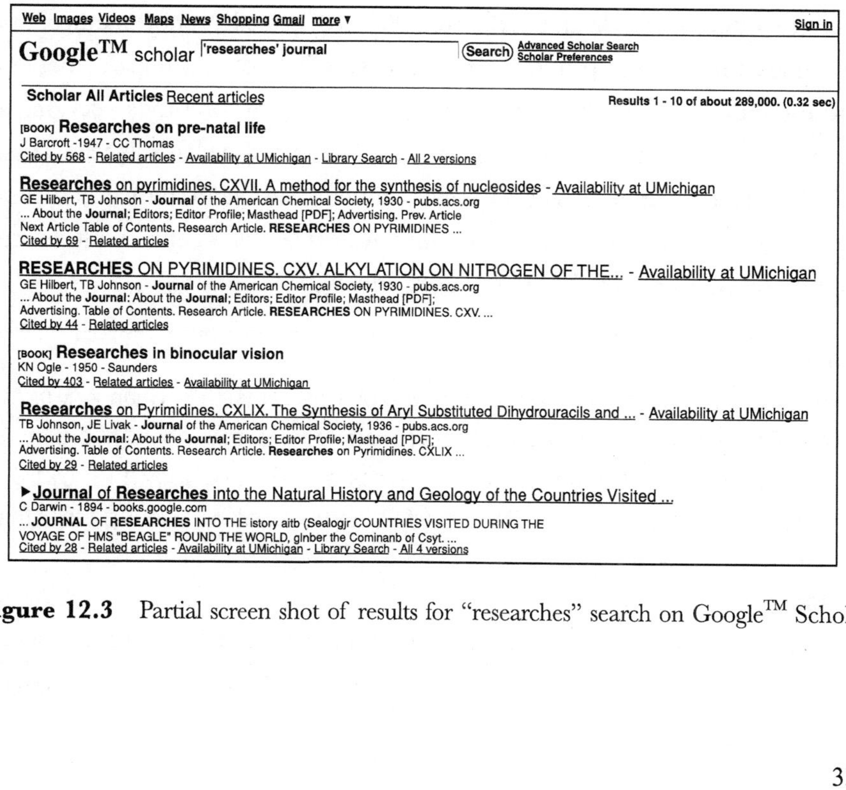

Figure 12.3 Partial screen shot of results for "researches" search on Google™ Scholar

The third task asked workshop participants to estimate frequencies of four ways of referring to nonverbal data. Since Sinclair (1991), corpus linguists, both full-time and occasional, have known that our intuitions are often highly unreliable when it comes to judging what is common and less common. Although we did not keep good notes of the group's opinions, it became clear that intuition alone could not provide a clear answer for Task Three and that only corpus data could offer some guidance. Our own study of a corpus of 50 RAs from thoracic surgery produced the following order (starting with the most frequent): A → C → B → D. Although the picture for perinatology would have to wait until the computer lab session, we were able to point out that there was a clear preference among a sample of medical texts for choosing for subject position the main results (e.g., *survival rates*) as opposed to fronting the nonverbal location reference (e.g., *Table* 4). This finding, if it be such, was eagerly noted by the group.

The material for writing introductions that followed is not discussed here since in EAP circles this is well-trod territory. Instead, we offer the final element of the first day's program on writing up methods. We discovered that many research papers in this field are what are termed "cohort studies," i.e., they track the medical progress or otherwise of selected groups of patients. These cohort studies typically describe, early in the Methods section, the subject/patient/participant characteristics that determined which subjects/patients were included or excluded from those studies. The materials we developed were entitled *Statements of inclusion and exclusion*. We opened with a recent sample text (most of which is reproduced below).

Task Four

Below are the first three paragraphs of a Methods section (C. Shannon, *et al.* 2006. Regimens of misoprostol with mifepristone for early medical abortion: A randomised trial. *British Journal of Obstetrics and Gynaecology* 113: 621-8), published by Wiley-Blackwell. Read the text and discuss with your partner the four questions that follow.

Methods

We conducted a multicentre randomised trial to compare three regimens

(to be continued)

(continued)

of mifepristone-misoprostol medical abortion. Between February 2001 and September 2001, women at three clinics in Canada who requested a medical abortion for termination of an early pregnancy were recruited for this study. The three centres were .... All 971 women who were enrolled gave a written informed consent.

Participants included in the study were women aged 16 years or older, seeking elective abortion of pregnancies less than 57 days as measured since the onset of their last menstrual period (LMP). Participants were required to provide written informed consent prior to participation in the study, to have evidence of an intrauterine pregnancy of 56 days LMP or less on vaginal ultrasound, to be willing to undergo surgical aspiration in case of failed medical abortion, and to have access to a telephone.

Women were excluded if haemoglobin was less than 9.5 g/dl or if they had active hepatic or renal disease, type I diabetes mellitus, adrenal insufficiency, glaucoma, sickle cell anaemia, coagulopathy, uncontrolled seizure disorder, severe cardiovascular disease, allergy or intolerance to mifepristone or misoprostol, used chronic oral steroid medications or anticoagulants, or had any other medical conditions that, in the opinion of the investigator, would compromise their health during the procedure.

1. In paragraph 2, inclusion criteria are given. How many criteria are there?
2. In paragraph 3, we find the exclusion criteria. How many conditions are given for exclusion?
3. What linguistic differences do you note between the two paragraphs?
4. What would you expect the next paragraph to deal with?

Figure 12.4 Writing up methods

Commentary

The first two questions really involve close reading, and, in fact, as readers may discover, are not that simple to answer. (Are the answers 5 and 15?) More importantly, the text demonstrates how important it is in cohort studies to be meticulously clear about inclusion and exclusion – and hence justifies our choice of this topic. The fourth question is also content-based, although in this case of a predictive nature. (As it happens, the next paragraph opens "On day 1, participants were given ...") The third alone asks for some linguistic analysis. The questions were thus designed so that the one we were really interested in was sandwiched between those that the participants would have been more accustomed to thinking about. Perhaps fortunately and certainly not surprisingly, Q3 was responded to the least effectively. As a result, some kind of motivation was established for our main teaching point – corpus-informed differences when writing about inclusions and exclusions. Here is the next part of our handout (slightly tidied up):

DESCRIBING INCLUSIONS

The Shannon paper used different constructions for inclusions and exclusions:

Participants included in the study were women ...

Women were excluded if ...

The difference was that inclusions were firm statements, while exclusions were expressed through a conditional clause. More generally, however, the wider corpus results suggest that the noun *inclusion* is a preferred choice over the verb. Read the sample sentences, and discuss the tasks that follow.

a) A total of 294 patients had adequate ultrasound images and all antenatal and labor data to *meet the study inclusion criteria*.
b) *The inclusion criteria for this study* were singleton pregnancy, live fetus with CRL between 45 and 84mm, and normal fetal karotype.
c) In addition, we used strict and precise definitions that were developed prior to the initiation of the study *for inclusion criteria*, outcomes, and potential confounding variables.
d) Among 38 fetuses scanned between October and December 2003, 18 (11 with normal hearts, 7 with CHD) *were selected for inclusion in this study*. Subjects with exceptionally poor volume image quality *were excluded*, but a deliberate attempt was made to *include* subjects with average (not exceptionally good) volumes.
e) Women *eligible for inclusion* were those who initiated prenatal care prior to 16 weeks gestation. Women *were ineligible if* they were younger than 18 years of age, did not speak or read English, did not plan to carry the pregnancy to term, did not plan to deliver at either of the two research hospitals, and/or were past 16 weeks gestation.

(to be continued)

(continued)

f) *We did not include* patients with prophylactic cerclage, placenta previa, major fetal anomaly, twin-twin transfusion syndrome, ruptured membranes or undetermined gestational age. Oral informed consent preceded each patient's *inclusion in this observational study. An inclusion form* was completed for each patient; it listed the inclusion and exclusion criteria as well as the procedure for collecting the indicators to be analyzed.

1. Are all the finite verbs in the past tense?
2. Inclusions in (a) through (e) all used the nominal form, while (f) used both the nominal and verbal forms. What about *exclusions*? Why might *inclusions* be often nominal, but exclusions typically verbal? (This last is a tough question!)
3. In fact, one of the six examples above was the opening to the Results section. Which one do you think it was?
4. *Meet the criteria* is a common collocation in perinatal research articles. On the next page, you will find all the examples of "meet/meets/met " in the 140-article perinatal corpus. What might you want to conclude?

Figure 12.5 Corpus-based analysis

Commentary

Participants were adamant that Methods should basically be described in the past. On Q2, some of the interesting observations made were that "inclusions" were predetermined and planned, so the "fixed" noun was appropriate; on the other hand, at least some of the "exclusions" would occur "as they arose" and so the verb might be better for a more fluid situation. For Q3, most correctly identified (d), showing their close familiarity; some plausibly argued that (a) would also be possible. There is insufficient space to show the full 37-line concordance for *meet* that we prepared for Q4, but the right collocation outcomes were little short of amazing due to the high degree of restrictedness, which is much greater than that found in Hyland's corpus of 240 research articles drawn from eight fields (e.g., Hyland 2004). The breakdown of the 37 instances was as in Table 12.2 (ignoring intervening modifiers).

Table 12.2 Right collocation outcomes for "meet"

Number	Noun (singular or plural)
29	criterion
3	recommendation
2	standard
1	assumption
1	goal
1	requirement

As often with corpus results, it is equally interesting to notice collocations that might have but did not occur, such as *meet deadlines/demands/difficulties/ targets* and so on. We then turned to Exclusion Statements, dealing first with the fact that 75 percent of these employed past tense verbs (including a few in the present perfect). We then asked participants to comment on the grammatical structure of the following.

A. 1. *Also excluded were* those women for whom the outcome of pregnancy was unknown ...
   2. *Also excluded were* women who experienced a spontaneous (N = 25) or induced (n = 6) abortion ...

B. 1. From these 215, *congenital abnormalities and chromosomal disorders excluded* 47, ...
   2. *The sampling frame for the survey excluded* those without a telephone or those who rely only on cell phones.

C. 1. Of the 36 patients, 1 was removed on day 2 by her physician without completing the protocol and another *was excluded* because of failure to meet early pregnancy failure criteria.
   2. From this group *we excluded* 316 men with missing data for father's occupation ...
   3. Of these, 15 *were excluded* because of CSF findings suggestive of ...
   4. From a total of 75 patients who *were excluded* at the beginning of the study, 31 patients were delivered elsewhere; ...
   5. Of the remaining 874 infants, 68 *were excluded* because of missing information on ...

6. Of 207 datasets, seven *were excluded* due to incomplete clinical data ...
7. Of the 12 fetuses which *were excluded* from the study, seven had isolated CDH ...

In the ensuing discussion, we pointed out in regard to A that these kinds of inversion were rare in English – in fact, these were the only two examples we found – and that nonnative speakers could be advised to avoid attempting them. On B we noted that these active verbs (themselves uncommon in this section) were functionally passives, perhaps somewhat along the lines of "The house sold quickly." Again, we suggested caution in the use of this structure. In contrast, we strongly advocated incorporating C; these prefronted prepositional phrases are pretty common in these perinatal articles and are usefully "snappy." We closed this section then with the following quick oral exercise, which was suitably enjoyed.

Task Five

Rephrase the following so they conform to C above:

1. Michael Jordan is the most famous of all recent basketball players.
2. 65 percent of those who failed to respond to treatment had some form of diabetes.
3. Only two of the six variables investigated produced statistically significant results.
4. 1,509 women were excluded if there was missing information of leisure activities out of a total sample of 48,145.
5. 2% (N = 36) of the total cohort were lost to follow-up (i.e., moved, delivered elsewhere, records not found) and were excluded from the analysis.

Figure 12.6 Rephrasing activity

Abstracts and the writing of abstracts

One topic in the seminar series, which until recently has received little attention in the EAP/ESP literature, is RA abstracts. RA abstracts in perinatology, according to journal policy, can be either unstructured or structured (i.e., divided into sections with section headings, Hartley 1997). Here is a typical example of the former.

Abstract

The object of this study was to evaluate postpartum women for psychiatric symptomatology including cognitive disturbances, anxiety, depression, and anger to better meet their needs for support and involve them in the care of their infants. We interviewed 52 postpartum mothers at the Bronx Lebanon Hospital Center within 5 days of delivery and determined the presence of psychiatric symptoms using the 29-item Psychiatric Symptom Index. Despite the fact that adult mothers were happier they were pregnant (71.4% versus 29.4%; $p = 0.010$) and less likely to be worried about their baby's health (25.7% versus 52.9%; $p = 0.003$), adult mothers demonstrated higher depressive symptomatology ($p = 0.009$), higher amounts of anger ($p = 0.004$), and greater overall psychiatric symptomatology ($p = 0.005$) than adolescent mothers. Mothers whose infants were in the neonatal intensive care unit did not report significantly higher psychiatric symptomatology than mothers whose infants were healthy. Physicians need to be aware of the high levels of depression and anger present among postpartum women so appropriate support can be given. (Hand, I. L., Noble, L., North, A., Kim, M. H., & Yoon, J. J. 2006)

We chose to include abstracts in our workshops because of their importance in attracting readers to read the full article, as well as because of the challenge of compressing the whole of one's work into 100-200 words.

To begin, we built the concept of "moves" already introduced in earlier workshops, using a move structure based on Hyland (2004). We then proposed the moves in Table 12.3 as a guide for deciding which information could potentially be included in an unstructured abstract.

Table 12.3 Abstract moves

Move #	Typical labels	Implied questions
Move 1	Background/introduction/situation	What do we know about the topic?

(to be continued)

(continued)

Move #	Typical labels	Implied questions
Move 2	Present research/purpose	What is this study about?
Move 3	Methods/materials/subjects/ procedures	How was it done?
Move 4	Results/findings	What was discovered?
Move 5	Discussion/conclusion/significance	What do the findings mean?

As can be seen, the illustrative abstract above did not start with an introductory background Move 1, but rather with a Move 2 (purpose/objective), raising the question of what type of opening might be preferred in perinatology RAs. To address this issue we created the following task.

Task Six

In our analysis of 20 perinatology ***unstructured*** abstracts from the corpus, we found that there were four types of opening sentence:

Type a: Purpose/objective (8 instances)

The purpose of this study was to identify risk factors and to characterize infants with transient tachypnea of the newborn (TTN).

Type b: Medical phenomenon (7 instances)

Mild postnatal anemia is common.

Type c: Medical practice (3 instances)

Continuous monitoring by pulse oximetry is a common practice for preterm and critically ill newborns.

Type d: Researcher action (2 instances)

Premature infants <1500 g were randomly assigned to study and control groups.

1. Which type of opening sentence would you prefer to write? Discuss in small groups.
2. Quickly create an example sentence for each of the four kinds of openers presented above.

Figure 12.7 Open sentence analysis

Commentary

The first of these two tasks was done quickly and efficiently, at least by the majority of the group who had good command of English (including a number of native speakers). Overall, there seemed a clear preference for openings describing a medical phenomenon or statement of practice, with several subsequently commenting that they would hope to attract more readers that way. We did the second activity orally round the class, with much successful ad-libbing by the perinatologists.

The second activity we illustrate from the abstract material asks participants to examine some concordance lines from the corpus, although we edited out various highly technical bits (these are shown by ellipses).

Task Seven

Below are 20 sample concordance lines from the corpus of *structured* perinatology journal article abstracts. All the extracts *immediately* follow the uppercase heading *Objective*. Scan the lines and do the tasks that follow. Work in pairs if possible.

Objective

1. To determine whether there is an unconfounded association between ...
2. The purpose of this study was to evaluate how this change affected the rate of ...
3. To examine maternal and neonatal outcomes in expectant management of ...
4. To compare immediate changes in lung compliance following the administration of ...
5. This study was conducted to examine the relation between iron status and ...
6. To determine whether apnea in preterm infants is associated with ...
7. The optimal method of epinephrine administration during ... is not known.
8. To determine if either CPR or continuous IV EPI in NICU is of benefit ...
9. To evaluate the impact of birth weight on development of ...
10. To describe current NICU practices with respect to wrapping preterm infants ...
11. Despite the high frequency of ..., there has been no previous investigation ... to ...

(to be continued)

(continued)

12. The epidemiology of ... in developing countries has been poorly studied.
13. Prospectively validate an antenatal ... risk score ... at two public health ... clinics.
14. To evaluate the mechanism of oxidative stress at glucose levels accompanying...
15. The purpose of this study was to determine whether ... concentrations ... can identify ...
16. The aim of this cohort prospective study was to compare the diagnostic value of ...
17. To systematically identify and synthesize investigations of the effectiveness of ...
18. Insufficient tools for bedside prediction of ... initiated this study.
19. To determine the threshold of metabolic acidosis associated with ...
20. To study the effect of phenobarbital given within six hours of life to... neonates....

1. Which of the above do you consider not to be Objective or Purpose statements? What is the function of the statements that do not point to an objective or purpose? What do you imagine would be the function of the sentence that immediately follows these statements?
2. Of the objective/purpose statements, how many go immediately to a "to + verb" formulation? What are the advantages and disadvantages of this formulation? In this regard, you might like to compare number 16 and number 17.
3. How do you interpret number 13?
4. List all the purposive verbs used (i.e., those following to) and calculate their frequencies. What might this tell us about research in this field?
5. What are the common purposive verbs in your writing? For homework, have a quick scan of some of your texts, using the "find" feature on your computer if you like. E-mail any results to us.

Figure 12.8 Statements of objective analysis

Commentary

In some ways, this activity turned out to be rather easy, and there was some tendency (in our view, at any rate) to digress into discussions of vocabulary and content issues. On question (1) there was wide agreement that items 7, 11, 12, and 18 differed from the majority of statements that clearly began with a purpose, but that a purpose could be nevertheless understood from the statement. Further, if a purpose could not be understood, then a purpose statement would likely follow. No one missed the fact that 13 is lacking a *to*, which none of us could explain as a strategic choice. On question (4) it was clear to all that the choice of verbs (evaluate, validate, identify, synthesize, and so on) suggests rigor and might contribute to an overall positive impression of the research. For most participants there seemed to be little reason to include the phrase, *The purpose of this study*, because the beginning of the abstract was labeled Purpose. One exception is item 16, which provides some detailed information on the nature of the study. In particular 16 indicates that the study is a prospective study[2], a kind of study that is highly valued in medical research because data collection can be tailored to the goals of the research. Given that one goal of an abstract is to attract a readership, this exercise did allow for some discussion of whether beginning with the purpose without any background statement would indeed be engaging.

We also provide this task here to explain that there is some advantage in reconstructing concordance lines in the ways laid out above. First, we can "delete and zap" lines that are linguistically odd; second, the editing out of obscure content helps focus attention on the language; and, third, providing all the beginnings of the sentences is facilitative for those who are less accustomed to reading KWIC (key word in context) concordance lines from the middle.

Some concluding thoughts

Up to this point, and in the spirit of this volume, we have focused primarily on how our corpus informed our materials development. However, we first offer here a word or two about how the corpus increased our sensitivity to certain lexical choices. One of the challenges of developing materials for a highly specialized group, such as the PRB fellows, is dealing with general words or

[2] In a prospective study, people are divided into one of two groups: one that receives an intervention of interest and one that does not.

phrases that may be used in idiosyncratic ways. Take, for instance, the verb *predict*. If we look at the uses of *predict/predicts/predicted* in the Hyland corpus, we notice a certain consistency in the kinds of things that can *predict*. Of course, researchers and scholars can predict, as also can models, hypotheses, theories, analyses, laws, and simulations. In the perinatology corpus, however, we see a broader range of agents that can predict; for example, quantifiable characteristics such as *paternal birth weight, gestational age*, and *endometrial volume* can also be subjects for *predict*, as in

Paternal birth weight *predicts* offspring birth weight.

More generally, in perinatology, *indicators*, *features*, and *characteristics* are also able to predict, but no instances of these collocates were found in the Hyland corpus. For example,

We examined which factors *predict* a rapid delivery of twin B ...

When questions about unexpected collocations arose, we found that our intuitions – indeed our longstanding writing instructor practice – can seduce us into overcorrection. For instance, we may be tempted to propose the following "improvements":

Paternal birth weight *can be used to predict* offspring birth weight. We examined which *factors allow* a rapid delivery of twin B ... to be predicted.

This perception has been reinforced by a 2007 poster presented by Kerans and Maher in which the authors also showed a tendency of language professionals to overedit. Inter alia, they took the case of "done" in sentences like "the analysis was done .... " Their medical corpus showed that this was standard language, even if we would be inclined to substitute something like "carried out" or "performed."

A second concluding observation we would make is that the corpus-informed material we have developed was, as described in Osborne (2004), entirely "top-down," i.e., based on a corpus of target discourses. There was nothing "bottom-up," which he glosses as "drawing data from a learner corpus and using the learners' own productions as a starting point for error correction and gradual enrichment" (p. 251). Even a small corpus of the fellows' drafts would have been useful for classroom editing, for identifying areas of grammatical uncertainty, and for demonstrating that rhetorical success is not impaired by minor language errors.

Some of our more general conclusions verge toward the banal, such as first-time materials are almost always in need of further attention and revision, and running ELT courses for busy people in their own workplaces can be problematic. Beyond these, there are trade-offs between concentration on corpus building/concordancing and on needs analysis/ethnography, as indeed interestingly discussed by Harwood (2007). A corpus-informed approach such as ours can certainly capture interesting features of the *disciplinary surface* of the target discourses, which in turn may well lead to adequate participant interest and rhetorical consciousness raising, but it does tend to focus on the well-machined final product to the detriment of understanding the processes (epistemological, methodological, social, and linguistic) leading to the creation of that product. In our particular case, however, we were fortunate to have other resources to inform our understanding of the process of getting published in medical journals. We had, for instance, complete RA manuscript reviews and associated editorial correspondence from the *Annals of Thoracic Surgery* (Benfield & Feak 2006). The vast majority of this correspondence indicated that good science is acknowledged even when a manuscript requires more language editing than usual. Doubtless, though, further insights might have been gained and further adjustments made if the University of Michigan and Wayne State University had been fewer than 40 miles apart.

Discussion questions and tasks

Reflection

1. What, if anything, have you learned from this chapter about ESP materials development? How could you use this information when developing materials?
2. How easy or difficult do you think it would be to use the corpus-informed approach outlined in this chapter to develop materials?

3. The materials presented in this chapter were designed for learners from the field of perinatology. To what extent could the same approach be taken when designing materials for another context such as law or business?
4. The materials described in this chapter were created for a group that was quite advanced in terms of linguistic ability and professional experience. Are there any aspects of what you read that could easily be adapted for, say, a presessional program for new graduate students from a range of disciplines?

Evaluation

5. Look at some materials you have used recently and examine them critically in relation to what you have learned from this chapter. What improvements could be made?

Adaptation/Design

6. Adapt Task Six on page 339 so that it would be relevant for a particular group of students you know. Explain why you think your adaptation would be meaningful and appropriate for that group.

Appendix: The Perinatology Corpus

Journal name	First file	Number of files	Total words
American Journal of Perinatology	PC.AJP.01.txt	20	51,687
Journal of Maternal-Fetal and Neonatal Medicine	PC.JMM.01.txt	20	56,462
American Journal of Obstetrics and Gynecology	PC.JOG.01.txt	20	62,343
Journal of Perinatology	PC.JOP.01.txt	20	56,561
Journal of Perinatal & Neonatal Nursing	PC.JPN.01.txt	20	101,533
Paediatric & Perinatal Epidemiology	PC.PPE.01.txt	20	65,153
Ultrasound in Obstetrics and Gynecology	PC.UOG.01.txt	20	57,042
	Total:	140	450,781

References

Benfield, J., & Feak, C. B. (2006). Corresponding with journal editors and reviewers. Workshop presented at the 42nd Annual Meeting of the Society of Thoracic Surgeons. Chicago, Illinois, January 24, 2006.

Connor, U., & Upton, T. A. (2004). The genre of grant proposals. In U. Connor & T. A. Upton (eds.). *Discourse in the professions: Perspectives from corpus linguistics*. Amsterdam: John Benjamins, pp. 235-55.

Flowerdew, L. (2004). The argument for using English specialized corpora to understand academic and professional language. In U. Connor & T. A. Upton op cit., pp. 11-33.

Hand, I. L., Noble, L., North, A., Kim, M. H., & Yoon, J. J. (2006). Psychiatric symptoms among postpartum women in an urban hospital setting. *American Journal of Perinatology* 23: 329-34.

Hartley, J. (1997). Are structured abstracts easier to read than traditional ones? *Journal of Research in Reading* 20: 122-36.

Harwood, N. (2005). Nowhere has anyone attempted ... In this article I aim to do just that. A corpus-based study of self-promotional *I* and *we* in academic writing across four disciplines. *Journal of Pragmatics* 37: 1207-31.

Harwood, N. (2007). Political scientists on the function of personal pronouns in their writing: An interview-based study of "I" and "we." *Text and Talk* 27: 27-54.

Hyland, K. (2004). *Disciplinary discourses: Social interactions in academic writing*. Ann Arbor: University of Michigan Press.

Hyland, K. (2006). *English for Academic Purposes: An advanced resource book*. London: Routledge.

Kerans, M. E., & Maher, A. (2007). Discipline & genre-specific language corpus analysis: A handy tool for clarifying language usage. Poster presentation at the PPRISEAL Conference, University of La Laguna, Tenerife, January.

Lee, D., & Swales, J. (2006). A corpus-based EAP course for NNS doctoral students: Moving from available specialized corpora to self-compiled corpora. *English for Specific Purposes* 26: 56-75.

McCall, J. J. (1965). Maintenance policies for stochastically failing equipment: A survey. *Management Science* 11: 493-524.

Osborne, J. (2004). Top-down and bottom-up approaches to corpora in language teaching. In U. Connor & T. A. Upton (eds.). *Applied corpus linguistics: A multidimensional perspective*. Amsterdam: Rodopi, pp. 251-65.

Scott, M. (1996). *Wordsmith Tools*. Oxford: Oxford University Press.

Shannon, C., Wiebe, E., Jacot, F., Guilbert, E., Dunn, S., Sheldon,W., & Winikoff, B. (2006). Regimens of misoprostol with mifepristone for early medical abortion: A randomised trial. *BJOG* 113(6): 621-8.

Sinclair, J. (1991). *Corpus, concordance, collocation*. Oxford: Oxford University Press.

Swales, J. M., & Feak, C. B. (2000). *English in today's research world: A writing guide*. Ann Arbor: University of Michigan Press.

Swales, J. M., & Feak, C. B. (2004). *Academic writing for graduate students*. Ann Arbor: University of Michigan Press.

The Writing Committee of the World Health Organization (WHO) Consultation on Human Influenza A/H5. (2005). Avian influenza A (H5N1) infection in humans. *New England Journal of Medicine* 353: 1374-85.

13

Research-based materials to demystify academic citation for postgraduates

Nigel Harwood

Summary

Learning to cite appropriately is an important skill for student writers at university to acquire. Although citation is mentioned in many English for Academic Purposes (EAP) textbooks, some researchers claim that these textbook writers often limit themselves to teaching writers *how* to cite, rather than *why*. This chapter therefore presents activities aimed at postgraduate learners that focus on the functions of citations in academic writing. The materials are based on the results of interviews with computer scientists and sociologists about citations in their own writing. These writers looked at the citations in one of their recent journal articles or book chapters and identified eleven different citation functions, the most common being (i) *signposting* citations, which direct readers to other sources; (ii) *supporting* citations, which help writers justify the topic of their research; (iii) *credit* citations, which acknowledge authors' debt to other researchers; (iv) *position* citations, which allow authors to identify different viewpoints and arguments; and (v) *engaging* citations, which help authors criticize their sources. A critical pragmatic approach to materials design is taken, whereby learners are provided with models of how to cite like the computer scientists and sociologists, but are also asked to consider how (in)appropriate it is for them to cite in the same way as these authors. The chapter considers ways in which teachers may wish to adapt the materials presented here for different EAP classes, and closes by considering ways in which teachers could extend their treatment of citation.

Introduction

A number of applied linguistics studies of citation have appeared in recent years, following Swales's (1981, 1986, 1990) pioneering work (e.g., Charles 2006; Hunston 1993; Hyland 1999, 2000, 2002; Petrić 2007; G. Thompson & Ye 1991; P. Thompson 2001, 2005; P. Thompson & Tribble 2001). As a result, our understanding of how reporting verbs combine with citation has been enhanced (e.g., Hyland 2002; Thomas & Hawes 1994; G. Thompson & Ye 1991). And Hunston (1993) and others (Burgess & Fagan 2002; Martín-Martín & Burgess 2004; Salager-Meyer 1999) have shown how criticism can be enacted via (unfavorable) citing. Most notably, perhaps, these studies have provided evidence of inter- and intradisciplinary similarities and differences in academic prose in both "expert" and student writing. Thus Hyland (1999, 2002) describes variation in citation and reporting between journal articles in the humanities, social sciences, and sciences, while P. Thompson (2001, 2005) describes differences in student writing in postgraduate theses. Given all of this variation, then, and given that student writers are often unsure of what lecturers expect their writing to look like (e.g., Lillis 2001), it is not surprising that nonnative university students often struggle to understand how they should cite correctly (e.g., Abasi *et al.* 2006; Angélil-Carter 2000; Borg 2000; Campbell 1990; Chandrasoma *et al.* 2004; Errey 2007; Pecorari 2003, 2006; Pennycook 1996; Petrić 2007; Sherman 1992). Indeed, students not only lack the knowledge of *how* to cite with regard to style and format; they often also fail to understand *why* references are used and what functions they perform (Angélil-Carter 2000).

Although there are EAP textbook materials that focus on citation, apart from Swales and Feak's (2000, 2004) activities, these have not met with widespread acclaim, the main criticism being that they focus on the mechanics but not the functions of citation (Borg 2000; Campbell 1990; Harwood 2004; P. Thompson 2001; P. Thompson & Tribble 2001). The materials I discuss in this chapter accordingly focus on this latter aspect, which has to date been investigated largely by information scientists and sociologists of science rather than by applied linguists. As Swales (1986, 2004) has noted, it is regrettable that the main strands of citation research from information science and sociology of science remain unknown to many applied linguists, despite recent attempts to bridge this gap (Harwood 2004; White 2004). One of the aims of this chapter, then, is to continue to raise awareness of work from all three disciplines.

I start by briefly reviewing some of the literature focusing on the functions citations perform in academic writing, with a particular focus on a recent interview-based research project investigating this issue. I then draw on the results of this research to create teaching materials designed for postgraduate EAP classes, which raise students' awareness of these citation functions and enable students to compare and contrast their own citation patterns with those by informants in my study.

The function of citations in academic writing

There is no shortage of research by information scientists and sociologists of science on citation functions in academic writing, Small (1982) and White (2004) being two excellent reviews of this body of work. Small (1982) shows that early studies conducted in the 1960s and 1970s identify a number of common citation functions, despite terminological differences. All feature some type of "use" category, "when the citing author ... employs some aspect of the cited work" (Small 1982: 300), such as Lipetz's (1965) "used" category, or Oppenheim and Renn's (1978) "use of equation, methodology" category. Those sources that the citing author "improves, modifies, or extends," like Moravcsik and Murugesan's (1975) evolutionary type, are a subclass of this "use" category. Similarly, most schemes feature categories in which sources are reviewed, compared, and/or contrasted (e.g., Frost's [1979] "state of present research"; Oppenheim & Renn's [1978] "information or data for comparison"). The supporting/substantiating category was only introduced once researchers began to look at citations in the humanities and social sciences (e.g., Spiegel-Rösing's 1977 "substantiates statement or assumption"), but more recent classifications (e.g., Bonzi & Snyder 1991; Vinkler 1987), which focus on the sciences, have also included it. Finally, all the schemes include negative citation. In some of the schemes (e.g., Cole 1975; Moravcsik & Murugesan 1975), this merely consists of a single category, whereas others (e.g., Chubin & Moitra 1975) distinguish between full and partial negation.

An interview-based study of citation functions

I decided to conduct my own research into citing functions using a very different method from that used by these early studies, which were criticized because of the way they were designed: The analysts relied on textual analysis to identify the pragmatic effect of citations, neglecting to consult the authors themselves, thereby potentially assigning citation functions that the authors did not intend (Borgman & Furner 2002). Intended citation functions may not be apparent to the analyst, partly because specialist knowledge in the discipline of the texts being studied is required; but also because, as Cronin (1984, 2005) has argued, citation is a private and subjective process, and functions cannot straightforwardly be read off from the text, however specialized the researcher's knowledge. And although more recent studies *have* consulted citers (e.g., Bonzi & Snyder 1991; Brooks 1985, 1986; Cano 1989; Case & Higgins 2000; Liu 1993; Shadish *et al.* 1995; Snyder & Bonzi 1998; Vinkler 1987), they have done so by presenting informants with ready-made checklists, which informants are encouraged to equate with their own citation functions.

My own study therefore provided informants with no categories or checklists at all, eliciting citation functions by means of the discourse-based interview approach (Odell *et al.* 1983), whereby 12 authors reexamined the citations in one of their recent journal articles or book chapters. This study was thus intended to be an emic account of citation functions, since "the concern is to catch the subjective meanings placed on situations by participants" (Cohen *et al.* 2000: 139) rather than by the interviewer. Other applied linguistic studies of citation (e.g., Charles 2006; Hyland 1999; P. Thompson 2001) have found evidence of disciplinary differences in citing patterns. Unlike recent information science studies, then, which focus on one discipline only (Case & Higgins 2000; Shadish *et al.* 1995;Wang & White 1999; White &Wang

1997), I focused on two – computer science and sociology – to determine whether citation functions also show signs of variation. Computer science and sociology were chosen as exemplars of hard and soft fields respectively (see Becher & Trowler 2001) in order to study disciplines with different traditions and epistemologies. In line with the applied linguists' research, my results indicate inter- and intradisciplinary differences with regard to (i) the most frequent citation functions; and (ii) how specific citation functions are used. Full details can be found in Harwood (2009) and further results are reported in Harwood (2008a, b), but I summarize some principal findings here in order to contextualize the materials and teaching activities that follow.

Eleven citation functions were identified and are summarized in Table 13.1. The terminology used to describe each function is derived from the informants.

Table 13.1 Citation functions and brief definitions

Citation function	Definition
Advertising	To alert readers to authors' own work or to the work of others
Building	To help authors develop methods or ideas
Competence	To underscore authors' expertise
Credit	To acknowledge authors' debts
Engaging	To help authors have a critical dialogue with their sources
Future	To establish future research plans
Position	To help authors identify viewpoints and findings
Signposting	To direct readers to other sources
Supporting	To help authors justify their research topic, method, or claim
Topical	To show authors are concerned with state-of-the-art issues
Tying	To align authors with others' methods or with other schools of thought or debates

While we cannot make confident generalizations about citation functions in the two disciplines from such a small sample of writing, a brief consideration of quantitative aspects of the data suggests some marked inter- and intradisciplinary similarities and differences that materials designers can focus on, as I will show later. Table 13.2 shows that three functions – position, supporting, and credit – are relatively frequent across both disciplines, and that the engaging function is far more frequent in the sociology texts, while the signposting function is far more frequent in the computing texts.

I now focus exclusively on these five categories, since over 80 percent of citations fell into one or more of these groups.[1] I provide brief extracts from informants' interview data, which explicate these functions more clearly, and supplement this with anonymized extracts from the informants' texts where appropriate. The computer scientists are identified as CS1-6 and the sociologists as SOC1-6.

Table 13.2 Most frequent citation functions across each discipline (number of occurrences)

Computer science	Sociology
1. Signposting (117)	1. Position (390)
2. Position (112)	2. Engaging (146)
3. Supporting (91)	3. Supporting (129)
4. Credit (68)	4. Credit (78)
5. = Building (30)	5. Building (54)
= Tying (30)	
7. Advertising (21)	6. Signposting (31)
8. Competence (6)	7. Tying (21)
9. Engaging (4)	8. Advertising (10)
10. Future (1)	9. = Competence (6)
	= Topical (6)
11. Topical (0)	11. Future (0)

[1] Recall that informants were free to identify as many functions for each citation as they wished; and in fact they frequently did so: Over 50 percent of citations in both disciplines were said to have more than one function.

Signposting citations

Signposting citations direct readers to other sources. They do so for three main reasons, namely (i) to help/interest less informed readers; (ii) to keep the argument on track; and (iii) to save space. The first group allows authors to address different audiences with varying amounts of specialist knowledge, directing readers to basic sources they are more likely to understand. CS4 explains the function of the second group as "helping keep the argument clear": "If you want to know how the technique works, you gotta go back and read it up, because this is not the place for it," the reference directing the reader to the appropriate source. The final group helps those computer scientists whose papers are more mathematical save space by condensing pages of equations and algorithms into a few words. CS1 writes, for instance: "The derivation of [equation] (4) is described by [reference]," explaining:

> The original papers referred to there went through this derivation ... [which] took several pages in the original paper. And we don't want to spend several pages just repeating that derivation here. So it's basically a way of saying I'm going to give you a brief description now ... If you want the full details they're there, and you can track them down there.

Space-saving citations are also found in the sociologists' texts. SOC4 talks about a very important anthropological concept at the beginning of his article, signposting the reader to the source for more details ("X's essay on the nature of anthropological understanding was first published in [year] and the debate ... has raged strongly ... [reference]"). He explains that

> ... having raised a complex issue, I don't have to go into huge detail which I don't have time to do or space to do in the article. So what I've got to do is to raise it and immediately chop it off. So the strategy is to raise it, to get the concept out of the box ..., and then shut the box, cos it could go on for ever, by saying "If you want to know more about this, read [reference]."

Supporting citations

Supporting citations can help authors justify the topic of their research by, for instance, creating a research space (Swales 1990). CS3's text features the following example:

> ... this research has so far not focused on the use of x but on y or z [references].[2]

Supporting citations can also help justify the method/methodology employed and/or the authors' claims. As an example of this third group, consider the following extract from CS6's text:

> The exact manner in which x interact with y ... has yet to be fully understood although the concept is by no means new [references 1, 2].

As CS6 makes clear, the supporting sources add weight to his argument:

> [I]t's still a debatable idea ..., some people don't agree with it .... And I did make a point to mention two pieces of work that are fairly old ... because these were the first two experimental pieces of evidence supporting the idea .... So giving support here, because I am one of those people who actually sees that there's enough experimental evidence for this .... And the point [of] this reference [is] to say that we have evidence as far back as 30 years ....

Credit citations

Credit citations acknowledge authors' debt to others for ideas or methods. SOC2, for instance, speaks of using citations to "pay respect and honor the ideas of those that have gone before," while SOC5 talks about a citee's "very influential and important" work. At other times, however, informants foreground a "self-defense" motivation, the citation making clear that they, the citer, are not claiming to be the originator of the citee's concept. In the following extract, for instance, SOC1 explains how the citations ensure he will not be attacked by reviewers for failing to acknowledge the work of others:

> ... to show that it wasn't me that discovered this, it was actually [name of source]. And to give [name of source] his due for discovering this overlooked thing .... I'm not just making a claim that it's me, cos that

---

[2] Textual extracts have been anonymized by substituting letters like x, y, and z for salient information that would make identifying the informant's text easier.

> would be wrong. And the reviewer could pick up on that, say, "Well hang on, someone else did this and so did some other person." So again it's saying that whilst this is an original argument to be made in [SOC1's sub-field], I haven't just magicked it out of thin air, there's a kind of pedigree to it .... [I]t's just setting out the provenance of the position ....

Position citations

Position citations allow authors to identify exemplars of different viewpoints. SOC2 memorably calls these citations "dip samples," agreeing they are "representatives and vivid examples of a particular line of argument." An example of an extract that includes this type of position citation in SOC2's text is:

> [The debate] is now polarized between the advocates (cf. reference 1, 2) and the opponents (cf. reference 3) of legislation.

This type of citation can also explicate researchers' standpoints in detail, or trace the development of a researcher's or field's thinking over time. Consider the following extract from SOC1's text, for instance:

> The origins of the x perspective lie in nineteenth-century Europe ..., and was most famously associated with [reference 1, orig. pub. 18xx] .... In twentieth-century American social science, x was replaced by y ....

Engaging citations

Engaging citations appear when authors are in critical dialogue with their sources. This criticality can be more or less marked: A "mild" engaging citation may appear when authors simply argue that an otherwise excellent source suffers from a minor flaw; the harsher type identifies a more serious flaw, or may even baldly state that the source is wrong. Both SOC1's and SOC6's texts contain detailed reviews and discussions of seminal sources that are praised, but that are then critiqued, as in the following from SOC1's article:

> The problem with such a characterization [i.e., a position advocated by the book SOC1 is attacking] is that .... Whilst [the book's authors]

> note that [the] notion of "x" is extremely useful ..., they do not consider the full implications of [the] argument ....

Demystifying citation functions: A critical pragmatic approach

My approach to designing teaching materials that explicate citation functions for learners is similar to Harwood and Hadley's (2004), which they call *critical pragmatic*. That is, whereas their materials provide prototypical models and examples students can adopt if they wish – the pragmatic element – they also ensure students question the relevance of these models to their own situation – the critical element. They argue for a critical pragmatic approach to materials design as a result of their view that adopting either a purely critical or pragmatic approach suffers from a number of weaknesses. Briefly, whereas a pragmatic approach aims to teach students a set of dominant discourse practices, this apparently straightforward objective can be problematized. A number of studies (e.g., Dudley-Evans 2002; Hewings & Hewings 2002; Hyland 2000; Samraj 2002, 2004) have concluded that these practices vary from discipline to discipline. Furthermore, although pragmatic approaches normally model "expert" texts (i.e., journal articles), it is unclear how relevant these models are to student writing (Harwood 2005a, b; Ivanič 1998). And it is also apparent that different lecturers have different ideas about what "good" academic writing should look like (Lea & Street 2000). A critical approach, on the other hand, questions the validity of transmitting dominant norms to students: It sees these norms as being open to contestation and change, and strives to create a more just, open university that is tolerant of different voices and different styles of academic discourse (see, for instance, Benesch 2001; Pennycook 1997, 2001). However, many students want and expect teachers to demystify and explicate dominant discourse practices (Belcher & Braine 1995). Furthermore, there is evidence that postgraduate students and novice researchers must conform to certain writing conventions to obtain their degrees and get their work published (e.g., Flowerdew 2000; Johns 1997). For all of these reasons, then, I follow Harwood and Hadley (2004) in claiming that a critical pragmatic approach gives us the best of both worlds.

Materials and activities

A range of materials and activities on citation functions now follow, accompanied by explanations and justifications.

Activity 1

(a) Why do people cite in their academic writing? Think about different types of academic writing, e.g., student assignments, journal articles, and so on.

(b) Why do *you* cite when you write assignments?

(c) Make a list of as many reasons as you can, compare your answers with someone else, then compare these with other groups.

Activity 1 could be criticized on the basis that the students' responses will be based merely on speculation rather than on empirical evidence about citing. However, in this case it is speculation and introspection that I wish to encourage: Some of the interviewees in my study told me they had never consciously considered their reasons for citing before, CS5 and SOC2 saying it had been an "automatic" process. Any demystification must therefore start by getting writers to consider what functions citing effects. Questions (a) and (b) are designed to encourage students to discuss similarities and differences in citing in different genres, given that researchers like Hyland and Samraj have shown that student and expert writing is likely to differ. While a number of citing functions will be identified, providing the class with a preliminary (pragmatic) model of citing, students are already being asked to (critically) assess the relevance of expert practices in their writing contexts. Question (c) is also designed to alert students to the possibility of difference, in that the teacher can encourage students from different disciplines to compare and contrast their lists. It may be that students from some scientific fields are aware that signposting citations save space by enabling the writer to avoid lengthy derivations of equations, although this function may not have occurred to a student in the humanities or social sciences. Again, therefore, students begin to realize citation functions and the frequencies with which these functions occur may not be equivalent across different fields.

Activity 2 provides students with an empirically derived model of citation functions, based on my research reported above.

Activity 2

Interviews with academic writers have revealed that citations have a number of different functions. Match the functions in List 1 with their definitions in List 2.

LIST 1	**LIST 2**
Citation function	**Definition**
Advertising	To help authors have a critical dialogue with their sources
Building	To help authors justify their research topic, method, or claim
Competence	To align authors with others' methods, or other schools of thought or debates
Credit	To alert readers to authors' own work or to the work of others
Engaging	To acknowledge authors' debts
Future	To help authors identify viewpoints and findings
Position	To direct readers to other sources
Signposting	To establish future research plans
Supporting	To show authors are concerned with state-of-the-art issues
Topical	To help authors develop methods or ideas
Tying	To underscore authors' expertise

I suggest all 11 citation functions could be introduced initially, and teachers could then focus on the most common functions found in my study (which are broadly in line with those found in earlier citation studies). Activity 3 below focuses on the five most frequent functions my informants identified. However, given that the engaging function was much less frequent in the computing texts (and apparently in scientific disciplines generally: see Small 1982), EAP practitioners teaching students in this field could decide to omit this function from an adapted version of this task. Alternatively, those practitioners who teach classes of social science/humanities students may decide it is appropriate to analyze engaging citations in greater depth.

Activity 3

(a) Now match comments by academic writers about their citations with each function in the table below.

Citation function	Academic's comment
Signposting: Directing less knowledgeable readers to introductory reading	"The original papers referred to there went through this derivation ... [which] took several pages in the original paper. And we don't want to spend several pages just repeating that derivation here. So it's basically a way of saying I'm going to give you a brief description now .... If you want the full details they're there, and you can track them down there."
Signposting: Directing readers to sources that discuss details that are not relevant here	"... there I rallied all of the literature that I found that made that point, or provided some research evidence ..."
Signposting: Directing readers to full explanations elsewhere to save space	"And I just adopted somebody else's methods for this particular purpose and said OK this is what we're doing, and this is what they've done in a similar experiment ..."
Supporting: Justifying the research topic	"... this [reference] was one of those attempts to address the general audience. This is more like the kind of book I tell my students to read in the beginning, it's general reading to become more interested, know about the main questions in the area."
Supporting: Justifying claims	"... those references are telling a story .... This is what was happening. This person said this, this person said that."

(to be continued)

(continued)

Credit: Acknowledging writer's debt to others for ideas	"... it explains in more detail how to do this ..., but ... I want to keep the argument clear .... If you want to know how the technique works, you gotta go back and read it up, because this is not the place for it."
Credit: Acknowledging writer's debt to others for methods	"... [these sources] are the most commonly cited examples of arguments in the field."
Position: The sources represent specific viewpoints	"... it's just to say that other people have done similar studies .... So it's just to make the case stronger really."
Position: The sources show how arguments have developed over time	"... I'm going to draw arguments from [the references]. And I'm drawing out their points to shoot them down ... I'm setting them up ... to then challenge their argument."
Engaging: Criticizing a source	"It was to really pay respect and honor the ideas of those that have gone before."

Again, these extracts have been chosen in part to try to raise awareness of different disciplinary epistemologies: Whereas I found that some of the sociologists were more prone to account for credit citations in terms of "paying respect" and "honoring" originators, some computer scientists' descriptions were more instrumental (compare CS3's more prosaic "I just adopted somebody else's methods" to acknowledge indebtedness). It may be that even at this early stage students will intuit that they use certain functions more or less frequently than others in the table; and, as a result of peer discussions in a follow-up activity, they will recognize that there are likely to be interdisciplinary differences in how (in)frequent certain functions are.

Having unjumbled the table, students are asked question (b), which explicitly raises the issues of interdisciplinary and intergeneric difference:

(b) Which of these citation functions do you think your lecturers use the most and least when they write articles? Why? Compare your answers with those of other students who are studying in different fields.

Whereas the purpose of 3(b) is to raise awareness of and encourage speculation about the frequency of different citation functions, Activity 4 below provides empirical data, which students can compare and contrast with their intuitions. Learners are given some quantitative information regarding the (in)frequency of the various citation functions, as follows.

Activity 4

Here are the results of some research that identifies the most frequent citation functions in articles and book chapters from two disciplines computer science and sociology:

Less frequent ↓	**Computer Science**	**Sociology**
	1. Signposting	1. Position
	2. Position	2. Engaging
	3. Supporting	3. Supporting
	4. Credit	4. Credit

(a) What similarities and differences can you see between the two disciplines? Suggest possible reasons for these similarities and differences.

(b) Now look at some of the pieces of writing you've done recently, which contain citations.

(i) What function(s) do *your* citations have? Are they the same functions as the ones in the list above? Or are they different? If they're different, write brief definitions of these functions and provide two or three extracts from your writing that illustrate these functions clearly.

(ii) Are you using citations in the same way as the "expert" writers in the tables above? Why (not)?

(iii) How frequently do you use different functions? Take two or three pieces of your writing and calculate how many times you use each function. Which are the three most frequent citation functions in your texts? Why?

(iv) Now compare your results with colleagues (i) who are studying the same discipline as you; and (ii) who are studying a different subject. To what extent are your results similar or different? Why do you think this is? Discuss this, and compile a list of possible reasons.

Whereas Activity 4 only provides students with quantitative data from two disciplines and from the "expert" genre, it does at least show how citation practices can vary across fields. Question (b) reveals how these practices also vary across genres, encouraging students to identify citation functions in a very small corpus of their own writing. Although I have criticized early citation studies for relying solely on textual analysis, in this case, it is the *writers themselves* who are doing the classifying, and who will therefore be in a better position to identify their functions than a nonspecialist analyst who did not author the text.

By the close of Activity 4, then, students will have compared and contrasted citation functions qualitatively and quantitatively across disciplines and genres. They will have "models" of experts' citation patterns (albeit in only two disciplines) and an understanding of how their own use of citations in a small selection of their writing resembles or deviates from these models. They can then reflect on how (in)appropriate these models of citation are for the writing they are asked to do, and how (in)appropriate their own citation patterns appear to be. The next stage is to seek their lecturers' input, to determine the extent to which the (in)appropriacy of the students' citation patterns are (dis)confirmed, which is one of the aims of Activity 5. Activity 5 aims to get students to take on

Activity 5

You are now going to solicit your lecturer's views on appropriate and inappropriate uses of citation functions.

(a) Ask your lecturer for a copy of a recent article they have written. Then read this text carefully, highlighting all the citations, and interview him/her, asking about the functions of each citation. Also show the lecturer your own writing assignments, and ask him/her to identify the functions of your citations. Does your lecturer feel you have cited in an appropriate way? Why (not)?

(b) Prepare a report summarizing the results of your research. In what ways were the lecturer's citation functions similar to and different from your own? Why? How (in)appropriate are your citation patterns, according to the lecturer? Why? Share these results with the class.

the role of disciplinary researchers (see Ivanič 1998; Johns 1997) of intergeneric variation in citation functions. How and why do lecturers' practices differ from those of students? Eliciting lecturers' beliefs regarding (in)appropriate citation usage further demystifies faculty expectations. It is likely, however, that in line with Lea and Street (2000), students' interviews will reveal that citation patterns and beliefs vary considerably, even among lecturers in the same discipline. Hence the critical aspect of the materials is reintroduced: Students will become aware that "appropriate," "one size fits all" citation patterns cannot be easily described. Activity 5 also draws on critical pedagogy because it aims to contribute to raising *lecturers'* awareness of the complexities of citation use, and may lead to faculty creating a more transparent system of institutional assessment, since once lecturers realize how complex citation practices are, they may also recognize the need to provide more explicit guidance and feedback on student writing generally. This is what Angélil-Carter's (2000) study of citation and plagiarism achieved, causing lecturers to reflect on their own writing practices and on the methods they use to socialize students into becoming proficient at these practices.

Continuing to demystify citation: Other possibilities

In what ways could these materials be extended by EAP practitioners and future researchers? Several possibilities come to mind.

Investigating student citation functions

I have stressed throughout that student and expert writing are different genres, and that therefore it would not be surprising to find that (successful) student writing features different citation patterns from its expert equivalent. Hence students' citation functions could be researched more systematically and the results incorporated into my activities. The necessity of interviewing students about their citing behavior can be seen by looking at Oppenheim and Smith's (2001) study, one of the few that focuses on student, rather than expert, behavior. Although Oppenheim and Smith's method can be criticized – they used a questionnaire rather than an interview to elicit functions and motivations of information science students and asked students to account for their motivations in general, rather than with reference to a specific piece of writing, thus raising reliability issues – it is clear that students professed to some very different motivations than experts. Whereas the most common citation function was support, almost 40 percent of the student writers

> ... had included citations in their work because they believed that the more references they included in a piece of work, the better the mark they would receive for that piece of work. They included references, therefore, because they considered it important to show that they had read widely around the subject. (p. 313)

Indeed, one of the student writers Angélil-Carter (2000) interviewed claimed a similar motivation. Even if such (over)citing is misguided, and *not* something we would wish to encourage student writers to do, it is worth introducing this data to compare and contrast it to experts' practice, and to challenge any mistaken motivations on the part of students.

Investigating inter- and intradisciplinary differences

While the focus of my materials has been on interdisciplinary difference in citation patterns – recall the marked differences between the (in)frequency of the engaging function in computing and sociology, for instance – my study also found evidence of marked *intra*disciplinary differences within each field, just as P. Thompson (2005) found that citation patterns varied within the discipline of agricultural botany. These differences can be accounted for by considering the type of audience the text was being written for, the type of paper that informants were writing (e.g., theoretical/empirical), and the publication outlet (see Harwood 2008a, 2008b, 2009). Future materials designers could explore these intradisciplinary aspects with students in more depth.

Investigating (in)appropriate citation and selection of sources

Activity 5 ensures that students investigate their lecturers' beliefs about (in)appropriate citation, something which the informants in my study were also asked about, with some fascinating patterns emerging. For instance, informants sometimes intentionally cited sources' first names to indicate the source was important; alternatively, other informants liked the more personalized, informal style citing that first names effected. I also investigated informants' reasons for choosing one source to cite over another, my results complementing those found in White and Wang's innovative studies (Wang &White 1999; White &Wang 1997), which identify 28 criteria potentially affecting citing decisions. Materials writers could draw on this body of research to design materials that will further develop students' understanding of (in)appropriate citation and selection of sources.

Investigating other literature

I began by reviewing a small selection of the vast array of work that has been done on citation in three fields: information science, sociology of science, and applied linguistics. A final suggestion, then, is that EAP practitioners could extend these activities by introducing students to other researchers' work on citation from any or all of these areas.[3] And Swales and Feak (2000, 2004) offer a range of EAP textbook activities that draw upon citation research in a similar way to my materials here, providing practitioners with alternative exercise types.

Discussion questions and tasks

Reflection

1. How do you use citation in your own writing? How does it differ from the ways the computer scientists and sociologists cite as reported in this chapter? How might this affect the way you decide to teach students about citation?
2. What are the pros and cons of using expert writing (i.e., journal articles or book chapters) as the basis for designing materials to teach students how to write?
3. What are the pros and cons of using the critical pragmatic approach to design materials focusing on citation? What alternative approaches and activities could you use instead?
4. If it is true that "different lecturers have different ideas about what

[3] For instance, the body of research now available on how reporting verbs combine with citations (e.g., Hyland 2002; Thomas & Hawes 1994; G. Thompson & Ye 1991) could inform tasks to develop students' ability to introduce sources into their writing effectively. The critical pragmatic approach could be taken by making students aware of the most frequent reporting verbs used to introduce sources across the disciplines by experts, and then asking learners to consider how (in)appropriate it would be for them to use these same reporting verbs in their own writing.

'good' academic writing should look like," what are the implications for designing English for Academic Purposes (EAP) writing activities?

Evaluation

5. Look at a selection of EAP textbook materials on citation and evaluate these on the basis of what you have learned in this chapter.
6. If you have taught EAP students about citation in the past, look at the materials and activities you used to do this. In light of this chapter, what changes would you make to these materials now? Why?

Adaptation/Design

7. What adaptations would you make to these materials if you were teaching an EAP class with students from a number of different disciplines? Why?
8. Design some other activities you could use to teach student writers about citation. If possible, pilot these on a group of learners. What did you learn?

References

Abasi, A. R., Akbari, N., & Graves, B. (2006). Discourse appropriation, construction of identities, and the complex issue of plagiarism: ESL students writing in graduate school. *Journal of Second Language Writing* 15: 102-17.

Angélil-Carter, S. (2000). *Stolen language? Plagiarism in writing*. Harlow, UK: Longman.

Becher, T., & Trowler, P. R. (2001). *Academic tribes and territories: Intellectual enquiry and the culture of disciplines*. Buckingham, UK: The Society for Research into Higher Education and Open University Press.

Belcher, D., & Braine, G. (1995). Introduction to D. Belcher & G. Braine (eds.). *Academic writing in a second language: Essays on research and pedagogy*. Norwood, NJ: Ablex, pp. xiii-xxxi.

Benesch, S. (2001). *Critical English for Academic Purposes: Theory, politics, and practice*. Mahwah, NJ: Lawrence Erlbaum Associates.

Bonzi, S., & Snyder, H. W. (1991). Motivations for citation: A comparison of self citation and citation to others. *Scientometrics* 21(2): 245-54.

Borg, E. (2000). Citation practices in academic writing. In P. Thompson (ed.). *Patterns and perspectives: Insights into EAP writing practice*. Reading, UK: Centre for Applied Language Studies, University of Reading, pp. 26-44.

Borgman, C. L., & Furner, J. (2002). Scholarly communication and bibliometrics. In B. Cronin (ed.). *Annual Review of Information Science and Technology* (Vol. 36). Medford, NJ: Information Today, pp. 3-72.

Brooks, T. A. (1985). Private acts and public objects: An investigation of citer motivations. *Journal of the American Society for Information Science* 36: 223-9.

Brooks, T. A. (1986). Evidence of complex citer motivations. *Journal of the American Society for Information Science* 37: 34-6.

Burgess, S., & Fagan, A. (2002). (Kid) gloves on or off? Academic conflict in research articles across the disciplines. *Revista Canaria de Estudios Ingleses* 44: 79-96.

Campbell, C. (1990). Writing with others' words: Using background reading text in academic compositions. In B. Kroll (ed.). *Second language writing: Research insights for the classroom*. Cambridge: Cambridge University Press, pp. 211-30.

Cano, V. (1989). Citing behavior: Classification, utility, and location. *Journal of the American Society for Information Science* 40: 284-90.

Case, D. O. & Higgins, G. M. (2000). How can we investigate citation behavior? A study of reasons for citing literature in communication. *Journal of the American Society for Information Science* 51: 635-45.

Charles, M. (2006). Phraseological patterns in reporting clauses used in citation: A corpus-based study of theses in two disciplines. *English for Specific Purposes* 25: 310-31.

Chandrasoma, R., Thompson, C., & Pennycook, A. (2004). Beyond plagiarism: Transgressive and nontransgressive intertextuality. *Journal of Language, Identity, & Education* 3(3): 171-93.

Chubin, D. E., & Moitra, S. D. (1975). Content analysis of references: Adjunct or alternative to citation counting? *Social Studies of Science* 5: 423-41.

Cohen, L., Manion, L., & Morrison, K. (2000). *Research methods in education* (5th ed.). London: RoutledgeFalmer.

Cole, S. (1975). The growth of scientific knowledge: Theories of deviance as a case study. In L. A. Coser (ed.). *The idea of social structure: Papers in honor of Robert K. Merton*. New York: Harcourt Brace Jovanovich, pp. 175-220.

Cronin, B. (1984). *The citation process: The role and significance of citations in scientific communication*. London: Taylor Graham.

Cronin, B. (2005). *The hand of science: Academic writing and its rewards*. Lanham, MD: Scarecrow Press.

Dudley-Evans, T. (2002). The teaching of the academic essay: Is a genre approach possible? In A. M. Johns (ed.). *Genre in the classroom: Multiple perspectives*. Mahwah, NJ: Lawrence Erlbaum Associates, pp. 225-35.

Errey, L. (2007). What is it about other people's words? In O. Alexander (ed.). *New approaches to materials development for language learning*. Bern: Peter Lang, pp. 209-22.

Flowerdew, J. (2000). Discourse community, legitimate peripheral participation, and the nonnative-English-speaking scholar. *TESOL Quarterly* 34(1): 127-50.

Frost, C. O. (1979). The use of citations in literary research: A preliminary classification of citation functions. *Library Quarterly* 49: 399-414.

Harwood, N. (2004). Citation analysis: Academic literacy for postgraduates. In M. Baynham, A. Deignan, & G. White (eds.). *Applied linguistics at the interface*. London: Equinox, pp. 79-89.

Harwood, N. (2005a). "I hoped to counteract the memory problem, but I made no impact whatsoever": Discussing methods in computing science using *I*. *English for Specific Purposes* 24: 243-67.

Harwood, N. (2005b). What do we want EAP teaching materials for? *Journal of English for Academic Purposes* 4: 149-61.

Harwood, N. (2008a). Citers' use of citees' names: Findings from a qualitative interview-based study. *Journal of the American Society for Information Science & Technology* 59(6): 1007-11.

Harwood, N. (2008b). Publication outlets and their effect on academic writers' citations. *Scientometrics* 77(2): 253-65.

Harwood, N. (2009). An interview-based study of the functions of citations in academic writing across two disciplines. *Journal of Pragmatics* 41: 497-518.

Harwood, N., & Hadley, G. (2004). Demystifying institutional practices: Critical pragmatism and the teaching of academic writing. *English for Specific Purposes* 23: 355-77.

Hewings, M., & Hewings, A. (2002). "It is interesting to note that ... ": A comparative study of anticipatory "it" in student and published writing. *English for Specific Purposes* 21(4): 367-83.

Hunston, S. (1993). Professional conflict: Disagreement in academic discourse. In M.

Baker, G. Francis, & E. Tognini-Bonelli (eds.). *Text and technology: In honour of John Sinclair*. Amsterdam: John Benjamins, pp. 115-34.

Hyland, K. (1999). Academic attribution: Citation and the construction of disciplinary knowledge. *Applied Linguistics* 20: 341-67.

Hyland, K. (2000). *Disciplinary discourses: Social interactions in academic writing*. Harlow, UK: Longman.

Hyland, K. (2002). Activity and evaluation: Reporting practices in academic writing. In J. Flowerdew (ed.). *Academic discourse*. Harlow, UK: Longman, pp. 115-30.

Ivanič, R. (1998). *Writing and identity: The discoursal construction of identity in academic writing*. Amsterdam: John Benjamins.

Johns, A. M. (1997). *Text, role, and context: Developing academic literacies*. Cambridge: Cambridge University Press.

Lea, M. R., & Street, B. V. (2000). Student writing and staff feedback in higher education: An academic literacies approach. In M. R. Lea & B. Stierer (eds.). *Student writing in higher education: New contexts*. Buckingham, UK: The Society for Research into Higher Education & Open University Press, pp. 32-46.

Lillis, T. M. (2001). *Student writing: Regulation, access, desire*. London: Routledge.

Lipetz, B.-A. (1965). Improvement of the selectivity of citation indexes to science literature through inclusion of citation relationship indicators. *American Documentation* 16: 81-90.

Liu, M. (1993). A study of citing motivation of Chinese scientists. *Journal of Information Science* 19: 13-23.

Martín-Martín, P., & Burgess, S. (2004). The rhetorical management of academic criticism in research article abstracts. *Text* 24(2): 171-95.

Moravcsik, M. J., & Murugesan, P. (1975). Some results on the function and quality of citations. *Social Studies of Science* 5: 86-92.

Odell, L., Goswami, D., & Herrington, A. J. (1983). The discourse-based interview: A procedure for exploring the tacit knowledge of writers in nonacademic settings. In P. Mosenthal, L. Tamor, & S. A. Walmsley (eds.). *Research on writing: Principles and methods*. New York: Longman, pp. 221-36.

Oppenheim, C., & Renn, S. P. (1978). Highly cited papers and the reasons why they continue to be cited. *Journal of the American Society for Information Science* 29: 225-31.

Oppenheim, C., & Smith, R. (2001). Student citation practices in an Information Science Department. *Education for Information* 19: 299-23.

Pecorari, D. (2003). Good and original: Plagiarism and patchwriting in academic second-language writing. *Journal of Second Language Writing* 12: 317-45.

Pecorari, D. (2006). Visible and occluded citation features in postgraduate second language writing. *English for Specific Purposes* 25: 4-29.

Pennycook, A. (1996). Borrowing others' words: Text, ownership, memory, and plagiarism. *TESOL Quarterly* 30(2): 201-30.

Pennycook, A. (1997). Vulgar pragmatism, critical pragmatism, and EAP. *English for Specific Purposes* 16(4): 253-69.

Pennycook, A. (2001). *Critical Applied Linguistics: A critical introduction*. Mahwah, NJ: Lawrence Erlbaum Associates.

Petrić, B. (2007). Rhetorical functions of citations in high- and low-rated master's theses. *Journal of English for Academic Purposes* 6(3): 238-53.

Salager-Meyer, F. (1999). Contentiousness in written medical English discourse: A diachronic study (1810-1995). *Text* 19: 371-98.

Samraj, B. (2002). Texts and contextual layers: Academic writing in content courses. In A. M. Johns (ed.). *Genre in the classroom: Multiple perspectives*. Mahwah, NJ: Lawrence Erlbaum Associates, pp. 163-76.

Samraj, B. (2004). Discourse features of the student-produced academic research paper: Variations across disciplinary courses. *Journal of English for Academic Purposes* 3(1): 5-22.

Shadish, W. R., Tolliver, D., Gray, M., & Sen Gupta, S. K. (1995). Author judgements about works they cite: Three studies from psychology journals. *Social Studies of Science* 25: 477-98.

Sherman, J. (1992). Your own thoughts in your own words. *ELT Journal* 46(2): 190-8.

Small, H. (1982). Citation context analysis. In B. Dervin & M. J. Voight (eds.). *Progress in communication sciences* (Vol. III). Norwood, NJ: Ablex, pp. 287-310.

Snyder, H., & Bonzi, S. (1998). Patterns of self-citation across disciplines (1980-1989). *Journal of Information Science* 24: 431-5.

Spiegel-Rösing, I. (1977). Science Studies: Bibliometric and content analysis. *Social Studies of Science* 7: 97-113.

Swales, J. M. (1981). *Aspects of article introductions*. Birmingham, UK: Language Studies Unit, University of Aston.

Swales J. M. (1986). Citation analysis and discourse analysis. *Applied Linguistics* 7(1): 39-56.

Swales, J. M. (1990). *Genre analysis: English in academic and research settings.* Cambridge: Cambridge University Press.

Swales, J. M. (2004). *Research genres: Explorations and applications.* Cambridge: Cambridge University Press.

Swales, J. M., & Feak, C. B. (2000). *English in today's research world: A writing guide.* Ann Arbor: The University of Michigan Press.

Swales, J. M., & Feak, C. B. (2004). *Academic writing for graduate students* (2nd ed.). Ann Arbor: The University of Michigan Press.

Thomas, S., & Hawes, T. P. (1994). Reporting verbs in medical journal articles. *English for Specific Purposes* 13(2): 129-48.

Thompson, G., & Ye, Y. (1991). Evaluation in the reporting verbs used in academic papers. *Applied Linguistics* 12(4): 365-82.

Thompson, P. (2001). A pedagogically-motivated corpus-based examination of PhD theses: Macrostructure, citation practices and uses of modal verbs. Unpublished PhD thesis, University of Reading, UK.

Thompson, P. (2005). Points of focus and position: Intertextual reference in PhD theses. *Journal of English for Academic Purposes* 4: 307-23.

Thompson, P., & Tribble, C. (2001). Looking at citations: Using corpora in English for academic purposes. *Language Learning & Technology* 5(3): 91-105.

Vinkler, P. (1987). A quasi-quantitative citation model. *Scientometrics* 12: 47-72.

Wang, P., & White, M. D. (1999). A cognitive model of document use during a research project. Study II. Decisions at the reading and citing stages. *Journal of the American Society for Information Science* 50: 98-114.

White, H. D. (2004). Citation analysis and discourse analysis revisited. *Applied Linguistics* 25(1): 89-116.

White, M. D., & Wang, P. (1997). A qualitative study of citing behavior: Contributions, criteria, and metalevel documentation concerns. *Library Quarterly* 67: 122-54.

14

Making professional academic writing practices visible: Designing research-based heuristics to support English-medium text production

Mary Jane Curry and Theresa Lillis

Summary

Pressure is growing for scholars around the world to publish their research in English, thus prompting the need to support multilingual writers in gaining access to the social practices of English-medium text production. Drawing on data from a longitudinal ethnographic study of the English-medium writing and publishing experiences of scholars outside of Anglophone contexts, we present a heuristics approach to supporting academic publishing. Our findings suggest that designers of teaching materials should take into account the social practices of professional text production as well as the features of academic writing. We propose the use of heuristics as a teaching and thinking tool designed to connect research data and findings with the experiences of multilingual scholars to support their English-medium text production. Heuristics provide an opportunity for a structured examination of the often informal or hidden social practices of developing academic texts for publication. They serve as tools for exploring various aspects of text production, ideally helping to explain or resolve problems in the contexts of scholars' work lives. The heuristics use data and analyses ("text histories") from our ethnographic research in order to link multilingual scholars' experiences and expertise with their efforts to publish in English. The heuristics include six sections: (1) background to the text history, from our research; (2) guiding hypothesis, from our analysis; (3) primary data, from our research; (4) key questions about the data, for reflection; (5) thinking about your practice, to make connections; and (6) suggestions for taking action and ideas on how to apply the knowledge created through the heuristics.

Multilingual scholars publishing in English: Key research findings

Pressure is increasing on scholars around the world to publish their research in English, particularly in high-status, international, English-medium journals. Such publications count as a key form of "currency" of academic life, used for annual evaluations, promotion, and acquiring research grants (Shi 2002; Tardy 2004). Likewise, postgraduate students are facing similar pressures to publish their research, often before finishing their degrees (Cho 2004; Dong 1998; Li 2002). As pressure grows, researchers have begun to study the conditions under which scholars respond to these external demands and act on their personal desires to publish in English (e.g., Braine 2005; Canagarajah 1996; Casanave 2002; Flowerdew 1999, 2000). Since 2001, we have been investigating the English academic writing and publishing experiences of some 50 multilingual scholars and postgraduates in southern and central Europe working in education and psychology. Our "text-ethnographic" study, Professional Academic Writing in a Global Context (PAW), has documented the success of many of these scholars and postgraduates in disseminating their research to local and other national academic and applied communities, in local and other national and regional languages (Curry & Lillis 2004). At the same time, multilingual scholars, whether they have studied and worked in Anglophone contexts or learned English locally, are actively producing English-medium texts, often for international outlets. PAW participants typically achieve their publishing success despite having limited resources for crucial scholarly activities, such as travel to conferences (Curry & Lillis 2004), like many scholars outside of Anglophone contexts (Canagarajah 1996, 2002a). Key resources can be material (e.g., supplies, equipment, books, journals, databases), financial (release time, funds for research and conference travel, opportunities to improve their English), and social (e.g., research collaborators, journal and book editors, participating in research networks) (Lillis & Curry 2006a, 2006b). Given the constraints they often work under, multilingual scholars manage their limited resources strategically in order to disseminate their work (see also Canagarajah 2002a).

PAW study findings have identified two types of social resources that appear to be key to the production of English-medium professional academic texts: research networks and "literacy brokers." Scholars' production of English-medium texts often takes place within research networks, involving a range of resources and members with different types of knowledge and experience along axes of linguistic, rhetorical, research, and disciplinary expertise. Indeed, for many scholars, participating in research networks seems to carry as much or more weight as their individual facility with English in terms of English-medium publishing success (Lillis & Curry 2006b). Another key resource is literacy brokers – a range of people who contribute to and influence the production of texts in various ways in relation to publishing opportunities, supporting scholars' writing, suggesting target journals, and shaping aspects of multilingual scholars' texts, as well as providing feedback on texts (Lillis & Curry 2006a). Literacy brokers may form part of a scholar's network or operate outside of it, as with editors and peer reviewers. These findings about the social nature of multilingual scholars' English-medium academic text production prompt the question of how scholars can increase their participation in these key social practices. Our research highlights the need to go beyond a focus purely on texts in designing materials to support the English-medium professional academic text production of scholars and postgraduates, toward an approach that foregrounds social practices. We use "design" here not only in the widely used sense of the application of research-generated understandings to pedagogy and materials development, but also to signal a connection with "design" as a specific move from critical theoretical research paradigms toward critical application (see discussion in Lillis 2003).

The need for materials designers to take account of the social practices of academic text production

Virtually all aspects of research involve writing – including formal and informal written communication among research network members (e.g., partners, colleagues, assistants, literacy brokers) while developing and conducting research; drafting, revising, and submitting texts for presentation or publication; and responding to literacy brokers' input after submission (Hengl & Gould 2006; Lillis & North 2006; Richardson 2000). Further, conducting and disseminating research involves social practices that may not traditionally be considered part of academic writing, for example, from deciding how to divide up research project findings for presentation at a conference by multiple collaborators, to transforming L1 research findings into English-medium text, to selecting an appropriate target journal (see also Li 2007). Such important practices are often left out of formal discussions about how to write and publish academic research. As Canagarajah (2002b) points out, scholars usually "have to learn [publishing practices] informally through their peers and mentors, for example, documenting conventions, copyright regulations, refereeing processes, and styles of interactions with the editorship of a journal" (p. 285). Indeed, these often hidden practices can mystify the ways that research is disseminated and create barriers to doing so.

In contrast, EAP courses and teaching materials usually take a text-based approach to English-medium academic writing, focusing chiefly on the rhetorical structure and language used in learners' texts (e.g., Swales & Feak 2004; Weissberg & Buker 1990) rather than addressing learners' participation in the social practices of academic writing for various purposes (but see Swales & Feak 2000). In addition, whereas many books and articles on academic writing and publishing are aimed at L1 scholars and postgraduates (e.g., Belcher 2009; Kitchen & Fuller 2005; Klingner *et al.* 2005; Thyer 2005; Wepner & Gambrell 2006), EAP materials are usually designed for undergraduate or postgraduate students. These materials usually assume that EAP learners are located in Anglophone rather than in other settings (Yakhontova 2001). In this chapter, recognizing the expertise of multilingual scholars in writing for a range of communities, we discuss an approach to designing materials that forges links between scholars' experiences and the English-medium publishing practices they engage with. As Harwood (2005) points out, EAP materials are frequently based on the intuitions of materials developers rather than on empirical data about academic writing practices. Our research suggests that designers of teaching materials should take into account not only the features of academic writing but also the social practices of professional text production. We therefore focus on the design of practical applications based on the findings of our text-ethnographic PAW study of multilingual scholars' experiences with English-medium professional academic text production. This research-based approach to materials design should be useful for supporting multilingual scholars and postgraduate students who may be starting to participate in the often hidden social practices of professional text production.

In the rest of this chapter, we will first discuss how social practice and social network theories ground our approach to designing materials for professional academic text production. We then propose the use of heuristics as a reflective teaching and thinking tool designed to connect research data and findings with the experiences of multilingual scholars to help them explore English-medium text production. Heuristics are approaches to identifying, exploring, and solving problems that draw on people's lived experiences, knowledge, and goals. Below we discuss how heuristics can offer a way for designers of pedagogical materials to support scholars and postgraduates in reflecting on their practices and experiences and connect them with the practices of English-medium academic writing and publishing. We provide three heuristics designed from empirical data drawn from the experiences of some of the multilingual scholars in the PAW study. The heuristics foreground the highly social and contextualized nature of academic research collaboration, focusing on two key writing activities – conference proposals and journal articles – going on in local and international networks and often involving interactions with literacy brokers. Such collaborative publishing practices have long taken place across many disciplines, particularly in the natural sciences, and increasingly in the social sciences and humanities (Akkerman *et al.* 2006). However, they are often ignored or downplayed in designing materials to teach writing. We aim to offer an understanding of the usefulness of research-based heuristics grounded in the experiences of multilingual scholars and postgraduates across specific cultural and linguistic contexts and academic disciplines.

Using research findings to design materials exploring social practices and social networks

Social practice theories of learning conventionally view learners as novices to situated social practices who learn by increasing their participation in the practices of specific communities (Barton & Tusting 2005; Lave & Wenger 1991; Wenger 1998). The notion that expert participants guide less-experienced participants into key practices may shed light on how some multilingual scholars and postgraduate students engage in English-medium text production by participating in networks and interacting with literacy brokers (Cho 2004). However, the expertise of multilingual scholars demonstrated in the PAW study challenges simple conceptualizations of a novice-to-expert trajectory based on increasing participation. The production of texts by scholars and postgraduates for a number of different communities signals the inadequacy of construing them as "novices" who are in the process of becoming "experts." Rather, multilingual scholars draw, in complex and sometimes contradictory ways, on their previous experiences as they engage with English-medium text production practices (see also Casanave 1998; Martin 2005). Thus, although increased participation in certain publishing practices is clearly central to multilingual scholars' ability to contribute research findings to a wider range of communities, we want to avoid invoking notions of deficit that may be inherent in novice-to-expert-trajectory apprenticeship models.

Findings from the PAW study also support critiques that the notion of participation is messier and more amorphous than earlier conceptions proposed (see also Barton & Tusting 2005; Keating 2005; Rock 2005). For multilingual scholars contributing to a range of communities, a particular scholar's experience and expertise involves the overlapping or intersecting domains of content knowledge, research experience, collaboration, and linguistic and rhetorical knowledge. Likewise, members of research networks may have different types of knowledge and expertise to contribute to a joint enterprise. As we illustrate in the heuristics, members of a research network may contribute complementary forms of expertise, for example, a student with greater control over English working with a professor with decades of research experience but less proficiency in writing academic English.

The multidimensionality of the expertise distributed among members of research networks demonstrates a key aspect of social network theory: that the social ties constituting networks act as an important form of social capital providing access to resources and the opportunities to use these resources (Bourdieu 1985; Granovetter 1983; Lin 2001; Portes 1998). Networks tend to operate on the basis of mutual exchange and reciprocity, albeit typically with unequal exchanges and power relations (Mace 2002; Polodny & Page 1998). As the heuristics drawn from our research illustrate, scholars enter or create networks, make various contributions, and take up the opportunities that networks afford in a range of ways, depending on what they can offer and the resources supplied by other network members (Lillis & Curry 2006b). Thus a perspective on academic text production that situates scholars within research networks captures the complex mix of participants and practices involved in professional English-medium text production.

Making research useful: Heuristics as a design tool

As noted above, heuristics can be defined as frameworks or approaches to identifying, exploring, and solving problems that draw on people's lived experiences and goals without resorting to prescriptivism. That is, they present ways of contemplating issues or problems without claiming to have predetermined answers. In the case of writing for publication in English, heuristics offer a means to apply our research findings to practical applications that connect research findings to users' immediate concerns about English-medium text production. The heuristics below comprise sets of questions about data and research findings designed to stimulate reflection and develop understandings of the practices that the data illustrate. Rather than offering generic advice, the heuristics are designed on the basis that users will find the primary data meaningful; the data prompt users' reflections on their experiences, and users connect these reflections to their own practices of English-medium text production. Although each user may not have had experiences related to all of the questions posed in the heuristics, engaging with the questions should stimulate reflection on the practices under discussion and may prompt further action.

The main focus of the heuristics is on how multilingual scholars with a range of levels of individual English proficiency engage in professional academic writing and publishing practices by participating in local and international networks and interacting with literacy brokers. The heuristics draw from a key unit of analysis from the PAW study, "text histories," which we have created in order to explore the trajectories of multilingual scholars' texts toward publication or presentation. We create text histories by drawing on these data sources: multiple drafts of particular texts, such as conference abstracts, journal articles, and book chapters, collected from PAW participants; correspondence between the author(s) and literacy brokers, including brokers' comments on submissions and journal editors' and reviewers' reports; our interviews with the main author(s) about the target outlet and history of a particular text, including the contributions and interventions of those involved in its production; and informal discussions and e-mails with the author(s).[1] The heuristics include six sections:

1. **Background to text history** – a brief narrative about the context and key participants involved in this text history
2. **Guiding hypothesis** – one or more key principles arising from the specific text history included in the heuristic
3. **Primary data** – PAW data or analysis of findings to support reflection and discussion about the guiding hypothesis
4. **Key questions about the data** – questions prompting analysis and reflection on the topic of the heuristic, followed by a section discussing these ethnographic findings
5. **Thinking about your practice** – questions to link users' reflections on the data to their participation in practices

[1] See Lillis and Curry (2006a) for a fuller discussion of text histories in the PAW data.

6. **Suggestions for taking action** – how users might increase participation in research networks and interact with literacy brokers. Whereas not all users will have access to some resources that are mentioned, these suggestions should prompt them to consider steps for moving forward.

Heuristics on the role of networks and brokers in professional academic text production

The heuristics we present here focus on two key research dissemination activities: preparing proposals for a conference and submitting articles for publication. As scholars engage in these activities in both local and international networks, the heuristics aim to tease out the practices connected with different types of networks and to examine the literacy brokering going on.

Heuristic 1: Participating in a local network to prepare conference abstracts[2]

1. BACKGROUND TO TEXT HISTORY: FIDEL IN HIS NETWORKS

Fidel is a senior lecturer in education and has been working in his southern European university for some 14 years. He has a high level of expertise in English, which he has been learning since he was eight years old. His academic career has been punctuated by extended visits to the United States and UK as a student and visiting scholar. These visits afforded him opportunities to engage in English-medium academic discourse related to his field of education and his specialist subfield of vocational education. Fidel sees himself as a typical of his generation in that his level of English is high, as is evident in both his written and spoken communication. Fidel has some 46 publications, nine of which are in the medium of English. He has secured national and international grant funding for research. For several years, Fidel has been involved in two interconnecting funded projects focusing on vocational identity, one national and the other international. Both projects involve him working closely with colleagues, research assistants, and students across disciplines as part of a

[2] Adapted from Lillis and Curry (2006b).

local network. Three scholars including Fidel can be considered "core" to the local network in that they work closely together to generate ideas for research activity and collaborate extensively (see FG, MN, and JK in Figure 14.1).

2. GUIDING HYPOTHESIS

Multilingual scholars with busy work lives provide each other with different kinds of support in local research networks in order to produce English-medium professional texts, such as writing conference abstracts to meet deadlines.

3. PRIMARY DATA: FIDEL'S LOCAL NETWORK IN ACTION

Data 1: Diagram of Fidel's local network working across two projects

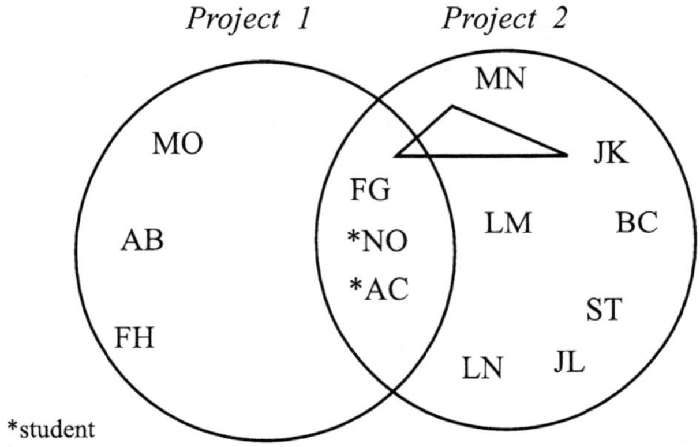

Figure 14.1 Participants in Fidel's [FG] networks

Data 2: Ethnographic description of activity: Preparing conference submissions

It is early evening, around 6 p.m. Fidel is busy, walking in and out of his office from his desk to the printer in another office. NO and AC [postgraduate students] are discussing in L1 the draft submissions they are preparing for an English-medium European conference. The deadline is imminent and they are all anxious to get these proposals in. Fidel is engaged in several tasks at the same time. He is trying to write a single-authored proposal in English, as well as support NO in producing his single-authored text in English. Fidel sits at his desk. AC comes in and looks at NO's draft and also adds comments. The phone rings and Fidel is talking on the phone to MN and they are discussing in L1 a version of another proposal they are preparing together on behalf of two other colleagues [JK and JL in Figure 14.1], also involved in one of the research projects. Fidel listens and responds in L1 on the phone as he writes at his computer in English, and MN writes at hers (field notes, TL, Jan. 2001).

4. KEY QUESTIONS ABOUT THE DATA

1. What does the diagram in Figure 14.1 tell you about this network? How many people in total are involved across the two projects? Who are involved in both projects? Who seems to have a pivotal role?
2. What does the ethnographic account tell you about the different tasks people are undertaking?
3. What does the ethnographic account tell you about the specific role played by Fidel (FG) in preparing the conference abstracts?
4. What do you notice about the involvement of postgraduates in the production of the conference abstracts? In particular, what does the ethnographic account tell you about the ways in which NO is supported to produce a conference abstract?

Discussion of the ethnographic data

From the diagram, it is clear that 13 people are involved in total in the two projects, with some working and writing across both – FG, NO, and AC. The triangle with FG, MN, and JK indicates their key roles in the local research activity: They work closely together in setting up research and writing. The ethnographic account provides a snapshot of the specific ways in which they work together within the context of very busy academic and teaching lives to meet pressured deadlines. All participants contribute to different parts of the research activity – such as research design, data collection, and analysis – through regular team meetings and more ongoing informal collaboration. In specific relation to writing, Fidel draws on the participants in his close research network as a resource for his text production – in this instance a conference abstract (see MN's activity in Data 2). But he also clearly acts as an important resource for others in the network, notably on NO's draft as indicated in Data 2. NO is a postgraduate student who played a key part in the data collection and analysis of one strand of the project: Here Fidel is following NO's lead in relation to analysis but supporting the representation of this analysis in English.

The result of this networked activity was as follows: Nine proposals of approximately 1,000 words were produced to schedule, involving 13 scholars working across two projects; three scholars were involved in the EU project, seven were involved in the national project, and three were working across both projects. All nine proposals were accepted for the conference and, following the conference, of the nine presented papers, six were later submitted and published as conference proceedings. The overall activity was clearly successful.

5. THINKING ABOUT YOUR PRACTICE

1. What local research networks are you involved in? These networks may be directly related to specific research projects – as is the case with Fidel and colleagues – or may be more spread out, such as contacts through conferences and seminars that you attend, or more informal, such as friends or colleagues who share similar interests.
2. What kind of role(s) do you play in supporting the English-medium research and text production of others, such as conference abstracts? Are you a resource in terms of the content of texts (e.g., data analysis)? The English language? The specific rhetorical moves or argument?
3. What kind of support for research and academic text production do you seek from others? Fidel's network is obviously closely knit; you may have more informal support, for example, asking a colleague for comments on an abstract you are drafting.
4. Could you map out a diagram indicating the key members of your research network? Your network may look quite diffuse or closely knit, like Fidel's.

6. SUGGESTIONS FOR TAKING ACTION

1. **Enhance your text-production opportunities**. With other members of your research network, pool your knowledge of upcoming conferences, calls for papers for special issues of journals or edited books, seminars, and other professional activities related to your research interests and topics.
2. **Work more effectively by working with others**. If you are currently writing in English, consider how to save time and effort in your text

production. Identify which members of your network have particular expertise that can be a resource to contribute. Think about when to start certain stages of text production such as writing or translating research findings into English, obtaining submission guidelines for target outlets, or other logistics that might be distributed among network members and/or started on early.

3. **Work at building your local network**. If you do not identify yourself as a member of a network, think about developing ways of working with others that would support both your and their English-medium text production. Find out whether other scholars or postgraduates locally are interested in English-medium publishing and what each of you might be able to contribute to a local network.

Heuristic 2: Participating in an international network to write a journal article[3]

1. BACKGROUND TO TEXT HISTORY: ISTVAN IN HIS NETWORKS

Istvan is a professor of psychology and director of an institute at the medical school of a central European university where he has worked for 25 years. Although Istvan feels comfortable reading academic English, he is frustrated with his abilities in conversation and writing. Istvan's prolific publishing record in his L1 and English (some 25 books and 15 book chapters and articles in his L1, plus some 15 articles and book chapters in English) has enabled him to establish two laboratories, one in the psychology department and one in the medical school, with many doctoral students and postdoctoral researchers. Istvan's chief and longest-lasting research network began in 1997, when two US researchers read an article on cognition Istvan had published and invited him to visit them. Istvan has since coauthored seven articles with them, working by e-mail and occasional visits. He has a strong understanding of the rhetorical conventions of the journals in his discipline(s); thus, what he typically seeks help with are aspects of English related to word choices and sentence construction.

[3] Drawing on data discussed in Lillis and Curry (2006b).

2. GUIDING HYPOTHESIS

Multilingual scholars often participate in international research networks that support their ability to publish in English-medium academic journals and in turn enable them to help others with their English-medium publishing. Various members of these networks make different contributions to their joint work.

3. PRIMARY DATA: ISTVAN'S INTERNATIONAL NETWORK IN ACTION

Data 1: Diagram of Istvan's international network

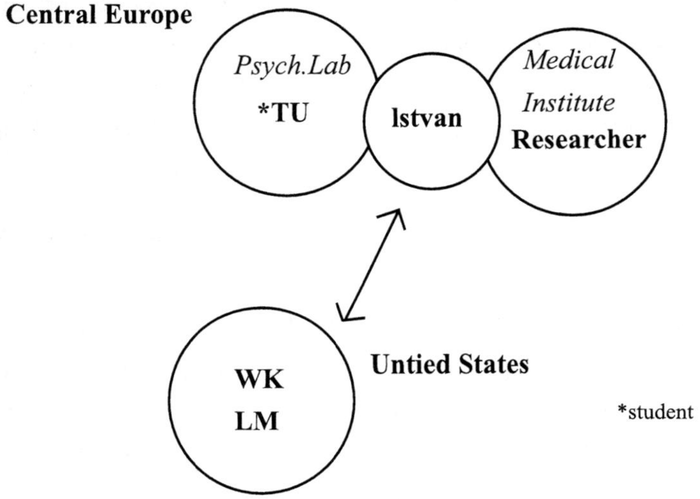

Figure 14.2 Participants in Istvan's network

Data 2: An account of the development of the article by international network members

Based on interviews and communications with Istvan, we know that the networked activity in his text history took place in two main stages over the course of three years and resulted in the publication of an article in a British journal. **Stage 1:** Istvan conducted the experiments with TU, who was then one of his students, and two other local researchers, in their L1 using local female university students as research subjects. Previously, Istvan had jointly developed these experimental methods with his US colleagues (WK and LM in Figure 14.2). Using these research results, Istvan drafted an article in English and enlisted TU's help with the writing, as TU has greater control of English than does Istvan. After minor feedback from WK, Istvan submitted the manuscript to an international English-medium journal. The article was rejected primarily because the study had used only female subjects.

Stage 2: Istvan secured funding for TU to reconduct the experiments with male subjects, again local university students. Then Istvan drew on TU's new findings to craft a quite different version of the article. He sent this draft to WK in the United States, who suggested detailed word- and sentence-level changes and pointed to confusing areas such as explanations of the research methodology. Istvan submitted the next revision to a new English-medium international journal, which accepted the article pending specified changes. Istvan enlisted his student TU's help in making these revisions, which were accepted and the article was published.

4. KEY QUESTIONS ABOUT THE DATA

1. How do you think the members of Istvan's network have gained access to both these local and international networks? What benefits might they find in belonging to these networks?
2. What different roles do these members of the networks have? What do they contribute in terms of methodology, data collection and analysis, writing, reviewing drafts, making revisions to text? How might these contributions be connected to their geographical locations in the network?
3. At what stages of research activity and text production do network members make these different contributions? When does Istvan's student appear to contribute? Who seems to be managing these various contributions?
4. Which contributions from network members might be the most relevant for getting the article published in an English-medium international journal?

Discussion of the ethnographic data

Istvan plays a pivotal role in these networks, connecting his local network of students and researchers in his laboratories to his US network, thereby providing opportunities for local network members to publish in international English-medium journals. At the same time, the experimental research findings from his local laboratory contribute to his academic field internationally. Istvan's student TU made important contributions in terms of conducting experiments and working on the English writing. The laboratory's researchers also assisted with the experiments. WK, the US colleague, contributed scientific, linguistic, and rhetorical knowledge that played an important role in helping Istvan shape the article to meet the expectations of an international English-medium journal.

5. THINKING ABOUT YOUR PRACTICE

1. Are you involved in research networks that extend beyond your local context? If so, how? If not, do you know of any international networks that you might want to join?
2. What contributions do you make to the research and writing that occurs in such networks?
3. Who plays a pivotal role in the international networks that you can identify?
4. What do you (or could you) offer to and receive from others in the network, particularly in relation to writing an academic journal article?

6. SUGGESTIONS FOR TAKING ACTION

1. **Make contact with other researchers.** Connecting with others in your discipline who are doing work that interests you or is related to your research may enable you to exchange ideas and develop collaborations. Speaking with presenters at conferences about connections with your research may be the beginning of a future collaboration. It is also possible to make connections electronically, as many scholars' e-mail addresses are available in their published articles, institutional or personal Web sites, or on the Internet.
2. **Look for resources.** Your institution, government, or professional association may have funding for conference travel and other research-related activities. You may find exchange grants to support stays to work with colleagues. Some journals offer reduced subscription rates to scholars in certain areas of the world. Many academics will fulfill requests for reprints of their publications, sending them by e-mail or post.

3. **Discuss your contributions.** Participants in networks may have different ideas about the purposes of collaborating, and the roles, tasks, and responsibilities of various network members. Identify what you hope to contribute and hope to gain from participating in a network and plan to discuss these issues with network members as you begin to work together in order to foster successful collaboration.

Heuristic 3: Involving literacy brokers in producing English-medium texts[4]

1. BACKGROUND TO TEXT HISTORY: CARLA INTERACTING WITH LITERACY BROKERS

Carla is an associate professor of psychology at a southern European university, where she has worked for 17 years. Having studied English since she was nine, her level of expertise in English is quite high. She had previously published five articles in English-medium journals and 10 in journals in her L1. A few years before the activity that took place in connection with this text history, she had spent six weeks working in the laboratory of a colleague in the United Kingdom. The experiments that she reports on in the article in this text history continue a line of research she has been involved with for a long time and collaborated on with the British colleague. In addition, Carla often conducts and writes on this research with a colleague from a nearby city with whom she did her graduate study, as is the case here.

2. GUIDING HYPOTHESIS

Scholars call on different people – whom we call "literacy brokers" – to support their English-medium text production. This heuristic explores some of the ways in which literacy brokers, a range of people who contribute to and influence the production of texts, intervene in text production and the ways that brokers orient to text. They may act in this process in various ways, such as providing or gatekeeping publishing opportunities, supporting scholars' writing about research, helping choose target journals, and shaping linguistic and rhetorical aspects of multilingual scholars' texts, as well as providing feedback on submitted texts.

---

4 Drawing on data discussed in Lillis and Curry (2006a).

3. PRIMARY DATA: IDENTIFYING LITERACY BROKERS AND THEIR ORIENTATIONS TO TEXT

Data 1: Text interventions by different kinds of literacy brokers

Example 1: Broker's suggestions for textual changes to the introduction*

Before changes by the broker	After changes by the broker
The aim of the present work is to study the effects of continuous noise, when the onset of the speech signal is delayed relative to the onset of the masker, on the recognition of voiced plosives.	The **purpose** of the present **study** is to examine the effects of continuous noise **on the recognition of voiced plosives**, when the onset of the speech signal is delayed **with regard** to the onset of the masker.

* Salient changes are indicated in boldfaced type.

Example 2: Broker's comments on submitted manuscript

[The manuscript] needs more reader guidance. In many parts, it lacks a little more introduction to the used procedures, and often a few sentences to describe the motivation for a certain method would be very helpful for a reader which is not deeply involved in this area of research.

pp. 5-7, it seems necessary to me to add some more details about the mentioned literature and why they are important for this study, so that the reader can at least get a basic idea of what is meant without having read each of the papers.

p. 23, para 2, this is a summary of the results but the discussion and interpretation of the results is missing.

4. KEY QUESTIONS ABOUT THE DATA

1. What kinds of changes do these different literacy brokers suggest? Which aspects of the article do these brokers seem to be considering in their comments?
2. What effects would the suggestions in each extract have, if Carla implemented them? That is, how would the meaning of the text change as a result of these comments?

3. What kind of literacy brokers do you think have made the changes suggested here? That is, what kind of knowledge of content, research methodology, English language, and academic writing do you think the brokers might be drawing on or orienting toward?
4. Which changes in these examples seem the most useful for improving the text for English-medium presentation or publication? Why?

Discussion of the ethnographic data

In the PAW study, we have identified a number of types of literacy brokers, two main categories of which are as follows:

Language professional brokers. These are people who work professionally in some way with the linguistic medium of English, such as translators, copyeditors, proofreaders, and English teachers. Language professional brokers tend to adopt what we can call a "language orientation" to academic texts. Example 1 shows interventions made by a language professional broker whom Carla hired to edit the article text before submission to the journal. The language professional broker's orientation here was toward sentence-level word and syntax choices.

Academic professional brokers. These are academics who work in universities or research institutes; depending on how their professional expertise relates to a particular text, they can be subclassified as a *general academic*, someone from a different disciplinary area than the author(s), or as a *discipline expert* who shares a disciplinary background. The academic professional broker's primary orientation tends to be toward the content of the text and research methodology and how these relate to current research in the discipline – this can be called a "content orientation." Example 2 above shows comments from one of the journal reviewers, who would be classified as academic professional brokers. In this case, the broker oriented mainly toward the research methodology, the research literature, and meeting the expectations of the journal.

5. THINKING ABOUT YOUR PRACTICE

1. Whom do you typically ask for help with your English-medium academic writing?
2. When in the development of your text do you seek input from such

literacy brokers?

3. How would you categorize the ways in which the literacy brokers orient to your texts? Do they tend to have a disciplinary content or language orientation? Or both?
4. What types of comment and feedback would you find most helpful to receive from these literacy brokers?

6. SUGGESTIONS FOR TAKING ACTION

1. **Identify what kinds of feedback might be useful**. If you have not previously asked anyone to read and comment on your English-medium academic writing, think about the specific kinds of feedback you might want at different moments as you develop your text. Do you want comments on the knowledge content, argument, research methodology, or ideas you are putting forward? On the article structure? On English-language expressions, grammatical aspects, disciplinary terminology, word or phrase choices?
2. **Make connections with literacy brokers.** Connections with brokers may happen just once or over time. Depending on the type of feedback you want, you may ask a local colleague or someone else, perhaps someone you have met at a conference, to read and comment on a particular text. Some publishers are now providing contact information for proofreaders on their Web sites. Literacy brokers may also be people such as journal editors, who may work with you on a text after submission to the journal if the referees' reviews of your submission have been encouraging.
3. **Consider what may be at stake for you in working with different types of literacy brokers.** Literacy brokers are not neutral participants in text production – they have their own implicit and explicit views about what makes a good text and what constitutes a significant contribution to knowledge. So you need to consider what might be at stake in asking different literacy brokers to read and comment on your texts. You may react differently to the comments of different types of brokers, such as a language professional broker compared

with an academic professional broker. Keep a critical perspective on brokers' proposed interventions, reserving your ability to disagree with suggested changes.

Conclusion: Supporting multilingual writers through research-based heuristics

In this chapter, we have focused on how the growing pressure for multilingual scholars and postgraduates to disseminate their research in English is driving a need to support such academic writers in the practices of English-medium text production. We have highlighted the importance of drawing on empirical research findings in the design of materials to support this participation. Our heuristics are intended to make visible some of the dynamic practices involved in participating in networks and interacting with literacy brokers in the development of professional academic texts, such as conference abstracts and journal articles. They draw on key research findings from the PAW study about the importance of research networks and literacy brokers to English-medium text production. These heuristics use empirical data that give a glimpse of the experiences of certain scholars and postgraduates in specific contexts working in particular academic disciplines. Because of the specificity of ethnographic research findings, we do not want to claim that these particular scholars' experiences will be shared across all other contexts or disciplines or, thus, that these heuristics would be useful to all scholars or postgraduates. Nonetheless, an approach to designing materials that illuminates the social practices of professional academic writing and publishing by multilingual scholars and postgraduates – as documented by empirical research – appears to be a much-needed complement to approaches concerned primarily with textual aspects of English-medium academic writing. In addition, we have foregrounded the social nature of English-medium text production, in contrast to models of learning that implicitly use an orientation to individual competence.

As we have illustrated, research-based heuristics can offer a tool for translating our empirical findings about the actual practices and experiences of multilingual scholars writing professional English-medium texts into ways of supporting reflection and subsequent action linked to the specific contexts, interests, and goals of users of the heuristics. We hope this focus will further designers' understandings of both the complexity of professional academic text production practices and the need for designing materials that are based on research about these practices rather than on intuitions alone. In this chapter we have not, however, included discussion of issues involved in designing materials based on empirical research conducted by other investigators, or materials created in collaboration with scholars and postgraduates in response to their interests and needs (Cargill & O'Connor 2006). Both of those directions would be worth further exploration.

In advocating a social-practice approach to supporting the English-medium text production of multilingual scholars, we do not mean to downplay the tensions inherent in the spread of English as the medium of scholarly text production. Along with other researchers (e.g., Braine 2005; Li 2007; Swales 2004; Tardy 2004) who have shed light on the numerous demands confronting multilingual scholars, our research brings into relief some of the contradictions created by the growing dominance of English. On the one hand, the spread of English as an "academic lingua franca" is viewed as neutrally benefiting the global circulation of knowledge by enabling authors to disseminate their work more widely and allowing readers greater access to research by virtue of needing to know fewer languages (Sano 2002). On the other hand, the dominance of English in academic publishing is seen as bolstering the gatekeeping power and privileges of those in Anglophone contexts (deSwaan 2001; Mauranen 1993) and creating barriers for nonnative users of English outside of Anglophone contexts (Ammon 2003). Although the dominance of English offers some benefits to global scholarship, they come with clear costs to many scholars working outside of Anglophone contexts. The constraints on multilingual scholars' access to the global "marketplace" of English-medium scholarship documented in the PAW study argue for concerted efforts to support those working outside Anglophone contexts. We hope that our research-based heuristics approach focusing on social practices will be useful for materials designers who are considering how to support multilingual scholars and postgraduates in English-medium text production.

Discussion questions and tasks

Reflection

1. Look at the sample heuristics provided in the chapter. What are the implications of using a heuristics approach for materials design and development? How might this approach differ from conventional approaches?
2. When – and for which learners – would a heuristics approach to teaching about the practices of professional academic publishing be most suitable?
3. What have you learned from this chapter about supporting multilingual graduate students and scholars in professional academic publishing? How could you use this information to select, adapt, and/or develop materials to support professional academic publishing differently than you currently do? Why?
4. What are some of the difficulties students might experience when using materials focusing on the social practices of professional academic publishing? How could you try to minimize these difficulties as (i) a teacher; and (ii) a materials designer?

Evaluation

5. Look at textbook materials on advanced academic writing/publishing and critically evaluate these on the basis of what you have learned in this chapter. Do they engage with the social practices of writing for publication?
6. Choose three of the following ethnographic studies about the experiences of multilingual scholars or postgraduate students writing in English to form the basis for developing materials to teach advanced academic writing: Belcher and Connor (2001); Casanave (1998, 2002); Casanave and Vandrick (2003); Flowerdew (2000); Li (2002, 2007); Lillis and Curry (2006a, 2006b); Shi (2002); St. John (1987). What potential problems might you face in turning these texts into heuristics-based materials? How culturally appropriate are these studies to your teaching context?

Adaptation/Design

7. Choose one of the studies listed above and develop suitable heuristics from the research data for a group of students. Explain why these materials you develop are suitable. Now try these materials out on the students in your group. Discuss their views on your materials.

References

Akkerman, S., Admiraal, W., & Simons, R. J. (2006). Collaborative activities in academic work. Unpublished manuscript.

Ammon, U. (2003). Global English and the non-native speaker: Overcoming disadvantage. In H. Tonkin & T. Reagan (eds.). *Language in the twenty-first century*. Amsterdam: Benjamins, pp. 23-34.

Barton, D., & Tusting, K. (eds.). (2005). *Beyond communities of practice: Language, power, and social context*. Cambridge: Cambridge University Press.

Belcher, D., & Connor, U. (eds). (2001). *Reflections on multiliterate lives*. Clevedon, UK: Multilingual Matters.

Belcher, W. L. (2009). *Writing your journal article in 12 weeks: A guide to academic publishing success*. Thousand Oaks, CA: Sage.

Bourdieu, P. (1985). The forms of capital. In J. G. Richardson (ed.). *Handbook of theory and research for the sociology of education*. New York: Greenwood, pp. 241-58.

Braine, G. (2005). The challenge of academic publishing: A Hong Kong perspective. *TESOL Quarterly* 30(4): 707-16.

Canagarajah, A. S. (1996). "Nondiscursive" requirements in academic publishing, material resources of periphery scholars, and the politics of knowledge production. *Written Communication* 13(4): 435-2.

Canagarajah, A. S. (2002a). Multilingual writers and the academic community: Towards a critical relationship. *Journal of English for Academic Purposes* 1: 29-44.

Canagarajah, A. S. (2002b). *A geopolitics of academic writing*. Pittsburgh, PA: University of Pittsburgh Press.

Cargill, M. & O'Connor, P. (2006). Developing Chinese scientists' skills for publishing in English: Evaluating collaborating-colleague workshops based on genre analysis. *Journal of English for Academic Purposes* 5: 207-21.

Casanave, C. (1998). Transitions: The balancing act of bilingual academics. *Journal of Second Language Writing* 7: 175-203.

Casanave, C. (2002). *Writing games: Multicultural case studies of academic literacy practices in higher education*. Mahwah, NJ: Lawrence Erlbaum.

Casanave, C. P., & Vandrick, S. (2003). *Writing for scholarly publication: Behind the scenes in language education*. Mahwah, NJ: Lawrence Erlbaum.

Cho, S. (2004). Challenges of entering discourse communities through publishing in English: Perspectives of nonnative-speaking doctoral students in the United States of America. *Journal of Language, Identity, and Education* 3(1): 47-72.

Curry, M. J., & Lillis, T. (2004). Multilingual scholars and the imperative to publish in English: Negotiating interests, demands, and rewards. *TESOL Quarterly* 38(4): 663-89.

deSwaan, A. (2001). English in the social sciences. In U. Ammon (ed.). *The dominance of English as a language of science*. Berlin/New York: Mouton de Gruyter, pp. 71-83.

Dong, Y. (1998). Non-native graduate students' thesis/dissertation writing in science: Self-reports by students and their advisors from two U.S. institutions. *English for Specific Purposes* 17(4): 369-90.

Flowerdew, J. (1999). Writing for scholarly publication in English: The case of Hong Kong. *Journal of Second Language Writing* 8(2): 123-45.

Flowerdew, J. (2000). Discourse community, legitimate peripheral participation, and the nonnative-English-speaking scholar. *TESOL Quarterly* 34(1): 127-50.

Granovetter, M. (1983). The strength of weak ties: A network theory revisited. *Sociological Theory* 1: 201-33.

Harwood, N. (2005). What do we want EAP teaching materials for? *Journal of English for Academic Purposes* 4: 149-61.

Hengl, T., & Gould, M. (2006). *The unofficial guide for authors (or how to produce research articles worth citing)*. Luxembourg: Office for Official Publications of the European Communities. EUR 22191 EN. Available at: http://eusoils. jrc.it/ESDB_Archive/eusoils_docs/other/EUR22191. pdf (accessed April 14, 2009).

Keating, M. C. (2005). The person in the doing: Negotiating the experience of self. In D. Barton & K. Tusting (eds.). *Beyond communities of practice: Language, power, and social context*. Cambridge: Cambridge University Press, pp. 105-38.

Kitchen, R., & Fuller, D. (2005). *The academic's guide to publishing*. Thousand Oaks, CA: Sage.

Klingner, J., Scanlon, D., & Pressley, M. (2005). How to publish in scholarly journals. *Educational Researcher* 34(8): 14-20.

Lave, J., & Wenger, E. (1991). *Situated learning: Legitimate peripheral participation.* Cambridge: Cambridge University Press.

Li, Y. (2002). Writing for international publication: The perception of Chinese doctoral researchers. *Asian Journal of English Language Teaching* 12: 179-93.

Li, Y. (2007). Apprentice scholarly writing in a community of practice: An intraview of an NNES graduate student writing an article. *TESOL Quarterly* 41(1): 55-78.

Lillis, T. (2003). Student writing as "academic literacies": Drawing on Bakhtin to move from critique to design. *Language and Education* 17(3): 192-207.

Lillis, T., & Curry, M. J. (2006a). Professional academic writing by multilingual scholars: Interactions by literacy brokers in the production of English-medium texts. *Written Communication* 23(1): 3-35.

Lillis, T., & Curry, M. J. (2006b). Reframing notions of competence in scholarly writing: From individual to networked activity. *Revista Canaria de Estudios Ingleses* 53: 63-78.

Lillis, T., & North, S. (2006). Academic writing. In S. Potter (ed.). *Doing postgraduate research* (2nd ed.). London: Sage, pp. 114-51.

Lin, N. (2001). Building a network theory of social capital. In N. Lin, K. Cook, & R. Burt (eds.). *Social capital: Theory and research.* New York: Aline de Gruyter, pp. 3-29.

Mace, J. (2002). *The give and take of writing: Scribes, literacy, and everyday life.* Leicester, UK: National Institute of Adult and Continuing Education.

Martin, D. (2005). Communities of practice and learning communities: Do bilingual co-workers learn in community? In D. Barton & K. Tusting (eds.). *Beyond communities of practice: Language, power, and social context.* Cambridge: Cambridge University Press, pp. 139-57.

Mauranen, A. (1993). *Cultural differences in academic rhetoric: A text linguistic study.* Frankfurt: Peter Lang.

Polodny, J., & Page, K. (1998). Network forms of organization. *Annual Review of Sociology* 24: 57-76.

Portes, A. (1998). Social capital: Its origins and applications in modern sociology. *Annual Review of Sociology* 24: 1-24.

Richardson, L. (2000). Writing: A method of inquiry. In N. K. Denzin & Y. Lincoln (eds.). *Handbook of qualitative research* (2nd ed.). Thousand Oaks, CA: Sage, pp. 923-48.

Rock, F. (2005). "I've picked some up from a colleague": Language, sharing and communities of practice in an institutional setting. In D. Barton & K. Tusting (eds.).

Beyond communities of practice: Language, power, and social context. Cambridge: Cambridge University Press, pp. 77-104.

Sano, H. (2002). The world's lingua franca of science. *English Today* 18(4):45-9.

Shi, L. (2002). How western-trained Chinese TESOL professionals publish in their home environment. *TESOL Quarterly* 36(4): 625-34.

St. John, M. J. (1987). Writing processes of Spanish scientists publishing in English. *English for Specific Purposes* 60(2): 113-20.

Swales, J. (2004). *Research genres: Exploration and applications.* Cambridge: Cambridge University Press.

Swales, J., & Feak, C. (2000). *English in today's research world: A writing guide.* Ann Arbor: University of Michigan Press.

Swales, J., & Feak, C. (2004). *Academic writing for graduate students: Essential skills and tasks* (2nd ed.). Ann Arbor: University of Michigan Press.

Tardy, C. (2004). The role of English in scientific communication: Lingua franca or Tyrannosaurus rex? *Journal of English for Academic Purposes* 3: 247-69.

Thyer, B. (2005). *Successful publishing in scholarly journals.* Thousand Oaks, CA: Sage.

Weissberg, R., & Buker, S. (1990). *Writing up research: Experimental research report writing for students of English.* Englewood Cliffs, NJ: Prentice Hall Regents.

Wenger, E. (1998). *Communities of practice: Learning, meaning, and identity.* Cambridge: Cambridge University Press.

Wepner, S., & Gambrell, L. (2006). *Beating the odds: Getting published in the field of literacy.* Newark, DE: International Reading Association.

Yakhontova, T. (2001). Textbooks, contexts, and learners. *English for Specific Purposes* 20: 397-415.

15

English for nursing: Developing discipline-specific materials

Susan Bosher

Summary

Despite the increase in immigrant students in nursing programs in the United States and the difficulties many of these students encounter in their programs, remarkably little attention has been given in the field of English Language Teaching to preparing ESL students for the language, cultural, and academic demands of nursing. Although a plethora of articles about ESL students in nursing has been published in recent years in nursing journals, most of the proposed interventions have addressed the sociocultural and academic needs of students, rather than their language needs, despite the fact that language has been cited by students and faculty as the most significant barrier faced by the majority of ESL nursing students. There has also been little collaboration between ESL and nursing faculty, and few courses have been developed to prepare students for the language-related demands of nursing programs. This chapter reviews the literature on ESL students in nursing, describes the results of a needs analysis that was conducted to determine the language skills and cultural knowledge necessary for students to succeed in baccalaureate-degree nursing programs, and presents materials that were developed for use in an English for Cross-cultural Nursing course, a four-credit, writing-intensive course for ESL prenursing students preparing to enter the baccalaureate-degree nursing program at St. Catherine University in St. Paul, Minnesota. The materials address nursing-specific language skills and cultural content, such as critical thinking skills, writing progress notes, listening to change-of-shift reports, understanding culturally sensitive topics in nursing, and analyzing multiple-choice test items.

Introduction

In the field of English Language Teaching, remarkably little attention has been given to nursing and to the language-learning needs of nursing students who are nonnative speakers of English or English-as-a-second-language (ESL) students.[1] Although some materials have been published for entry-level ESL health-care workers (Pogrund & Grebel 1998), and some programs have been developed for internationally educated nurses reentering the workforce in English-speaking countries (Hussin 2002), little has been done in response to the increasing number of immigrant students in nursing programs in the United States.

Immigrant students in nursing

Nurse educators in the United States are well aware of the increase in ESL students in their classes and in their programs and are eager to address their needs, as illustrated by the number of articles that have been published in various nursing journals since the early 1990s. Most of these students are immigrants rather than international students, a distinction that is often made in the literature on ESL in higher education (Bosher & Rowekamp 1998). In general, international students are well educated, in contrast to immigrant students, many of whom have experienced interruption in their schooling and may, therefore, not have developed full academic proficiency in either their native language or in English. In addition, international students are often single and without families or children to care for. Because they are not allowed to work off-campus or for more than the ten hours their work-study

[1] In the nursing literature, the term "ESL" is used to identify this population of students even though English may be one of several other languages students speak; in addition, many of these students have either been placed out of traditional ESL classes – preacademic courses in reading, writing, listening, and speaking – or have grown up in an English-speaking country of residency and are fluent in spoken English. In this paper, ESL refers to students for whom English is not their native language regardless of other languages they speak or their proficiency in English.

positions on campus will allow, they are able to focus more exclusively on their education. In contrast, immigrant students are often part of an extended family, including small children, and have responsibilities toward their families, both in the United States and in their country of origin, and might even work a full-time job in addition to going to school full-time.

Nursing organizations have long called for greater diversity in the nursing profession. In 1997, the American Association of Colleges of Nursing (AACN) released a position statement on diversity and equality of opportunity, which emphasized the nursing profession's commitment to "accelerating the inclusion of ... cultures ... that traditionally have been underrepresented...." In addition, the US Department of Health and Human Services has funded various initiatives to recruit and retain multicultural and economically disadvantaged students in nursing programs. Some of this funding has been used to explore ways to address the needs of ESL students in nursing (Bosher 2006; Guhde 2003). Despite an emphasis on creating a more diverse workforce, the National League for Nursing (NLN) reported "no significant increase in minority enrollment or graduation" (Nugent & Cook 2002: 31) from nursing programs between 1995 and 2000.

Although nursing programs tend to be demanding for all students, ESL nursing students experience greater difficulty being successful than do native speakers of English (Memmer & Worth 1991; Phillips & Hartley 1990), especially during their first and second semesters (Femea *et al.* 1995). One study found that the attrition rate was twice as high for ESL students compared to native English speakers (Jalili-Grenier & Chase 1997). In addition, ESL students are less likely to be successful on the national licensure examination for nurses, the NCLEX (Cunningham *et al.* 2004; Klisch 1994). In one study, the average pass rate on the NCLEX was 40 percent less for ESL students than for native speakers of English (Johnston 2001). Surprisingly, there has been little input from professionals in English language teaching in efforts to address the needs of ESL nursing students, even though language is often cited as the most significant barrier to their success (Amaro *et al.* 2006; Yoder 1996). One study of 30 retention strategies used in nursing programs in California (Memmer & Worth 1991) did not identify a single strategy that called upon the expertise of ESL professionals in preparing students specifically for nursing programs or working with students currently in nursing programs on language and culture-related issues. Indeed, several programs reported a decrease in language issues by requiring applicants to take a language proficiency test or by increasing the cut-off score on the TOEFL from 500 to 550 for admission, initiatives that seem counterproductive to the goal of increasing diversity in nursing.

Although one article did call for collaboration with ESL faculty (Malu *et al.* 1994), the purpose was to assist in screening applicants for their language proficiency. As part of that screening process, the authors also called for assessing applicants' current level of understanding of the educational process in nursing programs and standards of professionalism in nursing prior to their acceptance, criteria that would most certainly work against immigrant applicants with very different educational experiences from those in the United States and with very different expectations of the teaching/learning process. If the goal is to increase diversity in the profession of nursing, more emphasis should be given to preparing ESL students for the language, cultural, and academic demands of nursing, as well as to creating a more culturally inclusive environment in nursing education (Bosher & Pharris 2008), rather than focusing on ways to reduce access. In short, the benefits for ESL nursing students and nursing faculty alike that could result from collaboration between nursing and ESL faculty remain largely unrecognized and untapped.

Review of the literature

Studies that have investigated the needs of ethnically diverse students in nursing programs (Amaro *et al.* 2006; Yoder 1996) have identified four types of needs: personal, academic, language, and cultural. Overall, students felt their primary barrier in nursing was language, in terms of both the difficulties they encountered with reading, writing, listening to lectures, and oral communication, and the prejudice they experienced from others because of their accent. In addition, language plays a significant role in the academic issues that students encounter in nursing programs. For example, students felt overwhelmed by the amount of work in the nursing program, the complexity of the material, and the time needed to study – issues that for ESL students are that much more difficult and time-consuming because of the language.

Language also plays a role in the cultural issues students encounter in nursing programs, for example, when communicating with peers, instructors, clinical staff, and patients (Amaro *et al.* 2006). Behaviors that are the norm in the dominant culture and are part of the expectations that instructors have of students, such as asking questions when students do not understand, may pose problems for students who were raised with a different set of cultural norms. In some cultures, asking questions of the instructor or being assertive in any way is considered rude because of the respect and authority that are afforded teachers in those cultures (Kataoka-Yahiro & Abriam-Yago 1997).

In addition to language, culture plays a role in difficulties ESL students encounter communicating in the clinical setting, for example, using therapeutic communication and assertiveness skills (Bosher & Smalkoski 2002). Overall, clinical courses tend to be more difficult for ESL students than for native English speakers (Cameron 1998; Jalili-Grenier & Chase 1997). Though difficult for some students, communication in the clinical setting provides ESL students with exposure to authentic, meaningful language, an ideal setting for developing communicative competence in the language. Role plays can help students address cultural issues and give them practice interacting with patients and colleagues in preparation for the clinical setting. Bosher and Smalkoski (2002) developed a course on health-care communication for ESL students and used role plays to simulate authentic interaction in the target setting, thereby helping students gain confidence and proficiency in communicating effectively in the health-care setting.

Cameron (1998) identified five types of communicative behavior needed in the clinical setting: (1) getting information; (2) transmitting information; (3) translating information from one medium to another or from one audience to another; (4) utilizing different channels of communication; and (5) interacting socially as well as professionally in the clinical site. In the course that was subsequently developed, students worked on a variety of skills and tasks related to these communicative behaviors, as well as on accuracy in speech production at the levels of pronunciation, vocabulary, grammar, and discourse.

Culture also plays an important role in the successful outcomes of teaching ethnically diverse nursing students. Yoder (1996, 2001) describes various teaching approaches distinguished by the degree to which nursing faculty incorporate cultural awareness and appreciation. In the most effective teaching approach, the bridging approach, instructors recognize the importance of culture and its role in students' understanding of basic concepts in nursing as well as in students' perceptions of the teaching/learning process. In this approach, instructors integrate culture into their curriculum and adapt their teaching in response to the needs of their students. They value cultural diversity in the classroom, acknowledge the reality of prejudice in the lives of their students, and encourage students to maintain their ethnic identity rather than assimilate into the majority culture. The bridging approach has a positive impact on the ethnic identity, self-confidence, and self-esteem of ethnically diverse students in contrast to other teaching approaches, which deny or ignore cultural differences to varying degrees (Yoder 2001). Students find the educational environment created by the bridging approach to be welcoming, supportive, and empowering.

Another model that has been proposed for teaching ESL nursing students is based on Cummins's (1979) language interdependence hypothesis. Although no longer widely cited in ESL, it has inspired numerous articles in nursing in an attempt to explain why students who are fluent in spoken English struggle academically. In this model, Cummins (1979; Cummins & Swain 1986) distinguishes between context-embedded and cognitively undemanding ways of using the language, or basic interpersonal communication skills (BICS), that can take from two to three years to acquire, and context-reduced and cognitively demanding tasks, or cognitive academic language proficiency (CALP), that can take five to seven years to develop, or even longer, depending on the student's age on arrival in the United States and the degree of academic literacy developed in the student's native language (Collier 1989). Nurse educators (Abriam-Yago *et al.* 1999; Guhde 2003; Malu & Figlear 1998; Phillips & Hartley 1990) have enthusiastically embraced this distinction between language proficiencies and proposed ways to provide linguistic and contextual support for ESL nursing students to enhance their learning, participation, and success in nursing programs.

Other theorists (Hawkins 2001) have proposed an alternative explanation for the degree of difficulty that ESL students encounter in academic reading and writing. According to them, it is not that academic content or discipline-specific content is decontextualized, but that it is so highly contextualized that it seems decontextualized to outsiders. Likewise, social language is not cognitively undemanding or unrelated to academic content instruction, but rather a great deal of cognitive effort is required to become socialized into a discipline. Indeed, learning how to write successfully in nursing requires a certain degree of socialization into the profession of nursing, a process that is greatly facilitated for ESL students when instructors make explicit their assumptions and expectations for acceptable writing in the discipline (Bosher 2001).

On the other hand, some nurse educators have challenged what is considered acceptable writing in nursing. Alster (2004) claims that nursing students produce poor writing because that is what they have been exposed to. Students have not been given the opportunity to discuss and critique models of writing in nursing, so they imitate the writing they have seen, especially the stilted and often convoluted language of many nursing journals. In addition, students import the characteristics of writing in the clinical setting to writing academic papers, resulting in "flat, affectless text ... perhaps suitable for informing, but not for inspiring, challenging, or persuading" (Alster 2004: 172). Furthermore, nursing faculty often value form over substance, insisting on APA rules of style and formatting, to the detriment of encouraging students to focus on their ideas and analysis. Alster (2004) advocates providing a greater variety of writing assignments, such as reflective journals about clinical experiences, to which faculty would respond at the level of content only. She also proposes a writing-to-learn approach, where students use writing not only to communicate knowledge, but also to discover and create it. Such an approach would help initiate students into the nursing discourse community by giving them the opportunity to develop "confidence in their own authority to develop and communicate clinical knowledge" (p. 167), as well as "evaluate the soundness and significance of their own ideas as well as those of health care 'experts'" (p. 168). Becoming a member of a discourse community involves being able to claim authority and agency in the creation of knowledge in the profession. A more open approach to writing in nursing would encourage students to develop writing skills that are both more personally engaging, as well as grounded in critical thinking, especially for ESL students who might otherwise focus on language issues in their writing.

Another proposed strategy for effective teaching of ESL nursing students is to create learning activities that stimulate more than one sense (Jalili-Grenier & Chase 1997) or that speak to more than one learning style (Keane 1993; Phillips & Hartley 1990). Typically, information is conveyed in nursing courses through lectures that rely on audio input or auditory learning, and knowledge is assessed through multiple-choice tests. Although overheads, videos, and lecture outlines often accompany lectures and can help students learn the content visually, nursing courses are often front-loaded with theory the first half of the semester, followed by hands-on learning in a clinical setting the second half. If students do not pass the first half of the semester, they are not allowed to complete the clinical portion of the course, thereby missing the opportunity for learning through tactile and kinesthetic means, which are preferred learning styles for many ESL students (Reid 1987).

Despite the plethora of articles that have been published in nursing journals about ESL students in nursing, most of the proposed interventions address sociocultural or academic needs of students. There have been just a few studies that have focused on language-related skills and tasks that students need to succeed in nursing programs (Bosher 2006; Cameron 1998; Hussin 2002), even though, as mentioned earlier, language has been cited as the most significant barrier faced by the majority of ESL nursing students (Amaro *et al.* 2006; Yoder 1996). Furthermore, no articles have specifically proposed ESL for nursing courses, either for prenursing or nursing students, or collaboration in other ways with ESL faculty, besides preadmissions screening, despite indications that existing academic support is insufficient to meet the needs of ESL nursing students (Amaro *et al.* 2006).

Needs analysis of ESL nursing students

In 2000-2001, a needs analysis was conducted of ESL students in a baccalaureate-degree nursing program[2] (Bosher 2006). This needs analysis combined target-situation analysis with means analysis and learning situation analysis (Dudley-Evans & St John 1998; West 1994). The objective needs of the students (Hutchinson & Waters 1987), defined as the language-related tasks and activities that students need to perform as nursing students, were determined at the global and rhetorical levels (Tarone & Yule 1989) through observations of first-year course lectures, labs, and clinicals; discussions with faculty about various tasks and assignments; analysis of faculty questionnaires, specifically faculty perceptions of the degree of difficulty of each of the language-related skills and tasks identified in the target-situation analysis; and document analysis of course syllabi, writing assignments, and students' written products. Constraints on the learning situation were identified through discussions with faculty and administrators and through structured interviews with ESL students about their experiences in the nursing program. Subjective needs (Hutchinson & Waters 1987) were determined by analysis of student questionnaires, specifically students' perceptions of the degree of difficulty of each of the language-related skills and tasks identified in the target-situation analysis, and through structured interviews with students.

The results of the interviews and questionnaires led to the development of course objectives (see Appendix 15.1), which served as the framework for designing the English for nursing course (Bosher 2006). Materials were then developed that addressed each of the course objectives. Students' comments from interviews, conducted as part of the needs analysis, and written comments from student and faculty questionnaires are integrated into the discussion of sample materials and activities.

Academic versus clinical skills in nursing

The results of the needs analysis clearly indicate the importance of addressing both academic skills and clinical skills for ESL students, both of which are necessary for success in nursing programs, particularly at the baccalaureate-degree

[2] In the United States, there are basically two different educational paths to a nursing degree: an associate-degree program, usually at a two-year community or technical college, or a four-year baccalaureate-degree program. Graduates from both programs take the same national nursing licensure exam, the NCLEX.

level. Academic skills in nursing are similar to academic skills in the social and natural sciences. Nursing students must be able to understand complex reading material, usually in textbook format; comprehend lectures; take notes to supplement lecture outlines; study effectively for tests; participate actively in discussions; ask questions; and write research papers on various topics in nursing.

When students begin the clinical portion of their coursework, that is, the portion of their nursing education that brings them in contact with patients in various health-care settings and requires them to apply what they have learned in their classes to direct patient care, they are required to prepare nursing care plans and write clinical papers. These plans require students to research a patient's medical diagnosis and write out a detailed plan of care that reflects the nursing process of assessing the patient, including both his or her physical and psychosocial health; determining an appropriate nursing diagnosis; creating appropriate goals or desired outcomes for the patient; implementing the interventions that have been identified in the plan; and evaluating the patient's progress toward achieving the desired outcomes. Successful nursing care plans and clinical papers must demonstrate the ability to think critically, integrate information from multiple sources, and document the use of outside sources using the American Psychological Association (APA) system.

In addition, students need to be able to communicate effectively in the clinical setting, for which they need interviewing skills to gather information from patients; therapeutic communication skills to help patients cope with their situation; and assertiveness skills to speak up in difficult situations. Nursing students also need to chart accurately and appropriately the nursing care they provide, using any one of several types of documentation systems. In addition, change-of-shift reports are used to transmit information about a patient from one nurse to another. Sometimes, this information is passed orally from one nurse to the next; sometimes it is done through taped reports. Either way, nursing students must be able to understand critical information about the care of a patient, communicated orally to them, with or without face-to-face interaction, as well as pass it on to a nurse on the next shift.

Description of teaching context and learner profile

Based on the findings of the needs analysis, materials were developed for an English for Cross-cultural Nursing course, a four-credit, writing-intensive course for ESL prenursing students preparing to enter the baccalaureate-degree nursing program at St. Catherine University in St. Paul, Minnesota. The students in the course include recent and second-generation immigrants and international students, many of whom have been exempted from ESL classes but elect to take the course because they want to work on their writing skills and learn about cultural issues in nursing.

Intersect between theory/literature and materials/activities

The materials and activities developed for the course reflect a combination of English for academic and specific purposes. The materials are based on nursing-related topics, such as the profession of nursing; contemporary issues in nursing; the role of culture in nursing; as well as culturally sensitive topics, including mental health and illness, and sexuality in nursing. For each topic, students engage in various learning activities that require them to apply language and academic skills necessary for success in the nursing program. For example, they apply reading strategies to articles and chapters from nursing journals and textbooks; engage in discussions and give oral presentations on nursing-related topics; listen to nursing lectures and take notes using different note-taking systems; practice test-taking skills by taking quizzes and multiple-choice tests; write reflective journals, exploring the role of culture in nursing; and write various types of papers, including research papers on various nursing-related topics, using nursing journal databases. In addition, students work on discipline-specific language skills, such as therapeutic communication, interviewing, listening to morning reports, understanding nursing abbreviations, and writing progress notes on patients.

Sample materials and activities

The following materials and activities provide a representative sampling of language-related skills and cultural knowledge needed to succeed in a baccalaureate-degree nursing program. Whereas many academic skills and strategies are also important for success in nursing, the majority of activities that are described and discussed in this section are specific to nursing or have nursing-specific applications.

Critical reading/thinking: Evaluating sources of information

The ability to think critically is an important skill in nursing. Nurses often claim that ESL nursing students have difficulty thinking critically and independently (Malu & Figlear 1998; Sanner, Wilson, & Samson 2002). Although this is not necessarily the case, students may very well have difficulty expressing an opinion or evaluating an idea or a reading that may seem contrary to that of the instructor or another authority figure. They may also have difficulty supporting their points with theoretical evidence from textbooks or assessment data from patients' charts. As part of the needs analysis, one faculty member wrote that ESL/multicultural nursing students have the most difficulty with "critical thinking – application of theory and/or analysis of data." A student concurred: "The subjective and objective [assessment data] ... is easy for me to identify. The part that's very hard for me to do is the analysis and the planning piece .... Once I have all these data, I didn't know how to analyze it or how to plan for my intervention for my clients."

Various activities in the English for Nursing course address the need for students to read and think critically about information. This activity presents students with two articles about a topic of importance in nursing: the current nursing shortage. One article, written by a nurse, was published in a popular magazine (Gordon 2000); the other, written by a doctor, was published in a medical journal (Steinbrook 2002) (see Appendix 15.2). Although the articles are both about the nursing shortage, they are quite different in tone and content, reflecting the differing perspectives of the authors. The purpose of this activity is for students to evaluate the two sources of information and realize the authors' differing perspectives on the topic and, as a result, how the tone and content of the articles are different, as well. Similar to the authors' different perspectives are their different purposes in writing and the different audiences they are writing for.

Through this activity, students recognize the need to think critically about information they encounter while reading. In recognizing and discussing differences between the two perspectives on the nursing shortage, a broader context for the two readings is provided, a context that makes explicit some of the assumptions in nursing about appropriate sources of information. Discussion about the articles also provides a social context in which ideas can be discussed and exchanged, allowing for additional ways for students to interact meaningfully with text, thereby enhancing their comprehension. Writing about the differences between the two articles gives students additional practice working with the material in meaningful ways and challenges them to communicate their ideas clearly and coherently to an academic audience, supporting their ideas with evidence from the articles.

Developing a critique: Using metadiscourse to evaluate information

A critical perspective in writing is important in nursing. Nursing highly values, indeed demands, independent, critical thinking in writing. However, students must learn to express their ideas and opinions in ways that are appropriate in nursing. For example, the objective voice is preferred in writing in nursing except for journal entries and evaluations of clinical experiences (Bosher 2001). In formal writing, particularly research-based writing, the personal pronoun "I" is not used.

In preparation for this activity, students are provided with an explanation of how to evaluate information using metadiscourse or commentary about information. They are given examples of paragraphs that summarize and critique research articles from nursing journals (see Appendix 15.3). Students identify and discuss in small groups the words in the paragraphs that convey the author's agreement or disagreement with an idea, but without using the pronoun "I." Each group then rewrites one of the paragraphs using the personal pronoun "I" and discusses the rhetorical effects of the two different versions of the paragraphs.

Studies have shown that success in discipline-specific writing is related to the students' ability "to internalize the discipline's knowledge claims and institutional culture" (Parks & Maguire 1999: 148), an ability that is developed through a collaborative process of "socialization into the ways of doing, seeing, and valuing particular to the discipline" (p. 148). This activity develops in students an awareness of writing conventions in nursing, specifically the use of metadiscourse to evaluate information, by making explicit those rules and assumptions and giving students the opportunity to practice applying those rules to their own writing in a social context.

Writing progress notes: Writing in thought units

One type of discipline-specific writing that all nursing students must learn is writing progress notes. Although much of the documentation of direct patient care is now done through computerized charts, nurses still need to write progress notes, a task that is especially challenging for ESL students. As one student commented during the needs analysis: "I know all the information that I need to know about that patient and I know what's wrong, but how do I word it, pick up which one is relevant or how to write that piece so that it's accurate according to procedure or policy of the hospital setting."

Writing progress notes is done using telegraphic writing or writing that has been reduced from full prose to phrases and clauses (Schneller & Godwin 1983). In preparation for this activity, students practice a number of skills required for writing progress notes: using the metric system, specialized terminology and common abbreviations, and being precise and concise in descriptions. For this activity, students transform regular prose into concise, telegraphic writing, by eliminating words that are understood by the context and words that have a grammatical function only, and in the process, develop basic charting skills (see Appendix 15.4).

Listening in the clinical setting: Change-of-shift reports

In the clinical setting, as Cameron (1998) documented, nurses transmit information and translate information from one medium to another. In many hospitals, when nurses begin their shift, they listen to taped reports, or change-of-shift reports. During these reports, nurses find out who their patients are, what their conditions are, and what treatments are in place that they will need to continue or modify. Nurses take notes on their patients as they listen to the change-of-shift report, translating information from aural to written form, and then at the end of their shift, they transmit information from the patients' charts to the next shift of nurses via taped reports. Because the delivery of information is rapid and there are no visual cues to follow, taped reports are especially challenging for ESL nursing students. As one student wrote: "Reports are given very fast [and there are] many medical terminology and abbreviations." Guhde (2003) noted in her work with an ESL nursing student that even though the most difficult language-related task for this student was listening and taking notes from taped reports, with practice, there was a 40 percent increase in the amount of important information the student recorded accurately.

For this activity, students listen to taped reports and record important information. The first time they listen to the reports, they write down as much information as they can. The second time, they refer to the cloze exercise (see Appendix 15.5). As they listen, they read along and fill in the blanks with the words, numbers, or abbreviations that they hear. Through this activity, students practice listening for specific nursing information, including common medical and nursing terminology and abbreviations, and transmitting that information from aural to written form.

Communicating in the clinical setting: Learning to be assertive

Some ESL nursing students have difficulty being assertive, particularly if the cultural norms with which they were raised equate assertiveness with aggressiveness (Bosher & Smalkoski 2002; Klisch 2000). In preparation for this activity, students learn about assertiveness and how it differs from being passive or aggressive. They discuss the cultural implications of assertiveness and situations in health care that call for a nurse to be assertive. Students learn the model of assertiveness referred to as DESC (Davis, 2006), which stands for Describe the situation; Express your feelings OR indicate the problem the behavior is causing; Specify the change you want; and Consequences: Identify the results that will occur.

For this activity, students practice role plays of various situations that require assertiveness, using the DESC format in constructing their responses (see Appendix 15.6). Role-playing is an especially effective technique in helping students develop communicative competence in the target setting. Through role plays, students acquire the habit of using those skills and strategies, increasing the likelihood they will use them with actual patients and colleagues in the health-care setting (Bosher & Smalkoski 2002). Regarding the value of role plays, a student who had taken the health-care communication course, commented: "I got over my shyness about asking you know the taboo type of questions, and so that ... helped a lot because before I just wasn't willing to ask those questions at all." The student also improved in her ability to respond assertively. For example, in response to a particularly aggressive and demanding patient, the student recalled that she "handled this situation really well. From performing or doing role plays ... I learned how to just kind of put it in me and do it and not [just] sit there thinking, okay, what kind of question should I ask her?"

Cultural content: Validating students' perspectives

The culture of nursing reflects the values, beliefs, and practices of the dominant culture in the United States. Consequently, there are many ways in which the various cultures of ESL students can come into conflict with the culture of nursing. One topic that was frequently mentioned during the needs analysis was asking patients about sexuality-related concerns. One graduating student revealed that she had never been able to ask patients about their sexual habits: "Maybe we're [supposed to ask]. I mean I just didn't know how to start asking someone about that, you know (laughs) ... The instructors would give you feedback and tell you how you could do it, but still, I'll never be real comfortable about it."

Another area of potential conflict concerns end-of-life issues. Health care in the United States is based on the patient's right to know their diagnosis and prognosis and to make decisions about their course of treatment, even if the patient has a terminal illness. In contrast to the practice of truth disclosure, one student, who was interviewed as part of the needs analysis, admitted that "up until this moment I don't know if I could really tell somebody ... that they're dying .... But I think that's a good thing to let them know. Then again I still have my belief that I had going [in] that that would make them lose hope, but I still think maybe they should know because it could be nice to know." Her comments clearly suggest a certain degree of ambivalence and discomfort with the practice of truth disclosure in US health care.

Through readings, discussions, and reflective writing assignments, students have the chance to consider what their values, beliefs, and attitudes are about these topics and to become aware of any differences they may have with the dominant culture in the United States. The intent of having students reflect on the role of culture in nursing is not to pressure them to adapt the values of the dominant culture. On the contrary, nursing needs the cultural insights that students from various cultural backgrounds bring to the program and profession, insights that will be critical in meeting the health-care needs of an increasingly diverse population. Furthermore, assignments that build on students' cultural knowledge and perspective validate them and their experiences and strengthen their self-esteem and confidence, as discussed in the bridging approach to nursing education (Yoder 2001).

In preparation for this activity, students read and discuss an article on end-of-life decisions from a cross-cultural perspective. Students learn about ethical principles, such as patient autonomy, beneficence, truth disclosure, informed consent, and family well-being, which guide health-care professionals in the United States in providing end-of-life care. Using the case studies presented in this article, students discuss how cultural values can influence patient and family decision-making behavior regarding truth disclosure and ways in which cultural conflicts between patients, families, and health-care providers can be effectively resolved.

For the activity, students write a short reflective paper applying the ethical principles they have learned and their own cultural insight to a similar case study (see Appendix 15.7). Through this activity, ESL students have an opportunity to share their knowledge and insights about cultural influences in nursing, thereby validating their personal experiences and perspectives and enriching the discussion and educational experience of other students in the class, an important aspect of the bridging approach (Yoder 2001). Understanding and respecting how other cultures make their decisions regarding end-of-life care has direct implications for all nursing students, who need to provide culturally competent care for all their patients. This activity allows students to focus on their cultural understanding and interpretation of material, an approach that some researchers have argued also promotes critical thinking in ESL students (Sanner *et al.* 2002). Furthermore, through discussion, students have the opportunity to talk about an issue they will eventually write a paper about: the cultural influences on nursing practice, creating a degree of familiarity and comfort with the topic and building a strong foundation of spoken fluency on which to strengthen the student's proficiency in written academic English.

Study strategy: Deconstructing multiple-choice test items

Taking multiple-choice tests has been rated by both students and nursing faculty alike as the most difficult language-related task for ESL students in a baccalaureate-degree nursing program (Bosher 2006). As one student who was interviewed as part of the needs analysis stated: "I think it was just reading the questions and trying to understand what they're asking for ... it's the questions ... how it's worded." Another student commented: "I didn't understand what was being asked. Some of the questions I felt were not really clear." Indeed, studies analyzing multiple-choice tests in nursing classes have found that many test items do not reflect best practices in multiple-choice test-item writing (Bosher 2003; Bosher & Bowles 2008). For example, the lead-in of many test items is written using the completion format, rather than the question format. Options are written to complete the lead-in, rather than answer a question. In the test-item-writing literature, the question format is considered preferable to the completion format, as it is less taxing on the test taker's short-term memory (Haladyna 1994). It is also more consistent with the rhetorical function of multiple-choice testing, to create plausible clinical situations, ask *questions* about problems or gaps in information, and elicit correct *answers* from examinees (Bosher 1999; Trimble 1986). Many items also contained unnecessary linguistic complexity, such as embedded and reduced clauses; numerous grammatical errors, such as ambiguous referents and dangling modifiers; and lack of clarity or consistency in the wording (Bosher 2003).

In this activity, students are introduced to linguistic features that add unnecessary complexity to test items (see Appendix 15.8). Students are instructed in ways to unpack linguistic structures, so that instead of rereading a test item over and over again the way it is written, students take it apart and put it back in a way that is more straightforward and easier to understand. In the process, students learn that teachers do not always write test items that are clearly worded and that they have the right to challenge test items that are not easily comprehensible.

Conclusion

The materials and activities in the English for Cross-Cultural Nursing course, of which these are just a few, prepare students for the nursing-specific language skills and cultural content necessary for success in a baccalaureate-degree nursing program in the United States. The materials also address cultural content in nursing from a critical, cross-cultural perspective. Materials and activities are evaluated at the end of every semester that the course is offered. Feedback from students and the instructors' own critical assessment of the usefulness of various materials and activities have resulted in numerous changes over the years.

Discussion questions and tasks

Reflection

1. The materials described in this chapter were developed based on the results of a needs analysis that identified the objective needs of students in the target language setting. Are the materials you use based on the results of a needs analysis of your students? Why or why not?
2. How are discipline-specific materials different from general academic materials?
3. What are the advantages and disadvantages of using discipline-specific materials versus general academic materials in an advanced ESL class?
4. In your institution, is there collaboration between English language teachers and content instructors? Why or why not? If so, has such collaboration been helpful in meeting the needs of ESL students in nursing? In what ways?

Evaluation

5. Examine textbook materials focusing on English for nursing and English for medical purposes. How are they similar or different? What

factors appear to explain those similarities and differences?

Adaptation/Design

6. Based on what you have learned in this chapter, adapt or design some materials for English for nursing or English for medical purposes. Then pilot these materials with students in your class. Discuss how effective the materials were and what changes could be made to improve their effectiveness.

Appendix 15.1: English for Cross-cultural Nursing course objectives

At the end of the English for Nursing course, students will be able to:

Reading skills

- Apply reading strategies and skills to chapters from nursing textbooks and journal articles.
- Understand, define, and use medical and nursing terminology and abbreviations from readings and change-of-shift reports.

Writing skills

- Write coherent, well-organized, and well-developed papers on various nursing/health-care topics that have been carefully edited for errors.
- Research a nursing/medical topic using online nursing databases, including CINAHL, Health Source, and Alt-health Watch.
- Integrate appropriate information from outside sources, demonstrating effective paraphrasing, quoting, and documenting, for both in-text citations and reference lists, using the system of documentation of the American Psychological Association (APA).
- Demonstrate understanding of basic principles of charting and writing progress notes.

Listening and note-taking skills

- Demonstrate effective note-taking skills while listening to authentic lectures by nursing faculty.
- Demonstrate effective note-taking skills while listening to taped change-of-shift reports for clinicals.

Oral communication skills

- Present effectively and with confidence about a variety of topics in front of the class.
- Demonstrate understanding and effective use of therapeutic communication, interviewing techniques, and assertiveness skills, and avoidance of blocks to effective communication.
- Participate actively in class and group discussions.

Background knowledge and cultural issues

- Demonstrate an understanding of the profession of nursing and reflect on the student's personal reasons for wanting to become a nurse.
- Demonstrate an understanding of cultural influences on nursing and health care, including the student's own culture.
- Demonstrate background knowledge and increased comfort level talking about culturally sensitive topics, such as sexuality and mental illness.

Study skills

- Demonstrate effective multiple-choice test-taking strategies.
- Demonstrate understanding of basic time management skills.

Appendix 15.2: Critical reading/thinking: Evaluating sources of information

Activity: Evaluating sources of information

Preview the readings for information about the authors, their credentials and professional background, the magazine or journal the reading was published in (the source), the intended audience, and purpose of the article. For each reading, answer the following questions:

1. Who are the authors?
2. What are their credentials? Are they credible sources of information about nursing? Why or why not? How might their professional background influence their perspective about the nursing shortage in the United States?
3. When were these articles originally published? Are any of these articles out-of-date, do you think? Why or why not?

4. In what journals or magazines were these articles originally published? What kind of journals or magazines are they? (Check your library or the Internet for more information about them.) Who reads these journals or magazines, do you think?
5. Who do you think was the author's intended audience?

Now write a short essay that analyzes and evaluates each of these articles as an appropriate source of information about the nursing shortage. Consider the author, type of publication, and intended audience of each article. Discuss how the source of information has influenced the tone and content of each article. Provide specific examples from each of the articles to support your points.

Appendix 15.3: Developing a critique: Using metadiscourse to evaluate information

Activity: Communicating your position objectively

In the following example, the writer has made it clear what she agrees or disagrees with, but without using personal pronouns or possessive adjectives. Words that convey agreement or disagreement or that are evaluative in some way are italicized.

> **Example**
>
> The results of the study done by Liamputtong (2003) are *very compelling*. Overall, there were some *strengths* and *weaknesses* in the study. Some of the *strengths* were ... Even though there were *strengths*, there were also some *weaknesses* in the study.

In the excerpt below, circle the words that convey the author's agreement or disagreement or that are evaluative in some way.

> Overall, Miller (1995) points out common Cambodian health-care values and beliefs. Information regarding wind illness along with self-care techniques are described accurately. As a registered nurse, Miller provides excellent suggestions on how to be an effective caregiver for Cambodian patients. However, Miller misinterprets the use of the coining and cupping techniques. For instance, cupping is only used to treat headaches. Also,

> cooking oil and wax are rarely used as a lubricant during coining. In addition, Miller's findings were not based upon cultural research of the Cambodian ethnic groups. The author failed to provide statistics from past research findings. Her conclusions seem to be based only upon her experiences as a registered nurse.

Now, rewrite the paragraph above using the personal pronoun "I." Discuss the rhetorical effects of the two different versions of the paragraph.

Appendix 15.4: Writing progress notes: Writing in thought units

Activity: Practice charting skills

For each of the situations below, write a narrative nursing note for the patient's medical record. Change the full sentences to thought units, using telegraphic language. Refer to previous exercises for the specialized terminology, concise wording, precise wording, and common abbreviations that you need to complete this activity. The first one has been done for you.

Example

On January 6, 2005, at 9 a.m., Mr. A. tells you that he took a long time to void and that he had pain while voiding. He stated that he flushed about half a cup of urine down the toilet.

Narrative nursing note

1/6/2005 0900 States that he voided with difficulty. Approx 125 ml amber urine discarded by self.

S. Mohammed, RN

1. On January 7, 2005, at 3 p.m., Mrs. B. said that she had a bad pain just under her breastbone that went toward her left shoulder. The pain lasted 10 minutes. During that time, she had trouble catching her breath. She was sweating.
2. Ms. C., on January 8, 1005, at 10 a.m., said that she had pins and needles in her toes and fingers. She could feel her heart beating. She had no appetite.

3. Mr. D. had abdominal surgery yesterday. Today, 1/9/2005, at 8 a.m. his dressing is in place. At 10 a.m. there is a yellow stain, about an inch in diameter in the center of the dressing. At 10:30 a.m. there is a red stain, about 4 inches over the yellow stain.
4. Mr. F. complained of being constipated; he has not moved his bowels for three days. It is 1/10/2005.
5. Ms. G. says that she has a pain that comes and goes in her left eye. Both eyelids appear swollen. It is 1/11/2005.

Appendix 15.5: Listening in the clinical setting: Change-of-shift reports

Activity: Listening for specific information

Listen to the taped change-of-shift reports. The first time you listen to each report, write as much information as you can without any assistance. The second time, refer to the cloze exercise. As you listen, read along and fill in the blanks with the words, numbers, and abbreviations that you hear. After you have listened to each report, compare notes with a partner or small group. Put your answers up on the board. The instructor will play the taped report a third time, at which time you can make any necessary corrections.

1. First patient is **George Pitzel**, in room 110, bed 2, admitted with ________ Heart ________ and a right leg ________ ulcer. He is a ________ Code. He is on ________ Precautions. He is a 65-year-old gentleman. His ________ signs have been ________; his lung sounds are ________. He doesn't seem to have any ________ in his lower today. ________ change was done once on my shift; I did it earlier on the shift, so you'll have to be doing it at ________ tonight. The wound is ________. There is a moderate amount of serous ________ drainage on the dressing, but the wound is ________ in size. He's had his ace ________ on all of my shift. Both his right and left toes are to touch, though, and ________ pulses are ________ bilaterally.
2. In Room 215 is **Mrs. Yang** with a ________ obstruction. Her granddaughter spent the night; her family members have been taking

turns. Mrs. Yang speaks ________ English; her family interprets or you can call ________ for an ________. She is still ________ except ________ chips. We had to re-insert her ________ tube, which she was most unhappy with. We did get ________ cc's of ________ returns right away so she needs it still. Her IV is ________ at ________ per hour. Hemoglobin is ________. I'm not sure if she will get that ________ today or not. They ________ labs this morning. I haven't seen ________ yet. She wakes up ________ and appears ________.

Appendix 15.6: Communicating in the clinical setting: Learning to be assertive

Activity: Practicing DESC in role plays

Practice the following role plays. For each scenario, a different student will role-play the nurse while the instructor role-plays the patient. Practice using the DESC/DISC format for your assertive responses. After each role play, discuss how well the student did with each of the components of a DESC/DISC response: D = Describe the situation; E = Express your feelings about the situation (or I = Indicate the problem the behavior is causing); S = Specify the change you want; and C = Consequences or identify the results that will occur.

1. You have been working as a nurse for a year now. You have a colleague who always takes advantage of others. She comes up to you in front of a patient and asks you to cover for her, as she has to make an important phone call. She disappears and does not return for two hours. When she returns, you confront her.
2. You are a nurse who needs to interview a patient to get more postoperative information from him. When you walk into the patient's room, he is watching television. When you attempt to introduce yourself, the patient never takes his eyes off the TV. He acts as if you are not present in the room. How do you handle the need to turn off the TV, so that you can get the information you need from the patient?
3. You are a nurse providing care for a patient who states that he does not understand you because of your accent. He also states that he has never

had to work with a foreign nurse before. He wants another nurse. It is your responsibility to interview the patient to find out how he is feeling and determine how much pain he is experiencing. The patient is recovering from an appendectomy, but there seem to be complications. You need to interview the patient right away and get the information to the doctor. How do you respond to the patient's concerns about working with you? How do you get the information you need?

4. You are a nurse caring for an elderly man who has just had below-the-knee amputation on his left leg. He is concerned about returning home as he is a widower and lives alone. After looking for the surgeon for a while, you have just found him. You want to discuss tentative discharge plans for the patient and say: "Good morning, Dr. Alvarez. I want to talk with you about Mr. Smith's concerns about his discharge." Dr. Alvarez replies: "Listen, I'm really busy, and you'll just have to deal with this on your own. Can you get me his chart?"

Appendix 15.7: Cultural content: Validating students' perspectives

Ethical dilemma: End-of-life decision making

You are taking care of a 36-year-old patient from Vietnam, who has been diagnosed with a terminal illness. The family does not want the patient to know about her diagnosis, but in private, the patient has asked you what her prognosis is. How do you handle this situation? What factors and principles, both ethical and cultural, do you consider in your response to this ethical dilemma?

Write two to three pages in response to this ethical dilemma. Discuss the ethical dilemma that is posed by end-of-life decisions from a cross-cultural perspective. Include reference to the concepts of autonomy, beneficence, truth disclosure, informed consent, and family well-being in your response. Include, as well, your own cultural knowledge, experiences, and insights about end-of-life decisions.

In small groups, discuss your responses to this dilemma. Be prepared to share one of your responses with the class.

Appendix 15.8: Study strategy: Deconstructing multiple-choice test items

Activity: Understanding multiple-choice test items

Read the following test item and complete the task that follows. Note the revision of the test item below, which has incorporated the outcomes of the task.

Original

The nurse is planning a presentation on noise prevention for a display booth at a local health fair. The nurse plans to incorporate which of the following concepts in the display that is designed to minimize individual risk of hearing loss?

Task

1. Underline the question word or phrase in the lead-in above.
2. Does the question word or phrase occur at the beginning of the lead-in? Yes or no?
3. Is there additional information that is added to the lead-in after the question word? If so, circle the additional information.
4. Is there any unnecessary detail in the stem or lead-in? If so, cross it out.
5. Are there any words that you do not understand? If so, look them up and replace them with words you do know.
6. Rewrite the lead-in, so that the question phrase occurs at the *beginning* of the lead-in. Place the additional information in a separate sentence in the stem *before* the lead-in.

Revision

A nurse plans a presentation on noise prevention. The nurse wants to teach individuals how they can reduce their risk of hearing loss. Which concept does the nurse include?

References

Abriam-Yago, K., Yoder, M., & Kataoka-Yahiro, M. (1999). The Cummins Model: A framework for teaching nursing students for whom English is a second language.

Journal of Transcultural Nursing 10: 143-9.

Alster, K. B. (2004). Writing in nursing education and nursing practice. In V. Zamel & R. Spack (eds.). *Crossing the curriculum: Multilingual learners in college classrooms*. Mahwah, NJ: Lawrence Erlbaum, pp. 163-80.

Amaro, D. J., Abriam-Yago, K., & Yoder, M. (2006). Perceived barriers for ethnically diverse students in nursing programs. *Journal of Nursing Education* 45(7): 247-54.

American Association of Colleges of Nursing (October 27, 1997). Position Statement on Diversity and Equality of Opportunity. Washington, DC.

Bosher, S. (1999). Discourse analysis of the Mosby Assess Test. Conference presentation, Annual Conference of the American Association for Applied Linguistics (AAAL), Stamford, CT.

Bosher, S. (2001). Discipline-specific literacy in a second language: How ESL students learn to write successfully in a B.S. degree nursing program. ERIC Clearinghouse on Reading, English, and Communication. *ERIC Document 454 707.*

Bosher, S. (2003). Barriers to creating a more culturally diverse nursing profession: Linguistic bias in multiple-choice nursing exams. *Nursing Education Perspectives* 24: 25-34.

Bosher, S. (2006). ESL meets Nursing: Developing an English for Nursing course. In M. A. Snow & L. Kamhi-Stein (eds.). *Developing a new course for adult learners.* Washington, DC: TESOL, pp. 63-98.

Bosher, S., & Bowles, M. (2008). The effects of linguistic simplification on ESL students' comprehension of nursing course test items. *Nursing Education Perspectives*, May-June 29(3): 165-72.

Bosher, S., & Pharris, M. D. (2008). *Transforming nursing education: The culturally inclusive environment.* New York: Springer.

Bosher, S., & Rowekamp, J. (1998). The refugee/immigrant in higher education: The role of educational background. *College ESL* 8(1): 23-42.

Bosher, S., & Smalkoski, K. (2002). From needs analysis to curriculum development: Designing a course in health-care communication for immigrant students in the USA. *English for Specific Purposes* 21: 59-79.

Cameron, R. (1998). Language-focused needs analysis for ESL-speaking nursing students in class and clinic. *Foreign Language Annals* 31: 203-18.

Collier, V. P. (1989). How long? A synthesis of research on academic achievement in a second language. *TESOL Quarterly* 23: 509-31.

Cummins, J. (1979). Linguistic interdependence and the educational development of bilingual children. *Review of Educational Research* 49: 222-51.

Cummins, J., & Swain, M. (1986). *Bilingualism in education: Aspects of theory, research, and practice.* London: Longman.

Cunningham, H., Stacciarini, J.-M., & Towle, S. (2004). Strategies to promote success on the NCLEX-RN for students with English as a second language. *Nurse Educator* 29(1): 15-19.

Davis, C. M. (2006). *Patient practitioner interaction: An experiential manual for developing the art of health care* (4th ed.). Thorofare, NJ: SLACK.

Dudley-Evans, T., & St. John, M. J. (1998). *Developments in ESP – A multidisciplinary approach.* Cambridge: Cambridge University Press.

Femea, P., Gaines, C., Brathwaite, D., & Abdur-Rahman, V. (1995). Sociodemographic and academic characteristics of linguistically diverse nursing students in a baccalaureate degree nursing program. *Journal of Multicultural Nursing & Health* 1: 24-8.

Gordon, S. (2000). Nurse, interrupted. *The American Prospect* 11: 79-88.

Guhde, J. A. (2003). English-as-a-Second-Language (ESL) nursing students: Strategies for building verbal and written language skills. *Journal of Cultural Diversity* 10: 113-8.

Haladyna, T. M. (1994). *Developing and validating multiple-choice test items.* Hillsdale, NJ: Lawrence Erlbaum.

Hawkins, B. (2001). Supporting second language children's content learning and language development in K-5. In *Teaching English as a Second or Foreign Language* (3rd ed.). Boston: Heinle & Heinle, pp. 367-83.

Hussin, V. (2002). An ESP program for students of nursing. In T. Orr (ed.). *English for specific purposes.* Alexandria, VA: TESOL, pp. 25-39.

Hutchinson, T., & Waters, A. (1987). *English for specific purposes.* Cambridge: Cambridge University Press.

Jalili-Grenier, F., & Chase, M. (1997). Retention of nursing students with English as a second language. *Journal of Advanced Nursing* 25: 199-203.

Johnston, J. G. (2001). Influence of English language on ability to pass the NCLEXRN. In E. Waltz & L. Jenkins (eds.). *Measurement of nursing outcomes* (2nd ed.). New York: Springer, pp. 204-7.

Kataoka-Yahiro, M., & Abriam-Yago, K. (1997). Culturally competent teaching strategies for Asian nursing students for whom English is a second language. *Journal of Cultural Diversity* 4: 83-7.

Keane, M. (1993). Preferred learning styles and study strategies in a linguistically diverse baccalaureate nursing student population. *Journal of Nursing Education* 32: 214-21.

Klisch, M. L. (1994). Guidelines for reducing bias in nursing examinations. *Nurse Educator* 19: 35-9.

Klisch, M. L. (2000). Retention strategies for ESL nursing students: Review of literature 1990-99 and strategies and outcomes in a small private school of nursing with limited funding. *The Journal of Multicultural Nursing & Health* 6(2): 18-25.

Liamputtong, P. (2003). Abortion – It is for some women only! Hmong women's perceptions of abortion. *Health Care for Women International* 24: 230-41.

Malu, K. F., & Figlear, M. R. (1998). Enhancing the language development of immigrant ESL nursing students. *Nurse Educator* 23: 43-6.

Malu, K. F., Figlear, M. R., & Figlear, E. A. (1994). The multicultural ESL nursing student: A prescription for admission. *The Journal of Multicultural Nursing* 1(2): 15-20.

Memmer, M. K., & Worth, C. C. (1991). Retention of English-as-a-second-language (ESL) students: Approaches used by California's 21 generic baccalaureate nursing programs. *Journal of Nursing Education* 30: 389-96.

Miller, J. A. (1995). Caring for Cambodian refugees in the emergency department. *Journal of Emergency Nursing* 21(6): 498-501.

Nugent, K. E., & Cook, P. (2002). Call to action: The need to increase diversity in the nursing workforce. *Nursing Forum* 37: 28-32.

Parks, S., & Maguire, M. H. (1999). Coping with on-the-job writing in ESL: A constructivist-semiotic perspective. *Language Learning* 49: 43-6.

Phillips, S., & Hartley, J. T. (1990). Teaching students for whom English is a second language. *Nurse Educator* 15: 29-32.

Pogrund, P., & Grebel, R. (1998). *Make your mark in health service jobs*. Lincolnwood, IL: Contemporary Books.

Reid, J. M. (1987). The learning style preferences of ESL students. *TESOL Quarterly* 21(1): 87-111.

Sanner, S., Wilson, A. H., & Samson, L. F. (2002). The experiences of international nursing students in a baccalaureate nursing program. *Journal of Professional Nursing* 18(4): 206-13.

Schneller, T., & Godwin, C. (1983). *Writing skills for nurses: A practical text/workbook.* Reston, VA: Reston.

Steinbrook, R. (2002). Nursing in the crossfire. *New England Journal of Medicine* 346: 1757-66.

Tarone, E., & Yule, G. (1989). *Focus on the language learner*. Oxford: Oxford University Press.

Trimble, L. (1986). *English for science and technology*. Cambridge: Cambridge University Press.

West, R. (1994). Needs analysis in language teaching. *Language Teaching* 27(1): 1-19.

Yoder, M. K. (1996). Instructional responses to ethnically diverse nursing students. *Journal of Nursing Education* 35: 315-21.

Yoder, M. K. (2001). The bridging approach: Effective strategies for teaching ethnically diverse nursing students. *Journal of Transcultural Nursing* 12(4): 319-25.

16

Using textbook and real-life data to teach turn taking in business meetings

Jo Angouri

Summary

Research has repeatedly shown that a meeting is one of the most frequent and central work-related events where successful communication is crucial both for the individual and the company. Accordingly, "meeting skills" are seen as an integral part of work-related language-training programs and business textbooks. At the same time, participating effectively in meeting talk is self-evidently related to managing turn taking and handling overlapping talk as the latter constitutes a "signal event in interaction" (Schegloff 2000: 2). Against this backdrop, the purpose of this chapter is to discuss turn taking and overlapping talk in Business English textbooks and real-life data. Specifically, data drawn from a sample of meetings in seven multinational companies in Europe are compared to transcripts and expressions that feature in chapters dealing with meetings in bestselling Business English textbooks in the UK. The discussion is focused on the similarities/differences between real-life/textbook interactions and on the level of explicitness of the textbooks' suggested "useful expressions." My findings show a discrepancy between the textbook language taught and the actual language used in the meetings corpus. Furthermore, the level of explicitness suggested by textbook authors does not always correspond with the practices of the interactants in the real-life dataset. Hence this paper lends support to other research, which suggests that textbook material *alone* cannot prepare the students for the dynamic nature of work-related communication. This paper closes by showing how real-life data can be used in the language classroom to *complement* the Business English textbook in order to develop the learners' analytical skills.

Introduction

A growing body of research from different fields has emphasized the importance of business meetings for inter-/intraorganizational communication. Justifiably then, "meeting skills" are seen as an integral part of many work-related language-training programs. Against this backdrop, Williams's seminal work (1988) some time ago showed a disquieting discrepancy between the textbook language *taught* for meetings and the actual language *used* in the meetings she analyzed. In fact, the language taught in business English materials has been criticized on two fronts. First, the interactions featured do not seem to be based on concrete workplace data. Subsequently, the material is often prescriptive and fails to reflect the nature of actual workplace interactions (see also Ewer & Boys 1981; Harwood 2005; Williams 1988). Second, typical textbook material presents workplace interactions, and therefore the workplace in general, as being homogenous (with the boundaries of any minimal variation that is present set by the author rather than suggested by empirical data). Both limitations can have a negative impact with regard to both the appropriacy of the language the student selects and also her/his ability to integrate into her/his workplace as a result of the language selected. To make matters more complicated, recent research into workplace communication has stressed the importance of *context* in shaping the discourse practices of employees (Angouri & Harwood 2008; Holmes & Stubbe 2003; Rogerson-Revell 1999; Sullivan & Girginer 2002; Swales 2000) and the effects that socioeconomic changes have on discourse (e.g., Angouri 2007; Louhiala-Salminen 1996).

In light of the above, the purpose of this chapter is to take a closer look at *meeting talk* and to illustrate how it can be presented to learners. Since the increasing need to train large numbers of students to cope with meeting talk is commonly recognized (e.g., Holmes & Stubbe 2003; Rogerson-Revell

1999), I provide an alternative to Business English teaching materials widely used by Language for Specific Purposes (LSP) practitioners. Given the space limitations, my purpose is not to report the findings of an extensive investigation similar to Williams's research. I do, however, compare my findings to transcripts and expressions published in six best-selling Business English textbooks in the UK. The discussion is focused on the level of *explicitness of the forms* (i.e., I examine whether the speakers preannounce their acts and how they lexicalize them) and especially on *turn-taking patterns* and *overlapping talk in business meetings*. This chapter draws on a dataset of 21 audiorecorded meetings from seven multinational companies. I compare and contrast *turn-taking patterns* in my dataset and in the textbooks. I also discuss the language the textbooks suggest for handling overlapping talk. Finally, I show the ways in which real-life data can complement commercial materials.

This chapter is organized into the following parts: In order to place the discussion in context, a working definition of what constitutes a *business meeting* is provided. I next outline the theoretical framework that underpins this study and then move on to present the methodology and procedures I followed to gather my data. Finally, I discuss the interactional feature I use to analyze the excerpts, namely overlapping talk (OT), the findings of my study, and the conclusions that can be drawn.

Defining a meeting

Research has repeatedly shown that "meetings are the very stuff of 'work'" for corporate businesses (Holmes & Stubbe 2003: 56; Marra 2003; Tannen 1994). Despite their high frequency and importance, however, the definition of what constitutes a meeting seems to be debatable. Cuff and Sharrock (1985: 158) provide arguably the most flexible definition of business meetings as they suggest that the participants "commonsensically" understand what a meeting is. Although there have been more restricted and detailed definitions (e.g., Bargiela-Chiappini & Harris 1997; Holmes & Stubbe 2003; Schwartzman 1989), the working definition I adopt for the needs of the present study is the following: A meeting is *a gathering of at least three participants for a work-related business event, which is acknowledged as a formal or informal meeting by the participants.*

I now say a few words about the context-bound nature of workplace interactions and meeting talk in particular and the theoretical framework that underpins this study.

The context-bound nature of workplace interactions

Existing research has shown (e.g., Holmes & Stubbe 2003; Marra 2003) that interactions in the workplace in general and in business meetings in particular are context-bound. Specifically, factors such as the *formality* of the interaction, the *nature of the tasks*, and the *setting*, among others, are likely to affect the discourse. Hence, along with a growing body of work, I argue that workplace talk is firmly embedded on the one hand in the social and organizational context of a particular group/team and on the other in the wider social or institutional order (Holmes & Stubbe 2003: 2 ff; see also Bargiela-Chiappini & Harris 1997; Bargiela-Chiappini & Nickerson 2002; Bargiela-Chiappini *et al.* 2007; Sarangi & Roberts 1999). Accordingly, Lave and Wenger's (1991) concept of Communities of Practice (CofP) is employed as a theoretical framework here. In his later work, Wenger (1998: 73) identifies three dimensions of a CofP: namely, (a) what it is about – its *joint enterprise* as understood and continually renegotiated by its members; (b) how it functions – the *mutual engagement* that binds members together into a social entity; and (c) what capability it has produced – the *shared repertoire* of communal resources (routines, sensibilities, artifacts, vocabulary, styles, etc.) that members have developed over time. The latter is of interest to the present paper, as research has shown that CofPs have developed a specific discourse repertoire that distinguishes one community from others. Hence, newcomers, to use Lave's terminology, have to grasp these norms in order to fit in (Holmes 2005). In other words, "becoming a member of a CofP actively interacts with the process of gaining control of the discourse of that CofP" (Holmes & Marra 2002: 1685).

By now, then, the complexity of teaching students appropriate language for work-related interactions should be evident. In order for the language teacher to equip the students with the necessary skills for successful encounters, s/he would need to know in which CofP the student will need/desire to participate as well as the repertoire of these CofPs. In addition, a further complication is that the CofPs' repertoires are not static but dynamic processes coconstructed and negotiated between the participants and the wider social context (Holmes & Stubbe 2003; Linell 2001). Despite the pedagogical challenge this presents, I acknowledge the need for some classroom models and materials, and I suggest that thorough empirical research on workplace talk can provide these. Hence, my objective is to discuss how the dynamic nature of workplace talk in general, and of floor management (and turn-taking patterns[1]) in business meetings in particular, can be captured/presented for pedagogical purposes. I now turn to my study and briefly discuss in more detail the method and procedures followed.

Companies and participants

The research reported here constitutes part of a larger study of communicative activity in seven multinational[2] companies in Europe (Angouri 2007), which employed a combination of quantitative and qualitative techniques. Salient information about each company is provided in Table 16.1. Pseudonyms are used since all the firms wished to remain anonymous, and anything that could identify either the firm or the participants, as assessed by the HR managers or the participants themselves,[3] has either been replaced by pseudonyms, omitted, or deleted from the excerpts that will be discussed later on.

Table 16.1 Company profiles

Pseudonym	Site studied in	Company's working language
a) Andromeda	Greece	Greek & English
b) Apus	Greece	English

(to be continued)

[1] I do not aspire to exhaust the discussion on turn taking here or to analyze different theoretical and/or methodological approaches to the study of floor management. The discussion focuses solely on how real-life data can complement textbook materials.

[2] For the purposes of my study, the term *multinational* is defined as a company that has subsidiaries or branches in at least three countries and undertakes business activities in at least two industry sectors (see also Starke-Meyerring 2005).

[3] Due to the sensitive issue of confidentiality, I adopted a "hands-off " approach to the actual data collection (Stubbe 2001: 5), giving total control of the data collection process to the participants, in line with the guidelines set out by the University of Wellington's Language in the Workplace project.

(continued)

Pseudonym	Site studied in	Company's working language
c) Cassiopeia	UK	English
d) Lacerta	Sweden	English
e) Carina	Greece	English
f) Lyra	Greece	English
g) Vela	Italy	English

All the companies undertake activities across a range of industries and are considered leaders in their fields as far as turnover and volume of trade are concerned. However, the specific businesses of each company are not relevant here and will not be discussed.

I now say a few words about the participants in this study. My sample consists of two strata: line managers and post holders. The sample was stratified according to the participants' level of responsibility. Hence the line managers are responsible for a subsection of the department or groups of employees within the department, and the post holders are responsible for no one but themselves. In contrast to Williams's study, which involves native speakers interacting, in this study the workforce is multilingual. I consider this to be very important, as most modern workplaces, especially the multinational companies that form my sample, are by nature multilingual (see Angouri 2007). Hence my informants are either NS or NNS speakers of English. Insofar as the NNS are concerned, I consider my sample to be competent users of the language, as they have worked in an English-speaking, white-collar environment and in relatively senior positions for at least five years. The particular dataset consists of 21 audio recordings of meetings which lasted 56 minutes on average.

In order to analyze the data, I focus on one interactional feature here, namely *overlapping talk.*

Turn taking and overlapping talk (OT)

Turn taking in business meetings is widely seen as subject to a number of rules and constraints that have to do, largely, with the preallocation of certain turns to the chairperson but also with interactional patterns in the different workplace settings (e.g., Emmitt & Gorse 2003). Research has also shown, however, that the exact *context* of the interaction and the *status* the participants have in the company affects, if not determines, the turn-taking patterns (Vine 2004). At the same time, research on turn taking has paid special attention to the study of overlapping talk, as the latter constitutes, undoubtedly, a "signal event in interaction" (Schegloff 2000: 2). In this section, turn taking and overlapping talk are briefly discussed in order to contextualize the analysis of data later on. Overall, I take the stance that turn-taking procedures are embedded practices in the "culture" of each CofP. Therefore, the norms of when to speak and how to hold/pass the floor are negotiated and coconstructed by all members of the CofP.

The first influential work in the field of turn taking, and one that has undoubtedly attracted a lot of attention (see, for instance, Bennett 1981; Coates 1989; Edelsky 1981), is Sacks *et al.* (1974), who stated that "overwhelmingly, one party speaks at a time," and that "transitions from one turn to the next for the most part, with little or no gap and little or no overlap between them are common," and finally that "occurrences of more than one speaker are common but brief" (1974: 696 ff).

Instances of OT are often operationalized as "interruptions" and they have been seen as a form of "violation," and "rude and disrespectful acts" (Goldberg 1990: 885), being indicative of power and dominance. Many researchers (e.g., James & Clarke 1993; Tannen 1981, 1990, 1993), however, have suggested that not all interruptions are an "exercise of power" (Tannen 1994: 62) in conversation and that overlapping talk is not necessarily dominance-related (see, for instance, Beattie 1981, 1982; Coates 1993; Dindia 1987; Goldberg 1990; Murray 1987). In fact, Goldberg (1990: 885) states that "interruptions arise from a multitude of personal, relational and conversational sources." Therefore, overlapping talk is a complex phenomenon and does not derive solely from a person's desire to dominate. This is particularly relevant to the present study, as my research shows how instances of overlapping talk can have a facilitative function and are often highly appropriate and desirable acts (Angouri 2007).

Table 16.2 Handling interruptions in the textbook and real-life data

Textbooks: Suggested expressions (instances in real-life data)	Real-life data[4]
Sorry – can I just say ... (1)	Yes/no, connectives (and, but) + proposition (e.g., Excerpt 16.2 Line 99) (42)
I would just like to add that ... (0)	No exponent (the second speaker overlaps with a semantically complete proposition) (e.g., Excerpt 16.4 Line 44) (33)
(Pete) – you were saying? (0)	Pragmatic particle (uh, uhh, hmmm) + proposition (e.g., Excerpt 16.2 Lines 91, 92) (31)
Can I just finish what I was saying ... (0)	
If I could just interrupt you ... (0)	
I see your point but ... (0)	
Sorry, if I could just finish what I'm saying ... (0)	
Sorry, just one more thing ... (0)	
Before we move on, could we just ... (0)	
Sorry to interrupt but ... (0)	
Could I just come in here? (0)	

[4] Instances in recordings of meetings from where the reproduced excerpts are taken. On a methodological level, I remind the reader that the aim of the comparison here is indicative, and a more detailed analysis would require a discussion of the exact context of the interaction (for detailed discussions, see Angouri 2007).

Findings and discussion

Handling/countering OT

For the needs of this chapter, the following six textbooks were analyzed: *Business Basics, Business Class, Business Objectives, Business Options, Business Vision* and *Market Leader* (see Appendix 16.1 for details). And Table 16.2 presents a summary of the findings with respect to OT.

Column 1 of Table 16.2 shows the suggested expressions in the textbooks for handling or countering interruptions, and the number of instances of these expressions in my real-life dataset. One could then interpret these results as showing that most of the "linguistic strategies" the six textbooks are providing learners with never occur in real meetings. However, this is not the case. It may in fact be the case that this language *does* occur, albeit with a lower frequency than the textbooks imply. In any case, the likelihood of specific strategies (and of OT occurring) will depend on the discourse practices of each CofP (and is contingent upon a range of local factors such as the topic of interaction and the participants among others). To complement this brief discussion it is worth considering Column 2 of Table 16.2, which shows that OT in my dataset is not explicitly "preannounced" (cf. Column 1, Table 16.2) but is initiated with either a pragmatic device (*uh*, *mmm*, *hmm*), or with explicit (dis)agreement with the current speaker's utterance (*yes, yeah, no*). Alternatively, the speakers just "jump in." Examples of these means of effecting OT will be reproduced and discussed below.

I make one final remark regarding the findings presented in this section: Even though I have not surveyed as many textbooks as Williams, I consider my findings to lend support to her work in so far as politeness and explicitness is concerned. Specifically, Williams argues that "speakers [in the real-life meetings she analyzed] appeared to be more blunt than we normally allow our learners to be" (1988: 52), which seems indeed to be the case as regards overlapping talk as well. Similarly, in the same work it is suggested that "we might be in danger of teaching our students to be over-explicit" (Williams 1988: 52). It is indeed the case that speakers do not seem to be over-explicit and they do not "preannounce" their acts. To conclude this discussion here, I now compare two excerpts (see Appendix 16.2 for transcription conventions) from two textbooks with two excerpts from my dataset in order to discuss similarities/discrepancies between real-life/textbook interactions.

Excerpts from business meetings

Excerpt 16.1 comes from *Market Leader* (Appendix 16.1, Cotton *et al.* 2001), which includes the largest number of excerpts from business meetings of the books examined. Consider the following passage.

According to the authors (ibid. p. 19) this excerpt is the first part of an authentic brainstorming meeting between three employees. Information about the exact context or the status of the participants is not given. Hence, the reader does not know the relationship between participants or the background context of the interaction. It is noticeable that the meeting is rather smooth flowing and collaborative, as there is explicit agreement and all interactants work together. Interestingly, however, the participants do not share the floor and the turn-taking patterns follow a rather linear procedure (Rogerson-Revell 1999). Even though the transcript at the back of the textbook does not feature instances of OT that actually occur in the recording, there is a small amount of overlap between the speakers.

Excerpts

2.3 (P = Paul, S = Stephanie, C = Courtney)

P - OK, thanks for coming along this morning. As I said in my e-mail, the purpose of the meeting this morning is for us to brainstorm ideas, promotional activities that we are going to carry out to make sure that the launch of the Business Solutions website is a success from the start. I'm going to open up to you to come up with the ideas that you've formulated over the past couple of weeks. Anything goes, we've got no budget at the moment but you know, fire away.

S - Oh great, no budget constraints.

C - That's great. Television and radio.

S - Well, it's starting big.

P - Excellent.

C - Well, we haven't got a budget, err, well, I think we could reach a wide audience, something like that, and err, we could focus on some of the big sort of business financial network television if we want to reach a global market, if that's what we're working to do and extending to all areas I think.

S - Yeah, that's been quite successful for some of the banks and stuff.

P - That's right, but definitely focused advertising.

C - Focused on specific networks that would reach, that you know ... businessmen are watching network television.

S - Well, I've been working more on cheaper solutions than that just in case there are budget problems. I thought we could do some effective online promotion, which is actually very cheap, and I think we should aim to do anyway. Direct mailing but also register the site effectively with search engines so anybody who goes onto the Internet and is looking for business solutions would come up with our website.

C - Yeah, we should definitely do some of that.

P - Absolutely, yes.

C - What about press advertising, traditional newspapers, business magazines, journals?

P - Yes.

S - Yes, great, I mean we've done that very effectively in the past.

P - Yes, we've had some very good response rates to for the ads we've placed before.

S - Yes, and that could be something we could do, not just once but a kind of campaign over a period of time.

C - Yes, build it up.

P - Yep, use a campaign, OK.

Excerpt 16.1: Transcript from *Market Leader* (Cotton *et al.* 2001: 157).

88 L - -- =yeah I mean it could
89 be in an trading center or somet[hing]
90 N - ------------------------------------ [hmh [ye]ah]
91 S - ---[hmh yea]h I mean
92 exactly why was she avoiding the question
93 lik [e that]
94 L - --- [I mean i]t's fine her work b[ut]
95 N - --------------------------------------[y[eah] of] c[ourse]

96 S - --[hmh]

97 L - ---[is she re]ady

98 to face problems [like this]

99 S - ---------------------[and to comm]it to these pr[oblems]

100 N - --- [hmh yea]h yeah

101 that's true I agree w[ith you]

102 L - ----------------------[hmh yeah [ri]ght]

103 N - -----------------------------------[and I mea]n I thought as you

104 did that she was arrog[ant]

105 S - ------------------------ [hmh] (.) h[mh]

Excerpt 16.2: Transcript from a Cassiopeia meeting

I now compare Excerpt 16.1 to Excerpt 16.2, where three line managers from Cassiopeia are discussing whom to promote and put in charge of a new project. They have conducted job interviews and are evaluating an interviewee's performance. L, N, and S are all senior managers who work together on a big project, and L is chairing the meeting. As can be seen, the three Cassiopeia managers complete or extend each others' utterances and there are many instances of explicit agreement, positive reinforcements of the previous speaker's utterance (see, for instance, line 95, where N overlaps L and is overlapped in turn by S and similarly in line 100), as well as continuous backchanneling (e.g., lines 90, 91). Overlapping talk and turn-taking patterns in this particular meeting are indicative of the system the three managers have developed to manage their interactions here, although turn-taking patterns differ during other meetings even within the same workplace (Angouri 2007). Hence, even a cursory analysis of the two excerpts (Exc. 16.1 and Exc. 16.2) suggests a different system of turn taking.

19

A The next item on the agenda is the new Spanish sales organization. As you know, we're going to open the new sales office in March and so we need to discuss recruitment. Basically we have two alternatives. We can either take on new Spanish sales representatives and train them. Or we can teach our French sales reps Spanish and transfer them. Any views on this, Marcel?

B Yes. The important thing here is product knowledge, not language. The French sales staff have already got the product knowledge. They know how the company operates too. I think we should teach them Spanish and transfer them.

A How do you feel about that proposal, Carlos?

C I don't agree. It takes years to learn a language. But why don't we employ Spanish staff, and send them to France for technical training?

B No. It's a waste of time, if they can't speak French.

C What do you think, Nancy?

A I don't know. How long does it take to train a new sales rep, Marcel?

B It depends on the rep. Usually about a year.

A Mmm. That is a problem. But I think nationality is important here. It's a Spanish branch so I don't think we should employ French nationals. Now I know you're not going to agree with me here, Marcel, but as I see it we have no choice …

20

Excerpt 16.3: A business exchange. Transcript reproduced by permission of Oxford University from *Business Objectives*. New edition Student's Book by Vicki Hollett © Vicki Hollett 1996

To further illustrate the discrepancies between textbook and authentic language, I now compare another set of meetings from real-life data and textbooks. Excerpt 16.3 comes from *Business Objectives* (Hollett 2001). The background information provided suggests that three managers are discussing "the recruitment of sales representatives (reps.) for their new Spanish sales organization" (Hollett 2001: 68).

This textbook presents a similar picture of OT to *Market Leader*. By and large, the speakers take turns one at a time and the pattern seems to be "current speaker selects next," which "provide[s] for the allocation of a next turn to one party and coordinate[s] transfer in order to minimise gap and overlap" (Larrue

& Trognon 1993: 180). Interestingly, there is the necessary "disagreement in order to reach agreement" (Bargiela-Chappini & Harris 1997) between the speakers, but this still does not seem to affect the turn-taking pattern, as the speakers neatly take turns and very explicitly state what the problem seems to be in their eyes. If we now compare this to the interaction in Excerpt 16.4, one could justifiably claim that Excerpts 16.1 or 16.3 provide a somewhat different "real feel" (Williams 1988).

39 F - Ahmmm the one about walkthr[oughs]
40 J - ((All examining pictures)) [but you d]idn't find a walkt[hrough] uhh?
41 ((to P))
42 P - ---[no goo]d no
43 good on[es I'm afraid] ((speaking to J))
44 L - ----------[where is this] ((pointing at the picture))
45 F - Th[is is beh]ind the turbine house
46 P - [behind]hmmm
47 J - This walkthrough is uhm (.) how shall I put it and what can I s[ay (.)]
48 P - --- [looks
49 s]a[fe] perhaps ((general laughter))
50 J - [thi]s wood plank is (.) uhm ready to coll[apse]
51 F - ---[the stair] case [too]
52 J - --- [yes b]ut
53 the wood plank will coll[apse]
54 P - ---------------------------- [no it won]'t I am not worried about that (.) OK
55 J - OK then what is this guys? ((pointing at another picture))
56 F - well we have several ope[nings in the slab]
57 L - -----------------------------[yes the trenches I] know

Excerpt 16.4: Transcript from an Andromeda/Carina meeting

Excerpt 16.4 comes from a meeting of two managers (J and P) and two post holders (L and F). J and F work for Carina and P and L for Andromeda. These two companies (together with Lyra: see Table 16.1) work in a consortium, and the main topic being discussed is the safety and security of the worksite. A cursory examination of the transcript is again sufficient to indicate the differences between these excerpts and the two textbook ones with regard to turn-taking patterns. The excerpt constitutes another example of collaborative and supportive OT. All participants both overlap and are overlapped, and J, who is the Chair, "exercises light control over the meeting" (Holmes & Stubbe 2003: 82) and allows F (see 39 in Excerpt 16.4) to introduce the topic of the walkthroughs. Even though OT is more likely to occur among equals (as it does in this excerpt and in Excerpts 16.2 and 16.5), we see that it also occurs even when two senior managers interact with two post holders. In addition, the interactants share the floor without anybody attempting to monopolize. Even though both Excerpts 16.2 and 16.4 are collaborative in nature, the turn-taking patterns are very different. Consider, for instance, the lack of backchanneling in Excerpt 16.4, as well as the lack of pragmatic devices (such as hesitation markers).

29 J - [who is go]ing to do that wo[rk]
30 L - ---------------------------------[xxx]x and xxxxxx took the fob
31 D - How are you going to lift all this metal structures in their
32 places in the stack=
33 P - =we will be using the main winch used in the construction of
34 the stack too for the transfer of pe[rsonnel]
35 K - --------------------------------------- [you know tha]t it has to
36 be certified by xxxx or oth[erwise]
37 F - --------------------------------[it is certi]fied we did it before
38 the construction of the stack
39 P - It is certified. For the lift of the metal structures we will
40 use the four electric winches used in the stack of the first
41 phase.
42 A - Are this winches long enou[gh?]
43 P - --------------------------------[no tha]t's why we will use metal
44 cables as well as the winches. So we will lift
45 to the point the winches allow to then stabilize the
46 structure lifted with the metal cables, and then release the

winches and lift them to a higher place and then reconnect
them to the metal structure lifted to go higher, and so on
and so forth

Excerpt 16.5: Transcript from an Andromeda/Carina/Lyra meeting

This lends further support to the earlier argument about interactions in general and turn-taking patterns in particular being context-bound. This is not to suggest that turn-taking patterns as presented in Excerpts 16.1 and/or 16.3 are *not* likely to occur, but what is not apparent from the textbook extracts is that turn-taking patterns are *context* specific and contingent upon the practices and norms of each community. Hence, *no one* excerpt, even if it is authentic, can be considered to be representative of what turn-taking patterns in a given workplace would look like, as workplace talk (and meeting talk in particular) varies and is dynamic in nature. I will come back to this point to show how real-life data can complement commercial materials in the last section of this chapter.

To conclude this discussion, I now make one final comment. As both excerpts come from meetings of people who have developed specific repertoires, it is tempting to suggest that this is the reason why instances of OT are frequent. However, I would argue that this may not necessarily be the case, citing Excerpt 16.5, which comes from a general meeting of managers from Carina, Lyra, and Andromeda with the company who sponsors the work, with P acting as the chairperson. The participants have not had the chance to develop interpersonal relationships and/or discourse repertoires. Interestingly, even though there are seven participants in the room, only the senior managers interact. Hence this excerpt would lend support to the claim that OT is more frequent between equals (Vine 2004). Note however that the turn-taking system is again different from the "non-interactive" patterns presented in Excerpts 16.1 and 16.3. And even though the turns are longer and follow a "round-the-table" pattern (Rogerson-Revell 1999: 59), there are again frequent instances of OT.

Hence the question raised much earlier about whether the dynamic nature of interactions can be captured by pedagogical materials remains unanswered. I discuss this issue in the next section.

Implications

The brief analysis presented here lends support to the claim that textbooks do not seem to capture the dynamic and complex nature of interactions. At the same time, it is also the case that (a) textbooks are preferred to teacher-produced material by many practitioners, since they can reduce preparation time. Additionally, some practitioners may feel they lack the relevant training and existing resources to produce materials of their own (Harwood 2005; Jones 1990; Swales 1980). And (b) there are inherent difficulties textbook authors face when trying to encapsulate the dynamic nature of discourse, so compromises are inevitable. Insofar as business meetings are concerned, textbook authors/practitioners rarely have access to real-life interactions, not least because companies are reluctant for copies/recordings of their documents and interactions to leave work sites (see, for instance, Edwards 2000). Textbook authors also need to make their material readily comprehensible and accessible, and self-evidently the transcripts provided are much clearer than the ones deriving from real-life data. Furthermore, overlapping talk in particular, and interactional features in general, may not be considered a pedagogical priority and as such may not be clearly marked. This is rather problematic however, for the reasons outlined in the introduction of this chapter, and I now show how practitioners can exploit real-life data to overcome these limitations.

In line with other research (e.g., Holmes 2005; Holmes & Stubbe 2003), I argue that it is imperative to prepare future employees for the generic diversity (Angouri & Harwood 2008) and variation they will encounter in the workplace in order to enable them to more easily adapt their skills to the various situations and audiences. In order to achieve these ends, educators should also help future employees develop their "observational and analytical skills" (Holmes & Stubbe 2003: 173; Lutz 1989) so they are able to smoothly adapt and fit into the various CofPs they come across and/or become members of. Put differently, practitioners should teach (future) employees to analyze the practices of the various CofPs they come into contact with. To this end, I present below an illustrative set of pedagogical activities that exploit both textbook exchanges and real-life workplace data. The activities can be used for developing skills in handling turn taking and overlapping talk but could also be adjusted to focus on other interactional features (such as the use of discourse markers). Furthermore, the activities presented here could be used in either the Business English teaching context or in more "general" training programs on business communication.

A set of activities aimed at developing awareness of turn-taking patterns in business meetings

Overall aim: To develop students' observational skills, to familiarize them with workplace variability and diversity, and subsequently to raise awareness and facilitate adaptability. The set of materials below specifically aims at raising awareness regarding turn-taking patterns and overlapping talk in business meetings.

Find the difference

Level: Upper-intermediate and above

Time: three sessions, overall duration 5 hours: 2 hours for each of the first two sessions and 1 hour for the last (1st session: Activities a-d; 2nd session: Activities e-h; 3rd session: role plays)

Procedure:

a) Ask the students to reflect on their own experiences in participating in meetings. Do they have any? If not, encourage them to reflect on meetings they have seen (e.g., in films / on TV) and to describe what a meeting looks like. Get the students to discuss this.

b) Use any textbook material (e.g., on the brainstorming meeting from *Market Leader*). Play the recording (e.g., Excerpt 16.1) and ask the students to read the transcripts and to record their observations concerning:
   - the style and the formality level of the meeting
   - the turn-taking patterns
   - the frequency of overlapping talk

(to be continued)

(continued)

Consider explaining beforehand that there is no one right answer, but encourage them to make notes on what they observe.

c) Ask the students to compare their notes in groups. Guide them through a discussion concerning the formality level, the structure of the interactions, and the role of participants.
d) If applicable, ask them to compare these interactions with their own experiences.
e) Use Excerpts 16.2, 16.4, and 16.5, which present conversations featuring overlapping talk.
f) Ask the students to compare these excerpts with the ones you analyzed before.
g) If applicable, ask them to compare these excerpts with their own experiences.
h) Discuss the background context of the interactions. Is this information useful for them to draw conclusions as to the appropriateness of turn-taking patterns in the interactions?
i) In all the textbooks studied, the authors include an abundance of role-play activities. Choose one and ask students to apply in practice what you have discussed, focusing on turn-taking patterns and overlapping talk.

Discussion

The transcripts found in the textbooks present rather striking similarities in terms of their structure. The students should be able to notice a clear organization (opening, middle, and end) and also a very well-structured turn-taking system. Based on the textbook excerpt briefly discussed above, the students will form the idea that workplace meetings are "neat" and well-organized interactions. Insofar as the style is concerned, they all constitute semiformal interactions (as compared to casual conversation style). As is apparent, Activities (a)-(d) are intentionally not directly related to only a single interactional feature but address the "broader" context of the interaction. This is considered imperative given the importance of context as discussed earlier in this chapter: Without an understanding of both the wider and the local context it is impossible to interpret and understand workplace interaction (Bargiela-Chiappini & Harris 1997).

(to be continued)

(continued)

The main aim in Activities (e)-(h) should be to smoothly introduce the students to the concept of variation. The commercial materials fit in well with widely held stereotypes as to what business meetings look like. Consider encouraging students who have different experiences to reflect on them. This will lead to Activities (e)-(h) where students will be introduced to the context-specific, "messy" nature of workplace interactions (see also Freedman & Adam 1996). Allow time and encourage the students to observe the interactions. Guide them through possible patterns, such as a CofP (e.g., Excerpt 16.2) with a discourse repertoire as compared to a group of people that have not developed common practices (e.g., Excerpt 16.5). The students should be able to observe that a "round the table" turn-taking system is more likely in the second rather than the first setting. Get students to practice and encourage peer observation and feedback. Focus on turn-taking practices and frequencies of overlapping talk.

These materials share similarities with those suggested by Koester (2004), in that they also aim to raise awareness about diversity. Hence I conclude this section by suggesting that prescriptive ways of teaching workplace language are at odds with the generic diversity employees tend to encounter in their work life.

Conclusions

Overall, there is a pressing need for materials that are flexible enough to meet the needs of large numbers of students studying Language for Business Purposes. In the previous section, I showed how research findings on workplace discourse can inform materials so that the language taught is closer to the language used for work-related purposes.

Hence the dynamic nature of workplace talk *can* be captured in high-quality material that is based on research findings. Therefore, in line with other research (Bowles 2006; Harwood 2005), I argue that there should be ongoing collaboration between textbook writers, publishers, researchers, and academics. I acknowledge that this might sound unrealistic to many a reader, however I would also argue that if more researchers suggest ways in which the findings of their research can be used in classroom settings (e.g., Holmes 2005; Holmes & Stubbe 2003; Louhiala-Salminen 1996; Nickerson 2002; Sullivan & Girginer 2002), this will help bring the language used and the language taught closer together. Self-evidently, this would improve current teaching provision not only in the field of Business English but also more generally in any training program aiming at developing skills for efficient and effective workplace communication.

Overall, learning is part of the daily work life of employees both in terms of acquiring new skills as well as adapting to become *oldtimers*. Hence the ultimate aim of any work-related training program should be to develop understanding of the fact that *good* communication is context bound. Thus, students should be taught how to *observe* and *learn* the *local* discourse practices. To this end, the classroom environment should encourage collaboration and feedback between students as well as comparisons and discussions of authentic real-life workplace data from the target workplace, when and where possible. In other words, the language classroom should become a workshop (see Anson & Foosberg 1990). Due to the nature of the workplace, it is imperative for future employees to learn to work efficiently and constructively with others (Schneider & Andre 2005: 212). I close this chapter on a positive note by arguing that the increasing interest in professional discourse and the growing amount of published work are providing us with a better understanding of the nature of workplace communication and an abundance of real-life interactions that can be used to complement textbooks when and where tailored courses are not an option.

Discussion questions and tasks

Reflection

1. Look at Excerpt 16.2. In what ways does the talk here differ from that in the other excerpts?
2. What challenges may you face in applying the approach outlined in the chapter in order to find, select, and develop materials?

3. I state throughout the paper that "workplace talk" cannot be *easily* decontextualized, and subsequently, it is imperative to prepare students for the inherent variation and variability of workplace interactions. Do you agree? Discuss with reference to your own experiences.

Evaluation

4. Choose a textbook from Appendix 16.1 and critically examine a selection of activities focused on meeting talk.
5. Look at some textbook materials you have used with a class in the past. In light of what you have learned in this chapter, what changes would you make to these materials now? Why?

Adaptation/Design

6. Take the set of activities described on pages 448-50 and discuss how you would adapt these to meet the needs of a particular group of learners you are familiar with.
7. Use Excerpts 16.2, 16.4, and 16.5 to design suitable activities for a group of students you know.

Appendix 16.1

Cotton, D., & Robbins, S. (1996). *Business class*. London: Longman.

Cotton, D., Falvey, D., & Kent, S. (2001). *Market leader*. Harlow, UK: Longman Pearson.

Grant, D., & McLarty, R. (2001). *Business basics*. New York: Oxford University Press.

Hollett, V. (2001). *Business objectives*. Oxford: Oxford University Press.

Wallwork, A. (1999 [2001]). *Business options*. Oxford: Oxford University Press.

Wallwork, A. (2002). *Business vision*. Oxford: Oxford University Press.

Appendix 16.2: Transcription conventions

[	Left square brackets indicate a point of overlap onset.
]	Right square brackets indicate a point at which two overlapping utterances both end, where one ends while the other continues, or simultaneous moments in overlaps that continue.
=	Equal signs indicate continuous utterance with no break or pause and/or latch.

(.)	A dot in parentheses indicates a short pause.
↑ ↓	The up and down arrows mark rises or falls in pitch.
((NOTES))	Double parentheses are used to indicate transcriber's comments.
emphasis	Underlining is used to indicate some form of stress or emphasis.

References

Angouri, J. (2007). Language in the workplace. A multimethod study of communicative activity in seven multinational companies situated in Europe. PhD thesis. University of Essex.

Angouri, J., & Harwood, N. (2008). *This is too formal for us* ... A case study of variation in the written products of a multinational consortium. *Journal of Business and Technical Communication* 22: 38-64.

Anson, C. M., & Foosberg, L. (1990). Moving beyond the academic community. *Written Communication* 7: 200-31.

Bargiela-Chiappini, F., & Harris S. J. (1997). *Managing language: The discourse of corporate meetings*. Amsterdam: John Benjamins.

Bargiela-Chiappini, F., & Nickerson, C. (2002). Business discourse: Old debates, new horizons. *IRAL* 40(4): 273-86.

Bargiela-Chiappini, F., Nickerson, C., & Planken, B. (2007). *Business discourse*. New York: Palgrave Macmillan.

Beattie, G. W. (1981). The regulation of speaker turns in face-to-face conversation: Some implications for conversation in sound-only communication channels. *Semiotica* 34: 55-70.

Beattie, G.W. (1982). Turn-taking and interruption in political interviews: Margaret Thatcher and Jim Callaghan compared and contrasted. *Semiotica* 39: 93-114.

Bennett, A. (1981). Interruption and the interpretation of conversation. *Discourse Processes* 4: 171-88.

Bowles, H. (2006). Bridging the gap between conversation analysis and ESP: An applied study of the opening sequences of NS and NNS service telephone calls. *English For Specific Purposes* 25: 332-57.

Coates, J. (1989). Gossip revisited: Language in all-female groups. In J. Coates & D. Cameron (eds.). *Women in their speech communities*. London: Longman, pp. 94-121.

Coates, J. (1993). *Women, men and language*. London: Longman.

Cuff, E. C., & Sharrock, W. W. (1985). Meetings. In T. A. van Dijk (ed.). *Handbook of discourse analysis, vol. 3: Discourse and dialogue*. London: Academic Press, pp. 149-59.

Dindia, K. (1987). The effects of sex of subject and sex of partner on interruptions. *Human Communication Research* 13: 345-71.

Edelsky, C. (1981). Who's Got the Floor? *Language in Society* 10: 383-421.

Edwards, N. (2000). Language for business: Effective needs assessment, syllabus design and materials preparation in a practical ESP case study. *English for Specific Purposes* 19: 291-6.

Emmitt, S., & Gorse, C. (2003). *Construction communication*. Oxford; Malden, MA: Blackwell.

Ewer, J. R., & Boys, O. (1981). The EST textbook situation: An enquiry. *English for Specific Purposes* 1: 87-105.

Freedman, A., & Adam, C. (1996). Learning to write professionally: "Situated learning" and the transition from university to professional discourse. *Journal of Business and Technical Communication* 10: 395-427.

Goldberg, J. A. (1990). Interrupting the discourse on interruptions. *Journal of Pragmatics* 14(6): 883-905.

Harwood, N. (2005). What do we want EAP teaching materials for? *Journal of English for Academic Purposes* 4: 149-61.

Holmes, J. (2005). Leadership talk: How do leaders "do mentoring," and is gender relevant? *Journal of Pragmatics* 37: 1779-880.

Holmes, J., & Marra, M. (2002). Having a laugh at work: How humour contributes to workplace culture. *Journal of Pragmatics* 34: 1683-710.

Holmes, J., & Stubbe, M. (2003). *Power and politeness in the workplace*. London: Pearson Education.

James, D., & Clarke, S. (1993). Women, men, and interruptions: A critical review. In D. Tannen (ed.). *Gender and conversational interaction*. New York: Oxford University Press, pp. 231-80.

Jones, G. (1990). ESP textbooks: Do they really exist? *English for Specific Purposes* 9: 89-93.

Koester, A. (2004). *The language of work*. London: Routledge.

Larrue, J., & Trognon, A. (1993). Organization of turn-taking and mechanisms for turn-taking repairs in a chaired meeting. *Journal of Pragmatics* 19: 177-96.

Lave, J., & Wenger, E. (1991). *Situated learning. Legitimate peripheral participation*. Cambridge: Cambridge University Press.

Linell, P. (2001). Dynamics of discourse or stability of structure: Sociolinguistics and the legacy from linguistics. In N. Coupland, S. Sarangi, & C. Candlin (eds.). *Sociolinguistics and social theory*. Harlow, UK: Longman, pp. 107-26.

Louhiala-Salminen, L. (1996). The business communication classroom vs. reality: What should we teach today? *English for Specific Purposes* 15(1): 37-51.

Lutz, J. (1989). Writers in organizations and how they learn the image: Theory, research, and implications. In C. B. Matalene (ed.). *Worlds of writing: Teaching and learning in discourse communities of work*. New York: Random House, pp. 113-35.

Marra, M. (2003). *Decisions in New Zealand business meetings: A sociolinguistic analysis of power at work*. PhD thesis, Victoria University of Wellington.

Murray, S. O. (1987). Power and solidarity in "interruption": A critique of the Santa Barbara School Conception and its application by Orcutt and Harvey (1985). *Symbolic Interaction* 10: 101-10.

Nickerson, C. (2002). Endnote: Business discourse and language teaching. *IRAL* 40(4): 375-81.

Rogerson-Revell, P. (1999). Meeting talk: A stylistic approach to teaching meeting skills. In M. Hewings & C. Nickerson (eds.). *Business English: Research into practice*. London: Longman, pp. 55-71.

Sacks, H., Schegloff, E., & Jefferson, G. (1974). A simplest systematics for the organization of turn-taking for Conversation. *Language* 50: 696-735.

Sarangi, S., & Roberts, C. (eds.). (1999). *Talk, work and institutional order: Discourse in medical, mediation and management settings*. Berlin: Mouton de Gruyter.

Schegloff, E. (2000). Overlapping talk and the organization of turn-taking for conversation. *Language in Society* 29(1): 1-63.

Schneider, B., & Andre, J. (2005). University preparation for workplace writing: Perceptions of students in three disciplines. *Journal of Business Communication* 42(2): 195-218.

Schwartzman, H. B. (1989). *The meeting gatherings in organizations and communities*. New York, London: Plenum Press.

Starke-Meyerring, D. (2005). Meeting the challenges of globalization: A framework for global literacies in professional communication programs. *Journal of Business and Technical Communication* 19: 468-99.

Stubbe, M. (2001). From office to production line: Collecting data for the Wellington Language in the Workplace Project. *Language in the Workplace Occasional*

Papers 2. Accessed online at: www.vuw.ac.nz/lals/research/lwp/ docs/ops/op2.htm, April 2005.

Sullivan, P., & Girginer, H. (2002). The use of discourse analysis to enhance ESP teacher knowledge: An example using aviation English. *English for Specific Purposes* 21: 397-404.

Swales, J. (1980). ESP: The textbook problem. *English for Specific Purposes* 1: 11-23.

Swales, J. M. (2000). Languages for specific purposes. *English for Specific Purposes* 20: 59-76.

Tannen, D. (1981). New York Jewish Conversational Style. *International Journal of the Sociology of Language* 30: 133-49.

Tannen, D. (1990). *You just don't understand.* New York: Ballantine Books.

Tannen, D. (ed). (1993). *Framing in discourse*. Oxford: Oxford University Press.

Tannen, D. (1994). Interpreting interruption in conversation. In D. Tannen. (ed.). *Gender and discourse*. New York: Oxford University Press, pp 53-83.

Vine, B. (2004). *Getting things done at work: The discourse of power in workplace interaction*. Amsterdam/Philadelphia: John Benjamins.

Wenger, E. (1998). Communities of Practice. Learning as a social system. *Systems Thinker*. Accessed online at: www.co-i-l.com/coil/knowledge-garden/ cop/lss. shtml, November 2006.

Williams, M. (1988). Language taught for meetings and language used in meetings: Is there anything in common? *Applied Linguistics* 9: 45-58.

17

Designing materials for community-based adult ESL programs

Cori Jakubiak and Linda Harklau

Summary

This chapter examines approaches to materials design in community-based adult English as a Second Language programs in immigrant-receiving nations, particularly the United States. Adult ESL, otherwise known as "adult basic" ESL or "adult ESL literacy," focuses on the abilities that new residents need in order to live and work in an English-dominant host society. We identify three approaches to instruction and materials design. *Basic ESL/competency-based education*, the most widespread instructional approach, emphasizes notional/functional and daily life (or "survival") skills. It includes thematically driven instruction in areas such as occupations, consumer education, health, civics, and community resources. *Holistic approaches*, including whole language and language experience, focus on student-centered and student-generated materials and emphasize authentic, meaningful communication. *Freirean* or *participatory ESL literacy approaches* aim to help students to recognize, articulate, and resist potentially oppressive or marginalizing social conditions in order to meet their personal goals. We argue that although the materials themselves in each of these approaches may have similarities, there are nonetheless significant differences in how and why they are developed and used. It is therefore important for curriculum planners and materials designers to identify a coherent approach in order to clarify the values, beliefs, and goals underlying a community-based adult ESL program.

Designing materials for community-based adult ESL

Community-based ELT occurs around the world in a wide variety of settings. However, for the most part, the curriculum and materials in such programs are informally set, often ephemeral, and have not been subject to much scholarly scrutiny (Roberts & Baynham 2006). By far the most widespread and best-documented form of community-based English as a Second Language (ESL) instruction is adult ESL – sometimes termed "adult basic ESL" programs – in immigrant-receiving nations including the United States, Great Britain, and Australia. These programs focus on the English abilities that new migrants need in order to live and work in an English-dominant host society. Increased immigration in recent and coming decades (Rice & Stavrianos 1995) suggests that the need for adult ESL education programs is likely to grow (Allender 1998; Khanna *et al.* 1998; National Center for Adult ESL Literacy Education 2003; Rice & Stavrianos 1995). In the United States, for example, nearly half of all participants in federally funded adult education programs are English learners (Florez & Burt 2001). Similarly, large, recurrent waves of immigration to Australia in the last half century have prompted policy-makers to centralize adult English language learning; as a result, Australia's Adult Migrant English Program (AMEP) now provides 510 free hours of English language instruction to each new immigrant nationwide (Allender 1998; Murray 2005). Canada too has established a federal program, Language Instruction for Newcomers to Canada (LINC), to help unprecedented numbers of recent immigrants deal with the linguistic and social challenges they face upon resettlement (Murray 2005).

Despite the increasing need for comprehensive adult ESL programs in industrialized Anglophone nations around the world and in the United States in particular – where, as of the 2000 Census, more than 10 percent of the population was born outside of the country (National Center for Adult ESL Literacy Education 2003) – adult ESL as a field remains highly marginalized (Crandall 1993b). In the United States and Great Britain, for example, issues of teacher professionalization, inadequate funding and resources, and inappropriate curricula and materials strain the abilities of many adult ESL programs to meet their students' social and educational needs (Crandall 1993b; Khanna *et al.* 1998; Murray 2005). Adult ESL classes are often over-subscribed or poorly advertised, causing some learners to miss out on instruction entirely (Dreyden-Peterson 2007), whereas regular attendance can be problematic for those who do enroll. Reporting scheduling or childcare conflicts, transportation issues, or feelings that course content is irrelevant to their language needs, adult ESL students may come to class erratically or withdraw altogether (Skilton-Sylvester 2002).

In spite of the struggles faced by adult ESL programs, they are nonetheless vitally important to migrants' economic and social adjustment to the host society. Studies in the United States, for example, suggest that English proficiency is tied to wages and job security (Dreydon-Peterson 2007; Rice & Stavrianos 1995). Additionally, it facilitates participation in public affairs and access to public services and educational opportunities (Gordon 2004; Rice & Stavrianos 1995). English instruction might also help migrants to communicate with their children's schools (Crandall 1993a), understand their legal rights (Gordon 2004), increase their personal autonomy (Skilton-Sylvester 2002), and take more control over their social positioning in the host society (Gordon 2004; Peirce 1995).

Adult ESL classes thus have considerable potential to be sites of empowerment. Consequently, the instructional activities that take place in community-based adult ESL programs and the materials used to augment those activities merit careful attention. In this chapter, we outline issues salient to adult ESL education in general and to materials development in particular. We use adult ESL education in the United States as our exemplar. We begin with a brief description of adult ESL learners and review the background of adult ESL education in the United States. We then describe three different instructional approaches used in adult ESL classes and provide examples of materials and activities aligned with each.

Adult ESL students in the United States

If research indicates anything about the typical adult ESL student, it is that adult ESL students are difficult to typify. Students enrolled in adult ESL classes in the United States come from a variety of cultural and linguistic backgrounds: They may be newly arrived refugees, immigrants who have lived in the country for many years, or short-term residents who are visiting to work or study (Crandall 1993a). They are likewise heterogeneous in terms of their educational backgrounds. A large number are Spanish-speaking urban-dwellers who have completed secondary schooling in their home countries (Rice & Stavrianos 1995). Yet many others live in smaller towns, have little formal schooling, and may not be literate in their first languages (Wrigley 1993). Indeed, literacy is a major component of many American adult ESL programs. Some adult ESL students come from cultural groups characterized by limited literacy traditions (e.g., the Hmong), while other students, although literate in their first languages, may be unfamiliar with the Roman alphabet (Crandall 1993b). Adult ESL students may also differ considerably in their previous exposure to any formal study of English (Rice & Stavrianos 1995).

Adult ESL students in the United States enroll in language classes for a variety of reasons. Some may be orally conversant in English yet wish to improve their literacy skills for professional or educational advancement or to access public services (Crandall 1993a; Wrigley 1993). Alternately, some students join adult ESL as a required part of refugee settlement (e.g., Mahnen 1995), as a way to prepare themselves for the English language component of the US citizenship test (e.g., Orange County Public Schools 1999), or in an effort to better negotiate their domestic lives (Peirce 1995). Social or personal motives may figure prominently in an adult's decision to attend ESL class. For example, Skilton-Sylvester (2002) reports that female adult ESL learners were "coming to [ESL] class in part because of the social interaction it allowed, with language learning being an equal or secondary concern as they saw classroom participation as some much-needed time for themselves" (p. 12).

Educators have found that ESL students' expectations and experiences may be quite different from the native-born clientele of community-based adult basic education programs. For one, while many US-born adult education students have had previous, negative encounters with formal schooling, ESL students often have not faced similar barriers (Rice & Stavrianos 1995). As a result, they may view American public educational services more benevolently and stay in adult education programs longer than their non-ESL counterparts (Murray 2005). ESL students are also more likely than other adult education graduates to name program participation as a key factor in helping them find and succeed at later employment (Rice & Stavrianos 1995).

On the other hand, ESL students bring to class culturally mediated expectations of schooling and classrooms that may be different from those in the host society. In particular, students with prior schooling in their home countries may feel strongly about which topics are appropriate for classroom discussion, what the teacher's role should be, or what seating arrangements are culturally suitable, among other issues. In illustration, McGroarty (1993) reports that she inadvertently upset a Muslim husband and wife when she had her adult ESL class sit in a circle. The male student became uncomfortable with a seating arrangement that he felt put his wife on display.

Finally, adult ESL students differ from English monolingual adult education students in that they possess a key learning resource: fluency in one or more other languages. Second language acquisition research suggests that knowledge of another linguistic system – that is, familiarity with the concepts of grammar, syntax, and pragmatics – is positively correlated to learning an additional language (Gass & Selinker 1994). Adult language learners also bring personal learning strategies, advanced problem-solving skills, and frequently, good study habits to bear on the learning task (Scovel 2001). Moreover, many adult ESL students have already surmounted great political, personal, or economic obstacles to come to another country (cf. Hondagneu-Sotelo 2001). This fact alone is suggestive of qualities such as perseverance, risk taking, and high personal investment, all important elements in education and second language learning (Peirce 1995; Rubin 1975).

Adult ESL in the United States

Although national oversight and coordination of adult ESL programming in the United States has always been limited, especially in contrast to countries like Australia and Canada (Murray 2005), adult ESL came under federal auspices in 1964 with the Economic Opportunity Act. This initiative established Adult

Basic Education (ABE) programs throughout the United States to provide remediated and continuing education to adults who had not graduated from high school. Adult ESL classes were included under ABE.

ESL classes run under the aegis of ABE focused mainly on spoken, or "survival," English and, as they do at the present, operated in a variety of venues including community centers, voluntary organizations, and libraries (Crandall 1993b). However, with the arrival of many Southeast Asian refugees in the United States in the mid-1970s, adult ESL teachers faced a new pedagogical challenge: Many of these refugee students could neither read nor write. As the instructional strategies used in adult ESL programs up until that time were premised upon first language literacy, instructors struggled to meet students' needs (Holt 1995), and many programs shifted to a focus on teaching reading and writing. Since then, adult basic ESL education has become increasingly synonymous with ESL literacy (Murray 2005).

Federal legislation passed in the last two decades has furthered this congruence. The National Literacy Act of 1991, for example, tied funding for adult education programs to literacy gains. In order to secure federal monies, many adult ESL programs switched to primarily literacy instruction (Rice & Stavrianos 1995). The 1998 Adult Education and Literacy Act mandated the use of standardized competency tests in all adult education programs, further shifting the curricula of many adult ESL programs from spoken English to test-measurable literacy skills (Menard-Warwick 2005).

Many community-based adult ESL programs in the United States focus on family or "intergenerational" literacy. According to Weinstein-Shr and Quintero (1995), a main purpose of this approach "is to assist parents who desire more educational skills for themselves, so they can make sure that their children reach their full potential as learners. Central to this agenda is a focus on increased parental involvement in their children's schooling" (p. 5). English language and literacy skills are taught in tandem to both parents and children with the dual purpose of strengthening parent-child communication and improving children's academic success (Holt & Holt 1995). A popular model, advocated by the privately sponsored National Center for Family Literacy (NCFL) and supported in some federal legislation, defines *family literacy* as involving four components: (1) interactive literacy activities between parents and children; (2) improving parents' skills as primary teachers of their children; (3) parent literacy training for economic self-sufficiency; and (4) early childhood education (Lieshoff *et al.* 2004).

This conflation of community-based adult ESL with ESL literacy has not been without its detractors, however. Scholars in second language acquisition, for one, argue that fusing ESL with English literacy blurs the distinctions between students who are literate in their home language and those who are not (Crandall 1993b; Murray 2005). Moreover, family literacy programs that promote English use in the home disregard a wide body of research showing that it is the *quality* of linguistic interactions rather than the *language* of interactions that predict a child's academic success (Auerbach 1995). Studies in fact indicate that home language maintenance and multilingualism are tied to greater academic achievement (see, for example, Portes & Rumbaut 2001; Thomas & Collier 2002). Furthermore, a focus on monolingualism versus multilingualism may actually be inhibitive of immigrants' language rights (Skutnabb-Kangas 2000).

Additionally, the focus of many ABE programs is vocational or competency-based literacy (Mahnen 1995). Critics argue that this leads to a mismatch between program goals and the goals of attending students (Crandall 1993b; Rice & Stavrianos 1995). In illustration, while many adult learners enroll in ESL literacy classes in order to get a *better* job, the goal of vocational or competency-based literacy classes is often job *placement*. Thus, a program meets its goal if a student finds *any* job; it is irrelevant that doctors may work as janitors or engineers may work on the factory floor (Murray 2005). Caught between the need for federal funding and the desire to meet students' needs, then, adult ESL literacy programs frequently struggle.

The short-term, piecemeal nature of funding poses another challenge to community-based programs. While national and state governments are the largest sources of adult ESL funding in the United States (Rice & Stavrianos 1995), most programs must procure supplemental funding from corporations, local governments, and voluntary agencies (Crandall 1993b). As a result, programs beholden to funding agencies cannot devote their full attention and resources to curriculum and materials development, and instead must devote time and energy to "time-consuming counts: number of person hours of attendance, number of persons who complete the program, number of persons who are placed in jobs (without follow-up to see if they keep them), and the like" (Crandall 1993b: 13-4).

Finally, many adult ESL education programs in the United States have difficulty finding and retaining competent instructors. Limited resources, combined with interrupted funding cycles, force many programs to employ part-time workers or volunteers rather than full-time teachers (Rice & Stavrianos 1995; Wrigley 1993). Furthermore, while many instructors have experience teaching either ESL or English literacy, few have experience teaching both (Crandall 1993b). Lastly, although most states have established clear guidelines for the education of English language learners in preschool through secondary school and require teachers to be certified, few guidelines or certification programs exist for teaching ESL in community-based adult basic programs. If instructors hold credentials at all, they are likely to be in another content area or in a grade school subject, as if teaching ESL to adults were akin to teaching children (Crandall 1993b).

Instructional approaches

Given these conditions, it should not be surprising that there is wide diversity in instructional approaches used in community-based adult ESL programs. Overall, we might distinguish three main theoretical and methodological traditions guiding curriculum and materials development in these programs: (1) basic ESL/competency-based education (CBE); (2) whole language/language experience approach (LEA) ESL literacy; and (3) Freirean or participatory ESL literacy (Crandall & Peyton 1993).

Basic ESL or competency-based education (CBE)

The dominant instructional approach in community-based adult ESL programs in the United States is competency-based education (CBE), or "basic English" (Rice & Stavrianos 1995). This is a "functional approach to education that emphasizes life skills and evaluates mastery of those skills according to actual learner performance" (Savage 1993: 15). Within CBE, "life skills" are defined as tasks that allow one to function, or survive, in occupational, consumer, health, government and law, and community resource domains (Savage 1993). Accordingly, CBE ESL courses are usually organized around topics or themes such as visiting the doctor's office, using public transportation, or going to work. Within these topical units, students may learn how to perform tasks such as buying stamps, using public transportation, or filling out forms.

While literacy is a component of CBE, the focus is functional, or survival, literacy that "relates reading and writing instruction to what is required to meet basic life skill objectives" (Savage 1993: 26). Thus, CBE ESL instruction focuses on learning to read print items that students might see on a daily basis, such as signs, symbols, or important words. During a unit on shopping, for example, students might learn to read clothing labels or price tags; during a unit on food, students might learn to read menus. Competency-based education is likewise the dominant curricular approach in ESL family literacy programs in the United States (Morrow *et al.* 2003). These programs emphasize school-based literacy practices, such as the English parents' needs to read to their children, help with homework, and read home-school communication, such as report cards. During classtime, ESL parents and their children might also read picture books or write together in English. Parenting lessons may focus on home behaviors such as establishing routines or talking frequently with children in order to facilitate school success (Lieshoff *et al.* 2004).

As its name suggests, CBE operates on the premise that students arrive in class lacking certain competencies, and that students achieve success when they can demonstrate, or perform, these competencies. Consequently, a CBE approach pays particular attention to instructional objectives: They are written in task-based terms such as "students will be able to ...," and all objectives are performative. Verbs such as "understand" or "know," not being demonstrable, are not included in the instructional objectives of CBE (Savage 1993). Assessments, too, are task-based. Examples of assessments appropriate for CBE might be role plays (with a student ordering food, for example), fill-in-the-blank worksheets, or following directions. In sum, ESL literacy instruction "is competency-based if the needs of the students have been assessed, the competencies have been selected on those needs, the instruction is targeted to those competencies, and the students are evaluated based on performance of those competencies" (Savage 1993: 31).

Competency-based instructional approaches are popular in adult basic education programs, in part because performance-based assessments provide easily reducible data for funding agencies' accountability measures. Nevertheless, CBE has been accused of numerous faults. For one, research has found that in community-based programs, where enrollment is usually voluntary, preset curricula that are not well matched to students' goals may lead to high attrition. For example, themes focusing on parenting may be irrelevant for students who do not have children or whose children are not living with them (Skilton-Sylvester 2002). Likewise, family literacy programs focusing on the nuclear family overlook the fact that families are often separated in the immigration process and that children's aunts, older siblings, or grandparents (rather than parents) may be primary caregivers (Weinstein-Shr & Quintero 1995). Similarly, curricula focusing on English for the workplace neglect the fact that language proficiency is largely irrelevant for many unskilled jobs (Gordon 2004) or may be unhelpful to stay-at-home parents.

Another criticism is that CBE's focus on survival literacy over critical literacy or problem-solving skills encourages the status quo. As Murray (2005) puts it, "Competency-based ESL curricula often stress job-related tasks and include topics such as filling out forms, calling in sick, or developing listening skills to identify procedures to follow, but not the language needed for managerial or supervisory functions" (p. 68). Likewise, CBE-based family literacy approaches tend to focus on gaps in immigrant parents' knowledge rather than inadequacies in the schools their children attend. As Auerbach (1995) writes, "The goal [often seems] to be to transform home contexts into sites for mainstream literacy interactions and to inculcate parents with the skills and behaviors necessary to interact on the school's terms" (p. 64). Researchers also argue that the topical focus of CBE is highly ideological. For example, the topic of shopping and the teaching of how to read store advertisements, find bargains, and negotiate a department store hides a capitalist discourse in which accumulation, buying new items rather than used ones, and shopping for pleasure are rendered natural (Ilieva 2000).

Whole language and language experience approach (LEA) ESL literacy

Holistic approaches are based on practices widely used in teaching reading to children including "whole language" and the "language experience approach" (LEA). Alternately termed the reading/writing workshop approach (e.g., Atwell 1998) or the student-publications approach (e.g., Peyton 1993), these holistic models of community-based adult ESL view the four literacy modalities (i.e., listening, speaking, reading, and writing) as recursive, integrated processes embedded in particular social contexts. Central to holistic models of literacy instruction are the personal experiences of learners. Advocates of both whole language and LEA argue that any oral or written language exercise – even in the classroom – should be meaningful to the speaker/writer and serve a real purpose (Rigg & Kazemek 1993). Thus, whole texts (not segments) should always be used in class, and anything a student says or writes should be intrinsically meaningful, not simply a classroom exercise. Likewise, advocates eschew the breakdown or analysis of language skills associated with worksheets, abstracted proofreading exercises, or spelling lists (Rigg & Kazemek 1993).

As its name – language *experience* approach – suggests, students' life experiences form the subject matter of reading and writing in an LEA classroom. The approach asks students to relate a story about their own life experience orally in class. The story is then recorded in writing by the teacher and becomes a text for the class (Taylor 1993). This approach presents a significant contrast to CBE approaches, in which content arises from predetermined themes. Especially appropriate to community-based programs, holistic literacy approaches aim to upset the separation between the classroom and the outside world. Accordingly, off-campus field trips play an important curricular role in these approaches. Classes visit places in the community, and these field experiences then provide language content for reading, writing, and speaking (Taylor 1993). People outside of the classroom, too, are expected to influence holistic literacy programs. "Whole language teachers tie the classroom community to the larger community outside the school building," Rigg and Kazemek write. "Parents, grandparents, children, and other members of the community spend time in the classroom as experts on some topic – as storytellers, as observers, and as important contributors to the education of the community both in and out of the classroom" (1993: 38).

Finally, teachers take on different roles in holistic literacy classrooms. Rather than being viewed as the top-down font of knowledge, teachers in holistic literacy classrooms are expected to be facilitators: They assist students in drawing upon their own strengths, helping them use language for self-determined purposes and build upon the language they already know. Students are expected to share power with instructors and jointly negotiate the curriculum and evaluation (Rigg & Kazemek 1993).

Holistic models of community-based adult ESL literacy instruction face challenges in an age of accountability. Neither whole language nor LEA literacy approaches are conducive to standardized achievement testing, and critics thus argue that their success (or failure) is difficult to measure. Federal, state, and private funding agencies may exert considerable pressure on programs to abandon holistic approaches to literacy instruction in favor of CBE and other methods that can be aligned with criterion-referenced tests (Menard-Warwick 2005).

Freirean or participatory ESL literacy

Freirean approaches have been used in adult ESL and ESL family literacy program models (Auerbach 1995; Morrow *et al.* 2003). Similar to whole language and LEA approaches, adult ESL instruction in the Freirean, or participatory, tradition "revolves around the discussion of issues drawn from the real-life experience of adult learners" (Spener 1993: 75). Alternately referred to as the problem-posing approach or the liberatory approach, the model draws conceptually upon the work of Brazilian educator Paulo Freire. Freire's scholarship holds that language is a tool of emancipation: People need language and literacy skills not in and of themselves but in order to challenge oppressive social conditions (Freire 2003/1970). In a class in which the Freirean approach is used, then, the cultures of the students and the problems they face drive the themes covered in class (Spener 1993).

Critical literacy skills play a key role in Freirean-based programs. While more traditional adult ESL literacy courses may teach students how to decode, predict, or summarize texts, courses in the Freirean tradition additionally encourage critical-thinking skills and teach students to analyze the social, political, and ideological elements of texts (Hood 1998). For example, while a teacher in a traditional classroom might review a school-produced flyer on how parents can help their children with homework by focusing on comprehension of language and concepts, a teacher taking a Freirean approach might extend this activity by asking students to evaluate the feasibility of the school's suggestions and then to rewrite the flyer with more culturally appropriate alternatives (Auerbach 1995). In the Freirean approach, whether students possess literacy skills is seen as secondary to how they use them; critical literacy, in the Freirean sense, is the use of reading and writing to promote social change.

Freirean and participatory models of community-based adult ESL face similar criticisms as holistic approaches. Without a set curriculum, Freirean approaches tend to be incompatible with increasing mandates for standardized competency testing. Moreover, educators whose jobs are already made vulnerable by erratic funding might be reluctant to adopt the overtly political stance of Freirean instruction for fear of attracting the disapproval of funders or other stakeholders in the community. Others argue, however, that community-based adult ESL is an inherently advocative and political endeavor (Ferguson 1998). The model has thus far not been widely implemented (Menard-Warwick 2005).

Materials development in major instructional approaches

Materials development for basic ESL or competency-based education (CBE) classes

Because of the wide range of contexts and needs in community-based adult ESL programs, needs analysis is of major concern in developing a curriculum and materials. However, needs analysis takes considerably different forms in different approaches. In the case of CBE-focused programs, predetermined curricula are typically based on themes or topics deemed necessary for "survival" in English-dominant countries (Savage 1993). In family literacy programs, for example, topics might be related to home-school communication, parenting, and English literacy development (Lieshoff *et al.* 2004). Needs analyses in CBE-focused programs are also typically used as benchmark measures reported to funders and other stakeholders (Lieshoff *et al.* 2004) and therefore often take the form of preexisting placement tests. Students may answer oral or written questions such as, "What is your name?" "Where are you from?" "How long have you been in this country?" or "How many people are in your family?" so that instructors can place them in course levels (McKay & Tom 1999). Alternately, students are given picture prompts such as the John Test (cited in Brown *et al.* 1994) or cartoons with empty speech balloons above them; students then say or write what is happening in the pictures (McKay & Tom 1999). Lists and inventories are also commonly used in CBE-focused adult ESL needs analysis. Students are given possible reasons (or pictures representing reasons) why they want to learn English, and students check those that fit. Consistent with CBE's preset curriculum, however, the reasons from which students may choose (e.g., "shop for food," "talk to a dentist," "rent a house or apartment") are usually limited to the thematic domains that have already shaped course syllabi and materials (cf. McKay & Tom 1999).

A wide variety of commercial and public materials has been created for thematically organized, "basic English" programs, such as Gianola's *Health Stories: Readings and Language Activities for Healthy Choices* (2007), the Orange County Public Schools' *Citizenship Handbook* (1999), and Vacco and Jablon's *Conversations for Work* (2007). Family literacy materials in this vein include the NCFL and CAELA-sponsored *Practitioner Toolkit* (Lieshoff *et al.* 2004) and Fairfax County's *Family Literacy Curriculum* (Wong 2008). Correspondent with the CBE instructional approach, units are thematically organized and set measurable tasks (e.g., "Students will be able to talk about their jobs"), and activities aim to help students gain competency in stated areas. In Vacco and Jablon's (2007) *Conversations for Work*, for example, the text introduces vocabulary such as *bleach*, *sponges*, *soap*, *trash bags*, and *toilet paper* with corresponding pictures of each item. The following pages then present activities in which students are to use these words: a fill-in-the-blank exercise labeling items in a supply closet; a sentence-level exercise on prepositions of location instructing students to describe each item's location relative to other items; and a short paragraph reading and comprehension questions incorporating the words (e.g., Vacco & Jablon 2007).

Wordless picture books and illustrated children's stories are other important sources of reading materials for CBE ESL family literacy programs. Ancillary materials might include manuals for teachers on how to use these materials to model for parents how to engage their children in reading. Activities might include using illustrations to make predictions, pointing to the text as one reads along, stopping and asking questions about the story, and varying one's voice or expression (Lieshoff *et al.* 2004; Wong 2008). Alternatively, parents might be assigned to read their child a picture book at home and then report back on the experience (Lieshoff *et al.* 2004).

In addition to thematically organized textbooks and other readings, other materials commonly used in CBE adult ESL programs include flashcards, alphabet cards, and graphic organizers (McKay & Tom 1999). The CBE approach often involves discrete skills instruction in the alphabet, letter-sound correspondences, and sight words (Savage 1993). Materials thus include flip charts, picture cards, large-print flashcards, and photographic depictions of target vocabulary (e.g., shaking hands for "introducing yourself ") (see, e.g., Schlusberg 2006; Wong 2008) for practice in recognizing sight words, drilling letter-sound correspondence, and identifying word parts (e.g., suffixes, prefixes, roots).

Worksheets, too, are used with regularity in CBE-focused adult ESL. Materials may include short reading passages with comprehension questions; modifications of real-life print materials including leases, job applications, medical forms, and home-school correspondence (McKay & Tom 1999); lists of vocabulary words; puzzles including crosswords, word scrambles, or word searches; surveys; information-gap activities; cloze passages; or fill-in-the-blank forms (see, e.g., Lieshoff *et al.* 2004; Orange County Public Schools 1999; South Carolina Literacy Resource Center 1994; Wong 2008). For example, students studying food or nutrition might create menus or budget for a week of shopping (Lieshoff *et al.* 2004). Cross-cultural differences in behavior might be addressed in a worksheet asking students to label pictured behaviors as "ok" or "not ok" (Schlusberg 2006). Assignments may be completed in class or for homework; often, they are checked as a group. In alignment with the instructional philosophy behind CBE, promotion to a higher course level may be contingent upon the successful completion of all assignments and assessments (Rice & Stavrianos 1995).

Whole-group, teacher-led games are another mark of the CBE classroom. Materials here may include games, such as Jeopardy, bingo, or tic-tac-toe, to teach phonics, review vocabulary words, or "reinforce any unit which has over 30 terms" and equipment needed for such games, including cards, a pointer, small prizes, buzzers, and timers (Arnold *et al.* 1997). Additionally, materials developers can incorporate realia such as plastic fruits and vegetables, clocks, maps, calendars, and restaurant menus to create information-gap activities, role plays, and conversation practice (McKay & Tom 1999). For example, materials for students in an ESL family literacy program might practice school-associated phone calls, such as reporting a child's absence or rescheduling a teacher-parent meeting (Wong 2008). Alternatively, parents might be given scenarios of school-related problems – for example, "Ying's mother wants to go on a field trip, but doesn't know how to sign up" – and be asked to role-play solutions (Wong 2008).

Materials for whole language and language experience approach (LEA) ESL literacy classes

Holistically oriented community-based adult ESL programs also begin with needs analyses. However, unlike CBE approaches that gather information to determine where students fit in a predetermined course sequence, the objective of needs analyses in holistic approaches is to uncover students' individual educational goals. These goals are then used as a guide for designing curriculum (Wrigley, 1993). Moreover, unlike the norm or criterion-referenced inventories used in CBE approaches, holistic literacy programs' needs analyses are conducted through multiple methods, including instructor notes, observations of students, and informal conversations with pupils to gauge literacy levels and interests (Wrigley 2000). As Holt (1995) writes, students' unique behaviors can yield much data: "Informal assessment through classroom observation ... assist[s] the teacher in determining an individual learner's needs. Attention should be paid to how learners hold their pencils (awkwardly? Too tightly?) and their books (upside down?)" (p. 4).

Learners' personal experiences and goals likewise form the foundation of curriculum and materials in both the whole language and LEA approaches. In these approaches, then, the challenge for materials developers is that specific course topics and content cannot be identified beforehand. Instead, the developer's task is to specify activities, procedures, and resources that can be used by instructors to elicit student-generated content. Recommended elicitation tasks include the use of treasured objects or family photos as the basis of LEA stories: Students dictate information about objects or photos to the teacher, this information is transcribed, and transcribed stories then become texts for reading (Peyton 1993; Ullman 1997). Similarly, issues salient to students' lives, such as identity struggles or cultural conflicts, can provide rich fodder for LEA stories (Ullman 1997).

Advocates of holistic approaches believe that students' transcribed texts are advantageous as materials for several reasons. First, they are more engaging than a preset curriculum to both the tellers and other students. "[D]ictated texts that are scribed by the instructor can be meaningful reading materials that provide discussion about aspects of reading and writing, and explorations of society and the world," Rigg and Kazemek note (1993: 39). Additionally, proponents suggest that student-produced materials such as LEA stories use more accessible language and contain more relevant content than commercially or teacher-produced texts (Peyton 1993). As such, these texts are valuable for sustained silent reading, an activity on which holistic approaches place a strong emphasis. It is often difficult to find materials appropriate for adult ESL reading since "[m]any texts written in simplified English are juvenile, uninteresting, or even demeaning to adult readers" (Taylor 1993: 49). Holistic approaches circumvent this problem by using students' stories (Peyton 1993; Rigg & Kazemek 1993).

Besides student-generated texts, materials developers working with holistic approaches also look to children's and young adult literature and other trade books (e.g., Vaille & QuinnWilliams 2006), poetry authored by students or others (e.g., Fleischman 1988), popular magazines, songs, and local newspapers. Indeed, authentic materials – not textbooks or worksheets – are the mainstay of most holistic literacy programs. Above all, materials for these approaches are expected to be "purposeful, functional, and real," Rigg and Kazemek (1993) write. "Practice exercises from workbooks that are not authentic uses of language must be avoided ... complete and whole texts, such as whole stories and complete newspaper articles, must be used for reading" (pp. 36-7).

Holistic approaches also advocate teacher-student dialogue or writing journals. Research indicates, for one, that writing in journals can help adult ESL students explore social identities and investigate where and how they use English outside of the classroom (Peirce 1994; Ullman 1997). Second, journal writing can help adult language learners safely experiment with a new language to organize and express ideas and emotions (Rigg & Kazemek 1993). Lastly, journals offer a place for learners to record family and community histories as well as other stories from their native lands; these writings can form the basis of a future publication or simply be a means to share ideas (Peyton 1993).

Materials for Freirean or participatory ESL literacy classes

Similar to holistic approaches, Freirean – or participatory – models of adult community-based ESL instruction revolve around learners' lives. Needs analyses or intake assessments in Freirean-inspired courses are therefore unlikely to measure discrete skills or serve as a placement guide. Instead, they are used to gather information about students' identities (e.g., as a parent, as a spouse, as a worker, as an immigrant, as a community leader) and English language use. A sample needs analysis might solicit: (1) how often learners use English and with whom; (2) situations in which learners would like to use English but cannot; and (3) problems arising in learners' lives because of gaps in English language or literacy skills (Spener 1993). A family literacy program using a Freirean approach, for example, might employ interviews or focus groups with families as the basis of curriculum design (Holt & Holt 1995).

Freirean-based adult ESL curricula and materials likewise grow out of students' personal experiences, interests, and problems rather than prescribed frameworks. Accordingly, Freirean approaches, like holistic approaches, often eschew commercially produced materials, such as graded ESL textbooks, in favor of LEA stories, trade books, and authentic texts like newspapers or magazines. Themes in materials are elicited from students and may be quite unpredictable, from participants' joint concerns about the cultivation and harvesting of cotton (Huerta-Macías 1995), to finding and signing up for swimming lessons (Holt & Holt 1995), to learning English to speak with grandchildren (Weinstein-Shr 1995), to exploring the role reversals that can occur when children learn English more quickly than their parents (Auerbach 1995).

Freirean approaches, moreover, can be distinguished by their emphasis on situating learners' experiences in their identities and the broader sociocultural and sociopolitical contexts in which their identities are formed. Research in adult ESL has suggested that congruency between learners' social identities and the content of ESL courses bears strongly on student attrition (Peirce 1995; Skilton-Sylvester 2002; Ullman 1997). Curriculum and materials in these classes, then, focus on aspirations and goals that bring students to English classes as well as on helping them to identify and take collective action against oppressive social conditions that marginalize them or impede progress toward their goals (Auerbach *et al.* 1996).

The task for material developers working in this tradition is to identify tasks and activities that will facilitate the process of problem posing, critical literacy, and galvanizing for social change. Diaries or journals, for example, are used frequently in Freirean ESL and family literacy classrooms for students to explore their social identities vis-à-vis English, the problems they face in their lives, and their feelings about them (e.g., McGrail 1995). Students might be asked, for example, to write about the opportunities they have to communicate in English. As Peirce (1994) writes, such a task has liberatory possibilities:

> Learners can be encouraged to reflect critically on their engagement with target language speakers. That is, learners might investigate the conditions under which they interact with target language speakers;

> how and why such interactions take place; and what results follow from such interaction. This might help learners develop insight into the way in which opportunities to speak are socially structured and how social relations of power are implicated in the process of social interaction. As a result, they may learn to transform social practices of marginalization. (1994: 27)

As the ultimate goal of education, for Freire, was social change, writing materials might lead students to question the ways in which their language acquisition opportunities are embedded in matrices of power.

Dialogue journals between instructors and students are also common in Freirean-inspired classrooms. The informal, conversational tone of these products can empower students to write about issues of concern to them and to explore solutions to personal and social problems (Orem 2001). Furthermore, dialogue journals can be a space in which students can explore identity shifts or write about where and when they have experienced communication breakdowns (Peirce 1995).

In a Freirean-inspired family literacy program, wordless picture books and illustrated children's stories may be the basis of reading materials. Materials developers might also design activities for parents to write their own stories and read these aloud to their children. Materials also include ways to elicit students' oral stories, family histories, and traditions (perhaps in the home language) that may in turn serve as class texts. Students may then be asked to read or perform these stories at home or in class (Arrastía 1995). Materials might help families to compose and read intergenerational newsletters. As Weinstein-Shr (1995) reports, "Elders who once had little use for English have found themselves motivated to tell their stories, to read one another's, and to write them down in English for their grandchildren; these stories have become the curriculum" (p. 2).

Materials might also include directions for developing skits and role plays, class discussions, and readings to elicit students' personal challenges in day-to-day life. The politically charged issue of whether to drive without a license,[1]

---

[1] In most parts of the United States, only legal residents may get a driver's license. Yet driving is often essential to make a living in the United States. Undocumented immigrants therefore often drive without a license.

for example, could form the basis of written dialogues that are then performed (Menard-Warwick 2005). Alternatively, a class debate on US immigration policy and reading related newspaper editorials could help students articulate their own concerns in English (Ullman 1997). Materials developers might also use realia as a source of critical questions and class discussion. In the words of Menard-Warwick (2005), "even though teachers cannot provide easy solutions to the complex societal problems confronted by many immigrants, they can at least make their students' language-learning dilemmas explicit topics for classroom reading, writing, and discussion activities" (p. 182). Such is the Freirean approach.

Ultimately, within the Freirean approach, *what* materials are used is less important than *how* they are used. Informed by critical literacy theory, Freirean instructional models focus on helping learners use analytical skills to question, examine, and evaluate what they read (Florez 1998). Consequently, a traditional ESL textbook *could* actually be used in a Freirean-model classroom. However, what students would *do* with that textbook might look very different. For example, students in a Freirean class might critically examine an ESL textbook, looking for who and what are presented – and *not* presented – in its pages, rather than simply doing its prescribed exercises. As Ilieva (2000) discovered in examining Canadian adult ESL texts, shopping is usually presented in capitalistic terms as an activity one does for pleasure, such as buying new goods in a department store; alternative approaches to shopping, such as buying used goods or only buying when one needs something, are ignored altogether.

Conclusion

As we noted at the outset of this chapter, community-based adult ELT remains a marginalized and fragmentary field. Programs often have little to rely on to develop a principled approach to curriculum and materials design. Yet there are encouraging signs of renewed research and pedagogical interest in the UK (Roberts & Baynham 2006), United States (Condelli *et al.* 2002), Canada (Norton 2006), and Australia (Burns 2006). In this chapter, we have identified three major approaches informing materials design in community-based adult ESL programs in the United States and noted strengths and weaknesses in each.

Materials themselves may not differ markedly across these approaches, but there is a distinctive difference in how and why they are developed and used. Identifying an approach and, in so doing, clarifying a program's underlying values, beliefs, and goals, is a vital first step for any curriculum planner and materials designer. It is, however, particularly important for materials designers working with community-based adult ELT programs. Because of their marginalized and often underresourced status, community-based programs often include educators who are volunteers or out-of-field. Materials are thus not only instructional tools but also a means of teacher education and professional development. A coherent approach to curriculum and materials design also helps community-based ELT educators to articulate a strong vision of what their programs can accomplish and to act as effective advocates for their programs and students.

Discussion questions and tasks

Reflection

1. Which of the three approaches to developing materials for community-based adult ESOL programs do you support the most strongly? Why?
2. With a small group, make a chart of the strengths and weaknesses of each of the three approaches.
3. Now that you have read this chapter and discussed the approaches, would you approach materials development for community-based ELT programs differently? How so?
4. The approaches described in this chapter referred broadly to the context of US adult education. How are community-based programs in your area similar to and different from this context, and how might it affect your approach to materials development?

Evaluation

5. Look at some of the materials you have made or used. Which of these approaches are they most aligned with, and how might you improve them after reading this chapter?

Adaptation/Design

6. Identify one topic or theme likely to be covered in an adult community-based English program (e.g., health). Prepare materials and activities that represent each of the three approaches. Explain how and why the activities differ.

References

Allender, S. C. (1998). *Adult ESL learners with special needs: Learning from the Australian perspective. ERIC Q & A*. Washington, DC: National Clearinghouse for ESL Literacy Education (ERIC Document Reproduction Service No. ED421898).

Arnold, W., Blue, J., Bosma, A. S., Gillet, R., Korzhenyak, I., McCoy, A. L., *et al.* (1997). *The best of ESL: Practical strategy guide for ESL*. Flint: Michigan Adult Education Practitioner Project (ERIC Document Reproduction Service No. ED419433).

Arrastía, M. (1995). Our stories to transform them: A source of authentic literacy. In G. Weinstein-Shr & E. Quintero (eds.). *Immigrant learners and their families: Literacy to connect the generations*. McHenry, IL: Center for Applied Linguistics and Delta Systems, pp. 101-10.

Atwell, N. (1998). *In the middle: New understandings about writing, reading, and learning* (2nd ed.). Portsmouth, NH: Boynton/Cook.

Auerbach, E. R. (1995). From deficit to strength: Changing perspectives on family literacy. In G. Weinstein-Shr & E. Quintero (eds.). *Immigrant learners and their families: Literacy to connect the generations*. McHenry, IL: Center for Applied Linguistics and Delta Systems, pp. 63-76.

Auerbach, E., Barahona, B., Midy, J., Vaquerano, F., Zambrano, A., & Arnaud, J. (1996). *Adult ESL/literacy from the community to the community: A guidebook for participatory literacy training*. Mahwah, NJ: Lawrence Erlbaum.

Brown, B. H., Mendelsohn, P. P., & Wilson, D. L. (1994). *Teaching adults ESL: A practitioner's guide*. Nashville, TN: Tennessee Department of Education, Division of Adult and Community Education (ERIC Document Reproduction Service No. ED394363).

Burns, A. (2006). Surveying landscapes in adult ESOL research. *Linguistics and Education* 17: 97-105.

Condelli, L., Wrigley, H. S., & Yoon, K. (2002). *What works. Study for adult ESL literacy students. Study summary*. San Mateo, CA, and Washington, DC: Aguirre

International and American Institutes for Research (ERIC Document Reproduction Service No. ED482789).

Crandall, J. (1993a). *Introduction.* In J. Crandall & J. K. Peyton (eds.). *Approaches to adult ESL literacy instruction.* McHenry, IL: Center for Applied Linguistics and Delta Systems, pp. 1-14.

Crandall, J. (1993b). *Improving the quality of adult ESL programs: Building the nation's capacity to meet the educational and occupational needs of adults with limited English proficiency.* Washington, DC: The Southport Institute for Policy Analysis (ERIC Document Reproduction Service No. ED375684).

Crandall, J., & Peyton, J. K. (eds.). (1993). *Approaches to adult ESL literacy instruction.* McHenry, IL: Center for Applied Linguistics and Delta Systems.

Dreyden-Peterson, S. (2007). Editor's review of adult English language instruction in the United States and securing the future. [Electronic version]. *Harvard Educational Review* 77: 515-21.

Ferguson, P. (1998). The politics of adult ESL literacy: Becoming politically visible. In T. Smoke (ed.). *Adult ESL: Politics, pedagogy, and participation in classroom and community programs.* Mahwah, NJ: Lawrence Erlbaum, pp. 3-15.

Fleischman, P. (1988). *Joyful noise: Poems for two voices* (E. Beddows, Ill.). New York: HarperCollins.

Florez, M. C. (1998). Concepts and terms in adult ESL. CAELA November. Accessed online at: www.cal.org/caela/esl_resources/digests/termsQA.html, October 7, 2009.

Florez, M. C., & Burt, M. (2001). *Beginning to work with adult English language learners: Some considerations.* Washington, DC: National Clearinghouse for ESL Literacy Education (ERIC Document Reproduction Service No. ED458837).

Freire, P. (2003). *Pedagogy of the oppressed* (30th anniversary ed.) (M. B. Ramos, Trans). New York: Continuum (original work published 1970).

Gass, S. M., & Selinker, L. (1994). *Second language acquisition: An introductory course.* Hillsdale, NJ: Lawrence Erlbaum.

Gianola, A. (2007). *Health stories teacher's guide: Readings and language activities for healthy choices.* Syracuse, NY: New Readers Press.

Gordon, D. (2004). "I'm tired. You clean and cook." Shifting gender identities and second language socialization. *TESOL Quarterly* 38: 437-57.

Holt, G. M. (1995). *Teaching low-level adult ESL learners. ERIC Digest.* Washington, DC: National Clearinghouse for ESL Literacy Education (ERIC Document Reproduction Service No. ED379965).

Holt, G. M. & Holt, D. D. (1995). Literacy program design: Reflections from California. In G.Weinstein-Shr & E. Quintero (eds.). *Immigrant learners and their families: Literacy to connect the generations*. McHenry, IL: Center for Applied Linguistics and Delta Systems, pp. 11-8.

Hondagneu-Sotelo, P. (2001). *Dom'estica: Immigrant workers cleaning and caring in the shadow of affluence.* Berkeley: University of California Press.

Hood, S. (1998). Critical literacy: What does it mean in theory and practice? In H. Burns & S. Hood (eds.). *Teachers' voices 3: Teaching critical literacy*. Sydney: National Centre for English Language Teaching and Research, pp. 11-9.

Huerta-Macías, A. (1995). Literacy from within: The Project FIEL curriculum. In G.Weinstein-Shr & E. Quintero (eds.). *Immigrant learners and their families: Literacy to connect generations*. McHenry, IL: Center for Applied Linguistics and Delta Systems, pp. 91-9.

Ilieva, R. (2000). Exploring culture in texts designed for use in adult ESL classrooms. *TESL Canada Journal* 17(2): 50-63.

Khanna, A. L., Agnihotri, R. K., Verma, M. K., & Sinha, S. K. (1998). *Adult ESOL learners in Britain*. Clevedon, UK: Multilingual Matters.

Lieshoff, S. C., Aguilar, N., McShane, S., Burt, M., Peyton, J. K., Terrill, L., *et al.* (2004). *Practitioner toolkit: Working with adult English language learners*. Louisville, KY, and Washington, DC: National Center for Family Literacy and Center for Adult English Language Acquisition. Accessed online at: www.cal.org/caela/tools/program_development/prac_toolkit.html, May 20, 2008.

Mahnen, B. (1995). *Curriculum design for the Bosnian Refugee Resettlement Committee's adult ESL program*. Boulder, CO: Refugee Resettlement Committee (ERIC Document Reproduction Service No. ED282003).

McGrail, L. (1995). Memories of Miami in the family literacy class. In G.Weinstein-Shr & E. Quintero (eds.). *Immigrant learners and their families: Literacy to connect the generations*. McHenry, IL: Center for Applied Linguistics and Delta Systems, pp. 77-90.

McGroarty, M. (1993). Cross-cultural issues in adult ESL literacy classrooms. *ERIC Digest*. Washington, DC: National Clearinghouse on Literacy Education (ERIC Document Reproduction Service No. ED358751).

McKay, H., & Tom, A. (1999). *Teaching adult second language learners*. Cambridge: Cambridge University Press.

Menard-Warwick, J. (2005). Intergenerational trajectories and sociopolitical context: Latina immigrants in adult ESL. *TESOL Quarterly* 39: 165-85.

Morrow, L. M., Gambrell, L. B., & Pressley, M. (eds.). (2003). *Best practices in literacy instruction* (2nd ed.). New York: Guilford Press.

Murray, D. E. (2005). ESL in adult education. In E. Hinkel (ed.). *Handbook of research in second language teaching and learning*. Mahwah, NJ: Lawrence Erlbaum, pp. 65-84.

National Center for Adult ESL Literacy Education. (2003). *Adult English language instruction in the 21st century*. Washington, DC: Center for Applied Linguistics.

Norton, B. (2006). Not an afterthought: Authoring a text on adult ESOL. *Linguistics and Education* 17: 91-6.

Orange County Public Schools. (1999). *Citizenship handbook*. Tallahassee, FL: Bureau of Adult/Community Education (ERIC Document Reproduction Service No. ED429466).

Orem, R. A. (2001). Journal writing in adult ESL: Improving practice through reflective writing. *New Directions for Adult and Continuing Education* 90: 69-77.

Peirce, B. N. (1994). Using journals in second language research and teaching. *English Quarterly* 26(3): 22-9.

Peirce, B. N. (1995). Social identity, investment, and language learning. *TESOL Quarterly* 29: 9-31.

Peyton, J. K. (1993). Listening to students' voices: Publishing students' writing for other students to read. In J. A. Crandall & J. K. Peyton (eds.). *Approaches to adult ESL literacy instruction*. McHenry, IL: Center for Applied Linguistics and Delta Systems, pp. 59-73.

Portes, A., & Rumbaut, R. G. (2001). *Legacies: The story of the immigrant second generation*. Berkeley: University of California Press & Russell Sage Foundation.

Rice, J. K., & Stavrianos, M. (1995). *Adult English as a second language program: An overview of policies, participants, and practices*. Washington, DC, and Research Triangle Park, NC: Mathematical Policy Research and Research Triangle Institution (ERIC Document Reproduction Service No. ED388115).

Rigg, P., & Kazemek, F. E. (1993). Whole language in adult literacy education. In J. Crandall & J. K. Peyton (eds.). *Approaches to adult ESL literacy instruction*. McHenry, IL: Center for Applied Linguistics and Delta Systems, pp. 35-46.

Roberts, C., & Baynham, M. (2006). Introduction to the special issue: Research in adult ESOL. *Linguistics and Education* 17: 1-5.

Rubin, J. (1975). What the "good language learner" can teach us. *TESOL Quarterly* 9: 41-51.

Savage, K. L. (1993). Literacy through a competency-based educational approach. In J. Crandall & J. K. Peyton (eds.). *Approaches to adult ESL literacy instruction.* McHenry, IL: Center for Applied Linguistics and Delta Systems, pp. 15-34.

Schlusberg, P. (ed.). (2006). *Getting along with others. Living in America. Teacher's resource guide series*. Syracuse, NY: New Reader's Press.

Scovel, T. (2001). *Learning new languages: A guide to second language acquisition.* Boston: Heinle & Heinle.

Skilton-Sylvester, E. (2002). Should I stay or should I go? Investigating Cambodian women's participation and investment in adult ESL programs. *Adult Education Quarterly* 53(1): 9-26.

Skutnabb-Kangas, T. (2000). *Linguistic genocide in education, or worldwide diversity and human rights?* Mahwah, NJ: Lawrence Erlbaum.

South Carolina Literacy Resource Center. (1994). *An adult ESL curriculum.* Columbia, SC: South Carolina Literacy Resource Center (ERIC Document Reproduction Service No. ED393324).

Spener, D. (1993). The Freirean approach and literacy education for language minority adults in the United States. In J. Crandall & J. K. Peyton (eds.). *Approaches to adult ESL literacy instruction.* McHenry, IL: Center for Applied Linguistics and Delta Systems, pp. 75-98.

Taylor, M. (1993). The language experience approach. In J. Crandall & J. K. Peyton (eds.). *Approaches to adult ESL literacy instruction.* McHenry, IL: Center for Applied Linguistics and Delta Systems, pp. 47-58.

Thomas, W. P., & Collier, V. P. (2002). *A national study of school effectiveness for language minority students' long-term academic achievement.* Santa Cruz, CA: Center for Research on Excellence and Diversity in Education.

Ullman, C. (1997). *Social identity and the adult ESL classroom. ERIC Digest.* Washington, DC: National Clearinghouse for ESL Literacy Education (ERIC Document Reproduction Service ED413795).

Vacco, E., & Jablon, P. (2007). *Conversations for work.* Syracuse, NY: New Readers Press.

Vaille, B., & QuinnWilliams, J. (2006). *Creating book clubs in the English language classroom: A model for teachers of adults.* Ann Arbor: University of Michigan Press.

Weinstein-Shr, G. (1995). Learning from uprooted families. In G. Weinstein-Shr & E. Quintero (eds.). *Immigrant learners and their families: Literacy to connect the generations*. McHenry, IL: Center for Applied Linguistics and Delta Systems, pp. 113-34.

Weinstein-Shr, G., & Quintero, E. (eds). (1995). *Immigrant learners and their families: Literacy to connect the generations*. McHenry, IL: Center for Applied Linguistics and Delta Systems.

Wong, B. L. (2008). Fairfax County family literacy curriculum. Accessed online at: www.aelweb.vcu.edu/publications/famlitcurric, May 20, 2008.

Wrigley, H. S. (1993). *Adult ESL literacy: Findings from a national study. ERIC Digest*. Washington, DC: National Clearinghouse for ESL Literacy Education (ERIC Document Reproduction Service No. 365169).

Wrigley, H. S. (2000). Assessing progress: Are we progressing? In D. Holt & C. H. Van Duzer (eds.). *Assessing success in family literacy and adult ESL* (revised ed.). McHenry, IL: Delta Systems.

Author index

An italic number refers to information in tables, charts, figures, or footnotes.

Subject index

An italic number refers to information in tables, charts, figures, or footnotes.